THE
BEST
OF
Gourmet

THE BEST OF

OF

Gourmet

1992 EDITION

FROM THE EDITORS OF GOURMET

CONDÉ NAST BOOKS • RANDOM HOUSE, NEW YORK

LIBRARY OF CONGRESS CATALOGING-IN-PUBLICATION
DATA

(Revised for vol. 7)
Main entry under title:

The Best of Gourmet.
    Includes Indexes
    1. Cookery, International. I. Gourmet.
TX725.A1B4827   1986   641.5   87-640167
ISBN 0-679-41204-2 (v.7)
ISSN 1046-1760

Most of the recipes in this work were previously published in
Gourmet Magazine.

Manufactured in the United States of America

98765432   24689753   23456789
First Edition

Grateful acknowledgment is made to John Webber of the Kinnaird
Estate in Perthshire, Scotland for permission to reprint the
following recipes previously published in *Gourmet* Magazine:

"Bread and Butter Pudding" (page 240); "Cumberland Sauce"
(page 133); "Honey and Tarragon Coarse Mustard" (page 157);
"Potted Kippers" (page 120); "Turnip and Saffron Soup" (page
118); "Veal and Ham Terrine" (page 133). Copyright © 1991 by
John Webber. Reprinted by permission of the author.

The following photographers have generously given their
permission to use the photographs listed below. With the
exception of Mr. Oppersdorff's photograph, these photographs
have previously been published in *Gourmet* Magazine:

Ronny Jaques: "Cap-Ferrat" (Table of Contents);"Port D'Agres
on the River Lot in the Midi" (page 270); "Talloires on Lake
Annecy" (page 278). Copyright © 1981, 1985, and 1987 by
Ronny Jaques. Reprinted by permission of the photographer.

Mathias Oppersdorff: "Gordes in Provence" (page 262).
Copyright © 1991 by Mathias Oppersdorff. Printed by permission
of the photographer.

Adam Woolfitt: "Chateau Pichon-Longueville in Bordeaux"
(page 252). Copyright © 1983 by Adam Woolfitt. Reprinted by
permission of Susan Griggs Agency, London, England.

For Condé Nast Books

Jill Cohen, Director
Ellen Maria Bruzelius, Direct Marketing Manager
Kristine Smith-Cunningham, Advertising Promotion Manager
Mary Ellen Kelly, Fulfillment Manager
Katherine Ferrara, Assistant
Diane Pesce, Composition Production Manager
Serafino J. Cambareri, Quality Control Manager

For *Gourmet* Books

Diane Keitt, Editor
Judith Tropea, Associate Editor

For *Gourmet* Magazine

Gail Zweigenthal, Editor-in-Chief

Zanne Early Zakroff, Executive Food Editor
Kemp Miles Minifie, Senior Food Editor
Alexis M. Touchet, Associate Food Editor
Leslie Glover Pendleton, Food Editor
Amy Mastrangelo, Food Editor
Kathleen Nilon Atencio, Food Editor
Margaret Lawrence Binder, Food Editor
Elizabeth S. Imperatore, Food Editor

Romulo A. Yanes, Photographer
Marjorie H. Webb, Stylist
Nancy Purdum, Stylist

Produced in association with
Media Projects Incorporated

Carter Smith, Executive Editor
Lelia Wardwell, Project Editor
Martina D'Alton, Associate Project Editor
Marilyn Flaig, Indexer
Michael Shroyer, Art/Production Director

The text of this book was set in Times Roman by the Composition
Department of Condé Nast Publications, Inc. and U.S. Lithograph
Typographers. The four-color separations were done by The Color
Company, Seiple Lithographers, and Applied Graphic
Technologies—Kordet Division. The book was printed and bound
at R. R. Donnelley and Sons. Text paper is Citation Web Gloss.

Front Jacket: "Cheese Won Ton Ravioli Triangles with Tomato
Sauce and Confetti Vegetables" (page 172).

Back Jacket: "Pumpkin Soup with Cumin Breadsticks"
(page 116).

Frontispiece: "Banana Rum Ice Cream" (page 234).

ACKNOWLEDGMENTS

The editors of *Gourmet* Books would like to thank *Gourmet* colleagues and other contributors whose expertise helped to make *The Best of Gourmet, 1992 Edition* possible.

This year a new section, Cuisines of the World, is introduced with a study of French cooking. We would like to thank Georgia Chan Downard for her inspired menus and thorough research of current French cuisine and Zanne Early Zakroff for her insight and suggestions. Gerald Asher, *Gourmet's* Wine Editor, provided wine selections for each menu. Georgia's recipes were carefully prepared for photography by the *Gourmet* Kitchen staff, photographed by Romulo Yanes, and styled by Marjorie Webb and Nancy Purdum. Lorraine Alexander, a *Gourmet* editor, translated into French all of the menu and recipe titles throughout the section. Line drawings by Beverly Charlton, and regional photography by Ronny Jaques, Mathias Oppersdorff, and Adam Woolfitt add greatly to this section. We would also like to thank Steve Jenkins of Dean and DeLuca Inc. who provided valuable information on cheese for our piece on the French Cheese Course.

Our Addendum on spices could not have been organized without the scholarly help of Bernadette Callery at The New York Botanical Gardens. Once again, Georgia Chan Downard developed a lovely collection of recipes and Alexandra Schulz provided the informative drawings that appear in the section.

Many talented artists contributed the line drawings throughout the book. They are: Beverly Charlton, Daisy de Puthod, Barbara Fiore, Lauren Jarrett, Deborah Lanino, Zoe Mavridis, Jeanne Meinke, Jenni Oliver, Monique Fath Perry, Michael Rosen, and Agni Saucier.

And, we would like to thank Michael Shroyer who was called upon to give a new look to our expanded Table of Contents as well as to design the new Cuisines of the World chapter. Also, thank you to Blair Brown Hoyt for her careful proofreading of the manuscript.

CONTENTS

INTRODUCTION   9

PART ONE: THE MENU COLLECTION   11

INTRODUCTION

Shortly after *Gourmet* Magazine celebrated its 50th anniversary at the beginning of 1991, I began my first year as editor-in-chief. A whirl of celebrations to toast our 50 years has now passed, and I am able to appreciate at leisure all the wonderful tributes we have received. But, perhaps the most gratifying remarks have come from you, our readers, who have generously taken the time to write and express your thanks for the pleasure that *Gourmet* has provided throughout the years. In turn, I would like to thank you for your enthusiastic loyalty and support.

Time passes quickly, and as impossible as it seems, the book you now hold is the seventh edition of our annual, *The Best of Gourmet*. Since 1986, each volume has brought together over 500 recipes, including the very best recipes that appeared in our magazine during the previous year. A quick calculation will reveal that if you have been subscribing to our annual since it first appeared, over 3,500 recipes are at your fingertips!

And now we have a surprise for you! *Gourmet* has always celebrated the happy combination of food and travel: One of travel's main attractions is, of course, the opportunity to taste the cuisine of a foreign land and bring home a few of its secrets. This year we introduce Cuisines of the World, a new section in *The Best of Gourmet* that will transport you each year to a different corner of the world for a closer look at the foods enjoyed in a particular culture. Here we will combine *Gourmet*'s breathtaking travel photography with all-new *Gourmet* menus and food photography for a beautiful "getaway" that promises to be as informative as it is delicious.

Since French cuisine is considered one of the finest in the world, we appropriately introduce our new section with The Flavors of France. We begin with basic recipes, important cooking information, tips, and even a discussion of the French cheese course—all of these offer *Gourmet*'s insights into French cuisine. Then, three menus follow—A Summer Dinner *à la Campagne*, Sunday Lunch *en Famille*, and a *Buffet de Fête*—that put these essentials to use. A special effort has been made to keep these menus *au courant*, so for the latest in French cooking, turn to page 251 to see what you, too, can prepare.

This year our annual also holds a number of all-time favorite *Gourmet* recipes from our first 50 years that were reprinted in special articles during 1991. In fact, we even developed a very special menu from our own "old favorites" for Our Anniversary Party (see page 12). After all, what better way is there to celebrate the past than by reliving its best moments? We thought that you would like to have a more permanent copy of these recipes, so we have selected the finest ones and included them here.

You will also find an all-new addendum that shows you how to expand and enhance your culinary repertoire by cooking with spices. Our discussions of common and not-so-familiar spices help to unravel some of the mysteries of these gifts from nature. For example, did you know that mustard seeds lose their sharpness when heated? Try our Grated Carrot Salad with Mustard Seeds and Roasted Cashews for delicious proof! Twenty-four simple recipes using a variety of these natural food enhancers will add a little "spice" to your life.

This year's edition of *The Best of Gourmet* is the best ever! While we continue to collect our finest recipes, we also offer more all-new material than ever before. After six successful volumes, our series continues to grow with more and more beautiful photographs, exceptional recipes, and inventive entertaining ideas.

Gail Zweigenthal
Editor-in-Chief

THE MENU COLLECTION

As the seasons change, so do our ideas about entertaining. During the cold winter months thoughts turn to warming foods served in generous amounts. As spring approaches, fresh garden produce and flowers appear on our tables and the fare turns lighter and greener. During the hot months, cooking is light and easy. Portions are cut down, and the preferred informal setting is moved out-of-doors. By the fall, however, as the temperatures drop and the days become shorter, hearty menus filled with warming dishes are in demand once again. The Menu Collection gathers menus and photographs that appeared in our *Gourmet* Menus and Cuisine Courante columns throughout the year and arranges them chronologically. Our photography album captures a year of entertaining with an array of appropriate meals for each season that sparkle with creativity and style.

Our spectacular Anniversary Party opens The Menu Collection and toasts our 50 years in magazine publishing. Favorite dishes that appeared throughout the years were selected for each course—from the Croûtes au Fromage '69. . .to the Roast Fillet of Beef with Cornichon Tarragon Sauce '84. . .to the Winter Vegetables with Horseradish Dill Butter '84. . .to the newly created Chocolate Mousse and Raspberry Cream Dacquoise '91—the look is elegant, and the taste is sublime! This is the ideal menu to keep in mind for any large, special winter celebration, perhaps even your own birthday or anniversary party.

As the weather eases towards sunny days, you will want to plan a special dinner for Easter. We have just the one! Featuring make-ahead dishes, our surprisingly easy Easter Dinner begins with Mussels with Fennel and Roasted Red Pepper Butter, then offers a Ginger Rum-Glazed Ham that is complemented by Rhubarb, Onion, and Raisin Chutney; Garlic Bread Puddings; and Asparagus with Walnut-Chive Vinaigrette. A fabulous Strawberry Lemon Bavarian Cake brings our Easter Dinner, replete with lively spring flavor, to a close.

By summer's end you may want to host A Labor Day Cocktail Buffet in the garden. Unlike ordinary cocktail parties where only light hors d'oeuvres are served, our gathering offers an impressive nine-dish buffet where absolutely everything is special. An eclectic blend of international flavors is found here. For example, our Thai-Style Steamed Dumplings with Coriander Dipping Sauce and our Avocado and Crab-Meat Sushi bow to the East, while a nod to Italian favorites appears in our Olive, Rosemary, and Onion Focaccia and our Savory Mascarpone Cheesecake with Sun-Dried Tomato Pesto. Your guests will certainly not need to make dinner reservations on the day of your party!

Naturally, year's-end entertaining ideas turn toward the holidays. This year, as the last Thursday in November approaches, you will have in hand our Maryland Thanksgiving menu, complete with Crab Cakes, Roast Turkey with Country Ham Stuffing and Giblet Gravy, and a glorious two-dessert finale. And, by the time Santa arrives you will be able to plan an Elegant Little Christmas of Roasted Poussins with Fennel; Potato and Carrot Gratin Diamonds; and festive Raspberry Swirl Parfaits.

Choosing wines and spirits to accompany our menus has been made easy, thanks to Gerald Asher, *Gourmet*'s wine editor. Whether its a flamboyant Fleur de Champagne Perrier-Jouet '83 to add sparkle to Our Anniversary Party, or a cold Kingfisher beer to accompany our East Indian Dinner, his selections take the worry out of choosing the perfect beverage.

Ideally, entertaining should take place year-round, not just when the house is decorated for the holidays. After all, inviting friends into our home is one of the nicest pleasures in life. So, take the time to thoroughly enjoy the following 70 pages filled with exquisite photographs and outstanding menus. Complete with all the details that make even a simple event *Gourmet*, entertaining ideas for every season await!

OUR
ANNIVERSARY
PARTY

Fleur de Champagne
Perrier-Jouët '83

Croûtes au Fromage, p. 87

Blini with Three Caviars, p. 86

E. Guigal Côte Rôtie '85

Roast Fillet of Beef with Cornichon
Tarragon Sauce, p. 128

Lemon Bulgur Timbales with Chives, p. 176

Winter Vegetables with Horseradish
Dill Butter, p. 199

Spinach, Fennel, and Pink
Grapefruit Salad, p. 206

Muscat de
Beaumes-de-Venise

Chocolate Mousse and Raspberry
Cream Dacquoise, p. 220

Blini with Three Caviars

Roast Fillet of Beef with Cornichon Tarragon Sauce;
Lemon Bulgur Timbale with Chives;
Winter Vegetables with Horseradish Dill Butter

Chocolate Mousse and
Raspberry Cream Dacquoise

OPERA BROADCAST LUNCHEONS

Saintsbury's Vin Gris
of Pinot Noir '89

Poached Chicken with Vegetables, Coriander, and
Saffron Couscous, p. 148

Chopped Salad of Cucumber, Red Onion,
Lemon, and Parsley, p. 207

Cinnamon Cocoa Meringues with Vanilla Ice Cream
and Cinnamon Chocolate Sauce, p. 242

Boutari Nemea '88

Risotto with Artichoke Hearts, Prosciutto,
and Red Bell Pepper, p. 180

Fennel and Watercress Salad, p. 204

Ginger Butterscotch Pear Tart, p. 233

Poached Chicken with Vegetables, Coriander, and Saffron Couscous;
Chopped Salad of Cucumber, Red Onion, Lemon, and Parsley

Risotto with Artichoke Hearts, Prosciutto, and
Red Bell Pepper; Fennel and Watercress Salad

Ginger Butterscotch Pear Tart

Toasted-Coconut Streusel Coffeecake, Mocha Hot Chocolate

A PRE-SKI BREAKFAST

Pineapple Citrus Juice, p. 250

Vegetable and Cheese Strata, p. 163

Herbed Home-Fried Potatoes, p. 189

Spicy Sausage Patties, p. 138

Toasted-Coconut Streusel Coffeecake, p. 222

Mocha Hot Chocolate, p. 250

Vegetable and Cheese Strata; Herbed Home-Fried Potatoes;
Spicy Sausage Patties; Pineapple Citrus Juice

EASTER DINNER

Jekel Vineyards
Arroyo Seco
Johannisberg
Riesling '89

Mussels with Fennel and
Roasted Red Pepper Butter, p. 125

Ginger Rum-Glazed Ham, p. 134

Rhubarb, Onion, and Raisin Chutney, p. 216

Garlic Bread Puddings, p. 134

Asparagus with Walnut-Chive Vinaigrette, p. 182

Strawberry Lemon Bavarian Cake, p. 224

Mussels with Fennel and Roasted Red Pepper Butter

Ginger Rum-Glazed Ham; Rhubarb, Onion, and Raisin Chutney;
Garlic Bread Puddings; Asparagus with Walnut-Chive Vinaigrette

Strawberry Lemon Bavarian Cake

Red Lentil Soup with Spiced Oil; Pappadams

AN EAST INDIAN DINNER

Red Lentil Soup with Spiced Oil, p. 114

Pappadams, p. 115

*Kingfisher beer or
Clos du Bois
Alexander Valley
Malbec '87*

Braised Lamb with Spinach, p. 141

Spiced Saffron Rice, p. 178

Cauliflower with Ginger and Mustard Seeds, p. 184

Coconut Mint Sorbet, p. 243

Braised Lamb with Spinach; Spiced Saffron Rice;
Cauliflower with Ginger and Mustard Seeds

A
NEW ORLEANS-STYLE
DINNER

Artichokes with Garlic Pimiento Vinaigrette, p. 182

Crown Roast of Pork with Dirty Rice Stuffing
and Creole Mustard Sauce, p. 134

Château
Prieuré-Lichine
Margaux '85

Sweet Potato Purée, p. 192

Okra and Onion Pickle, p. 186

Pecan Chocolate Tart, p. 234

Muscat de Frontignan,
Vin Doux Naturel

Banana Rum Ice Cream, p. 234

Artichokes with Garlic Pimiento Vinaigrette

Crown Roast of Pork with Dirty Rice Stuffing
and Creole Mustard Sauce;
Sweet Potato Purée; Okra and Onion Pickle

Rhubarb Streusel Pie

PASTA DINNERS

Artichoke Croustades, p. 182

Antinori
Galestro '90

Pasta with Spring Vegetables and Prosciutto, p. 170

Red-Leaf and Bibb Lettuce Salad with Scallion, p. 205

Rhubarb Streusel Pie, p. 230

Marinated Vegetables, p. 198

Boutari
Santorini '89

Rigatoni with Shrimp in Tomato and Feta Sauce, p. 174

Fennel and Coarse Salt Breadsticks, p. 98

Fresh Pineapple Sherbet, p. 243

Pasta with Spring Vegetables and Prosciutto;
Red-Leaf and Bibb Lettuce Salad with Scallion

DINNER
À LA FRANÇAISE

Potage Saint-Germain, p. 116

Saint-Nicolas-de-
Bourgeuil '88

Poulet au Vinaigre à l'Estragon, p. 144

Pommes Anna, p. 190

Haricots Verts à la Vapeur, p. 184

Salade Verte avec Croûtes de Roquefort, p. 204

Pots de Crème Javanaise, p. 237

Potage Saint-Germain

Poulet au Vinaigre à l'Estragon;
Pommes Anna; Haricots Verts à la Vapeur

Mango Yogurt Mousses

A LUNCHEON IN BERMUDA

Onion Tart with Sherry Peppers Sauce, p. 188

Tomato Basil Concassé, p. 188

The Hogue Cellars
Washington State
Chenin Blanc '89

Avocado, Grapefruit, and Watercress Salad with
Roquefort and Paprika Dressing, p. 203

Mango Yogurt Mousses, p. 239

Onion Tart with Sherry Peppers Sauce; Tomato Basil Concassé;
Avocado, Grapefruit, and Watercress Salad with Roquefort and Paprika Dressing

A
SWEDISH
MIDSUMMER
DINNER

Assorted Canapés, p. 93

Aquavit, p. 249

*Oven-Poached Salmon Steaks
with Mustard Dill Sauce, p. 121*

*Zeltinger Himmelreich
Kabinett '89
Selbach-Oster*

Beet Orange Salad, p. 207

Parsleyed Yellow-Potato Salad, p. 209

*Swedish Meringue Cake with Strawberries
and Orange Filling, p. 225*

Assorted Canapés, Aquavit

Oven-Poached Salmon Steaks;
Mustard Dill Sauce; Beet Orange Salad;
Parsleyed Yellow-Potato Salad

Raspberry Summer Pudding

AN ELEGANT STOVE-TOP DINNER

Domaine du Couroulou '85
Côtes du Rhône-Villages,
Vacqueyras

Poached Loin of Lamb, p. 140

Coriander, Mint, and Chili Chutney, p. 140

Cumin-Scented Rice Timbales, p. 178

Ratatouille, p. 193

Assorted Breadsticks

Raspberry Summer Pudding, p. 240

Poached Loin of Lamb; Coriander, Mint, and Chili Chutney;
Cumin-Scented Rice Timbale; Ratatouille; Breadsticks

DINNER ALFRESCO

Minted Cucumber and
Bell Pepper Buttermilk Soup, p. 113

McDowell Valley Vineyards
Les Vieux Cépages
Grenache Rosé '90

Grilled Tuna Salad
with Sun-Dried Tomato Dressing, p. 202

Bruschetta with Caponata, p. 107

Summer Fruit Terrine, p. 247   Raspberry Peach Sauce, p. 248

Lemon Thins, p. 227

Minted Cucumber and Bell Pepper Buttermilk Soup

Grilled Tuna Salad with
Sun-Dried Tomato Dressing;
Bruschetta with Caponata

Summer Fruit Terrine
with Raspberry Peach Sauce;
Lemon Thins

Pickled Ginger and Plum-Wine Granita; Honeydew and Sake Granita

LUNCHEON IN A JAPANESE GARDEN

*Smoked Salmon, Watercress, and Daikon Salad
with Ginger Vinaigrette, p. 202*

Sake   *Chilled Japanese Noodles
. with Grilled Chicken and Vegetables, p. 168*

Honeydew and Sake Granita, p. 241

Pickled Ginger and Plum-Wine Granita, p. 241

Smoked Salmon, Watercress, and Daikon Salad with Ginger Vinaigrette;
Chilled Japanese Noodles with Grilled Chicken and Vegetables; Sake

DINNER
BY THE PACIFIC

Clams Marinière with Tomato and Onion, p. 124

Muscadet de Sèvres-et-Maine '90

Grilled Veal Chops and Zucchini with Rosemary, p. 132

Bricco dell'Uccellone, Barbera '86

Orzo with Dried Cherries and Almonds, p. 169

Tiramisù Parfaits, p. 238

Clams Marinière with Tomato and Onion

Grilled Veal Chops and Zucchini with Rosemary
Orzo with Dried Cherries and Almonds

Tiramisù Parfaits

Pistachio Cake with Orange Syrup; Fruit and Walnuts

PICNIC IN THE OLIVE GROVE

Hummus with Pita Toasts, p. 90

Qupé
Santa Barbara County
Marsanne '89

Shrimp, Feta, and Tomato Salad, p. 202

Couscous with Pine Nuts and Parsley, p. 176

Pistachio Cake with Orange Syrup, p. 224

Fruit and Walnuts

The Picnic

A LABOR DAY COCKTAIL BUFFET

*Thai-Style Steamed Dumplings with
Coriander Dipping Sauce, p. 88*

Avocado and Crab-Meat Sushi, p. 86

*Szechwan-Style Eggplant
with Pita Wedges, p. 186*

Cocktails

*Goat Cheese and
Tomato Tart, p. 196*

*Kendall-Jackson
Lake County
Sauvignon Blanc '89*

Smoked Trout Canapés, p. 94

*Shredded Pork with
Tomato Salsa
on Tortilla Chips, p. 94*

*Simi Winery
Rosé of Cabernet
Sauvignon '89*

*Olive, Rosemary,
and Onion Focaccia, p. 99*

*Bridgehampton
Winery
Chardonnay '88*

*Savory Mascarpone Cheesecake
with Sun-Dried Tomato Pesto, p. 160*

Assorted Greens with Vinaigrette

Thai-Style Steamed Dumplings with Coriander Dipping Sauce;
Avocado and Crab-Meat Sushi; Assorted Greens with Vinaigrette

Assorted Greens with Vinaigrette; Szechwan-Style Eggplant with Pita Wedges; Goat Cheese and Tomato Tart;
Smoked Trout Canapés; Shredded Pork with Tomato Salsa on Tortilla Chips;
Olive, Rosemary, and Onion Focaccia; Savory Mascarpone Cheesecake with Sun-Dried Tomato Pesto

Bread and Butter Pudding

A FISHING PICNIC IN SCOTLAND

Turnip and Saffron Soup, p. 118

Potted Kippers, p. 120

Veal and Ham Terrine, p. 133
Cumberland Sauce, p. 133

Château Franc-Mayne
Grand Cru Classé   *Grilled Sausages*, p. 157
Saint-Emilion '87   *Honey and Tarragon Coarse Mustard*, p. 157

Steamed Potatoes, p. 191

Frisée and Radicchio Salad with Bacon and Pine Nuts, p. 204

Assorted Rolls

Bread and Butter Pudding, p. 240

A MASQUERADE DINNER

Grilled Polenta with
Wild Mushrooms, p. 177

Chianti dei
Colli Senesi '88

Breast of Duck with Port Sauce, p. 156

Dried Cherry and Shallot Confit, p. 156

Wild Rice Pancakes, p. 180

Brunello di
Montalcino '79

Sautéed Watercress, p. 198

Radicchio, Fennel, and Arugula Salad
with Roquefort and Walnuts, p. 205

Chocolate and Prune Marquise
with Armagnac Crème Anglaise, p. 246

Vin Santo

Breast of Duck
with Port Sauce;
Dried Cherry
and Shallot Confi[t]
Wild Rice
Pancakes;
Sautéed Watercre[ss]

Grilled Polenta
with Wild Mushrooms

Radicchio, Fennel,
and Arugula Salad
with Roquefort
and Walnuts

66

Cinnamon Baked Apples with Yogurt Cheese

COUNTRY BREAKFAST

Cranberry, Pear, and Grapefruit Juice, p. 250

Cheddar French Toast with Dried Fruit in Syrup, p. 166

Honey-Marinated Canadian Bacon, p. 134

Cinnamon Baked Apples with Yogurt Cheese, p. 244

Tea   Coffee

A MARYLAND THANKSGIVING

Crab Cakes, *p. 124*

Roast Turkey with
Country Ham Stuffing
and Giblet Gravy, *p. 158*

Spiced Crunberry Sauce, *p. 215*

Candied Sweet Potatoes, *p. 192*

Kale-Stuffed Onions, *p. 187*

Potato Parsnip Purée, *p. 189*

Sauerkraut with Apples and Caraway, *p. 194*

Lady Baltimore Cake, *p. 223*

Lemon Buttermilk Chess Tartlets, *p. 234*

*Grand Cru Vineyards
Clarksburg
Dry Chenin Blanc*

*Beringer Vineyards
Gamay-Beaujolais
Nouveau '91*

Roast Turkey with Country Ham Stuffing and
Giblet Gravy; Spiced Cranberry Sauce; Candied
Sweet Potatoes; Kale-Stuffed Onions; Potato
Parsnip Purée; Sauerkraut with Apples and Caraway

DINNER AFTER THE GAME

Mixed Antipasto, p. 85

Valpolicella '89   *Baked Pasta with Tomatoes,*
Shiitake Mushrooms, and Prosciutto, p. 171

Escarole, Spinach, and Red Onion Salad
with Anchovy Garlic Dressing, p. 203

Assorted Italian Breads

Cappuccino Brownies, p. 226

Mixed Antipasto; Baked Pasta with Tomatoes, Shiitake Mushrooms,
and Prosciutto; Escarole, Spinach,
and Red Onion Salad with Anchovy Garlic Dressing

A NANTUCKET CHRISTMAS DINNER

Schramsberg Vineyards
   Blanc de Blancs '85 LD

Clos du Val
   Carneros Estate   Oyster Pan Roast with Pepper Croutons, *p. 126*
      Chardonnay '88

Clos de la Roche
   Domaine Armand Rousseau   *Roast Beef with Glazed Onions*
      Burgundy '85   *and Worcestershire Gravy, p. 128*

                    Mashed Celery Potatoes, p. 190

                    Acorn Squash Purée, p. 195

            Buttered Brussels Sprouts and Chestnuts, p. 184

                    Cornmeal Rolls, p. 102

Renaissance Vineyards
   Late-Harvest Special-Selection   *Cranberry Pear Tart*
      White Riesling '85   *with Gingerbread Crust, p. 232*

            Chocolate Almond Truffle Squares, p. 248

Roast Beef with Glazed Onions and Worcestershire Gravy;
Buttered Brussels Sprouts and Chestnuts;
Mashed Celery Potatoes; Acorn Squash Purée; Cornmeal Rolls

AN ELEGANT
LITTLE CHRISTMAS

Mâche Salad with
Chiffonade of Beet and Radish, p. 205

Crichton Hall
Napa Valley
Chardonnay '88

Roasted Poussins with Fennel, p. 150

Potato and Carrot Gratin Diamonds, p. 189

Sage Cloverleaf Rolls, p. 102

Raspberry Swirl Parfaits, p. 242

Roasted Poussins with Fennel; Potato
and Carrot Gratin Diamonds; Sage Cloverleaf Rolls

A RECIPE COMPENDIUM

*I*n Part Two of *The Best of Gourmet*, A Recipe Compendium, we have brought together the best recipes that appeared in *Gourmet* Magazine during 1991 and arranged them alphabetically by category. Here you will find all of the recipes from our *Gourmet* Menus and Cuisine Courante columns that are pictured in Part One, The Menu Collection, as well as a selection of the best recipes from the other columns of the magazine—Gastronomie sans Argent, In Short Order, and The Last Touch. Our anniversary year also prompted special articles that touted all-time *Gourmet* favorites, and many of these "best" recipes can be found here.

As its name implies, Gastronomie sans Argent offers exceptional yet inexpensive dishes. It is no secret that produce is always best in season, and it is then that it is the most reasonably priced. If you are lucky enough to live near a farm, you will be able to buy fresh produce by the bushel as it is harvested. But even if you must rely on supermarket produce, it makes economical and gastronomical sense to stock up on these goods when they are at their peak and to make as many dishes with them as possible. Recipes from this column also prove that inexpensive foods need not be handled in humdrum fashion. On the following pages you will find a multitude of frugal yet inspired dishes.

For example, the notoriously unpopular winter vegetables of rutabagas and turnips were recently given a new lease on life by our food editors. Who else would think of making a Rutabaga and Cheddar Soufflé—and who else would ever guess how delicious it is? Proof is in the tasting, and after making our soufflé, you'll want to try our Grated Turnip Cakes with Ham, or our Rutabaga and Potato Gratin, or perhaps our Crispy Braised Duck with Turnips and Olives.

Chicken, too, has inappropriately gained the reputation of being an unexciting food. We encourage you to reassess these thoughts as you try our Roasted Chicken Legs with Plum Chili Salsa, or our Red-Wine Marinated Fried Chicken with Onions, or our Grilled Lemon-Lime Chicken. These and other chicken delights will prove that this American favorite can be dressed up and served with pride on any occasion.

Even the pick of summer fruits, always popular dessert favorites, are often used merely to embellish ice cream or garnish cakes. Here, however, you will find creative fruit finales that add a splash of color and freshness to your table. Our Frangipane Tart with Strawberries and Raspberries, for example, combines the sweetness of ripe strawberries and the tartness of plump raspberries with an almond and Amaretto frangipane mixture for a riot of summer flavor. Rows of these sumptuous fruits (sliced strawberries and whole raspberries) are decoratively placed atop the frangipane for an impressive, bright-red display of summer's goodness. And, you will not want to miss our light-as-air Honeydew and Cantaloupe Mousse, an elegant, refreshing dessert that is delicately enhanced with Midori (melon-flavored liqueur) and Port. Layers of honeydew and cantaloupe mousse are alternated for a pretty, pastel dessert that says "summer." But it is probably the Jumbleberry Pie, a combination of blackberries, blueberries, and raspberries (or whatever other berry you might have on hand) that is our quintessential fruit finale of the year!

When time is of the essence you will want to turn to our recipes from In Short Order, our column that offers dishes for two that can be prepared in forty-five minutes or less. For easy access to these recipes, simply turn to our Index of 45-Minute Recipes. It is nice to know that when a friend drops in unexpectedly, you will have a source of special, quick, and easy recipes at your disposal.

For example, let's say it is lunchtime and a friend has stopped by for a visit. Using *Gourmet* staples that you will probably have on hand, why not prepare our Croques-Monsieurs with Tomato and Thyme (Grilled Ham and Gruyère Sandwiches) or our Spinach Salad with Fried Blue Cheese. For dessert, our Poached Pear and Dried Apricots with Chocolate Sauce or our Strawberry Italian Ice can be made in a matter of minutes. Recipes for these and scores of dishes like them make spontaneous entertaining a snap!

When a trip to the grocery store is possible, this column can be the source of truly inspired quick dinners. Poached Scrod with Herbed Vinaigrette is a healthful, simple dish that is sure to please. You may want to add our Vegetable Ribbons with Horseradish Lemon Butter for a unique accompaniment. This colorful side dish can be made in the microwave in seconds, but the look will not give you away! Or perhaps you have pasta on your mind. Our Fusilli with Carrots, Peas, and Mint is as quick and easy as it is delicious! Add a simple dessert, such as our Broiled Peaches with Cookie-Crumb Topping, and your meal is complete.

In Short Order recipes also should be used to please the whimsical nature in all of us. Here you will find combinations of ingredients that you might never have thought to try yourself. Creations such as our Cheddar Chutney Drop Biscuits, our Microwave Chocolate Puddings with Rum-Soaked Golden Raisins, our Spicy Peanut and Scallion Pilaf, and our Broiled Eggplant Rolls with Goat Cheese and Tomato are gems that will stretch your cooking imagination and bring a smile to your guest's lips.

Our Recipe Compendium also includes thematic recipes from The Last Touch column that add a special *Gourmet* accent to any meal. Variations on the subject of vinaigrettes include a Basic French Vinaigrette, a Sun-Dried Tomato Vinaigrette, a Raspberry and Walnut Vinaigrette, and many others. The more playful theme of peanut butter includes recipes for Peanut Butter Swirl Brownies, Cold Sesame Noodles, and Chocolate Peanut Butter Balls, to name a few. Recipes highlighting radishes even appear—Radish Slaw, Glazed Radishes, Stuffed Radishes, and Layered Radish Finger Sandwiches give you some exciting ideas on how to add zip to a menu that lacks taste and color. And, on a more practical note, various recipes for dips, potato salads, apple cider, and hard boiled eggs are offered. Often, the little things in life please us the most, so be sure to have a look at these simple recipes.

Whatever you need, it is all here! If you are in a hurry to find a particular dish, turn to one of our three handy indexes at the back of the book, or if you have more time, slowly thumb through our Recipe Compendium. You will be amazed at the number of recipes that you will want to try.

HORS D'OEUVRES, CANAPÉS, AND DIPS

HORS D'OEUVRES

Mixed Antipasto

For the marinade
1 large garlic clove, minced
2 tablespoons balsamic vinegar
2 tablespoons red-wine vinegar
½ teaspoon dried rosemary, crumbled
1 teaspoon dried basil, crumbled
1 teaspoon dried orégano, crumbled
¼ teaspoon dried hot red pepper flakes,
    or to taste
½ cup olive oil

3 large carrots, cut diagonally into
    ¼-inch-thick slices
2 small fennel bulbs (about 1½ pounds),
    cut crosswise into ¼-inch-thick slices
    (about 3 cups)
2 red bell peppers, roasted (procedure on
    page 126) and cut into strips
2 yellow bell peppers, roasted (procedure on
    page 126) and cut into strips
a 12-ounce jar *peperoncini* (pickled Tuscan
    peppers), rinsed and drained well
¾ pound black or green brine-cured olives or
    a combination
¼ pound sun-dried tomatoes packed in oil,
    drained and cut into strips

¾ pound marinated or plain *bocconcini* (small
    mozzarella balls, available at specialty
    foods shops and some supermarkets)
½ pound pepperoni or *soppressata* (hard
    Italian sausage, available at Italian markets,
    some butcher shops, and some specialty
    foods shops), cut crosswise into ¼-inch-
    thick slices and the slices quartered
two 7-ounce jars marinated artichoke hearts,
    rinsed and drained well
⅓ cup minced fresh parsley leaves plus, if
    desired, parsley sprigs for garnish

Make the marinade: In a small bowl whisk together the garlic, the vinegars, the rosemary, the basil, the orégano, the red pepper flakes, and salt and pepper to taste, add the oil in a stream, whisking, and whisk the marinade until it is emulsified.

In a large saucepan of boiling water blanch the carrots and the fennel for 3 to 4 minutes, or until they are crisp-tender, drain them, and plunge them into a bowl of ice and cold water. Let the vegetables cool and drain them well. In a large bowl toss together the carrots, the fennel, the roasted peppers, the *peperoncini*, the olives, the sun-dried tomatoes, the *bocconcini*, the pepperoni, the artichoke hearts, the marinade, and the minced parsley until the antipasto is combined well and chill the antipasto, covered, for at least 4 hours or overnight. Transfer the antipasto to a platter, garnish it with the parsley sprigs, and serve it at room temperature. Serves 6 to 8.

PHOTO ON PAGES 74 AND 75

Avocado and Crab-Meat Sushi

For the rice
1 cup white short-grain rice*
2 tablespoons rice vinegar (available at
    Oriental markets, specialty foods shops,
    and some supermarkets)
1 teaspoon sugar
1 teaspoon dry Sherry
½ teaspoon salt

½ avocado (preferably California)
fresh lemon juice for rubbing the avocado
three 8- by 7-inch pieces of toasted *nori*
    (dried laver)*
½ cucumber, peeled and cut lengthwise into
    8- by ¼-inch strips, discarding the seeds
about ¼ pound fresh King crab meat, thawed
    if frozen, picked over, and drained
wasabi (Japanese horseradish) paste* to taste
    for the *sushi* plus additional as an
    accompaniment if desired
soy sauce as an accompaniment
pickled ginger* as an accompaniment if desired

*available at Oriental markets, some specialty
    foods shops, and some supermarkets

Make the rice: In a large fine sieve rinse the rice under running cold water until the water runs clear with no milky residue and drain it well. In a large heavy saucepan combine the rice with 1¼ cups water, bring the water to a boil, and simmer the rice, covered tightly, for 15 minutes, or until the water is absorbed and the rice is tender. Remove the pan from the heat, let the rice stand, covered tightly, for 10 minutes, and transfer it to a jelly-roll pan, spreading it in an even layer. Keep the rice warm, covered. In a saucepan whisk together the vinegar, the sugar, the Sherry, and the salt, simmer the mixture until the sugar is dissolved, and let it cool. Sprinkle the rice with as much of the vinegar mixture as necessary to moisten it lightly, tossing it carefully, and cover it with a dampened cloth. (Do not chill the rice.) *The rice may be made 3 hours in advance and kept, covered with the dampened cloth, at room temperature.*

Peel and pit the avocado, rubbing it with the lemon juice, and cut it into ¼-inch-thick strips. Heat the *nori* in a preheated 350° F. oven for 10 minutes, or until it is softened slightly, and keep it warm. Working with one sheet of *nori* at a time and with a long side facing you, spread about ¾ cup of the rice in an even layer on each sheet, leaving a ½-inch border on the long sides. Arrange some of the avocado strips horizontally across the middle of the rice and arrange some of the cucumber strips and the crab meat on top of the avocado. Dab the crab meat with the *wasabi* and beginning with a long side roll up the *nori* tightly jelly-roll fashion. Cut each roll with a sharp knife into ¾-inch-thick slices and serve the rolls with the soy sauce, the additional *wasabi*, and the ginger. Makes about 24 to 30 pieces.

PHOTO ON PAGES 58 AND 59

Blini with Three Caviars
(Buckwheat Yeast Pancakes with Three Caviars)
a ¼-ounce package (2½ teaspoons)
    active dry yeast
2½ tablespoons sugar
2 cups milk
2 tablespoons unsalted butter, melted, plus
    additional for brushing the griddle
1 cup buckwheat flour (available at natural
    foods stores and specialty foods shops)
1 cup all-purpose flour
1 teaspoon salt
2 large eggs, separated
¾ cup well-chilled heavy cream
about 2 cups sour cream as an accompaniment
about 4 ounces each black caviar, golden
    caviar, and salmon roe

In a large bowl proof the yeast with ½ tablespoon of the sugar in ⅓ cup lukewarm water for 10 minutes, or until it is foamy. Stir in 1 cup of the milk, heated to lukewarm, the remaining 2 tablespoons sugar, 2 tablespoons of the butter, and the buckwheat flour, beat the batter for 1 minute, and let it rise, covered with plastic wrap, in a warm place for 2 hours or chill it, covered tightly, overnight. (Chilling overnight produces a tangier flavor. Let the batter come to room temperature before continuing with the recipe.) Stir in the remaining 1 cup milk, heated to lukewarm, the all-purpose flour, the salt, and the yolks, beat the mixture for 1 minute, and let it rise, covered with the plastic wrap, in a warm place for 1 hour, or until it is double in bulk and bubbly. In a bowl beat the cream until it holds soft peaks and fold it into the batter. In a metal bowl beat the egg whites until they just hold stiff peaks and fold them into the batter gently but thoroughly.

Heat a griddle or large skillet over moderate heat until it is hot, brush it lightly with the additional melted butter, and spoon tablespoons of the batter onto the griddle, spreading them to form 3-inch rounds. Cook the *blini* for 1 minute on each side, or until the undersides are golden. Transfer the *blini* as they are cooked to a platter and keep them warm, covered with a kitchen towel. Make *blini* with the remaining batter in the same manner, brushing the griddle lightly with the butter as necessary. *The* blini *may be made 2 days in advance and kept covered and chilled. Reheat the* blini, *covered with foil, in a 350° F. oven for 10 to 15 minutes, or until they are warm, or microwave them on a microwave-safe platter, covered with microwave-safe plastic wrap, at high power (100%) for 2 minutes, or until they are warm.*

Arrange 3 or 4 *blini* on each of 18 small plates, top them with some of the sour cream, and arrange some of the caviar decoratively on the sour cream. Serves 18 with *blini* to spare.

PHOTO ON PAGES 12 AND 13

Croûtes au Fromage
(Cheese Pastries)

1½ cups all-purpose flour
½ teaspoon salt
⅛ teaspoon cayenne

¾ stick (6 tablespoons) cold unsalted butter, cut into bits, plus 3 tablespoons, softened
1 cup coarsely grated sharp Cheddar
3 tablespoons heavy cream
1 large egg, beaten lightly
1½ cups finely shredded Swiss cheese

Into a bowl sift together the flour, the salt, and the cayenne, blend in the 6 tablespoons butter and the Cheddar, and stir in the cream, stirring until the mixture forms a dough. Chill the dough, wrapped in wax paper, for 2 hours.

Roll out the dough ¹⁄₁₆ inch thick on a lightly floured surface and using a 1½-inch round cutter cut out rounds, rerolling the scraps and cutting out additional rounds. Arrange the rounds on baking sheets, brush them lightly with the egg, and bake them in batches in the middle of a preheated 450° F. oven for 5 to 7 minutes, or until they are browned lightly. *The pastry rounds may be made 2 days in advance and kept in an airtight container.*

In a small bowl cream together well the Swiss cheese and the remaining 3 tablespoons butter. Arrange half the pastry rounds, bottom sides up, on baking sheets, divide the cheese mixture among them, and sandwich the mixture with the remaining pastry rounds, pressing the rounds together lightly. Bake the *croûtes* in the preheated 450° F. oven for 4 minutes, or until the cheese is just melted. Makes about 46 *croûtes*.

Chicken Liver Pâté with Fig Preserves

3 large onions (about ¾ pound), chopped
1 stick (½ cup) unsalted butter
1 pound chicken livers, trimmed
¼ cup Tawny Port
¼ teaspoon allspice
1 tablespoon fresh lemon juice
⅓ cup fig preserves (available at specialty
   foods shops and some supermarkets),
   chopped fine
toast points or water biscuits as an
   accompaniment

In a large skillet cook the onions in 2 tablespoons of the butter over moderate heat, stirring, until they are softened and transfer them to a food processor. In the skillet melt 2 tablespoons of the remaining butter over moderately high heat until the foam subsides and in it sauté the chicken livers, patted dry and seasoned with salt and pepper, stirring, for 2 minutes, or until they are browned on the outside but still pink within. Transfer the livers to the food processor. Add the Port to the skillet, bring it to a boil, and deglaze the skillet, scraping up the brown bits, for 1 minute. Add the Port to the food processor with the remaining 4 tablespoons butter, softened, the allspice, the lemon juice, and salt and pepper to taste, purée the mixture until it is smooth, and force it through a fine sieve into a bowl. Line an oiled 1½-quart terrine or straight-sided dish with plastic wrap and pour the pâté mixture into it. Chill the pâté, covered, for 6 hours, or until it is firm. *The pâté may be made 4 days in advance and kept covered and chilled.* Invert the pâté onto a plate, discarding the plastic wrap, smooth the top and sides, and spread the preserves on top. Serve the pâté with the toast points or water biscuits.

daisy

*Thai-Style Steamed Dumplings with
Coriander Dipping Sauce*

For the filling
¼ cup minced scallion
1 pound ground pork
2 teaspoons minced peeled fresh gingerroot
1 red bell pepper, minced
   (about ½ cup)
⅔ cup minced cabbage
1 garlic clove, minced
¼ teaspoon Oriental sesame oil
1½ tablespoons soy sauce
2 tablespoons finely chopped fresh coriander
1 large egg, beaten lightly

60 *shao mai* wrappers (round won ton
   wrappers, available at Oriental and
   Southeast Asian markets, specialty foods
   shops, and many supermarkets), thawed
   if frozen
cornstarch for dusting the baking sheet
For the sauce
1 tablespoon *naam pla* (fish sauce, available
   at Oriental and Southeast Asian markets
   and some specialty foods shops)
3 tablespoons fresh lime juice
1 tablespoon white-wine vinegar
1 teaspoon sugar,
   or to taste
2 teaspoons minced peeled fresh gingerroot
1 tablespoon shredded fresh mint leaves
1 tablespoon finely chopped fresh coriander

2 tablespoons vegetable oil
coriander sprigs for garnish

Make the filling: In a bowl combine well the scallion, the pork, the gingerroot, the bell pepper, the cabbage, the garlic, the oil, the soy sauce, the coriander, the egg, and salt and pepper to taste and chill the filling for at least 1 hour or overnight.

Put about 1 heaping teaspoon of the filling in the center of 1 of the wrappers and moisten the edge of the wrapper. Gather the edge of the wrapper up and around the filling and form a waist with the wrapper, pushing the dumpling from the bottom and keeping the filling level with the top of the wrapper. (The filling should not be enclosed.) Continue to make dumplings with the remaining wrappers and filling in the same manner and arrange them in one layer on a baking sheet lined with wax paper dusted lightly with the cornstarch. *The dumplings may be prepared up to this point 8 hours in advance and kept uncovered and chilled or 1 month in advance and kept covered tightly and frozen. (If the dumplings are frozen, do not thaw them in advance.)*

Make the sauce: In a bowl whisk together the *naam pla*, the lime juice, the vinegar, the sugar, the gingerroot, the mint, the coriander, and salt and pepper to taste.

In a large non-stick skillet heat 1 tablespoon of the oil over high heat until it is hot but not smoking and in it fry half the dumplings, flat sides down, over moderately high heat for 1 minute, or until the undersides are golden. Add ½ cup water and steam the dumplings, covered, over moderate heat for 3 minutes, or until the pork is cooked through. (If using frozen dumplings, fry them, frozen, for 1 minute, or until the undersides are golden, and steam them, adding ¾ cup water per batch, covered, for 8 to 10 minutes, or until the pork is cooked through.) Add the remaining 1 tablespoon oil to the skillet and cook the remaining dumplings in the same manner. Garnish the dumplings with the coriander sprigs and serve them with the sauce. Makes 60 dumplings.

PHOTO ON PAGE 58

Egg, Onion, and Apple Croquettes

6 hard-boiled large eggs,
   chopped fine
2 tablespoons chopped onion
¼ cup chopped dried apple
½ cup béchamel sauce (recipe follows)
1 teaspoon ground cumin, or to taste
1 tablespoon fresh lemon juice,
   or to taste
2 raw large eggs, beaten lightly
2 cups fresh bread crumbs
vegetable oil for deep-frying the croquettes
½ cup bottled applesauce
1 teaspoon bottled horseradish, or to taste

In a large bowl combine well the hard-boiled eggs, the onion, the apple, the béchamel, the cumin, the lemon juice, and salt and pepper to taste and chill the mixture for 30 minutes. Form the mixture into 1-inch balls, dip the balls in the raw eggs, shaking off the excess, and roll them in the bread crumbs, transferring the croquettes as they are made to a baking sheet lined with wax paper. Chill the croquettes, covered loosely, for 1 hour. In a deep fryer or heavy deep skillet heat 2 inches of the oil to 350° F. and in it fry the croquettes in batches, turning them and transferring them to paper towels to drain with a slotted spoon as they are done, for about 2 minutes, or until they are golden. In a small bowl stir together the applesauce and the horseradish. Serve the croquettes with the sauce. Makes 18 to 20 croquettes.

Béchamel Sauce

1 tablespoon minced onion
3 tablespoons unsalted butter
¼ cup all-purpose flour
3 cups milk
¼ teaspoon salt
white pepper to taste

In a saucepan cook the onion in the butter over moderately low heat, stirring, until it is softened. Stir in the flour and cook the *roux*, stirring, for 3 minutes. Add the milk in a stream, whisking vigorously until the mixture is thick and smooth, add the salt and the white pepper, and simmer the sauce for 10 to 15 minutes, or until it is thickened to the desired consistency. Strain the sauce through a fine sieve into a bowl and cover the surface with a buttered round of wax paper to prevent a skin from forming. Makes about 2¼ cups.

Eggs Stuffed with Capers, Olives, Anchovy, and Radish

6 hard-boiled large eggs, halved
2 tablespoons chopped green olives
2 tablespoons chopped drained bottled capers
2 tablespoons finely chopped radish
1 flat anchovy fillet, minced and mashed
   to a paste
1 tablespoon mayonnaise
1 heaping tablespoon plain yogurt
1 tablespoon minced fresh parsley leaves

In a bowl mash the yolks and combine them well with the olives, the capers, the radish, and the anchovy. Stir in the mayonnaise and the yogurt until the mixture is combined well and season the mixture with salt and pepper. Divide the mixture among the whites and sprinkle the stuffed eggs with the parsley. Makes 12 stuffed egg halves.

Hummus with Pita Toasts

two 6-inch *pita* loaves, split and each round
  cut into 8 triangles
3 tablespoons unsalted butter, melted
a 19-ounce can chick-peas (about 2 cups),
  rinsed and drained well
3 tablespoons *tahini* (sesame seed paste,
  available at natural foods stores
  and some supermarkets)
1 tablespoon olive oil
3 tablespoons fresh lemon juice
1 garlic clove, minced and mashed to a paste
  with 1 teaspoon salt
fresh parsley for garnish

Brush the rough sides of the *pita* triangles with the butter, sprinkle them with salt to taste, and on a baking sheet bake the triangles in the top third of a preheated 400° F. oven for 6 to 8 minutes, or until they are golden. *The pita toasts may be made 1 day in advance and kept in an airtight container.*

With a rubber spatula force the chick-peas in batches through a sieve or the fine disk of a food mill into a bowl, discarding the solids remaining in the sieve. In a small bowl whisk together the *tahini* and the oil and whisk in the lemon juice and ⅓ cup cold water. Whisk the *tahini* mixture into the chick-peas with the garlic paste and pepper to taste. *The hummus may be made 1 day in advance and kept covered and chilled.* Sprinkle the *hummus* with the parsley and serve it with the *pita* toasts. Serves 4.

PHOTO ON PAGE 57

Liptauer Cheese

6 ounces cream cheese, softened
½ stick (¼ cup) unsalted butter, softened
1 teaspoon sweet paprika
  (preferably Hungarian)
1 teaspoon drained bottled capers
2 flat anchovy fillets, rinsed, patted dry,
  and minced
1 shallot, minced
½ teaspoon caraway seeds
crackers or toast points as an accompaniment

In a bowl cream together the cream cheese and the butter, add the paprika, the capers, the anchovies, the shallot, the caraway seeds, and salt and pepper to taste, and combine the mixture well. Pack the cheese into a crock and chill it, covered, for 1 day to let the flavors develop. Serve the cheese with the crackers. Makes about 1 cup.

Marinated Mozzarella, Roasted Bell Pepper, and Olive Brochettes

¾ pound fresh or smoked mozzarella, cut into
  ½-inch cubes (about 2 cups)
¼ cup extra-virgin olive oil
1 garlic clove, minced
1 tablespoon white-wine vinegar
½ teaspoon dried orégano, crumbled
½ teaspoon dried basil, crumbled
¼ teaspoon dried thyme, crumbled
25 brine-cured black olives, halved and pitted
2 large red bell peppers, roasted (procedure on
  page 126) and cut into ¾-inch squares
about 50 wooden picks

In a bowl or resealable heavy plastic bag combine the mozzarella, the oil, the garlic, the vinegar, the orégano, the basil, the thyme, and salt and pepper to taste and let the cheese marinate for at least 4 hours at room temperature or chilled overnight. Thread a mozzarella cube, an olive half, and a roasted pepper square onto each of the wooden picks and arrange the brochettes on a platter. *The hors d'oeuvres may be made 4 hours in advance and kept covered.* Makes about 50 hors d'oeuvres.

Baked Cheddar Olives

1 cup grated sharp Cheddar
2 tablespoons unsalted butter, softened
½ cup all-purpose flour
⅛ teaspoon cayenne
a 3-ounce jar small pimiento-stuffed green
  olives (about 24), drained and patted dry

In a bowl combine the Cheddar and the butter, add the flour and the cayenne, and blend the dough until it is combined well. Drop the dough by tablespoons onto wax paper and wrap or mold each tablespoon of dough around each of the olives, covering each olive completely. Bake the wrapped olives on a baking sheet in the middle of a preheated 400° F. oven for 15 minutes, or until the pastry is golden, and serve them warm. Makes about 24 Cheddar olives.

Parsley Walnut Pinwheels

2 cups all-purpose flour
1 teaspoon salt
1 pound extra-sharp Cheddar, grated
1 stick (½ cup) unsalted butter, cut into bits
5 to 6 tablespoons ice water
1 garlic clove
2 cups loosely packed fresh parsley leaves
½ cup walnut pieces

In a food processor blend the flour, the salt, the Cheddar, and the butter until the mixture resembles meal. With the motor running add 5 tablespoons of the water and blend the mixture, adding more water if necessary, until it just forms a dough. (Do not overblend the dough.) Transfer the dough to a sheet of wax paper and halve it. With the motor running drop the garlic into the food processor and mince it. Turn off the motor, add the parsley and the walnuts, and blend them until they are chopped coarse. Add half the dough, reserving the other half, chilled, and blend the mixture, scraping down the sides, until the parsley mixture is distributed evenly throughout the dough. Pat half the parsley dough into a 7- by 5-inch rectangle on a sheet of wax paper, reserving the other half, top it with another sheet of wax paper, and roll it into a 12- by 7-inch rectangle. Transfer the dough in the wax paper to a baking sheet and chill it for 10 minutes, or until it is firm but flexible. Repeat the rolling and chilling procedure with half of the reserved plain cheese dough.

Discard the top sheet of wax paper from the plain cheese dough and arrange the parsley dough, unwrapped, on top, pressing the 2 layers together lightly with the rolling pin. Using the bottom sheet of wax paper as a guide and beginning with a long side, roll the doughs tightly together jelly-roll fashion (if the doughs are too firm to roll easily, let them stand at room temperature until they are pliable) and chill the roll, wrapped well, for at least 1 hour or overnight. Repeat the entire procedure with the remaining reserved parsley and plain cheese doughs. *The dough rolls may be made 1 week in advance and kept covered tightly and chilled.*

Unwrap the rolls and cut them crosswise into ¼-inch-thick slices. Bake the pinwheels in batches on greased baking sheets in the middle of a preheated 400° F. oven for 12 to 14 minutes, or until they are golden, transferring them as they are baked to racks, and let them cool. Makes about 100 pinwheels.

Pepperoni Cheddar Straws

2 cups all-purpose flour
1 teaspoon salt
1 pound extra-sharp Cheddar, grated
1 stick (½ cup) unsalted butter, cut into bits
5 to 6 tablespoons ice water
a 2½-ounce package sliced pepperoni
a pinch of cayenne

In a food processor blend the flour, the salt, the Cheddar, and the butter until the mixture resembles meal. With the motor running add 5 tablespoons of the water and blend the mixture, adding more water if necessary, until it just forms a dough. Do not overblend the dough. Transfer the dough to a sheet of wax paper and halve it.

In the food processor grind fine the pepperoni with the cayenne, add half the dough, reserving the other half, chilled, and blend the mixture until the pepperoni is just distributed. On the sheet of wax paper halve the pepperoni dough and divide 1 of the halves into thirds, reserving the other half, wrapped and chilled. Roll each third into an 8-inch rope. Repeat the rolling procedure with half of the reserved plain cheese dough.

On a new sheet of wax paper arrange the 6 ropes side by side, alternating the pepperoni with the plain, press them tightly together, and top them with another sheet of wax paper. With a rolling pin flatten the ropes between the sheets of wax paper and roll them into a ⅛-inch-thick rectangle (about 15 by 7 inches). Transfer the dough and the wax paper to a baking sheet and chill it for at least 1 hour or overnight. Repeat the entire procedure with the reserved plain cheese and pepperoni doughs. *The sheets of dough may be made 1 week in advance and kept covered tightly and chilled.*

Cut the sheets of dough crosswise into ½-inch-wide strips, discarding the wax paper. Bake the strips in batches on greased baking sheets in the middle of a preheated 400° F. oven for 10 minutes, or until they are golden, transferring them as they are baked to racks, and let them cool. Serve the straws freshly baked. Makes about 50 straws.

Layered Radish Finger Sandwiches

1 stick (½ cup) unsalted butter, softened
½ teaspoon anchovy paste
2 scallions, minced fine
12 very thin slices of whole-wheat bread
2 cups thinly sliced radishes

In a small bowl cream the butter and stir in the anchovy paste, the scallions, and salt and pepper to taste. Spread one side of each of 3 slices of the bread with some of the scallion butter and top the buttered side of one of the slices with an overlapping layer of the radishes. Top the radishes with another slice of the buttered bread, buttered side down, and butter the top of the slice. Top the butter with an overlapping layer of the radishes and top the radishes with the remaining slice of the buttered bread, buttered side down. Press the sandwich together gently, trim the crusts, and cut the sandwich lengthwise into thirds. Make sandwiches with the remaining bread, butter, and radishes in the same manner. *The sandwiches can be made 2 hours in advance and kept wrapped in plastic and chilled.* Makes 12 finger sandwiches.

Radishes Filled with Salmon Roe and Lemon Cream

35 to 40 radishes, halved crosswise
8 ounces cream cheese,
    softened
½ teaspoon freshly grated lemon zest
1 tablespoon fresh lemon juice
2 tablespoons minced fresh dill
3 tablespoons salmon roe

Trim the end of each radish half so that the half will stand upright and with a small melon-ball cutter hollow out the radishes. *The radishes may be hollowed out 8 hours in advance and kept chilled in a bowl of water.* Drain the radish shells, inverted, on paper towels for 5 minutes. In a bowl with an electric mixer beat the cream cheese on high speed for 5 minutes, or until it is very light and fluffy, beat in the zest, the lemon juice, the dill, and salt and pepper to taste, and fold in the salmon roe. Transfer the mixture to a pastry bag fitted with a ½-inch plain tip and pipe it into the radish shells. *The hors d'oeuvres may be made 1½ hours in advance and kept covered loosely and chilled.* Makes about 75 hors d'oeuvres.

Stuffed Radishes

1 pound (about eighteen 1¼-inch) radishes,
    halved crosswise
4 ounces cream cheese, softened
½ cup Kalamata or other brine-cured black
    olives, pitted and minced
1 tablespoon drained bottled capers,
    chopped fine
2 tablespoons minced fresh parsley leaves
    plus small sprigs for garnish

Trim the narrow end of each radish half so that the half will stand upright and with a small melon-ball cutter hollow out a ¾-inch cavity in each half, dropping the halves as they are hollowed into a bowl of ice and cold water. In a bowl cream the cream cheese, stir in the olives, the capers, the minced parsley, and salt and pepper to taste, and transfer the mixture to a pastry bag fitted with a ½-inch plain tip. Transfer the radishes, hollowed sides down, to paper towels, let them drain for 5 minutes, and pipe the cream cheese mixture into them. Garnish each stuffed radish with a parsley sprig. *The radishes can be stuffed 1½ hours in advance and kept covered and chilled.* Makes about 36 hors d'oeuvres.

Pickled Shrimp

¼ cup crab boil (available at fish markets and
    specialty foods shops) if desired,
    tied in cheesecloth
2½ pounds small shrimp, shelled
    and deveined
¾ cup distilled white vinegar
5 teaspoons celery seeds
2 teaspoons salt, or to taste
1 cup olive oil
1 large onion, sliced thin
3 bay leaves
crackers as an accompaniment if desired

In a kettle bring 6 cups water with the crab boil to a boil, simmer the mixture for 5 minutes, and add the shrimp. Boil the shrimp for 5 minutes and drain them. In a small bowl whisk together the vinegar, the celery seeds, the salt, and pepper to taste, add the oil in a stream, whisking, and whisk the dressing until it is emulsified. In a deep glass dish arrange half the shrimp in one layer, arrange half the onion slices over them, and top them with the bay leaves. Arrange the remaining shrimp over the onions, sprinkle the remaining onion slices over them, and pour the dressing over the mixture. Let the shrimp marinate, covered and chilled, for 24 hours and serve them skewered on wooden picks or with the crackers. Serves 8 to 10.

CANAPÉS

Assorted Canapés

For the shrimp canapés
6 slices of homemade-type white bread
3 tablespoons unsalted butter, softened
12 thin round slices of small tomatoes
48 slices of ripe olives
12 cooked small shrimp
¼ cup mayonnaise
1 tablespoon drained bottled horseradish
12 dill sprigs
For the pickled herring canapés
6 slices of rye bread
3 tablespoons unsalted butter, softened
½ cup minced fresh parsley leaves
2 tablespoons minced radish
2 tablespoons minced onion
twelve 4-inch thin strips of bottled pickled
    herring fillet, patted dry
24 drained bottled capers
For the smoked mackerel canapés
6 slices of pumpernickel bread
3 tablespoons unsalted butter, softened
⅔ cup finely grated carrot
2 teaspoons fresh lemon juice
2 teaspoons vegetable oil
1 small smoked peppered mackerel fillet
    (available at some specialty foods shops),
    separated into 12 pieces, discarding
    any bones

36 thin diagonal slices of scallion green
For the cheese canapés
6 slices of rye bread
3 tablespoons unsalted butter,
    softened
12 thin slices of salami, cut into twelve
    2-inch scallop-edged rounds
¼ pound *Västerbotten* cheese (available at
    Scandinavian markets and some specialty
    foods shops) or sharp Cheddar, sliced thin
    and cut into twelve 1½-inch rounds
thirty-six 1½-inch-long julienne strips of
    red bell pepper
about 2 tablespoons Swedish sweet mustard
    (available at Scandinavian markets and
    some specialty foods shops) or other
    sweet mustard
12 drained bottled cocktail onions

Make the shrimp canapés: Spread the bread with the butter, cut it into twelve 2-inch squares, and on it arrange decoratively the tomatoes, the olives, and the shrimp. In a small bowl combine well the mayonnaise and the horseradish, dot the shrimp with the mixture, and garnish it with the dill.

Make the pickled herring canapés: Spread the bread with the butter, cut it into twelve 2-inch squares, and press the buttered side of the bread gently into the parsley to coat it. In a small bowl combine well the radish and the onion and divide the mixture among the bread squares. Roll up each herring strip into a coil and arrange the herring and the capers decoratively on the bread.

Make the smoked mackerel canapés: Spread the bread with the butter and with a 2-inch scalloped cutter cut it into 12 rounds. In a small bowl combine well the carrot, the lemon juice, the oil, and salt and pepper to taste, divide the mixture among the bread rounds, and on it arrange decoratively the mackerel and the scallion green.

Make the cheese canapés: Spread the bread with the butter and with a 2-inch scalloped cutter cut it into 12 rounds. Arrange the salami, the cheese, and the bell pepper decoratively on the bread, spoon small dollops of the mustard onto the canapés, and press the onions into the mustard.

The canapés may be made 30 minutes in advance and kept covered and chilled. Arrange the canapés on a platter. Makes 48 canapés.

PHOTO ON PAGE 42

Peanut Butter, Scallion, and Bacon Canapés

½ cup peanut butter
6 scallions, chopped
2 tablespoons fresh lemon juice
1 tablespoon soy sauce
1 tablespoon mayonnaise plus additional for
   brushing the bread slices
1 teaspoon brown sugar or granulated sugar
9 slices of homemade-type white bread,
   crusts removed
6 slices of lean bacon, cut into 1-inch pieces
   and cooked until almost crisp

In a small bowl stir together the peanut butter, the scallions, the lemon juice, the soy sauce, 1 tablespoon of the mayonnaise, and the brown sugar. Spread the bread slices lightly with the additional mayonnaise, spread the peanut butter mixture on the slices, and cut the slices into quarters. Arrange the canapés on a baking sheet, put a piece of bacon on top of each canapé, and bake the canapés in the middle of a preheated 425° F. oven for 8 to 10 minutes, or until the bacon is crisp. Makes 36 canapés.

Shredded Pork with Tomato Salsa on Tortilla Chips

twelve 7-inch corn tortillas, each cut into
   4 rounds with a 2-inch cutter
vegetable oil for frying the tortillas
2½ pounds untrimmed boneless pork shoulder
   or butt, cut into 2- by ¾-inch strips
the zest of 1 lime removed in strips with a
   vegetable peeler
1 teaspoon salt
1 scallion, cut into 3 pieces
3 garlic cloves
¼ teaspoon cumin
For the salsa
2 tomatoes, chopped fine
3 tablespoons finely chopped onion
¼ cup finely chopped fresh coriander
1 teaspoon minced *jalapeño* chili
   (wear rubber gloves)
1 teaspoon fresh lime juice

coriander sprigs for garnish

Arrange the tortilla rounds in one layer on baking sheets, cover them with a kitchen towel, and let them stand for 1 hour. In a large heavy skillet fry the rounds in batches in ¾ inch of 375° F. oil for 30 seconds to 1 minute, or until they are pale golden and the bubbling subsides. Transfer the tortilla chips with a slotted spoon to paper towels to drain and season them with salt. *The tortilla chips may be made 1 day in advance and kept in an airtight container.*

In a heavy kettle arrange the pork strips in one layer, add enough water to barely cover them, and add the zest, the salt, the scallion, the garlic, and the cumin. Bring the water to a boil and simmer the mixture, covered partially, turning the pork occasionally, for 1 hour, or until the pork is just tender and the water is almost evaporated. Cook the pork, uncovered, over moderately low heat, turning it frequently, for 40 minutes to 1 hour more, or until it is browned well and begins to fall apart. Remove the pork with a slotted spoon from the kettle, discarding the zest, the scallion, and the garlic, and transfer it to paper towels to drain. Let the pork cool and using 2 forks or your fingers shred it. *The shredded pork may be made 2 days in advance and kept covered and chilled.*

Make the *salsa*: In a small bowl combine the tomatoes, the onion, the coriander, the *jalapeño*, the lime juice, and salt and pepper to taste.

Onto each tortilla chip spoon a heaping teaspoon of the pork and top it with some of the *salsa* and a coriander sprig. Makes 48 hors d'oeuvres.

PHOTO ON PAGE 61

Smoked Trout Canapés

½ pound smoked trout fillets (available at
   specialty foods shops and some fish
   markets), picked over and flaked
½ cup plain yogurt, drained in a fine sieve
   for 1 hour
¼ cup mayonnaise
1 teaspoon fresh lemon juice
1 tablespoon minced fresh dill plus dill sprigs
   for garnish
1 tablespoon minced onion, patted dry
12 slices of pumpernickel bread, each slice
   cut decoratively into 2-inch shapes

In a food processor purée the trout, the yogurt, the mayonnaise, the lemon juice, the minced dill, the onion, and salt and pepper to taste until the mixture is smooth. *The trout mixture may be made 1 day in advance and kept covered and chilled.* On each piece of bread spread a scant teaspoon of the mixture, mounding it, and garnish each canapé with a dill sprig. Makes about 36 canapés.

PHOTO ON PAGE 61

DIPS

Artichoke and Parmesan Dip

a 14-ounce can artichoke hearts, drained well
½ cup freshly grated Parmesan
¾ cup mayonnaise
¼ cup plain yogurt
1 garlic clove, minced and mashed to a paste
   with a pinch of salt
2 teaspoons fresh lemon juice, or to taste
1 scallion, chopped
Tabasco to taste
breadsticks or lightly toasted
   French bread slices

In a food processor purée the artichoke hearts, the Parmesan, the mayonnaise, the yogurt, the garlic paste, the lemon juice, the scallion, the Tabasco, and salt and

pepper to taste until the mixture is smooth. Serve the dip with the breadsticks or the toasts. Makes about 2¾ cups.

Avocado and Tomatillo Dip

2 avocados (preferably California*)*
1½ tablespoons fresh lemon juice
an 11-ounce can *tomatillos verdes* (Spanish
   green tomatoes, available at Hispanic
   markets and some specialty foods shops),
   drained
¼ teaspoon ground cumin
½ cup chopped fresh coriander
1 garlic clove, minced
1½ teaspoons finely chopped drained pickled
   jalapeño pepper (wear rubber gloves)
¼ cup chopped onion
¼ cup sour cream
tortilla chips or potato chips

In a food processor purée the avocados, pitted and chopped, the lemon juice, the *tomatillos verdes*, the cumin, the coriander, the garlic, the *jalapeño*, the onion, the sour cream, and salt and pepper to taste until the mixture is smooth. Serve the dip with the chips. Makes about 3 cups.

Layered White Bean, Tuna, and Vegetable Dip

For the cucumber layer

1½ cups plain yogurt

1 cucumber, peeled, seeded, and chopped fine

¼ teaspoon salt

1 large garlic clove, minced and mashed to a
    paste with ½ teaspoon salt

For the bean layer

½ pound dried white beans such as Great
    Northern, soaked in enough cold water
    to cover them by 2 inches overnight or
    quick-soaked (procedure on page 143)
    and drained

1 cup finely chopped onion

2 teaspoons minced garlic

½ teaspoon dried orégano, crumbled

2 tablespoons olive oil

½ cup dry white wine

For the tuna layer

a 6½-ounce can chunk-light tuna packed in
    oil, drained and flaked

⅓ cup finely chopped red onion

¼ cup finely chopped pitted Kalamata or other
    brine-cured black olives

½ cup minced fresh parsley leaves

1 tablespoon red-wine vinegar, or to taste

For the topping

2 plum tomatoes, diced

1 green bell pepper, diced

½ red onion, sliced thin

¼ cup sliced pitted Kalamata or other
    brine-cured black olives

toasted *pita* triangles

Make the cucumber layer: In a sieve set over a bowl and lined with a triple thickness of rinsed and squeezed cheesecloth let the yogurt drain for 1 hour. Put the cucumber in another sieve, sprinkle it with the salt and let it drain for 1 hour. Pat the cucumber dry between paper towels and transfer it to a bowl. Stir in the yogurt, the garlic, and salt and pepper to taste and combine the mixture well.

Make the bean layer: In a saucepan combine the beans with enough cold water to cover them by 2 inches, simmer them, covered, for 1 hour, or until they are tender, and drain them well, reserving the cooking liquid. In a skillet cook the onion, the garlic, the orégano, and salt and pepper to taste in the oil over moderately low heat, stirring, until the onion is softened. Add the

wine and simmer the mixture until the wine is reduced by half. In a food processor purée the beans and the onion mixture with ½ cup of the reserved cooking liquid and salt and pepper to taste, transfer the mixture to a bowl, and chill it, covered, until it is cool.

Make the tuna layer: In a small bowl toss together the tuna, the onion, the olives, the parsley, the vinegar, and salt and pepper to taste.

Assemble the dip: Spread the bean purée over the bottom of a 10-inch round shallow serving dish, top it with the tuna mixture, and spoon the cucumber mixture over the top. Chill the dip, covered, for at least 3 hours or overnight, sprinkle the top with the tomatoes, the bell pepper, the onion, and the olives, and serve the dip with the *pita* triangles. Serves 8.

Cheddar, Bacon, and Green Pepper Dip

2½ teaspoons Dijon-style mustard

¾ cup mayonnaise

¾ cup plain yogurt

½ pound sharp Cheddar, grated fine
    (about 3 cups)

1 large green bell pepper, minced

½ cup thinly sliced scallion
5 slices of crisp cooked lean bacon, crumbled
   fine, plus additional crumbled bacon
   for garnish
cayenne to taste if desired
lightly toasted *pita* triangles or crackers

In a serving bowl whisk together the mustard, the mayonnaise, the yogurt, and pepper to taste, add the Cheddar, the bell pepper, the scallion, and the finely crumbled bacon, and stir the mixture until it is combined well. Sprinkle the dip with the additional bacon and the cayenne and serve it with the *pita* toasts or the crackers. Makes about 3 cups.

Hard-Boiled Egg, Roquefort, and Scallion Dip

6 hard-boiled large eggs
1½ cups crumbled Roquefort
1 teaspoon fresh lemon juice, or to taste
⅓ cup plain yogurt
3 scallions, chopped
potato chips or *crudités*

In a food processor or blender purée the eggs with the Roquefort, the lemon juice, the yogurt, and salt and pepper to taste, transfer the mixture to a bowl, and stir in the scallions. Serve the dip with the potato chips or crudités. Makes about 2 cups.

Pesto Cottage Cheese Dip

2½ cups packed fresh basil leaves, rinsed and
   spun dry
½ cup pine nuts
2 cups cottage cheese
2 tablespoons olive oil
2 garlic cloves, minced and mashed to a paste
   with a pinch of salt
⅓ cup freshly grated Parmesan
breadsticks or *crudités*

In a food processor purée the basil, the pine nuts, the cottage cheese, the oil, the garlic paste, the Parmesan, and salt and pepper to taste, scraping down the side of the bowl occasionally and adding water to thin the mixture if desired, until the mixture is smooth. Serve the dip with the breadsticks or the *crudités*. Makes about 2½ cups.

Fried Shallot and Garlic Dip

vegetable oil for frying the shallot and garlic
¾ cup thinly sliced shallot
2 garlic cloves, sliced thin
1¼ to 1½ cups *crème fraîche*
   (available at specialty foods shops and
   most supermarkets) or sour cream
1½ tablespoons minced fresh parsley leaves
1 tablespoon thinly sliced fresh chives
potato chips or *crudités*

In a skillet heat ½ inch of the oil over moderately high heat until it is hot but not smoking and in it fry the shallot and the garlic, stirring, for 1 to 2 minutes, or until they are pale golden. Transfer the shallot and the garlic with a slotted spoon to paper towels, let the mixture cool, and crumble it fine. In a bowl whisk together 1¼ cups of the *crème fraîche*, the parsley, the chives, the shallot mixture, and salt and pepper to taste, adding some or all of the remaining ¼ cup *crème fraîche* to thin the dip if desired. Serve the dip with the chips or the *crudités*. Makes about 1¾ cups.

Sun-Dried Tomato and Roasted Red Pepper Dip

two 7-ounce jars roasted red peppers, drained
   and patted dry
8 sun-dried tomato halves, soaked in hot
   water for 5 minutes, drained well, and
   patted dry
1 garlic clove, minced and mashed to a paste
   with a pinch of salt
1 tablespoon fresh lemon juice
2 tablespoons chopped flat-leafed parsley
   leaves plus additional parsley for garnish
4 ounces cream cheese, cut into bits
   and softened
½ cup sour cream
lightly toasted *pita* triangles or *crudités*

In a food processor purée the peppers, the tomatoes, the garlic paste, the lemon juice, and 2 tablespoons of the parsley until the mixture is smooth, add the cream cheese, the sour cream, and salt and pepper to taste, and purée the mixture, scraping down the side of the bowl occasionally, until it is smooth. Transfer the dip to a serving bowl, garnish it with the additional parsley, and serve it with the *pita* toasts or the *crudités*. Makes about 2¼ cups.

BREADS

YEAST BREADS

Fennel and Coarse Salt Breadsticks

a ¼-ounce package (2½ teaspoons) active
   dry yeast
1½ teaspoons sugar
2½ to 3 cups all-purpose flour
1 teaspoon table salt
¼ cup olive oil
cornmeal for sprinkling the baking sheets
an egg wash made by beating 1 large egg with
   1 tablespoon water
fennel seeds for sprinkling the breadsticks
coarse salt for sprinkling the breadsticks

In the large bowl of an electric mixer proof the yeast with ½ teaspoon of the sugar in ¾ cup lukewarm water for 5 minutes, or until it is foamy. Add the remaining teaspoon sugar, 2 cups of the flour, the table salt, and the oil and beat the mixture with the dough hook until it is combined. Knead the dough, kneading in enough of the remaining 1 cup flour to make the dough form a ball, and knead the dough for 5 minutes, or until it is soft but not sticky. On a lightly floured surface let the dough rest, covered with a kitchen towel, for 15 minutes. Divide the dough into 12 pieces, working with 1 piece at a time and keeping the remaining pieces covered, roll the dough between the palms of the hands to form 14-inch ropes, and arrange the ropes as they are formed 2 inches apart on baking sheets sprinkled lightly with the cornmeal. Let the breadsticks rise, covered loosely, in a warm place for 40 minutes, brush them lightly with the egg wash, and sprinkle them with the fennel seeds and the coarse salt. Bake the breadsticks in the middle of a preheated 450° F. oven for 12 to 15 minutes, or until

they are pale golden, and let them cool on a rack for 10 minutes. *The breadsticks may be made 1 day in advance and kept in an airtight container.* Makes 12 breadsticks.

Thick Focaccia

a ¼-ounce package (2½ teaspoons) plus
   1 teaspoon active dry yeast
1 teaspoon sugar
1¾ cups lukewarm water
5½ cups bread flour
1 teaspoon table salt
5 tablespoons olive oil
1 tablespoon coarse salt, or to taste

In the bowl of an electric mixer fitted with the paddle attachment proof the yeast with the sugar in the water for 5 minutes, or until the mixture is foamy, add the flour, the table salt, and 3 tablespoons of the oil, and combine the dough well. With the dough hook knead the dough for 2 minutes, or until it is soft and slightly sticky. Form the dough into a ball, transfer it to an oiled bowl, and turn it to coat it with the oil. Let the dough rise, covered with plastic wrap, in a warm place for 1½ hours, or until it is double in bulk. *The dough may be made up to this point, punched down, and kept, covered and chilled, overnight. Let the dough return to room temperature before proceeding with the recipe.* Press the dough into an oiled jelly-roll pan, 15½ by 10½ by 1 inches, and let it rise, covered loosely, in a warm place for 1 hour, or until it is almost double in bulk.

Dimple the dough, making ¼-inch-deep indentations with your fingertips, brush it with the remaining 2 tablespoons oil, and sprinkle it with the coarse salt. Bake the *focaccia* in the bottom third of a preheated 400° F. oven for 30 to 40 minutes, or until it is golden, let it cool in the pan on a rack, and serve it warm or at room temperature.

Olive, Rosemary, and Onion Focaccia

a ¼-ounce package (2½ teaspoons) active
  dry yeast
1 teaspoon sugar
4½ to 5 cups all-purpose flour
1¼ teaspoons salt
3 tablespoons olive oil
2 teaspoons finely chopped fresh rosemary
  leaves plus whole rosemary leaves
¼ cup minced onion
½ pound Kalamata, Niçoise, or green Greek
  olives or a combination, pitted and cut into
  slivers (about 1 cup)
1½ teaspoons coarse salt,
  or to taste

In the large bowl of an electric mixer fitted with the dough hook stir together the yeast, the sugar, and 1¾ cups lukewarm water and proof the yeast mixture for 5 minutes, or until it is foamy. Stir in 4½ cups of the flour, the salt, and 2 tablespoons of the oil and knead the dough, scraping down the dough hook occasionally and adding as much of the remaining ½ cup flour as necessary to form a soft, slightly sticky dough, for 3 minutes. Transfer the dough to a lightly oiled bowl, turn it to coat it with the oil, and let it rise, covered, in a warm place for 1 hour, or until it is double in bulk. Knead in the chopped rosemary, press the dough with lightly oiled hands into a well-oiled 15½- by 10½-inch jelly-roll pan, and let it rise, covered loosely, for 30 minutes. *The dough may be made 8 hours in advance and kept covered and chilled.*

Dimple the dough with your fingertips, making ¼-inch-deep indentations, brush it with the remaining 1 tablespoon oil, and top it with the onion, the olives, the salt, and the whole rosemary leaves. Bake the *focaccia* in the bottom third of a preheated 400° F. oven for 35 to 45 minutes, or until it is golden and cooked through. Transfer the *focaccia* to a rack, let it cool for 10 minutes, and serve it, cut into squares, warm or at room temperature.

PHOTO ON PAGE 61

Beverly Charlton

Semolina Focaccia with Bell Peppers, Sun-Dried Tomatoes, and Garlic Confit

a ¼-ounce package (2½ teaspoons) active
    dry yeast
½ teaspoon sugar
1 cup lukewarm water
3½ cups semolina flour (durum
    wheat flour, available at specialty
    foods shops)
1 teaspoon table salt
a 4-ounce jar sun-dried tomatoes
    packed in oil, drained, reserving
    ¼ cup of the oil, and the
    tomatoes chopped
4 garlic cloves
¼ cup olive oil
3 large red bell peppers,
    sliced thin
1 teaspoon coarse salt,
    or to taste
dried hot red pepper flakes for sprinkling the
    focaccia if desired

In the bowl of an electric mixer fitted with the paddle attachment proof the yeast with the sugar in the water for 5 minutes, or until the mixture is foamy, add the flour, the table salt, and the sun-dried tomatoes with 1 tablespoon of the reserved tomato oil, and combine the dough well. With the dough hook knead the dough for 2 minutes, or until it is soft and slightly sticky. Form the dough into a ball, transfer it to an oiled bowl, and turn it to coat it with the oil. Let the dough rise, covered with plastic wrap, in a warm place for 1½ hours, or until it is double in bulk. *The dough may be made up to this point, punched down, and kept, covered and chilled, overnight. Let the dough return to room temperature before proceeding with the recipe.* Press the dough evenly into an oiled jelly-roll pan, 15½ by 10½ by 1 inches, and let it rise, covered loosely, in a warm place for 1 hour, or until it is almost double in bulk.

While the dough is rising, in a saucepan cook the garlic in the olive oil over moderately low heat for 20 minutes, transfer it with a slotted spoon to a cutting surface, discarding the oil, and chop it fine. In a bowl stir together the garlic, the bell peppers, the remaining 3 tablespoons reserved tomato oil, and pepper to taste, sprinkle the mixture evenly over the dough, and sprinkle it with the coarse salt. Bake the *focaccia* in the bottom third of a preheated 400° F. oven for 30 to 35 minutes, or until it is golden, sprinkle it with the red pepper flakes, and let it cool in the pan on a rack. Serve the *focaccia* warm or at room temperature.

Dried Cherry and Golden Raisin Sweet Focaccia

2 cups dried sour cherries (about
    ½ pound, available at specialty
    foods shops)
1 cup golden raisins
2 cups water
a ¼-ounce package (2½ teaspoons) active
    dry yeast
½ teaspoon granulated sugar
3½ cups unbleached all-purpose flour
1 teaspoon salt
½ cup firmly packed light brown sugar
¼ teaspoon cinnamon
¾ stick (6 tablespoons) cold unsalted butter,
    cut into bits

In a bowl combine the cherries, the raisins, and the water, let the fruit soak for 10 minutes, or until it is softened, and drain the mixture, reserving 1 cup of the liquid. In a small saucepan heat the reserved liquid over low heat until it is lukewarm. In the bowl of an electric mixer fitted with the paddle attachment proof the yeast with the granulated sugar in the warm liquid for 5 minutes, or until the mixture is foamy, add the flour, the salt, ¼ cup of the brown sugar, the cinnamon, and the butter, and combine the dough well. Knead the dough with the dough hook for 2 minutes, or until it is soft and slightly sticky, transfer it to a lightly floured surface, and knead in the fruit mixture, patted dry, until it is incorporated thoroughly. Form the dough into a ball, transfer it to an oiled bowl, and turn it to coat it with the oil. Let the dough rise, covered with plastic wrap, in a warm place for 1½ hours, or until it is double in bulk. *The dough may be made up to this point, punched down, and kept, covered and chilled, overnight. Let the dough return to room temperature before proceeding with the recipe.* Press the dough evenly into an oiled jelly-roll pan, 15½ by 10½ by 1 inches, and let it rise, covered loosely, in a warm place for 1 hour, or until it is almost double in bulk.

Dimple the dough, making ¼-inch-deep indentations with your fingertips, and sprinkle it with the remaining ¼ cup brown sugar. Bake the *focaccia* in the bottom third of a preheated 400° F. for 30 to 35 minutes, or until it is golden, let it cool in the pan on a rack, and serve it warm or at room temperature.

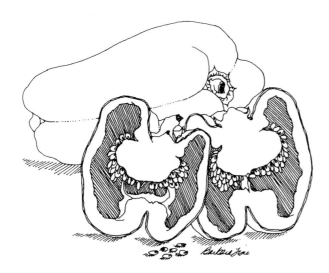

Grape and Walnut Sweet Focaccia

a ¼-ounce package (2½ teaspoons) active
   dry yeast
½ teaspoon granulated sugar
1 cup lukewarm water
3½ cups unbleached all-purpose flour
1 teaspoon salt
⅔ cup firmly packed light brown sugar
¼ teaspoon cinnamon
¾ stick (6 tablespoons) cold unsalted butter,
   cut into bits
1¼ pounds seedless grapes (preferably red),
   halved lengthwise (about 3 cups)
¾ cup finely chopped walnuts
2 tablespoons Marsala

In the bowl of an electric mixer fitted with the paddle attachment proof the yeast with the granulated sugar in the water for 5 minutes, or until the mixture is foamy, add the flour, the salt, ⅓ cup of the brown sugar, the cinnamon, and the butter, and combine the dough well. With the dough hook knead the dough for 2 minutes, or until it is soft and slightly sticky. Form the dough into a ball, transfer it to an oiled bowl, and turn it to coat it with the oil. Let the dough rise, covered with plastic wrap, in a warm place for 1½ hours, or until it is double in bulk. *The dough may be made up to this point, punched down,* *and kept, covered and chilled, overnight. Let the dough return to room temperature before proceeding with the recipe.* Press the dough evenly into an oiled jelly-roll pan, 15½ by 10½ by 1 inches, and let it rise, covered loosely, in a warm place for 1 hour, or until it is almost double in bulk.

In a bowl stir together the grapes, the walnuts, and the Marsala and sprinkle the mixture evenly over the dough. Sprinkle the *focaccia* with the remaining ⅓ cup brown sugar and bake it in the bottom third of a preheated 400° F. oven for 30 to 35 minutes, or until it is cooked through and the topping is caramelized. Let the *focaccia* cool in the pan on a rack and serve it warm or at room temperature.

Pepper, Rosemary, and Cheese Bread

a ¼-ounce package (2½ teaspoons) active
   dry yeast
3½ to 4½ cups unbleached all-purpose flour
1½ teaspoons salt
1 tablespoon dried rosemary, crumbled fine
1 teaspoon freshly ground pepper
2 tablespoons olive oil
1 cup freshly grated Parmesan
   (about 3 ounces)
1 cup grated provolone (about ¼ pound)
2 red bell peppers, roasted (procedure on
   page 126) and chopped fine

In a large bowl proof the yeast in 1⅓ cups warm water for 5 minutes, or until the mixture is foamy. Stir in 3½ cups of the flour, the salt, the rosemary, the pepper, the oil, the cheeses, and the bell peppers and stir the mixture until it is combined well. Knead the dough on a floured surface, incorporating as much of the remaining 1 cup flour as necessary to prevent the dough from sticking, for 8 to 10 minutes, or until it is smooth and elastic, transfer it to a lightly oiled bowl, turning it to coat it with the oil, and let it rise, covered with plastic wrap, in a warm place for 1 hour, or until it is double in bulk. Punch down the dough, halve it, and shape each piece into a loaf, about 14 inches long. Transfer the loaves to a lightly oiled baking sheet and let them rise, covered with a kitchen towel, for 45 minutes, or until they are almost double in bulk. Bake the loaves in the middle of a preheated 450° F. oven for 30 to 35 minutes, or until they are golden, transfer them to a rack, and let them cool. Makes 2 loaves.

Cornmeal Rolls

a ¼-ounce package (2½ teaspoons) active
    dry yeast
a pinch of sugar
1¼ cups lukewarm water
1 cup yellow cornmeal
about 2¾ cups all-purpose flour
2 teaspoons coarse salt plus additional for
    sprinkling the rolls
1 large egg, beaten lightly
caraway seeds for sprinkling the rolls

In the bowl of an electric mixer proof the yeast with the sugar in ¼ cup of the water for 10 minutes, or until the mixture is foamy. Beat in the remaining 1 cup water, the cornmeal, 2¼ cups of the flour, and 2 teaspoons of the salt and with the dough hook knead the dough for 5 minutes. Knead in enough of the remaining ½ cup flour so that the dough pulls away from the side of the bowl but remains sticky. Turn the dough out into a large bowl, dust it with flour, and let it rise, covered with plastic wrap, in a warm place for 1½ hours, or until it is double in bulk. Punch down the dough. *The dough may be prepared up to this point 1 day in advance and kept covered and chilled.* Let the dough rise again, covered, in a warm place for 1½ hours (longer if the dough was chilled), or until it is double in bulk.

Punch down the dough, knead it lightly on a lightly floured surface, and divide it into 16 pieces. Working with 1 piece of dough at a time, keeping the other pieces covered, form the dough into different shapes such as knots and wreaths. (To form wreaths, shape the dough into rings and with scissors snip the outer edges at intervals.) Arrange the rolls as they are formed on a greased baking sheet. (Use a black-steel baking sheet for crustier rolls.) Let the rolls rise, uncovered, in a warm place for 30 minutes, or until they are almost double in bulk, brush them lightly with the egg, and sprinkle them with the caraway seeds and the additional salt. Bake the rolls in the upper third of a preheated 450° F. oven for 10 to 12 minutes, or until they are golden. Serve the rolls warm. Makes 16 rolls.

PHOTO ON PAGE 78

Pumpkin Nutmeg Dinner Rolls

a ¼-ounce package (2½ teaspoons) active
    dry yeast
⅓ cup sugar
¾ cup milk, heated to lukewarm
7 to 8 cups all-purpose flour
1 teaspoon freshly grated nutmeg
1 teaspoon salt
1½ sticks (¾ cup) cold unsalted butter,
    cut into bits
1 large whole egg, beaten lightly
2 cups fresh pumpkin purée (page 230) or a
    16-ounce can pumpkin purée
an egg wash made by beating 1 large egg yolk
    with 1 tablespoon water

In a small bowl proof the yeast with 1 teaspoon of the sugar in the milk for 5 minutes, or until the mixture is foamy. In a large bowl combine well 7 cups of the flour, the nutmeg, the salt, and the remaining sugar and blend in the butter until the mixture resembles coarse meal. Add the whole egg, the pumpkin purée, and the yeast mixture and stir the dough until it is combined well.

Turn the dough out onto a floured surface and knead it, incorporating as much of the remaining 1 cup flour as necessary to prevent the dough from sticking, for 10 minutes, or until it is smooth and elastic. Form the dough into a ball, transfer it to a well-buttered large bowl, and turn it to coat it with the butter. Let the dough rise, covered with plastic wrap, in a warm place for 1 hour, or until it is double in bulk. Turn the dough out onto a work surface, divide it into 14 pieces, and form each piece into a ball. Fit the balls into a buttered 10-inch springform pan and let them rise, covered with a kitchen towel, in a warm place for 45 minutes, or until they are almost double in bulk. Brush the rolls with the egg wash and bake them in the middle of a preheated 350° F. oven for 40 to 50 minutes, or until they are golden. Let the rolls cool slightly in the pan, remove the side of the pan, and serve the rolls warm. *The rolls may be made 1 week in advance and kept wrapped well and frozen. Reheat the rolls, wrapped in foil, in a preheated 350° F. oven for 25 minutes, or until they are heated through.* Makes 14 rolls.

Sage Cloverleaf Rolls

⅔ cup milk
¾ stick (6 tablespoons) unsalted butter
1 tablespoon sugar
a ¼-ounce package (2½ teaspoons) active
    dry yeast
1 large whole egg, beaten lightly

1½ teaspoons salt
2½ to 3 cups all-purpose flour
¼ cup minced fresh sage or 2 tablespoons
   dried, crumbled
an egg wash made by beating 1 large egg
   with 1 tablespoon water

In a saucepan combine the milk, 4 tablespoons of the butter, and the sugar, heat the mixture over moderately low heat, stirring occasionally, until it registers between 110° F. and 115° F. on a candy thermometer, and in it proof the yeast for 5 minutes, or until the mixture is foamy. Stir in the whole egg, the salt, and 2½ cups of the flour, stirring until the mixture forms a dough. On a floured surface knead the dough, kneading in enough of the remaining ½ cup flour to form a soft dough, knead in the sage, and knead the dough for 8 to 10 minutes more, or until it is smooth and elastic. Form the dough into a ball and transfer it to a buttered bowl. Turn the dough to coat it with the butter. Let the dough rise, covered with plastic wrap, in a warm place for 1 hour, or until it is double in bulk.

Punch down the dough and divide it into 36 equal pieces. Form the pieces into balls, dipping the balls as they are formed into the remaining 2 tablespoons butter, melted, and put 3 balls in each of 12 buttered ⅓-cup muffin tins. Let the rolls rise in a warm place for 30 minutes, or until they are double in bulk, brush the tops with the egg wash, being careful not to let the egg drip down the sides, and bake the rolls in the middle of a preheated 400° F. oven for 15 to 20 minutes, or until they are golden. *The rolls may be made 1 day in advance and kept wrapped in foil at room temperature. Reheat the rolls, wrapped in the foil, in a preheated 350° F. oven for 15 minutes, or until they are hot.* Makes 12 rolls.

PHOTO ON PAGE 81

QUICK BREADS

Cheddar Chutney Drop Biscuits

1 cup all-purpose flour
1½ teaspoons double-acting baking powder
½ teaspoon salt
2 tablespoons cold unsalted butter, cut
   into bits
½ cup coarsely grated sharp Cheddar

2 tablespoons Major Grey's chutney, the
   solids chopped fine
⅓ cup milk

In a bowl whisk together the flour, the baking powder, and the salt, add the butter, and blend the mixture until it resembles coarse meal. Stir in the Cheddar. In a small bowl stir together the chutney and the milk, add the mixture to the flour mixture, and stir the mixture until it is just combined. Drop the dough into 6 mounds in a ring in a well-buttered 9-inch round glass baking dish and bake the biscuits in the middle of a preheated 450° F. oven for 15 minutes, or until they are golden. Makes 6 biscuits.

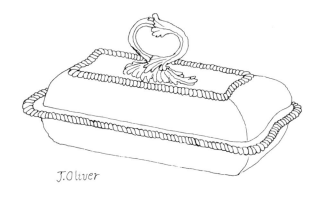

J. Oliver

Roasted Red Pepper and Parmesan Biscuits

¾ cup all-purpose flour
1½ teaspoons double-acting baking powder
¼ teaspoon salt
a pinch of cayenne
3 tablespoons cold unsalted butter, cut
   into bits
⅓ cup finely chopped drained bottled roasted
   red peppers, patted dry
¼ cup freshly grated Parmesan
3 tablespoons milk

In a bowl whisk together the flour, the baking powder, the salt, the cayenne, and a pinch of black pepper, add the butter, and blend the mixture until it resembles coarse meal. Add the roasted peppers, the Parmesan, and the milk and stir the mixture until it just forms a dough. Drop the dough in 6 mounds about 2 inches apart onto a buttered baking sheet and bake the biscuits in the middle of a preheated 425° F. oven for 15 to 18 minutes, or until they are golden and cooked through. Makes 6 biscuits.

Irish Soda Bread

4 cups bread flour
1 tablespoon double-acting baking powder
1 teaspoon salt
¾ teaspoon baking soda
1 cup raisins, rinsed in hot water and patted dry
1 tablespoon caraway seeds
2 cups buttermilk

Into a large bowl sift together the flour, the baking powder, the salt, and the baking soda and stir in the raisins and the caraway seeds. Add the buttermilk and stir the mixture until it forms a dough. Turn the dough out onto a well-floured surface and knead it for 1 minute. Halve the dough, with floured hands shape each half into a round loaf, and transfer the loaves to a lightly greased baking sheet. Cut an X ¼ inch deep across the tops of the loaves with a sharp knife and bake the loaves in the middle of a preheated 350° F. oven for 45 to 55 minutes, or until a tester comes out clean. Transfer the loaves to racks and let them cool. Makes 2 loaves.

Lemon Bread

½ cup vegetable shortening
1¼ cups sugar
2 large eggs
1¼ cups all-purpose flour
1 teaspoon double-acting baking powder
¼ teaspoon salt
½ cup milk
½ cup finely chopped walnuts
1 teaspoon freshly grated lemon zest
¼ cup fresh lemon juice

In a bowl cream together the shortening and 1 cup of the sugar until the mixture is light and fluffy and beat in the eggs, 1 at a time, beating until the mixture is smooth. Into another bowl sift together the flour, the baking powder, and the salt and stir the mixture into the egg mixture alternately with the milk, stirring until the mixture is just combined. Stir in the walnuts and the zest, transfer the batter to a well-buttered 9- by 5-inch loaf pan, and bake the bread in the middle of a preheated 350° F. oven for 1 hour, or until a tester comes out clean. Transfer the bread in the pan to a rack and with a small skewer poke it all over. In a small bowl stir together the remaining ¼ cup sugar and the lemon juice, pour the mixture over the hot bread, and let the bread cool.

Bacon and Onion Corn Muffins

8 slices of lean bacon
½ cup finely chopped onion
1 cup yellow cornmeal
⅔ cup all-purpose flour
1 teaspoon double-acting baking powder
1 teaspoon baking soda
½ teaspoon salt
2 large eggs
½ stick (¼ cup) unsalted butter, melted
  and cooled
1½ cups sour cream
¼ cup milk

In a heavy skillet cook the bacon over moderate heat until it is crisp, transfer it to paper towels to drain, and crumble it. Pour off all but 1 tablespoon of the fat from the skillet and in the fat remaining in the skillet cook the onion over moderately low heat, stirring, until it is softened. Into a bowl sift together the cornmeal, the flour, the baking powder, the baking soda, and the salt. In another bowl whisk together the eggs, the butter, the sour cream, and the milk, stir in the bacon, the onion, and the cornmeal mixture, and beat the batter well. Divide the batter among 12 well-buttered ⅓-cup muffin tins and bake the muffins in the middle of a preheated 425° F. oven for 20 minutes, or until they are golden. Turn the muffins out onto a rack and let them cool. Makes 12 muffins.

Caraway Cheese Muffins

2 cups all-purpose flour
1 tablespoon double-acting baking powder
2 teaspoons sugar
1¼ teaspoons salt
¼ teaspoon English-style dry mustard
1 cup coarsely grated sharp Cheddar
1 large egg
1 cup milk
½ stick (¼ cup) unsalted butter, melted
  and cooled
1½ teaspoons caraway seeds

Into a bowl sift together the flour, the baking powder, the sugar, the salt, and the mustard and stir in the Cheddar. In another bowl whisk together the egg, the milk, and the butter, add the mixture to the flour mixture, and stir the batter until it is just combined. Divide the batter among 12 well-buttered ⅓-cup muffin tins, sprinkle the muffins with the caraway seeds, and bake them in the middle of a preheated 350° F. oven for 25 to 30 minutes, or until they are golden. Let the muffins cool in the tins for 2 minutes and turn them out onto a rack. Makes 12 muffins.

Cranberry Upside-Down Muffins

2 cups cranberries, picked over and rinsed
1¼ cups sugar
1 teaspoon freshly grated nutmeg
2 cups all-purpose flour
1 tablespoon double-acting baking powder
½ teaspoon salt
1 large egg
½ stick (¼ cup) unsalted butter, melted and cooled
1 cup milk

In a saucepan combine the cranberries, 1 cup of the sugar, and the nutmeg, cook the mixture over moderately high heat, stirring, until the sugar is dissolved, and boil it, covered, for 3 minutes. Simmer the mixture, uncovered, stirring, for 3 minutes and let it cool.

Into a bowl sift together the flour, the baking powder, the remaining ¼ cup sugar, and the salt. In another bowl whisk together the egg, the butter, and the milk, add the mixture to the flour mixture, and stir the batter until it is just combined. Divide the cranberry mixture among 12 well-buttered ½-cup muffin tins, top it with the batter, and bake the muffins in the middle of a preheated 400° F. oven for 25 minutes, or until they are golden. Let the muffins cool in the tins for 2 minutes and invert them onto a rack. Makes 12 muffins.

Sour Cream Bran Muffins

1 stick (½ cup) unsalted butter, softened
¼ cup firmly packed light brown sugar
1 large egg, beaten lightly
1 cup sour cream
¼ cup dark molasses
½ cup raisins
1 cup all-purpose flour
1 teaspoon baking soda
¼ teaspoon salt
1 cup miller's bran (available at natural foods stores, specialty foods shops, and some supermarkets)

In a large bowl with an electric mixer cream together the butter and the brown sugar until the mixture is light and fluffy, beat in the egg, the sour cream, and the molasses, and stir in the raisins. In a bowl whisk together the flour, the baking soda, the salt, and the bran, add the mixture to the sour cream mixture, and stir the batter until it is just combined. (The batter will be lumpy.) Spoon the batter into 12 well-buttered ⅓-cup muffin tins and bake the muffins in the middle of a preheated 400° F. oven for 15 to 20 minutes, or until they are golden and springy to the touch. Turn the muffins out onto a rack and let them cool. Makes 12 muffins.

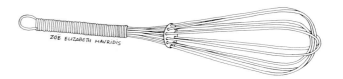

ZOE ELIZABETH MAVRIDIS

Cinnamon, Pecan, and Currant Cream Scones

¼ cup heavy cream plus additional for brushing
1 large egg yolk
½ teaspoon vanilla
1 cup all-purpose flour
3 tablespoons sugar plus additional for sprinkling
¼ teaspoon salt
1½ teaspoons double-acting baking powder
¼ teaspoon baking soda
½ teaspoon cinnamon
3 tablespoons cold unsalted butter,
    cut into bits
⅓ cup pecans, chopped
¼ cup currants

In a small bowl whisk together ¼ cup of the cream, the egg yolk, and the vanilla. Into a bowl sift together the flour, 3 tablespoons of the sugar, the salt, the baking powder, the baking soda, and the cinnamon, add the butter, and blend the mixture until it resembles coarse meal. Stir in the pecans, the currants, and the cream mixture with a fork until the mixture forms a sticky but manageable dough. Knead the dough gently on a lightly floured surface for 30 seconds, pat it into a ¾-inch-thick round, and cut it into 6 wedges. Transfer the wedges to a lightly greased baking sheet, brush them with the additional cream, and sprinkle them with the additional sugar. Bake the scones in the middle of a preheated 400° F. oven for 15 to 18 minutes, or until they are golden. Makes 6 scones.

Hot Onion Squares

2 cups very thinly sliced onion
7 tablespoons lard
cayenne to taste
2 cups bread flour
1 tablespoon double-acting baking powder
¾ teaspoon salt
⅔ cup milk
1 large egg
¾ cup sour cream

In a heavy skillet cook the onion in 2 tablespoons of the lard over moderately low heat, stirring, until it is golden, stir in the cayenne and salt and pepper to taste, and reserve the mixture. Onto a sheet of wax paper sift together the flour, the baking powder, and the salt and sift the mixture again into a bowl. Add the remaining 5 tablespoons lard and blend the mixture until it resembles fine meal. Stir in the milk, stirring until the dough is combined well, turn the dough out onto a floured surface, and knead it for 30 seconds. Pat the dough into a 9-inch square, press it evenly into a greased 9-inch-square pan, and top it with the reserved onion mixture. In a small bowl whisk together the egg, the sour cream, and salt and pepper to taste, pour the mixture over the onion mixture, smoothing it with a spatula to cover the onion mixture evenly, and bake the bread in the middle of a preheated 450° F. oven for 20 to 25 minutes, or until it is cooked through. Cut the onion bread into squares and serve it hot. Serves 6 to 8.

Popovers

1 cup sifted all-purpose flour
½ teaspoon salt
2 large eggs
1 cup milk
melted unsalted butter for brushing the pan

Into a bowl sift together the flour and the salt. In a small bowl whisk together the eggs and the milk. Add the milk mixture to the flour mixture, stirring, and stir the batter until it is smooth. In a preheated 450° F. oven heat a six-cup popover pan for 5 minutes, or until it is hot, brush the cups with the melted butter, and fill them half full with the batter. Bake the popovers in the middle of the 450° F. oven for 20 minutes, reduce the heat to 375° F., and bake the popovers for 20 minutes more, or until they are golden and crisp. Makes 6 popovers.

CRACKERS AND TOASTS

Spiced Yuca Chips

2½ pounds fresh yuca (cassava, available at most Hispanic produce markets), cut into 4-inch sections
vegetable oil for deep-frying
1 tablespoon chili powder
¾ teaspoon salt
a pinch of cayenne

With a paring knife make a ⅛-inch-deep slit down the length of each yuca section and with the aid of the knife pry off the brown and the white layers. In a food processor fitted with the 1-mm. slicing disk slice the yuca crosswise. In a kettle heat 1½ inches of the oil to 375° F. on a deep-fat thermometer. Separating the yuca slices, drop them, 1 at a time, into the oil and fry them in batches, turning them, for 1 to 2 minutes, or until they are pale golden, transferring them as they are fried to paper towels to drain. In a small bowl stir together the chili powder, the salt, and the cayenne and in a large bowl toss the chips with the spice mixture.

Cheddar Cornmeal Crackers

⅔ cup yellow cornmeal
⅓ cup all-purpose flour
½ teaspoon salt
1 teaspoon sugar
1½ teaspoons double-acting baking powder
⅔ cup cold water
2 tablespoons unsalted butter, melted and cooled
1 large egg
1 cup grated sharp Cheddar

In a blender blend together the cornmeal, the flour, the salt, the sugar, and the baking powder, add the water, the butter, and the egg, and blend the mixture for 15 seconds. Scrape down the sides, add the Cheddar, and blend the batter for 5 seconds, or until it is combined well. Spread ¼ cup measures of the batter into 4-inch circles on buttered baking sheets and bake the crackers in batches in the middle of a preheated 400° F. oven for 6 minutes. Turn the crackers and bake them for 5 to 6 minutes more, or until they are crisp. The crackers keep in an airtight container for 1 week. Makes about 10 crackers.

Bruschetta with Caponata

For the caponata

¼ cup olive oil

3½ cups ¼-inch dice unpeeled eggplant
    (about 1¼ pounds)

¾ cup finely chopped onion

¾ cup finely chopped celery

⅓ cup chopped pitted green olives

3 tablespoons chopped drained bottled capers

¼ cup red-wine vinegar

1½ tablespoons sugar, or to taste

3 tablespoons golden raisins

3 tablespoons pine nuts, toasted lightly

3 plum tomatoes, cut into ¼-inch dice
    (about 1 cup)

¼ cup finely chopped flat-leafed parsley leaves

For the bruschetta

eight to twelve ½-inch-thick diagonal slices of
    country-style Italian bread

olive oil for brushing the bread

flat-leafed parsley sprigs for garnish

Make the *caponata*: In a heavy skillet heat 2 tablespoons of the oil over moderately high heat until it is hot but not smoking, in it cook the eggplant, stirring, for 3 to 5 minutes, or until it is tender, and transfer it to a bowl. To the skillet add the remaining 2 tablespoons oil and in it cook the onion and the celery over moderate heat, stirring, for 5 minutes. Add the olives, the capers, the vinegar, the sugar, the raisins, the pine nuts, and the tomatoes and cook the mixture, stirring, for 2 minutes. Cook the mixture, covered, stirring occasionally, for 5 to 10 minutes, or until it is cooked through and the celery is tender, and transfer it to the bowl. Stir in the parsley, let the *caponata* cool, and chill it, covered, overnight. Season the *caponata* with salt and pepper.

Make the *bruschetta*: Grill the bread on an oiled rack set about 4 inches over glowing coals for 1 minute on each side, brush the toasts on one side with the oil, and sprinkle them with salt to taste.

Top each toast generously with some of the *caponata*, arrange 2 or 3 toasts on each of 4 plates, and garnish each serving with the parsley sprigs. Serves 4.

PHOTO ON PAGE 48

Genoa Toasts

⅔ cup olive oil

4 garlic cloves, minced and mashed to
    a paste with a pinch of salt

about ½ of a day-old thick *focaccia*
    (page 98), cut into ¼-inch-thick slices

coarse salt to taste for sprinkling the toasts

In a bowl stir together the oil and the garlic paste, brush both sides of the *focaccia* slices lightly with the oil mixture, and bake the slices in one layer on baking sheets in a preheated 250° F. oven for 30 minutes. Turn the slices, sprinkle them with the salt, and bake them for 30 minutes more, or until they are pale golden and crisp. Makes about 48 toasts.

SOUPS

Cream of Jerusalem Artichoke and Celery Soup

2 pounds Jerusalem artichokes (sunchokes), peeled, sliced, and reserved in a bowl of cold water
6 cups sliced celery plus celery leaves for garnish
2 cups water
1 quart (4 cups) chicken broth
⅔ cup dry white wine
1 tablespoon English-style dry mustard
2 cups half-and-half
⅛ teaspoon freshly grated nutmeg

In a stainless steel or enameled kettle combine the Jerusalem artichokes, drained, the sliced celery, the water, the broth, the wine, and the mustard and simmer the mixture, uncovered, for 30 minutes, or until the vegetables are tender. In a blender purée the mixture in batches, transferring it as it is puréed to a bowl, pour the purée into the kettle, cleaned, and stir in the half-and-half, the nutmeg, and salt and pepper to taste. Heat the soup over moderate heat, stirring, until it barely reaches a boil, ladle it into heated bowls, and garnish each serving with a celery leaf. Makes about 9 cups, serving 6 to 8 as a first course.

Asparagus and Leek Soup

1 cup finely chopped white and pale green part of leek, washed well
1 garlic clove, minced
2 tablespoons unsalted butter
1 pound asparagus, trimmed and cut into 1-inch pieces
1¼ cups chicken broth
⅓ cup sour cream

In a saucepan cook the leek and the garlic in the butter over moderately low heat, stirring, until the leek is softened, add the asparagus, the broth, and ½ cup water, and simmer the mixture, covered, for 10 to 12 minutes, or until the asparagus is very tender. Purée two thirds of the mixture in a blender until it is very smooth, stir the purée into the mixture remaining in the pan, and whisk in the sour cream and salt and pepper to taste. Cook the soup over moderately low heat until it is heated through, but do not let it boil. Serves 2.

Avocado and Smoked Salmon Soup

2 avocados (preferably California)
2 tablespoons fresh lemon juice
½ cup sour cream
3 to 3½ cups chicken broth
¼ teaspoon Tabasco
2 ounces smoked salmon

Peel and pit the avocados and in a blender blend them with the lemon juice, the sour cream, 3 cups of the broth, and the Tabasco until the mixture is smooth, adding enough of the remaining ½ cup broth to thin the mixture to the desired consistency. Transfer the soup to a bowl, season it with salt and pepper, and chill it, its surface covered with plastic wrap, for 1 hour, or until it is cold. (The soup will discolor if kept for more than 6 hours.) Stir half the salmon, chopped, into the soup, divide the soup among chilled bowls, and garnish it with the remaining salmon, cut into strips. Makes about 5 cups, serving 6.

Barley, Swiss Chard, and Lima Bean Soup

1 cup medium pearl barley
2 onions, chopped coarse
1 cup chopped carrot
2 large garlic cloves
2 tablespoons olive oil
3 quarts (12 cups) water
1 quart (4 cups) chicken broth
2 smoked ham hocks
4 parsley sprigs
1 cup chopped celery
1 pound Swiss chard, washed well and
   chopped coarse
a 10-ounce package frozen lima beans
1 teaspoon dried basil, crumbled
½ teaspoon dried thyme, crumbled

In a baking pan toast the barley in a preheated 375° F. oven, shaking the pan occasionally, for 5 to 7 minutes, or until it is aromatic. In a large kettle cook the onions, the carrot, and the garlic in the oil over moderate heat, stirring occasionally, until the vegetables are browned. Add the water, the broth, the ham hocks, and the parsley and simmer the mixture, uncovered, for 1 hour. Add the toasted barley and the celery and simmer the mixture, uncovered, for 45 minutes. Transfer the ham hocks with tongs to a cutting board, discard the fat and bones, and chop the ham coarse. To the kettle add the ham, the Swiss chard, the lima beans, the basil, the thyme, and salt and pepper to taste and simmer the soup for 15 to 20 minutes, or until the chard is tender. Makes about 15 cups, serving 6 as a main course.

Curried Bean and Bell Pepper Soup

a 19-ounce can *cannellini* beans, rinsed and
   drained well
½ cup chopped red bell pepper
1 small garlic clove, minced
2 tablespoons grated onion
¾ cup chicken broth
½ teaspoon curry powder
2 teaspoons fresh lemon juice, or to taste
a pinch of sugar
¾ cup half-and-half
finely chopped fresh basil leaves for garnish

In a blender purée the beans and the bell pepper with the garlic, the onion, the broth, the curry powder, the lemon juice, and the sugar. Add the half-and-half and blend the mixture until it is just combined. Strain the mixture through a sieve set over a bowl, pressing hard on the solids, discard the solids, and chill the soup for 1 hour, or until it is cold. Serve the soup garnished with the basil. Makes about 3 cups, serving 4.

Beverly Charlton

Kidney Bean and Sausage Soup

about ¼ pound *kielbasa* or other smoked
   sausage, cut into rounds
a 19-ounce can kidney beans, drained and
   rinsed
3 cups chicken broth
1 small onion, chopped fine
1 small green bell pepper, chopped fine
a dash of Worcestershire sauce
¼ cup thinly sliced scallion green
cayenne to taste

In a heavy skillet brown the sausage and transfer it to paper towels to drain. In a blender purée 1 cup of the beans with 1 cup of the broth. In a saucepan combine the sausage, the purée, the remaining 2 cups broth, the onion, the bell pepper, and the Worcestershire sauce and simmer the mixture for 10 minutes. Stir in the remaining beans, the scallion green, and the cayenne. Heat the soup until it is hot. Makes about 4 cups, serving 2.

Red Bean and Bacon Soup

½ pound lean bacon (about 8 slices), cut
  into ½-inch pieces
1½ cups finely chopped onion
2 large garlic cloves
1 bay leaf
1 tablespoon chili powder
1½ teaspoons ground cuminseed
¼ teaspoon cayenne, or to taste
1½ cups chopped celery
1½ cups chopped carrot
1 pound red beans such as kidney or pinto,
  soaked in enough cold water to cover them
  by 2 inches overnight or quick-soaked
  (procedure on page 143) and drained
4 cups chicken broth plus, if desired,
  additional for thinning the soup
a 28-ounce can Italian tomatoes, chopped,
  reserving the juice
½ cup medium-dry Sherry, or to taste
chopped scallion green as an accompaniment
sour cream as an accompaniment

In a heavy kettle cook the bacon over moderately low heat, stirring occasionally, until it is crisp, transfer it to paper towels to drain, and reserve it. Pour off all but ¼ cup of the fat and in the remaining fat cook the onion, the garlic, the bay leaf, the chili powder, the cuminseed, and the cayenne, stirring, until the onion is softened. Add the celery, the carrot, the beans, 4 cups of the broth, and 2 cups water and simmer the soup, covered, for 1 to 1½ hours, or until the beans are tender. Add the tomatoes with the reserved juice and simmer the soup, covered, for 20 minutes. Discard the bay leaf and force the soup in batches through a food mill into a large saucepan. Stir in the Sherry, salt and pepper to taste, and the additional broth or water to thin the soup to the desired consistency, simmer the soup for 5 minutes, and serve it with the reserved bacon, the scallion green, and the sour cream. Makes about 12 cups, serving 6.

Creamy White Bean Soup with Leeks

three 19-ounce cans white beans, rinsed
  well in a sieve
¼ teaspoon dried tarragon, crumbled
2 cups chicken broth
2 cups thinly sliced white and pale
  green part of leek, washed
3 garlic cloves, minced
¼ teaspoon dried hot red pepper flakes,
  or to taste
3 tablespoons olive oil
¾ cup half-and-half
1 tablespoon fresh lemon juice

In a blender purée the beans in batches with the tarragon and the broth and strain the purée through a fine sieve into a bowl, pressing hard on the solids. In a large saucepan cook the leek, the garlic, and the red pepper flakes in the oil over moderately low heat, stirring occasionally, until the leek is softened and begins to turn golden. Add the purée, the half-and-half, the lemon juice, and salt to taste and simmer the soup, stirring, for 5 minutes. Makes about 5½ cups, serving 6 as a first course.

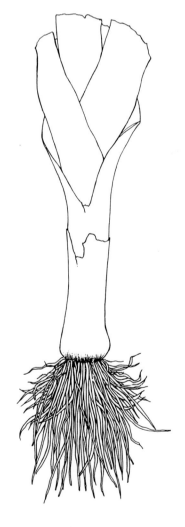

ZOE MAVRIDIS · 91

Beef Consommé with Herbed Crêpes Julienne

herbed crêpe batter (page 162)
4 pounds meaty beef shanks, sawed into
    1-inch pieces
2 onions, chopped coarse
1 carrot, chopped coarse
2 ribs of celery, chopped coarse
1½ teaspoons salt
a cheesecloth bag containing 4 parsley
    sprigs, 1 bay leaf, and a pinch of
    dried thyme
a 7-pound chicken, halved lengthwise
    and the giblets (excluding the liver), chopped
10 chives, cut into 2-inch pieces, for garnish

Make 2 crêpes (procedure on page 235) with the herbed crêpe batter and cut them into julienne strips. In a baking pan spread the shanks, the onions, and the carrot, brown the mixture well in a preheated 450° F. oven, and transfer it to a kettle. Add 2 cups water to the baking pan, deglaze the pan over moderately high heat, scraping up the brown bits, and add the liquid to the kettle with 3½ quarts cold water, the celery, the salt, and the cheesecloth bag. Bring the water to a boil, skimming the froth, and simmer the mixture, adding boiling water if necessary to keep the ingredients barely covered, for 3 hours. Add the chicken and enough water to cover the mixture and simmer the mixture, skimming it, for 2 to 3 hours, or until it is reduced to about 2 quarts. Remove the chicken and reserve it for another use. Strain the stock through a fine sieve into a bowl, pressing hard on the solids, and let it cool. Chill the stock, remove the fat, and clarify the stock (procedure follows). In a large saucepan heat the consommé over moderately low heat until it is hot. Serve the beef consommé garnished with the chives and the julienne herbed crêpes. Makes about 6 cups, serving 6.

To Clarify Stock

8 cups cool liquid stock,
    fat removed
the crushed shells of 4 large eggs
4 large egg whites,
    beaten lightly
4 scallions, chopped

In a kettle combine the stock, the shells, the egg whites, the scallions, and, if necessary, salt and pepper to taste. Bring the liquid to a boil, stirring, simmer the stock, undisturbed, for 20 minutes, and ladle it through a fine sieve lined with a double thickness of rinsed and squeezed cheesecloth into a bowl. Makes about 6 cups clarified stock.

Summer Borscht

1 fresh beet (about 3 inches in diameter),
    peeled and grated coarse
1 small onion, chopped
1 tablespoon sugar
3 tablespoons dry red wine
1 tablespoon red-wine vinegar
sour cream for garnish

In a large microwave-safe bowl stir together the beet, the onion, the sugar, and 1½ cups water and microwave the mixture, covered, at high power (100%) for 12 to 15 minutes, or until the beet is tender. Stir in the wine and microwave the mixture, uncovered, at high power (100%) for 3 minutes more. Stir in 1 cup cold water, the vinegar, and salt and pepper to taste, transfer the soup to a metal bowl set in a larger bowl of ice and cold water, and stir it until it is cold. Divide the soup between 2 bowls and garnish each serving with a dollop of the sour cream. Makes about 2¼ cups, serving 2.

Gingered Carrot Soup

1 tablespoon unsalted butter
4 carrots (about ¾ pound),
    grated coarse
½ teaspoon sugar
1 tablespoon grated peeled fresh gingerroot
¾ cup chicken broth,
    or to taste
2 cups boiling water
1 teaspoon fresh lemon juice,
    or to taste

In a 2-quart microwave-safe dish melt the butter in the microwave at high power (100%) for 15 seconds, stir in the carrots, the sugar, the gingerroot, the broth, and the water, and microwave the mixture at high power for 20 minutes, or until the carrots are tender. In a blender purée the mixture with the lemon juice and salt and pepper to taste and divide the soup between 2 bowls. Serves 2.

Cheddar Vegetable Soup

½ cup finely chopped onion
⅓ cup finely chopped carrot
⅓ cup finely chopped celery
½ teaspoon caraway seeds
1½ tablespoons unsalted butter
3 tablespoons all-purpose flour
⅓ cup dry white wine
1½ cups chicken broth plus additional to thin
    the soup if desired
¾ teaspoon Worcestershire sauce
1½ cups chopped cauliflower
¼ pound extra-sharp Cheddar, grated coarse
    (about 1¼ cups)
a dash of Tabasco, or to taste

In a saucepan cook the onion, the carrot, the celery, the caraway seeds, and salt and pepper to taste in the butter over moderately low heat, stirring, until the vegetables are softened, stir in the flour, and cook the mixture, stirring, for 3 minutes. Stir in the wine, 1½ cups of the broth, the Worcestershire sauce, and the cauliflower and simmer the mixture, covered, for 10 to 15 minutes, or until the cauliflower is tender. Remove the pan from the heat and stir in the Cheddar, a little at a time, stirring until it is melted. Stir in the Tabasco, the additional broth, if desired, and salt and pepper to taste and heat the soup over low heat, but do not let it boil. Makes about 3½ cups, serving 2.

Chicken Meatball Soup

½ pound ground chicken
3 tablespoons minced fresh parsley leaves
1 teaspoon Worcestershire sauce (preferably
    white-wine)
½ teaspoon salt
⅛ teaspoon dried sage, crumbled
⅓ cup thinly sliced white part of scallion plus
    ⅓ cup thinly sliced green part of scallion
1 tablespoon unsalted butter
¼ cup dry white wine
4 cups chicken broth
2 ounces snow peas, cut into ½-inch pieces
    (about ½ cup)

In a bowl combine well the chicken, the parsley, the Worcestershire sauce, the salt, the sage, and pepper to taste and form the mixture into 1-inch balls. In a large saucepan cook the white part of scallion in the butter over moderately low heat until it is softened, add the wine, and simmer the mixture until the wine is reduced by half. Add the broth, bring the liquid to a boil, and add the meatballs and the snow peas. Simmer the soup, covered, for 5 minutes, or until the meatballs are cooked through, and stir in the green part of scallion and salt and pepper to taste. Serves 2.

Corn and Oyster Bisque

5 ears of fresh or frozen corn
3 cups water
1 bay leaf
18 oysters, shucked (procedure follows),
    reserving the liquor
2 cups milk
¼ teaspoon Tabasco, or to taste
whole or minced fresh parsley leaves
    for garnish
paprika for garnish

Cut the corn kernels from the cobs on a work surface, transfer them to a large saucepan, and with the back of a knife scrape the milk from the cobs into the pan. Cut each cob into 3 pieces and add them to the pan. Add the water and the bay leaf and simmer the mixture, covered, for 30 minutes. Discard the cobs and the bay leaf, in a blender purée the corn mixture in batches, and strain the purée through a fine sieve into a bowl, pressing hard on the solids. Transfer the purée to the pan and pour the reserved oyster liquor through a fine sieve into the pan. Add the milk, the Tabasco, and salt to taste and heat the mixture over moderate heat, stirring, being careful not to let it boil, until it is hot. Add the oysters and heat the soup, stirring, being careful not to let it boil, for 3 minutes, or until the edges of the oysters curl. Ladle the soup into heated shallow bowls and garnish each serving with some of the parsley and the paprika. Makes about 7½ cups, serving 6 as a first course.

To Shuck Oysters

Scrub the oysters thoroughly with a stiff brush under running cold water. Hold each oyster flat side up on a work surface with the hinged end away from you, insert an oyster knife between the shells at the hinged end, twisting the knife to pop open the shell, and slide the blade against the flat upper shell to cut the large muscle and free the upper shell. If the shell crumbles and cannot be opened at the hinge, insert the knife between the shells at the curved end of the oyster, pry the shells open, and sever the large muscle. Break off and discard the upper shell and slide the knife under the oyster to release it from the bottom shell.

Herbed Cream of Corn Soup

4 cups cooked fresh corn kernels or two
    10-ounce packages frozen, thawed
1 cup chicken broth
2 tablespoons finely chopped white part
    of scallion
½ teaspoon dried thyme, crumbled
1 cup half-and-half
2 tablespoons minced fresh parsley leaves

In a blender blend the corn, the broth, the scallion, and the thyme until the mixture is smooth. Strain the mixture through a sieve set over a bowl, pressing hard on the solids, discard the solids, and stir in the half-and-half and the parsley. Season the soup with salt and pepper and chill it, covered, for 1 hour, or until it is cold. Makes about 4 cups, serving 4.

Cream of Crab Meat Soup

¼ cup minced onion
1½ tablespoons unsalted butter
4 teaspoons all-purpose flour
2 tablespoons medium-dry Sherry, or to taste
1 cup bottled clam juice
a pinch of Old Bay seasoning (available at
    fish markets and many supermarkets) if
    desired
½ teaspoon fresh lemon juice, or to taste
a dash of Tabasco, or to taste
1 cup half-and-half
½ pound lump crab meat, thawed if frozen
    and picked over
1 hard-boiled large egg, the white and yolk
    separated and each minced, for garnish

In a large saucepan cook the onion in the butter over moderately low heat, whisking, until it is softened, whisk in the flour, and cook the *roux*, whisking, for 3 minutes. Whisk in the Sherry, the clam juice, the Old Bay seasoning, the lemon juice, the Tabasco, the half-and-half, and salt and pepper to taste and simmer the mixture, whisking occasionally, for 15 minutes. Add the crab meat and heat the mixture until the crab meat is heated through. Divide the soup between 2 bowls and garnish it with the egg. Serves 2.

Minted Cucumber and Bell Pepper Buttermilk Soup

2 cucumbers, peeled and seeded
¾ cup plain yogurt
1 teaspoon salt
1½ teaspoons sugar, or to taste
2 teaspoons English-style dry mustard, or to taste
2½ cups buttermilk
1 large red bell pepper, diced fine
    (about 1 cup)
1 large yellow bell pepper, diced fine
    (about 1 cup)
2 tablespoons finely chopped fresh mint
    leaves plus shredded mint leaves for garnish
fresh lemon juice to taste

In a blender purée 1 of the cucumbers, chopped, the yogurt, the salt, the sugar, and the mustard, transfer the purée to a large bowl, and stir in the buttermilk, the bell peppers, the remaining cucumber, diced fine, and the 2 tablespoons chopped mint. Chill the soup, covered, for at least 3 hours or overnight and stir in the lemon juice and salt to taste. Divide the soup among 4 bowls and garnish it with the shredded mint. Makes about 6 cups, serving 4.

PHOTO ON PAGE 46

Gumbo Filé

6 live small hard-shelled crabs or
  ½ pound lump crab meat,
  picked over
¼ cup vegetable shortening
2 rounded tablespoons all-purpose flour
¼ cup chopped onion
1 pound okra, rinsed, trimmed,
  and sliced thin
½ cup chopped ham
a 14- to 16-ounce can tomatoes including
  the juice
2 tablespoons finely chopped green bell
  pepper
2 garlic cloves, minced and
  mashed to a paste with
  ½ teaspoon salt
1 bay leaf
6 parsley sprigs
1 thyme sprig
2 tablespoons chopped celery leaves
¾ pound medium shrimp,
  shelled
cayenne to taste
1 tablespoon filé powder (available at some
  specialty foods shops)

In a kettle blanch the crabs in boiling water for 2 minutes, drain them, and let them cool until they can be handled. Discard the top shells, the aprons, the gills, the sand sacs, and the mouths and reserve the crabs.

In a heavy skillet, preferably cast-iron, melt the shortening over moderately low heat, add the flour, and cook the *roux*, stirring constantly, for 30 minutes, or until it is the color of cocoa. Stir in the onion and cook the mixture, stirring, until the onion begins to brown. Add the okra and cook the mixture over moderate heat, stirring frequently, until the okra is golden. In a kettle bring 8 cups water to a boil, add the *roux* mixture, the ham, the tomatoes with the juice, the bell pepper, the garlic paste, the bay leaf, the parsley, the thyme, and the celery leaves, and simmer the mixture, stirring occasionally, for 50 minutes. Stir in the reserved crabs and simmer the gumbo for 5 minutes. Stir in the shrimp and the lump crab meat, if used, simmer the gumbo for 5 minutes, or until the shrimp are firm, and season it with the cayenne and salt. Discard the bay leaf and serve the gumbo sprinkled with the filé powder. Makes about 9 cups, serving 6.

Lentil and Brown Rice Soup

5 cups chicken broth
1½ cups lentils, picked over and rinsed
1 cup brown rice
a 32- to 35-ounce can tomatoes, drained,
  reserving the juice, and chopped
3 carrots, halved lengthwise and cut crosswise
  into ¼-inch pieces
1 onion, chopped
1 stalk of celery, chopped
3 garlic cloves, minced
½ teaspoon dried basil, crumbled
½ teaspoon dried orégano, crumbled
¼ teaspoon dried thyme, crumbled
1 bay leaf
½ cup minced fresh parsley leaves
2 tablespoons cider vinegar, or to taste

In a heavy kettle combine the broth, 3 cups water, the lentils, the rice, the tomatoes with the reserved juice, the carrots, the onion, the celery, the garlic, the basil, the orégano, the thyme, and the bay leaf, bring the liquid to a boil, and simmer the mixture, covered, stirring occasionally, for 45 to 55 minutes, or until the lentils and rice are tender. Stir in the parsley, the vinegar, and salt and pepper to taste and discard the bay leaf. The soup will be thick and will thicken as it stands. Thin the soup, if desired, with additional hot chicken broth or water. Makes about 14 cups, serving 6 to 8.

Red Lentil Soup with Spiced Oil

For the soup
1 cup red lentils (available at natural foods
  stores, East Indian markets, and some
  supermarkets), picked over
2 onions, chopped
2 tablespoons vegetable oil
5 garlic cloves, minced
4 teaspoons grated peeled fresh gingerroot
1 teaspoon ground cumin
1 teaspoon ground coriander seeds
3 cups chicken broth
1 cup drained canned tomatoes
For the spiced oil
2 tablespoons vegetable oil
1½ tablespoons minced seeded fresh red chili
  (wear rubber gloves) or ¼ teaspoon dried
  hot red pepper flakes

¼ teaspoon cuminseed
¼ teaspoon tumeric

fresh coriander sprigs for garnish if desired
pappadams (recipe follows) as an
    accompaniment

Make the soup: In a large bowl wash the lentils in several changes of cold water until the water runs clear and drain them in a fine sieve. In a large heavy saucepan cook the onions in the oil over moderate heat, stirring, until they are softened, add the garlic and the gingerroot, and cook the mixture, stirring, for 1 minute. Add the cumin and the ground coriander seeds and cook the mixture over moderately low heat, stirring, for 1 minute. Add the lentils, the broth, 1½ cups water, and the tomatoes and simmer the mixture, covered, for 15 to 20 minutes, or until the lentils are tender. In a blender or food processor purée the mixture in batches, transferring it to a bowl as it is puréed, return the soup to the pan, cleaned, and season it with salt and pepper. *The soup may be made 3 days in advance and kept covered and chilled. Reheat the soup and thin it, if necessary, with water.*

Make the spiced oil: In a small skillet or saucepan heat the oil over moderately high heat until it is hot but not smoking, add the chili, the cuminseed, and the tur-

meric, and fry the spices, stirring, for 10 to 15 seconds, or until the sizzling begins to subside. Remove the skillet from the heat.

Heat the soup over moderate heat, stirring, until it is hot and ladle it into bowls. Drizzle the spiced oil with a spoon over the soup, garnish each serving with a coriander sprig, and serve the soup with the *pappadams*. Makes about 6 cups, serving 6.

PHOTO ON PAGE 26

Pappadams
(Crisp Lentil Wafers)

pappadams (available at East Indian markets
    and specialty foods shops)
vegetable oil for frying the *pappadams*

In a skillet at least 2 inches wider than a *pappadam* heat ½ inch of the oil to 375° F. on a deep-fat thermometer and in it fry the *pappadams*, 1 at a time, turning them, for 10 to 15 seconds, or until they have expanded and turned pale golden. Transfer the *pappadams* as they are fried to paper towels to drain. *The pappadams may be fried 1 day in advance and kept, covered loosely, at room temperature.*

PHOTO ON PAGE 26

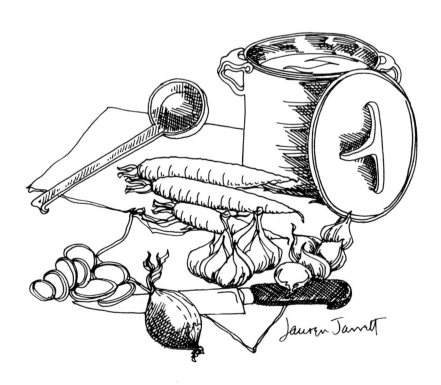

Minted Lettuce Soup

4 cups packed torn iceberg lettuce or romaine,
   rinsed and spun dry
1½ cups buttermilk
½ cup packed fresh mint leaves
a pinch of sugar

In a blender blend the lettuce, the buttermilk, the mint, and the sugar until the mixture is smooth. Transfer the soup to a bowl, season it with salt and pepper, and chill it, covered, for 1 hour, or until it is cold. Makes about 2½ cups, serving 2.

Onion and Cider Soup with Roquefort Croutons

3½ pounds onions, halved lengthwise and
   sliced thin
¼ cup olive oil
2 cups unpasteurized apple cider
3 cups beef broth
1 cup water
2 tablespoons brandy
six ½-inch-thick slices of Italian bread,
   toasted lightly
3 ounces Roquefort or Saga Blue, crumbled
   (about ¾ cup)

In a heavy kettle cook the onions in the oil over moderately high heat, stirring occasionally, for 1 hour, or until they are golden. Stir in the cider, the broth, the water, the brandy, and salt and pepper to taste and simmer the soup, uncovered, for 20 minutes. Arrange the toast slices on a baking sheet, sprinkle the Roquefort on them, and broil the croutons under a preheated broiler about 4 inches from the heat until the cheese begins to melt. Ladle the soup into heated bowls and float a Roquefort crouton in each serving. Makes about 7 cups, serving 4 to 6 as a main course.

Potage Saint-Germain
(*Fresh Pea Soup*)

For the croutons
1½ cups ½-inch cubes of French or
   Italian bread
2 tablespoons unsalted butter, melted
For the soup
the white part of 2 leeks, chopped and
   washed well

2 tablespoons unsalted butter
3 cups chicken broth
4 cups shelled fresh green peas or two
   10-ounce packages frozen
4 cups chopped lettuce, rinsed
   and drained
½ cup fresh mint leaves

¼ cup chilled heavy cream if desired

Make the croutons: In a bowl drizzle the bread cubes with the butter, tossing them to coat them well, and in a shallow baking dish bake them in a preheated 350° F. oven, stirring occasionally, for 10 minutes, or until the croutons are golden and crisp. Season the croutons with salt. *The croutons may be made 1 day in advance and kept in an airtight container.*

Make the soup: In a large saucepan cook the leeks in the butter over moderately low heat, stirring occasionally, until they are softened, add the broth and 2 cups water, and bring the mixture to a boil. Add the peas and the lettuce and simmer the mixture, covered partially, for 10 minutes, or until the peas are tender. Stir in the mint leaves and in a blender or food processor purée the soup in batches. *The soup may be made 1 day in advance and kept covered and chilled.* Return the soup to the pan, season it with salt and pepper, and reheat it over moderately low heat, stirring, until it is hot.

In a small bowl beat the cream until it is thickened slightly but still pourable and season it with salt. Ladle the soup into bowls, drizzle drops of the cream on each serving, and draw a skewer or knife through the drops, forming decorative patterns. Serve the soup with the croutons. Makes about 8 cups, serving 6.

PHOTO ON PAGE 35

Pumpkin Soup with Cumin Breadsticks

For the breadsticks
a loaf of Italian-style bread
¾ stick (6 tablespoons) unsalted butter
2 teaspoons ground cumin

a 6-pound pumpkin (preferably a sugar
   pumpkin)
3 tablespoons unsalted butter
1 onion, sliced thin
2 carrots, grated coarse
2 cups chicken broth

3 cups water plus, if desired, additional water
   for thinning the soup
1 bay leaf
½ cup heavy cream
6 ounces cooked smoked sausage such as
   kielbasa, 8 thin rounds cut off an end and
   the remaining sausage quartered lengthwise
   and sliced thin
⅓ cup minced fresh parsley leaves

Make the breadsticks: Halve the bread crosswise, cut the halves lengthwise into ½-inch-thick slices, and cut the slices into ½-inch-wide sticks. Let the breadsticks stand, uncovered, on racks overnight. In a small saucepan melt the butter with the cumin and salt and pepper to taste, brush the breadsticks with the cumin mixture, and bake them in batches on ungreased baking sheets in the middle of a preheated 350° F. oven for 8 to 10 minutes, or until they are golden. *The breadsticks may be made 1 day in advance and kept in an airtight container.*

Slice off the stem end of the pumpkin 2½ inches from the top, reserving it, scrape out the seeds and the membranes, reserving the seeds for toasting (procedure follows) if desired, and brush the inside of the pumpkin with 1½ tablespoons of the butter, melted. Top the pumpkin with the reserved stem end, bake it in a shallow baking pan in the middle of a preheated 375° F. oven for 1¼ hours, or until the pulp is tender, and let it cool in the pan until it can be handled. In a large heavy saucepan cook the onion in the remaining 1½ tablespoons butter over moderately low heat, stirring occasionally, until it is softened, add the carrots, the broth, 3 cups of the water, and the bay leaf, and simmer the mixture until the carrots are tender. Discard the bay leaf.

Discard any liquid that may have accumulated in the pumpkin and scoop out the pulp carefully, leaving a ¼-inch-thick shell. In a blender purée the pulp with the carrot mixture in batches, transferring the mixture to a kettle as it is puréed, and stir in the cream and salt and pepper to taste. *The soup may be prepared up to this point 1 day in advance and kept covered and chilled. Chill the pumpkin shell in the baking pan.*

In a heavy skillet cook the sausage rounds and the sausage pieces over moderate heat, stirring, until they are browned lightly and transfer them to paper towels to drain. Reserving the rounds, stir the pieces into the soup and heat the soup over moderate heat, stirring occasionally and, if desired, thinning it with the additional water, until it is hot. Heat the pumpkin shell if necessary in

a preheated 375° F. oven until it is warm and ladle the soup into the shell. Garnish the soup with the parsley and the reserved sausage rounds and serve it with the breadsticks. Makes about 12 cups, serving 8.

PHOTO ON BACK JACKET

Lauren Jarrett

To Toast Pumpkin Seeds
½ cup fresh pumpkin seeds, unrinsed
1 tablespoon vegetable oil

In a bowl toss the seeds with the oil and salt to taste and on an ungreased baking sheet bake them in the middle of a preheated 250° F. oven, stirring occasionally, for 1 hour to 1¼ hours, or until they are golden and crisp. (Alternatively the prepared seeds may be spread in a microwave-safe glass baking dish, microwaved at high power [100%], stirring after every minute, for 4 minutes, and microwaved at medium power [50%], stirring after every 2 minutes, for 6 to 8 minutes, or until they are crisp.) Makes ½ cup.

Fresh Tomato and Coriander Soup

2 pounds tomatoes, quartered
½ cup tomato juice
1 pickled *jalapeño* pepper, seeded (wear
    rubber gloves), or to taste
½ teaspoon sugar
2 tablespoons fresh orange juice
3 tablespoons minced fresh coriander
sour cream as an accompaniment if desired

In a blender blend the tomatoes, the tomato juice, the *jalapeño* pepper, and the sugar until the mixture is smooth. Strain the mixture through a sieve set over a bowl, discard the solids, and stir in the orange juice, the coriander, and enough water to thin the soup to the desired consistency. Season the soup with salt and pepper, chill it, covered, for 1 hour, or until it is cold, and serve it with the sour cream. Makes about 4½ cups, serving 4.

Turkey, Tortellini, and Watercress Soup

4 quarts (16 cups) water
the carcass of a turkey, broken into
    large pieces
1 carrot, sliced
2 ribs of celery
1 bay leaf
1 onion, quartered
½ teaspoon dried thyme, crumbled
3 parsley sprigs
1 teaspoon fennel seeds
½ pound fresh cheese *tortellini*
4 cups coarsely chopped rinsed watercress

In a large kettle combine the water, the turkey carcass, the carrot, the celery, the bay leaf, the onion, the thyme, the parsley, and the fennel seeds and simmer the mixture, uncovered, for 1½ hours. Strain the stock through a large sieve into a large bowl, transfer the tur-

key meat to a cutting board, discarding the bones and remaining solids, and chop it fine. Transfer the strained stock to the kettle, add the turkey meat, and bring the liquid to a boil. Add the *tortellini* and salt and pepper to taste and simmer the mixture until the *tortellini* are just tender. Add the watercress and simmer the soup for 1 minute. Makes about 12 cups, serving 6 as a main course or 8 to 10 as a first course.

Turnip and Saffron Soup

¾ pound turnips, peeled and sliced thin
¾ cup chopped white part of leek, washed well
¾ cup finely chopped onion
½ cup thinly sliced celery
3 tablespoons unsalted butter
4½ cups chicken broth
1 bay leaf
8 fresh parsley stems
a scant ½ teaspoon dried thyme, crumbled
a scant ¼ teaspoon crumbled saffron threads
⅓ cup heavy cream

In a large heavy saucepan sweat the turnips, the leek, the onion, and the celery, all seasoned with salt and pepper, in the butter, covered with a buttered round of wax paper and the lid, over moderately low heat for 8 minutes, or until the vegetables are softened. Add the broth, ¾ cup water, the bay leaf, the parsley stems, and the thyme, simmer the mixture, covered, for 30 minutes, and discard the bay leaf and the parsley stems. In a blender or food processor purée the soup in batches and return it to the cleaned pan. Stir in the saffron, let the soup stand for 5 minutes, and stir in the cream. Heat the soup over moderate heat, stirring, until it is heated through and season it with salt and pepper. *The soup may be made 1 day in advance and kept covered and chilled.* Makes about 6 cups, serving 6.

PHOTO ON PAGE 63

FISH AND SHELLFISH

FISH

Fried Fish with Moroccan-Style Herb Sauce

¼ cup coarsely chopped fresh coriander
¼ cup coarsely chopped fresh
    parsley leaves
1 garlic clove, minced
2 tablespoons fresh lemon juice
½ teaspoon paprika
½ teaspoon ground cumin
⅛ teaspoon cayenne, or to taste
3 tablespoons vegetable oil plus additional
    for frying the fish
1 pound skinless firm-fleshed white fish fillet,
    such as cod or halibut, cut into 4 equal
    pieces
all-purpose flour seasoned with salt and
    pepper for dredging the fish

In a food processor or blender purée the coriander, the parsley, the garlic, the lemon juice, the paprika, the cumin, the cayenne, 3 tablespoons of the oil, and salt and pepper to taste. In a skillet heat 1 inch of the additional oil to 375° F. on a deep-fat thermometer, dredge the fish in the flour, shaking off the excess, and in the oil fry it, turning it once, for 1½ to 2 minutes on each side, or until it is cooked through. Transfer the fish to paper towels to drain, divide it between 2 plates, and drizzle the sauce over it. Serves 2.

Steamed Fish Fillets with Scallion-Ginger Oil

1 pound white fish fillets
2 tablespoons vegetable oil
a 1½-inch-long piece of fresh gingerroot,
    peeled and cut into julienne strips
1 large scallion, cut into julienne strips
1 teaspoon Oriental sesame oil

soy sauce to taste as an accompaniment
white-wine vinegar to taste as an
    accompaniment

Arrange the fillets in one layer in a microwave-safe baking dish, season them with salt and pepper, and cover the dish tightly with microwave-safe plastic wrap. Microwave the fish at high power (100%) for 3 minutes, or until it is opaque and just cooked through, remove the plastic wrap carefully, and pour off the liquid in the dish. Keep the fish warm, covered loosely.

In a microwave-safe glass measure combine the vegetable oil, the gingerroot, and the scallion and microwave the mixture at high power (100%) for 1 minute. Add the sesame oil, let the mixture cool slightly, and pour it over the fish. Serve the fish sprinkled with the soy sauce and the vinegar. Serves 2.

Poached Cod with Parsley Horseradish Sauce

two ¾-inch-thick cod or scrod steaks (about
    1 pound total)
½ cup minced fresh parsley leaves
1 tablespoon distilled white vinegar
½ teaspoon paprika
1½ tablespoons drained bottled horseradish,
    or to taste
¼ cup olive oil

In a deep heavy skillet large enough to hold the cod steaks in one layer combine the steaks with enough salted cold water to cover them by 1 inch, bring the water to a simmer, and poach the steaks, covered, at a bare simmer for 5 to 6 minutes, or until they just flake. While the steaks are poaching, in a blender purée the parsley with the vinegar, the paprika, the horseradish, the oil, and salt and pepper to taste. Transfer the steaks with a slotted spatula, draining them well, to plates and spoon the sauce over them. Serves 2.

Poached Cod with Spinach and Pimiento-Cayenne Purées

a 4-ounce jar pimiento, drained
¼ teaspoon cayenne
4 cups packed fresh spinach leaves, washed well
1 tablespoon unsalted butter
two ¾-inch-thick cod or scrod steaks

In a blender purée the pimiento with the cayenne, season the purée with salt, and reserve it in a bowl. In a saucepan cook the spinach with the water clinging to its leaves over moderate heat, covered, until it is wilted, transfer it to the cleaned blender, or a food processor, and purée it with 2 tablespoons water. In the pan heat the spinach purée with the butter over moderately low heat, stirring occasionally, until the butter is melted and keep the purée warm, covered.

In a heavy saucepan large enough to hold the cod in one layer combine the cod with enough salted cold water to cover it by 1 inch, bring the water to a simmer, and in it poach the cod, covered, at a bare simmer for 5 to 6 minutes, or until it just flakes. Divide the spinach purée between 2 plates, spoon dollops of the pimiento purée on top of the spinach portions, and swirl them decoratively into the spinach purée. Transfer the cod with a slotted spatula onto the purées. Serves 2.

Potted Kippers

a 6- to 7-ounce can kippers (smoked herring, available at some specialty foods shops), drained, patted dry, and, if necessary, skinned
1 small shallot, minced
4 flat anchovy fillets
2 tablespoons fresh lemon juice
⅛ teaspoon cayenne
2 tablespoons olive oil
1½ tablespoons Scotch
1 stick (½ cup) unsalted butter, cut into 8 pieces and softened
fresh dill sprigs for garnish if desired
crackers or crusty rolls

In a food processor purée the kippers with the shallot, the anchovies, the lemon juice, and the cayenne, with the motor running add the oil in a stream, the Scotch, and the butter, and blend the mixture until it is combined well. Pack the mixture into small ramekins or a crock and chill it, covered, until it is firm. *The potted kippers may be made 2 days in advance and kept covered and chilled.* Garnish the potted kippers with the dill and serve them with the crackers or crusty rolls. Makes about 1 cup.

PHOTO ON PAGE 63

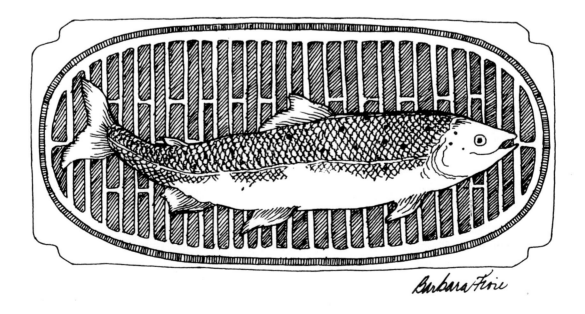

Barbara Fiore

*Oven-Poached Salmon Steaks with
Mustard Dill Sauce*

1½ cups dry white wine
¼ cup sugar
1 teaspoon peppercorns
1½ teaspoons coriander seeds
1 teaspoon mustard seeds
1½ teaspoons salt
1 onion, sliced
ten 1-inch-thick salmon steaks
For the sauce
⅓ cup distilled vinegar
½ cup Swedish coarse-grained mustard
    (available at Scandinavian markets and
    some specialty foods shops) or other
    coarse-grained mustard
2 teaspoons sugar
⅛ teaspoon ground cardamom
½ cup vegetable oil
⅓ cup finely chopped fresh dill

dill sprigs for garnish
1 lemon slice for garnish

In a saucepan combine the wine, 1½ cups water, the sugar, the peppercorns, the coriander seeds, the mustard seeds, the salt, and the onion, simmer the mixture for 15 minutes, and let it cool to room temperature. Halve the salmon steaks with a sharp knife, discarding as many bones as possible, and re-form the steaks. Arrange the steaks in 2 buttered shallow baking pans, ladle the wine mixture around them, and poach the steaks, covered with a buttered piece of foil, on the upper and lower racks of a preheated 375° F. oven, switching the positions of the pans after 15 minutes, for 30 minutes. Let the steaks cool, venting the foil, and chill them in the poaching liquid, covered, for at least 6 hours or overnight.

Make the sauce: In a bowl whisk together the vinegar, the mustard, the sugar, the cardamom, and salt and pepper to taste, add the oil in a stream, whisking, and whisk the sauce until it is emulsified. *The sauce may be prepared up to this point 1 day in advance, covered and chilled.* Whisk in the dill 1 hour before serving.

Separate the salmon steaks into halves, brush them with some of the poaching liquid, and arrange them on a platter. Garnish the salmon with the dill sprigs and the lemon slice and serve it with the sauce. Serves 12.

PHOTO ON PAGE 43

Scrod with Tomatoes, Bacon, and Sherry

2 slices of lean bacon
1 small onion,
    chopped
½ cup chopped drained canned tomatoes
3 tablespoons medium-dry Sherry
1 tablespoon soy sauce
⅛ teaspoon sugar
two 6-ounce scrod fillets

In a skillet cook the bacon over moderate heat, turning it, until it is crisp, transfer it with tongs to paper towels to drain, and crumble it. Pour all but 1 tablespoon of the fat from the skillet and in the remaining fat cook the onion, stirring, until it begins to turn golden. Add the tomatoes, the Sherry, the soy sauce, and the sugar and simmer the sauce for 5 minutes, or until it is thickened. Add the scrod and simmer it, covered, for 4 minutes. Turn the scrod and simmer it, covered, for 4 minutes more, or until it just flakes. Transfer the scrod with a slotted spatula to 2 plates and keep it warm, covered. (If desired, boil the sauce for 1 minute to thicken it slightly.) Spoon the sauce over the scrod and sprinkle the scrod with the bacon. Serves 2.

Poached Scrod with Herbed Vinaigrette

1 tablespoon white-wine vinegar
2 tablespoons extra-virgin olive oil
1 shallot, chopped fine
¼ cup finely chopped fresh mint leaves
¼ cup finely chopped fresh basil leaves
¼ cup finely chopped fresh parsley leaves
two ½-pound pieces scrod fillet

In a small saucepan combine the vinegar, the oil, the shallot, and salt and pepper to taste. In a small bowl combine well the mint, the basil, and the parsley and on each of 2 plates mound one fourth of the herb mixture. In a deep skillet bring 1 inch of salted water to a boil, add the scrod, skinned sides down, and poach it, covered, at a bare simmer for 8 minutes, or until it just flakes. Transfer each fillet with a slotted spatula, blotting it with paper towels and reserving the cooking liquid, to a bed of herbs and top the scrod with the remaining herb mixture. Add 1 tablespoon of the reserved cooking liquid to the vinegar mixture, bring the mixture to a boil, and spoon it over the scrod. Serves 2.

Curried Seafood Crêpes

For the filling

½ pound sea scallops, cut into
  ½-inch pieces
½ pound scrod fillet, cut into
  ½-inch pieces
3 tablespoons unsalted butter
2 carrots, halved lengthwise and cut crosswise
  into ¼-inch slices
¼ teaspoon salt
a pinch of sugar
2 tablespoons all-purpose flour
2 teaspoons curry powder
1 cup milk
2 tablespoons bottled Major Grey's chutney,
  minced
fresh lemon juice to taste
1 cup frozen peas, thawed
1 tablespoon minced fresh parsley leaves
  if desired

curry crêpe batter (recipe follows)
parsley sprigs for garnish
lemon slices for garnish

Make the filling: In a large saucepan bring 4 cups water to a simmer, add the scallops and the scrod, and poach the seafood, its surface covered with a buttered round of wax paper, at a bare simmer for 5 minutes. Drain the seafood and reserve the poaching liquid in a bowl. In the pan melt 1 tablespoon of the butter, stir in the carrots, 2 tablespoons water, the salt, and the sugar, and cook the carrots, covered, over moderate heat for 2 minutes. Remove the lid, cook the carrots, stirring, for 1 minute, or until they are just tender, and add them to the seafood. Melt the remaining 2 tablespoons butter in the pan, whisk in the flour, and cook the *roux* over moderately low heat, whisking, for 3 minutes. Whisk in the curry powder, add the milk in a stream, whisking, and salt and pepper to taste, and cook the mixture, whisking, until it is smooth. Simmer the mixture, whisking occasionally, for 5 minutes, or until it is very thick, and stir in the chutney and the lemon juice. Stir in the seafood and carrot mixture, the peas, the minced parsley, and enough of the reserved poaching liquid, by teaspoons, to thin the mixture to the desired consistency. *The filling may be made 1 day in advance and kept covered and chilled.*

Make 12 crêpes (procedure on page 235) with the curry crêpe batter. Working with one crêpe at a time, put 2 tablespoons of the filling on one quadrant of each crêpe, fold the crêpe in half over the filling, and fold it in half again to form a triangle. Arrange the crêpes on a buttered baking sheet and bake them in a preheated 400° F. oven for 10 minutes, or until they are heated through. Transfer the crêpes to serving plates and garnish them with the parsley sprigs and the lemon slices. Makes 12 filled crêpes, serving 4 to 6.

Curry Crêpe Batter

1 cup all-purpose flour
1 tablespoon curry powder
¼ teaspoon salt
1 cup chicken broth
2 large eggs
1 tablespoon unsalted butter, melted and
    cooled

In a blender or food processor blend the flour, the curry powder, the salt, the broth, the eggs, and the butter for 5 seconds. Turn off the motor, with a rubber spatula scrape down the sides of the container, and blend the batter for 20 seconds more. Transfer the batter to a bowl and let it stand, covered, for 1 hour. *The batter may be made 1 day in advance and kept covered and chilled.* Makes enough batter for about 15 crêpes.

Goujonettes of Sole with Creamy Lemon Noodles

½ pound fillet of sole, halved
    lengthwise along the seam
    and cut diagonally to
    form ½-inch strips
½ cup milk, seasoned with salt and pepper
about ½ cup all-purpose flour, seasoned
    with salt and pepper
    for dredging
vegetable oil for deep-frying
6 ounces dried medium egg noodles
1 teaspoon freshly grated lemon zest
3 tablespoons unsalted butter,
    softened
1 tablespoon dry white wine
½ cup heavy cream
1 teaspoon fresh lemon juice, or
    to taste
1 tablespoon freshly grated Parmesan, or
    to taste
2 teaspoons finely chopped fresh dill

In a small bowl combine the sole with the milk and let the mixture stand for 10 minutes. Drain the sole well, pat it dry, and dredge it in the flour to coat it well. In a large skillet fry the sole in 1½ inches of 360° F. oil in batches, turning it, for 2 to 4 minutes, or until it is crisp and golden. Transfer the sole as it is fried to paper towels to drain and keep it warm in one layer on a baking sheet in a preheated 200° F. oven.

In a kettle of boiling salted water cook the noodles until they are *al dente*, reserve ½ cup of the cooking water, and drain the noodles. In a large skillet cook the zest in 2 tablespoons of the butter over moderate heat, whisking, for 1 minute, add the wine, and cook the mixture, whisking, for 1 minute. Add the cream and cook the mixture, whisking, for 2 minutes. Add the noodles and cook the mixture, tossing it, for 1 minute. Add the remaining 1 tablespoon butter, the lemon juice, the Parmesan, and salt and pepper to taste and add by tablespoons enough of the reserved cooking water to achieve a smooth, creamy consistency. Divide the noodles between 2 heated plates, arrange the sole on top, and sprinkle it with the dill. Serves 2.

Foil-Baked Swordfish with Carrots, Leeks,
and Ginger Lime Butter

2 large carrots, cut into julienne strips
    (about 1½ cups)
the white and pale green part of
    2 small leeks chopped fine (about 1 cup),
    washed well, and drained
2 tablespoons unsalted butter, softened
1½ teaspoons freshly grated lime zest
1½ teaspoons grated peeled fresh gingerroot
two 6-ounce swordfish steaks
    (about ¾ inch thick)

In a heavy skillet cook the carrots and the leeks with salt and pepper to taste in 1 tablespoon of the butter over moderate heat, stirring, for 10 minutes, or until the carrots are crisp-tender, and keep the mixture warm. In a small bowl stir together the remaining 1 tablespoon butter, the zest, the gingerroot, and salt and pepper to taste. Fold 2 pieces of 20- by 12-inch foil in half by bringing the short ends together, unfold each piece, and arrange a swordfish steak, seasoned with salt and pepper, just to one side of each fold line. Top the swordfish with the vegetable mixture and dot it with the butter mixture. Fold the foil over the swordfish steaks with the vegetable mixture to enclose them, fold the edges of the foil together to form tightly sealed packets, and bake the packets on a baking sheet in a preheated 450° F. oven for 10 minutes. Open the packets carefully, transfer the swordfish steaks with the vegetable mixture to plates, and pour the juices over them, discarding the foil. Serves 2.

SHELLFISH

Clams Marinière with Tomato and Onion

1 cup dry white wine
2 garlic cloves, minced
2 pounds 1-inch hard-shelled clams or
   thirty-six 2-inch hard-shelled clams,
   scrubbed well
3 plum tomatoes, seeded and chopped
½ small red onion, sliced thin
2 tablespoons minced fresh basil leaves plus
   4 fresh basil sprigs for garnish if desired
2 tablespoons unsalted butter, cut into bits
2 teaspoons fresh lemon juice

In a large saucepan combine the wine and the garlic, bring the wine to a boil, and simmer the mixture for 2 minutes. Add the clams, steam them, covered, for 3 to 5 minutes, or until they have opened, and discard any unopened ones. Transfer the clams with a slotted spoon to a large bowl and keep them warm, covered. Strain the cooking liquid through a fine sieve lined with rinsed and squeezed cheesecloth into a bowl and return it to the cleaned pan. Add the tomatoes, the onion, and the minced basil and bring the liquid to a boil. Swirl in the butter and add the lemon juice. Divide the clams among 4 bowls, pour the sauce over them, and garnish each serving with a basil sprig. Serves 4.

PHOTO ON PAGE 52

Crab Cakes

1 large egg
3 tablespoons mayonnaise
1½ teaspoons English-style dry mustard, or
   to taste
¼ cup chopped drained bottled pimiento
3 tablespoons minced fresh parsley leaves
1 teaspoon Old Bay Seasoning (available at
   fish markets and some supermarkets)
   if desired
1 teaspoon Worcestershire sauce
2 dashes of Tabasco, or to taste
¼ teaspoon black pepper, or
   to taste
¼ teaspoon salt
1 pound backfin or lump crab meat,
   picked over

¾ cup finely crushed Saltines (about
   20 crackers)
2 tablespoons vegetable oil
1 tablespoon unsalted butter
lemon wedges as an accompaniment

In a large bowl whisk together the egg, the mayonnaise, the mustard, the pimiento, the parsley, the Old Bay Seasoning, the Worcestershire sauce, the Tabasco, the pepper, and the salt, add the crab meat and ¼ cup of the Saltines, and toss the mixture gently. Spread the remaining ½ cup Saltines on a plate, form the crab mixture with a ⅓-cup measure gently into eight ¾-inch-thick patties, and coat the top and bottom of each patty carefully with the Saltines, transferring the crab cakes as they are formed to a sheet of wax paper. In a large skillet heat the oil and the butter over moderately high heat until the foam subsides and in the fat sauté the crab cakes, in batches if necessary, for 1 to 2 minutes on each side, or until they are golden, transferring them as they are cooked to a heated platter. Serve the crab cakes with the lemon wedges. Serves 8 as a first course.

Sautéed Soft-Shelled Crabs

4 soft-shelled crabs, cleaned by the fishmonger
¾ cup milk
½ cup all-purpose flour
½ teaspoon dried thyme, crumbled
1 teaspoon salt
½ teaspoon black pepper
2 tablespoons unsalted butter
2 tablespoons vegetable oil
2 garlic cloves, quartered
2 slices of rye or white bread, toasted lightly
2 lemon wedges

In a bowl let the crabs soak in the milk for 15 minutes. While the crabs are soaking, in a shallow dish stir together the flour, the thyme, the salt, and the pepper. Remove the crabs from the milk, letting the excess drip off, and dredge them in the flour mixture, coating them thoroughly. In a large skillet heat the butter and the oil with the garlic over moderately high heat until the fat is hot but not smoking and in the fat sauté the crabs for 4 minutes on each side, or until they are just cooked through. Put 1 slice of the toast on each of 2 plates, top each slice with 2 of the crabs, and serve the crabs with the lemon. Serves 2.

bell pepper and cook the mixture over moderate heat, stirring occasionally, until the vegetables are softened. Add the clam juice, the tomatoes, and 1 cup water, bring the liquid to a boil, and simmer the mixture gently for 15 to 20 minutes, or until it is reduced and thickened. Stir in the crab meat and salt and pepper to taste, simmer the stew for 5 minutes, and stir in the scallion green. Serve the stew over the rice. Serves 2.

Mussels with Fennel and Roasted Red Pepper Butter

For the red pepper butter
1 stick (½ cup) unsalted butter, softened
2 red bell peppers, roasted (procedure on page 126)
1 garlic clove, chopped, if desired
¼ teaspoon dried hot red pepper flakes

3½ pounds mussels
1½ cups dry white wine
¼ cup medium-dry Sherry
2 cups thinly sliced fennel bulb
1½ cups thinly sliced shallot
¼ teaspoon dried hot red pepper flakes
1 teaspoon fennel seeds
2 fresh thyme sprigs or ¼ teaspoon dried, crumbled
½ teaspoon salt

Make the red pepper butter: In a food processor or blender blend the butter with the roasted peppers, the garlic, the red pepper flakes, and salt to taste until the mixture is smooth. *The red pepper butter may be made 2 days in advance and kept covered and chilled.*

Scrub the mussels well in several changes of cold water, scrape off the beards, and rinse the mussels. In a large kettle combine 4 cups water, the white wine, the Sherry, the fennel bulb, the shallot, the red pepper flakes, the fennel seeds, the thyme, and the salt and boil the mixture, covered, for 3 minutes. Add the mussels, boil them, covered, shaking the kettle occasionally, for 4 to 6 minutes, or until the shells have opened, and discard any unopened mussels. Arrange the mussels, the fennel bulb, and the shallot in shallow bowls, ladle the hot broth over them, and spoon about 1 tablespoon of the red pepper butter in the center of each serving. Serve the remaining red pepper butter separately. Serves 8 as a first course.

PHOTO ON PAGE 23

Lauren Jarrett

Crab Stew

2 tablespoons vegetable oil
3 tablespoons all-purpose flour
1 onion, chopped
1 small green bell pepper, chopped
an 8-ounce bottle of clam juice
2 fresh or canned plum tomatoes, seeded and chopped
½ pound lump crab meat, picked over
⅓ cup thinly sliced scallion green
cooked rice as an accompaniment

In a large heavy saucepan combine the oil and the flour and cook the *roux* over moderately low heat, stirring constantly with a metal spatula, for 8 to 10 minutes, or until it is a deep caramel color. Add the onion and the

To Roast Peppers

Using a long-handled fork char the peppers over an open flame, turning them, for 2 to 3 minutes, or until the skins are blackened. (Or broil the peppers on the rack of a broiler pan under a preheated broiler about 2 inches from the heat, turning them every 5 minutes, for 15 to 25 minutes, or until the skins are blistered and charred.) Transfer the peppers to a bowl and let them steam, covered, until they are cool enough to handle. Keeping the peppers whole, peel them starting at the blossom end, cut off the tops, and discard the seeds and ribs. (Wear rubber gloves when handling chilies.)

Oyster Pan Roast with Pepper Croutons

For the croutons
4 cups 1-inch cubes of Italian or French bread
2 tablespoons olive oil
½ teaspoon freshly ground pepper
½ teaspoon salt
For the pan roast
⅓ cup chopped shallot
1 tablespoon unsalted butter
2 tablespoons all-purpose flour
a 14- to 16-ounce can tomatoes, crushed and
    drained in a sieve
¼ teaspoon dried basil, crumbled
¼ teaspoon Tabasco
¼ teaspoon paprika
30 oysters, shucked (procedure on page 112),
    reserving the liquor
2 cups half-and-half
1 cup milk

finely chopped fresh parsley leaves
    for garnish

Make the croutons: In a baking pan toss the bread cubes with the oil, the pepper, and the salt and toast them in the middle of a preheated 350° F. oven, tossing them occasionally, for 15 minutes, or until they are golden. *The croutons may be made 2 days in advance, cooled, and kept in an airtight container.*

Make the pan roast: In a saucepan cook the shallot in the butter over moderately low heat, stirring occasionally, until it is softened, stir in the flour, the tomatoes, the basil, the Tabasco, and the paprika, and cook the mixture, stirring, for 8 minutes. Add the reserved oyster liquor, strained through a fine sieve to remove any grit,

stir in the half-and-half and the milk, and heat the mixture over moderately low heat, stirring and being careful not to let it boil, until it is hot. Add the oysters and salt to taste and heat the pan roast until it is hot, being careful not to let it boil.

Divide the pan roast among 6 shallow bowls and garnish it with the croutons and the parsley. Makes about 7 cups, serving 6.

Scallops Provençale

2½ tablespoons olive oil
1 pound large sea scallops, patted dry
2 garlic cloves, sliced thin
1 tomato, diced
⅛ teaspoon dried thyme, crumbled
¼ cup shredded fresh basil leaves

In a non-stick skillet large enough to hold the scallops in one layer heat 1 tablespoon of the oil over high heat until it is hot but not smoking and in it sear the scallops for 1 to 2 minutes on each side, or until they are golden and just cooked through. Transfer the scallops with a slotted spoon to a small platter and keep them warm, covered loosely. Add the remaining 1½ tablespoons oil to the skillet and in it cook the garlic over moderate heat, stirring, until it is pale golden. Add the tomato and the thyme and cook the mixture, stirring, for 1 minute. Season the tomato mixture with salt and pepper, spoon it over and around the scallops, and sprinkle the scallops *provençale* with the basil. Serves 2.

*Scallop Quenelles with
Gingered Tomato Sauce*

For the sauce
¼ cup minced onion
1 tablespoon vegetable oil
¾ teaspoon grated peeled fresh gingerroot
a 14- to 16-ounce can tomatoes, drained,
    reserving the juice, and chopped fine
For the quenelles
¾ pound sea scallops, rinsed and patted dry
½ teaspoon salt
½ cup chilled heavy cream

1 tablespoon minced fresh parsley leaves
    for garnish

Make the sauce: In a skillet cook the onion in the oil over moderately low heat, stirring, until it is softened, add the gingerroot, and cook the mixture, stirring, for 1 minute. Add the tomatoes with the juice and simmer the sauce, stirring occasionally, for 5 to 8 minutes, or until it is thickened slightly. Season the sauce with salt and pepper and keep it warm.

Make the quenelles: Discard the tough bit of muscle clinging to the side of each scallop if necessary and in a food processor purée the scallops with the salt. With the motor running add the cream in a stream and blend the mixture until it is just smooth. In a large deep skillet bring 1½ inches of salted water to a simmer. Scoop out and form oval mounds of the mousse with 2 soup spoons dipped in cold water, dropping each mound as it is formed into the simmering water, and poach the quenelles at a bare simmer, turning them occasionally, for 6 minutes, or until they are springy to the touch. Transfer the quenelles with a slotted spoon to paper towels, let them drain briefly, and divide them between 2 plates.

Spoon the sauce over and around the quenelles and garnish them with the parsley. Serves 2.

Shrimp and Scallops with White Bean and Herb Sauce
⅓ cup finely chopped onion
1 garlic clove, minced
2 tablespoons olive oil
¼ cup dry white wine
¼ cup packed fresh parsley leaves
¼ cup packed fresh basil leaves
1 cup drained rinsed canned *cannellini* (white beans)
¼ cup bottled clam juice
10 medium shrimp (about 6 ounces), shelled and deveined
¼ pound bay scallops

In a small saucepan cook the onion and the garlic in 1 tablespoon of the oil over moderately low heat, stirring, until the onion is soft, add the wine, and simmer the mixture until the wine is reduced by half. Add the parsley, the basil, ½ cup of the beans, and the clam juice, simmer the mixture, stirring, for 1 minute, and in a blender purée it. In the saucepan stir together the purée, the remaining ½ cup beans, and salt and pepper to taste and simmer the mixture for 2 minutes.

In a skillet, preferably non-stick, heat the remaining 1 tablespoon oil over moderately high heat until it is hot but not smoking and in it sauté the shrimp, seasoned with salt and pepper, for 1½ to 2 minutes on each side, or until they are cooked through. Transfer the shrimp with a slotted spoon to a plate and keep them warm. To the skillet add the scallops and sauté them, stirring, for 1 to 2 minutes, or until they are cooked through. Divide the bean sauce between 2 shallow bowls and arrange the shellfish over it. Serves 2.

MEAT

BEEF

Roast Fillet of Beef with Cornichon Tarragon Sauce

3 trimmed 3- to 3½-pound fillets of beef, tied,
    at room temperature
⅓ cup vegetable oil
2 sticks (1 cup) unsalted butter, softened
⅔ cup Dijon-style mustard
1¼ cups minced shallot
5 cups dry white wine
½ cup minced fresh tarragon leaves or
    2 tablespoons dried, crumbled
⅓ cup heavy cream
40 *cornichons* (French sour gherkins,
    available at specialty foods shops and some
    supermarkets), cut into julienne strips
    (about 1 cup)

Rub the fillets with the oil, season them with salt and pepper, and in a large roasting pan, leaving space between the fillets, roast them in a preheated 550° F. oven for 23 minutes, or until a meat thermometer registers 130° F., for medium-rare meat. Transfer the fillets to a platter and let them stand, covered loosely with foil, for 15 minutes. In a bowl with an electric mixer cream together the butter and the mustard. In a large saucepan combine the shallot, the wine, and the tarragon and cook the mixture over moderately high heat until the wine is reduced to about 1 cup. *The mustard butter and the shallot mixture may be made 1 day in advance and kept covered and chilled. Reheat the shallot mixture before continuing.* Add the cream and the *cornichons,* reduce the heat to low, and whisk in the mustard butter, a little at a time, and any meat juices that have accumulated on the platter. Season the sauce with salt and pepper and keep it warm, but do not let it boil. Slice the fillets and nap the meat with the sauce. Serves 18.

PHOTO ON PAGE 14

*Roast Beef with Glazed Onions and
Worcestershire Gravy*

3 large onions (about 1½ pounds), sliced thin
a 14- to 16-ounce can tomatoes, crushed and
    drained in a sieve
1 tablespoon vegetable oil
a tied boneless 3-pound rib roast at room
    temperature
1 tablespoon all-purpose flour
1 cup beef broth
1 cup water
2 tablespoons Worcestershire sauce
fresh rosemary sprigs for garnish

In a roasting pan combine well the onions, the tomatoes, the oil, and salt and pepper to taste and roast the mixture in the middle of a preheated 500° F. oven for 10 minutes. Stir the mixture, put the beef, seasoned with salt and pepper, on top of it, and roast the beef and the onion mixture in the oven for 15 minutes. Reduce the temperature to 350° F. and roast the beef for 12 minutes more per pound, or until a thermometer registers 135° F., for medium-rare meat.

Transfer the beef to a cutting board and let it stand for 30 minutes. Transfer three fourths of the onion mixture to a bowl and reserve it, keeping it warm, covered. To the mixture remaining in the roasting pan add the flour and cook the mixture over moderate heat, stirring, for 3 minutes. Whisk in the broth, the water, the Worcestershire sauce, and any juices that may have accumulated on the cutting board and simmer the gravy, whisking and scraping up the brown bits, for 10 minutes. Transfer the gravy to a small saucepan and skim the fat from the top. Just before serving, carve the beef, arrange it on a platter with the reserved onion mixture, and garnish it with the rosemary sprigs. Bring the gravy to a boil, transfer it to a gravy boat, and serve it with the beef. Serves 6.

PHOTO ON PAGE 79

Beef Roasted in Salt Crust

3 cups coarse kosher salt
a 6- to 8-pound standing rib roast,
    trimmed

In a bowl stir together the salt and ¾ cup water until the mixture forms a slightly stiff paste resembling wet snow. Arrange the rib roast, fat side up, in a roasting pan and coat it completely with the salt mixture, patting the mixture on about ¼ inch thick. Roast the beef in the middle of a preheated 325° F. oven for 2 hours (about 22 minutes per pound), or until it registers 130° F. on a meat thermometer for medium-rare meat. Transfer the beef to a cutting board and let it stand for 15 minutes. Remove the crust with a hammer and carve the meat. Serves 6 to 8.

Vietnamese-Style Grilled Steak with Noodles

6 ounces *capellini*, or other thin spaghetti
3 tablespoons white-wine vinegar
1½ tablespoons soy sauce
2 garlic cloves, minced
4 teaspoons sugar
¼ teaspoon dried hot red pepper flakes
¼ teaspoon salt
⅛ teaspoon anchovy paste
¼ cup packed fresh mint leaves, shredded, or
    1 teaspoon dried, crumbled, plus 2 mint
    sprigs for garnish
two ¾-inch-thick boneless shell steaks
    (about 1 pound)
¾ cup fresh bean sprouts, rinsed
    and drained
½ red bell pepper, cut into
    julienne strips

In a kettle of boiling salted water boil the *capellini* until it is just tender and drain it in a colander. Rinse the *capellini* under cold water and drain it well. While the noodles are boiling, in a blender blend the vinegar, 1 tablespoon water, the soy sauce, the garlic, the sugar, the red pepper flakes, the salt, and the anchovy paste until the sauce is smooth. In a bowl toss the noodles with the sauce and the shredded mint.

Heat a well-seasoned ridged grill pan over moderately high heat until it is hot and in it grill the steaks, patted dry and seasoned with salt and pepper, for 3 to 4 minutes on each side, or until they are springy to the touch, for medium-rare meat. (Alternatively the steaks may be grilled on an oiled rack set 4 to 5 inches over glowing coals for the same amount of time.) Transfer the steaks to a cutting board and let them stand for 5 minutes. Cut the steaks into thin slices.

Divide the noodles between 2 plates, mounding them, arrange the slices of steak on them, and surround the noodles with the bean sprouts and the bell pepper. Garnish each serving with a mint sprig. Serves 2.

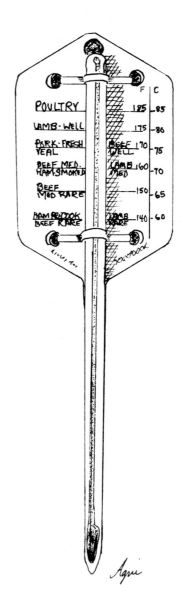

Beef and Mushroom Stew

¾ pound boneless beefsteak, such as blade or
    sirloin, cut into 1-inch cubes
1 teaspoon fresh lemon juice
1 tablespoon all-purpose flour
2 tablespoons unsalted butter
1 small onion, sliced thin
½ pound mushrooms, cut into eighths
¼ cup dry red wine
¼ cup canned beef consommé combined
    with ¼ cup water
1 teaspoon sweet paprika
cooked egg noodles as an accompaniment

In a small bowl toss the beef well with the lemon juice, add the flour, and toss the beef until it is coated with the flour. In a heavy skillet heat the butter over moderately high heat until the foam subsides and in it brown the beef. Transfer the beef with a slotted spoon to a bowl and in the fat remaining in the skillet cook the onion and the mushrooms over moderate heat, stirring, until they are just tender. Add the wine, simmer the mixture for 1 minute, and stir in the consommé mixture, the paprika, and salt and pepper to taste. Simmer the mixture, stirring, for 3 minutes, stir in the beef and the juices that have accumulated in the bowl, and cook the stew until the beef is heated through. Serve the stew over the noodles. Serves 2.

Grilled Skirt Steak with Parsley Jalapeño Sauce

2 tablespoons minced fresh parsley leaves
1 small garlic clove, minced and mashed to a
    paste with ¼ teaspoon salt
2 small pickled *jalapeño* peppers, seeded and
    minced to a paste (wear rubber gloves)
2 tablespoons olive oil
¾ to 1 pound skirt steak, halved crosswise

In a small bowl stir together the parsley, the garlic paste, the *jalapeños*, the oil, and salt and pepper to taste until the mixture is combined well. Grill the steak, seasoned generously with salt and pepper, on an oiled rack set about 6 inches over glowing coals for 4 minutes on each side for medium-rare meat. Transfer the steak to a cutting board, let it stand for 5 minutes, and cut it across the grain into thin slices. Divide the steak between 2 plates, top it with some of the parsley *jalapeño* sauce, and serve the remaining sauce separately. Serves 2.

Chinese-Style Braised Beef with Turnips

1 cup water
2 tablespoons soy sauce
2 tablespoons medium-dry Sherry
two ¼-inch slices of fresh gingerroot,
    flattened with the flat side of a large knife
a 3-inch cinnamon stick, broken into
    large pieces
1½ teaspoons sugar
½ teaspoon salt
⅛ teaspoon aniseed
1 pound boneless chuck, cut into
    ½-inch pieces
½ pound turnips, cut into ½-inch pieces
½ teaspoon cornstarch dissolved in
    1 tablespoon cold water
1 tablespoon chopped fresh coriander or
    parsley leaves for garnish if desired
cooked rice as an accompaniment if desired

In a 1½-quart microwave-safe dish stir together the water, the soy sauce, the Sherry, the gingerroot, the cinnamon, the sugar, the salt, and the aniseed, add the chuck, spreading it evenly, and microwave the mixture, covered, at high power (100%) for 20 minutes. Stir in the turnips and microwave the mixture, covered, at high power for 15 minutes. Stir the cornstarch mixture, stir it into the stew, and microwave the stew, covered, at high power for 2 minutes. Sprinkle the stew with the coriander and serve it with the rice. Serves 2.

Chili Our Way

six 3-inch-long dried hot chili peppers,
    or to taste
3 pounds boneless lean beef chuck, cut into
    ¼-inch pieces
6 tablespoons rendered beef suet
    (procedure follows) or vegetable oil
2 onions, chopped
4 garlic cloves, minced
1½ tablespoons ground cumin
1 pound canned tomatoes, drained
    and chopped
1 tablespoon unsweetened cocoa powder
1 bay leaf
½ teaspoon dried orégano, crumbled
Accompaniments
sour cream

finely grated Cheddar
minced onion
seeded and minced fresh green hot chili
    peppers (wear rubber gloves)
kidney beans or pinto beans
tortilla chips

Heat a griddle or cast-iron skillet over moderately high heat until it is hot and on it toast the chili peppers, turning them and being careful not to let them burn, for 1 to 2 minutes, or until they are several shades darker. Let the chili peppers cool until they can be handled, seed them (wear rubber gloves), and in a small saucepan combine them with 1 cup water. Bring the water to a boil, covered, simmer the mixture for 5 minutes, and in a blender purée it.

In a large casserole sauté the chuck in 4 tablespoons of the rendered beef suet over moderately high heat until it is colored lightly and transfer it to a bowl. Add to the casserole the remaining 2 tablespoons beef suet, the onions, and the garlic and cook the mixture over moderate heat, stirring, until the onions are softened. Add the cumin and cook the mixture over moderately low heat, stirring, for 1 minute. Add the chuck, the chili purée, the tomatoes, the cocoa powder, the bay leaf, and the orégano and combine the mixture well. Add enough water to barely cover the chuck, bring the liquid to a boil, and simmer the mixture, covered, stirring occasionally and adding more water if necessary to keep the chuck barely covered, for 2 hours. Add salt to taste, simmer the mixture, uncovered, for 1 hour more, or until the chuck is very tender and the liquid is reduced to the desired consistency, and discard the bay leaf. (The chili will improve in flavor if cooled and kept chilled, covered, overnight.)

Transfer the chili to a heated serving bowl and serve it with the sour cream, the Cheddar, the onion, the chili peppers, the beans, and the tortilla chips. Serves 6.

To Render Beef Suet

½ pound fresh beef suet

In a food processor chop fine the beef suet and in a skillet cook it over moderately low heat, stirring occasionally, until it is melted and the cracklings are golden. Strain the fat through a fine sieve into a heatproof bowl or crock and let it cool. The rendered suet keeps, covered and chilled, indefinitely. (A half pound beef suet yields about 1¼ cups rendered beef suet.)

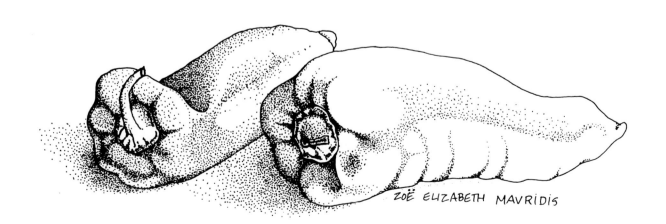

ZOË ELIZABETH MAVRIDIS

VEAL

Grilled Veal Chops and Zucchini with Rosemary

4 teaspoons freshly grated lemon zest
1 tablespoon minced fresh rosemary plus four
    4-inch woody branches
2 tablespoons fresh lemon juice
⅓ cup olive oil
four 1¼-inch-thick loin veal chops, boned,
    leaving the tails attached
2½ pounds zucchini, scrubbed and cut
    diagonally crosswise into ⅓-inch-thick
    slices

In a large shallow dish stir together 3 teaspoons of the zest, 2½ teaspoons of the minced rosemary, the lemon juice, the oil, and salt and pepper to taste until the marinade is combined well. Wrap each tail flush against the loin portion of each chop and with a metal skewer pierce a hole through the tail and the loin portion. Sprinkle the tail of each chop with ¼ teaspoon of the remaining zest, ⅛ teaspoon of the remaining minced rosemary, and salt and pepper to taste, wrap each tail flush against the loin portion, and skewer each chop through the pierced holes with a rosemary branch. Add the chops to the marinade and let them marinate, covered and chilled, turning them once and adding the zucchini to the marinade for the last hour, for at least 3 hours or overnight. Grill the chops on a rack set about 6 inches over glowing coals for 7 minutes on each side for medium-rare meat. Grill the zucchini for 3 minutes on each side, or until it is just tender. Serves 4.

PHOTO ON PAGE 54

Veal Birds Paprika

1½ cups finely chopped onion
½ cup finely chopped mushrooms
9 tablespoons unsalted butter
1 cup fine dry bread crumbs
1 teaspoon dried basil, crumbled
six ¼-inch-thick veal cutlets
    (about 1 pound total), flattened
    between sheets of plastic wrap
½ cup white veal stock (recipe follows) or
    chicken broth
½ cup tomato purée
2 tablespoons paprika

buttered noodles as an accompaniment
1 cup sour cream

In a heavy skillet cook ½ cup of the onion and the mushrooms in 6 tablespoons of the butter over moderate heat, stirring occasionally, until the onion is golden, stir in the bread crumbs, the basil, and salt and pepper to taste, and let the filling cool. Divide the filling among the cutlets and fold in the long sides of each cutlet ½ inch. Starting with a short side, roll up the cutlets and tie them at each end with kitchen string.

In a large heavy skillet heat 2 tablespoons of the remaining butter over moderately high heat until the foam subsides, in it brown the veal birds, patted dry, and transfer them as they are browned to a bowl. In the skillet cook the remaining 1 cup onion in the remaining 1 tablespoon butter over moderate heat, stirring, until it is golden, stir in the stock, the tomato purée, and the paprika, and add the veal birds with any juices that have accumulated in the bowl. Simmer the mixture, covered, for 15 to 20 minutes, or until the veal is tender. Arrange the noodles on a platter, remove the string from the veal birds, and transfer the veal birds with tongs to the platter. Reduce the heat to low, whisk the sour cream and salt and pepper to taste into the skillet, and cook the sauce, stirring occasionally, until it is hot, but do not let it boil. Serve the sauce separately. Serves 6.

White Veal Stock

2 pounds meaty veal knuckles, sawed into
    2-inch pieces
1 large onion stuck with 2 cloves
2 leeks, halved lengthwise and washed well
1 carrot
1 rib of celery, halved
1 teaspoon salt
a cheesecloth bag containing 4 parsley
    sprigs, ½ teaspoon dried thyme,
    and 1 bay leaf
1 pound chicken giblets (excluding the livers),
    chopped, or the chopped carcass of a raw or
    cooked chicken

In a kettle cover the veal knuckles with 12 cups cold water, bring the water to a boil, and skim the froth. Add ½ cup cold water, bring the stock to a simmer, and skim any froth. Add the onion, the leeks, the carrot, the celery, the salt, and the cheesecloth bag and simmer the stock, skimming the froth, for 4 hours. Add the giblets and simmer the stock, skimming the froth and adding boiling water if necessary to keep the ingredients barely covered, for 2 hours more. Strain the stock through a fine sieve set over a bowl, pressing hard on the solids, and let it cool. Chill the stock and remove the fat. The stock may be frozen. Makes about 6 cups.

Veal and Ham Terrine

a 1½-pound piece of top round of veal
¾ pound sliced bacon
1 cup finely chopped shallot
1 tablespoon unsalted butter
2 tablespoons minced fresh parsley leaves
2 tablespoons minced fresh chives
2 tablespoons minced fresh sage leaves
2 teaspoons minced fresh thyme plus a
    fresh thyme sprig
1½ pounds ⅛-inch-thick slices of cooked
    smoked ham
1 bay leaf
Cumberland sauce (recipe follows) as an
    accompaniment
fresh red currants for garnish if desired

Freeze the veal, wrapped in plastic wrap, for 30 to 45 minutes, or until it is firm but not frozen, cut it across the grain with a sharp knife into ⅛-inch-thick slices, and flatten the slices between sheets of plastic wrap. Line the bottom and sides of a 2-quart terrine with the bacon, letting the slices overhang. In a small skillet cook the shallot in the butter over moderately low heat, stirring, until it is softened, add the parsley, the chives, the sage, and the minced thyme, and cook the mixture, stirring, for 1 minute. Let the shallot mixture cool. Arrange the veal and the ham in layers in the lined terrine, sprinkling each veal layer with some of the shallot mixture and salt and pepper to taste. Fold the bacon over the top layer of meat, arrange the bay leaf and the thyme sprig on it, and cover the terrine tightly with a double thickness of foil and the lid or with a triple thickness of foil. Put the terrine in a baking pan, add enough hot water to the pan to reach one third of the way up the sides of the terrine, and bake the terrine in the middle of a preheated 375° F. oven for 1¾ hours, or until a meat thermometer registers 165° F. Let the terrine cool, uncovered, on a rack, pour off any excess liquid, and cover the terrine with foil. Weight the terrine evenly with a 5-pound weight and chill it overnight. Remove the weight and foil and invert the terrine onto a cutting board. Serve the terrine, sliced, with the Cumberland sauce and garnish it with the currants. Serves 6 with leftovers.

PHOTO ON PAGE 63

Cumberland Sauce

the zest of 1 orange, removed with a
    vegetable peeler and cut into fine
    julienne strips
½ cup fresh orange juice
½ cup red currant jelly
1 tablespoon minced shallot
2 tablespoons Tawny Port
2 teaspoons fresh lemon juice
1 teaspoon English-style dry mustard

In a saucepan of boiling water blanch the zest for 1 minute and drain it. In the pan bring the orange juice to a boil with the jelly, the shallot, and the Port, stirring until the jelly is melted, and boil the mixture until it is reduced to about ⅔ cup. In a small dish stir together the lemon juice and the mustard and stir the mustard paste into the jelly mixture with the zest. Transfer the sauce to a jar and chill it, covered. *The Cumberland sauce may be made 2 days in advance and kept covered and chilled.* Makes about 1 cup.

PHOTO ON PAGE 63

PORK

Ginger Rum-Glazed Ham

a 7- to 8-pound half (shank end) of a fully-
cooked cured ham
⅓ cup chopped preserved ginger in syrup
(available at specialty foods shops and
some supermarkets)
3 tablespoons firmly packed brown sugar
3 tablespoons dark rum
parsley sprigs for garnish if desired
garlic bread puddings (recipe follows) as an
accompaniment

If the ham comes with the skin still attached, remove
most of it with a sharp knife, leaving a layer of fat and a
collar of skin around the shank bone. Trim the fat, leaving a layer about ⅓ inch thick, and score the layer remaining into diamonds. Bake the ham on a rack in a
roasting pan in a preheated 350° F. oven for 55 minutes.
In a blender blend together the ginger, the brown sugar,
and the rum, spoon the glaze over the ham, spreading it,
and bake the ham for 30 to 35 minutes more, or until the
glaze is brown and bubbly. Transfer the ham to a platter,
garnish the platter with the parsley, and let the ham
stand for 15 minutes before carving. Serve the ham with
the garlic bread puddings. Serves 8.

PHOTO ON PAGE 24

Garlic Bread Puddings

2 cups milk
8 garlic cloves, chopped
2 large whole eggs
2 large egg yolks
3 tablespoons minced fresh parsley leaves
¾ teaspoon salt
2½ cups ½-inch cubes of Italian bread

In a saucepan scald the milk with the garlic, let the
mixture stand off the heat for 15 minutes, and strain it
through a sieve, discarding the garlic. In a bowl whisk
together the whole eggs and the yolks, add the milk in a
stream, whisking, and stir in the parsley, the salt, and
pepper to taste. Divide the bread cubes among 8 well-
buttered ⅓-cup muffin tins, ladle the custard mixture
over them, dividing it evenly, and let the bread puddings stand for 10 minutes. *The puddings may be pre-*

*pared up to this point 8 hours in advance and kept
covered and chilled.* Bake the puddings in a preheated
350° F. oven for 45 minutes, or until they are golden and
puffed. Let the puddings cool for 10 minutes (they will
sink as they cool), run a thin knife around the side of
each pudding, and lift the puddings out carefully with a
fork. Serve the garlic bread puddings warm. Serves 8.

PHOTO ON PAGE 24

Honey-Marinated Canadian Bacon

18 thin slices of Canadian bacon
(about ¾ pound)
¼ cup honey
¼ teaspoon allspice
1 tablespoon unsalted butter

In a shallow dish or resealable plastic bag combine
the bacon, the honey, and the allspice, coating the bacon well, and let the bacon marinate, covered and
chilled, overnight.

In a large skillet heat the butter over moderate heat
until the foam subsides and in it cook the bacon,
drained, in batches for 1 to 2 minutes on each side, or
until it is golden, transferring it to a baking pan as it is
cooked. Keep the bacon warm in a preheated 250° F.
oven. Serves 6.

PHOTO ON PAGE 69

Crown Roast of Pork with Dirty Rice Stuffing and Creole Mustard Sauce

2 teaspoons dried thyme, crumbled
2 teaspoons salt
1 tablespoon vegetable oil
a 12-rib crown roast of fresh pork
(about 6¾ pounds)
dirty rice stuffing (recipe follows)
¼ cup dry white wine
¼ cup heavy cream
⅓ cup Creole mustard (available at many
specialty foods shops)
flat-leafed parsley sprigs for garnish
cherry tomatoes for garnish

In a small bowl combine well the thyme, the salt,
pepper to taste, and the oil and rub the mixture all over
the pork, patted dry. Arrange the pork on an oiled round
of heavy-duty foil slightly larger than the bottom of the

pork in the middle of a lightly oiled shallow roasting pan and fill the center of the crown with some of the stuffing, mounding it. Roast the stuffed pork, the stuffing covered with another oiled round of foil, in a preheated 450° F. oven for 20 minutes, reduce the heat to 325° F., and roast the stuffed pork for 2¼ hours more, or until a meat thermometer registers 160° F., for medium-well meat, or for 2½ hours more, or until a meat thermometer registers 170° F., for well-done meat. In a 2-quart shallow baking dish bake the remaining stuffing in the 325° F. oven during the last 30 minutes of the pork's roasting time. Transfer the pork to a platter and let it stand for 15 minutes.

While the pork is standing add the wine to the roasting pan, deglaze the pan over moderately high heat, scraping up the brown bits, and strain the mixture through a fine sieve into a small saucepan. Add ½ cup water and boil the mixture until it is reduced to about ⅔ cup. Add the cream, boil the mixture, stirring, until it is reduced to about ¾ cup, and whisk in the mustard and salt and pepper to taste. Discard the foil from the stuffing, arrange the parsley and the tomatoes decoratively around the pork, and serve the pork with the mustard sauce and the remaining stuffing. Serves 6.

PHOTO ON PAGE 31

Dirty Rice Stuffing

1½ cups short-grain rice (available at Asian
   markets and some supermarkets)
1 pound chicken giblets including the livers
2 cups chicken broth
1 parsley sprig
½ teaspoon black peppercorns
2 onions
3½ tablespoons vegetable oil
¼ cup all-purpose flour
1 green bell pepper, chopped
1 rib of celery, chopped
½ cup thinly sliced scallion green
cayenne to taste

In a heavy saucepan combine the rice, 2½ cups cold water, and salt to taste. Bring the water to a boil, reduce the heat to low, and cook the rice, covered, for 15 minutes, or until it is tender and the water is absorbed.

In another heavy saucepan combine the giblets, the broth, 2 cups water, the parsley, the peppercorns, 1 of the onions, halved, and salt to taste, bring the mixture to

a boil, and simmer it for 8 to 10 minutes, or until the livers are just cooked through. Transfer the livers with a slotted spoon to a bowl, simmer the mixture for 30 minutes more, and strain the stock through a fine sieve into another bowl, reserving the giblets with the livers. Let the giblets cool, trim the kidneys, and remove the meat from the necks, discarding the skin and bones. Chop the giblets and the livers and return them to their bowl.

In a heavy skillet, preferably cast-iron, combine the oil and the flour and cook the *roux* over moderately low heat, stirring constantly with a metal spatula, for 30 minutes, or until it is the color of milk chocolate. Add the remaining onion, chopped, the bell pepper, and the celery and cook the mixture, stirring, until the vegetables are softened. Add the giblet stock, simmer the gravy for 30 minutes, and stir in the giblets. *The rice and the giblet gravy may be made 1 day in advance and kept covered and chilled. Let the rice return to room temperature before continuing with the stuffing.*

In a large bowl combine well the rice, the gravy, the scallion green, the cayenne, and salt to taste. Serves 6.

PHOTO ON PAGE 30

Pork Chops Creole

1 tablespoon vegetable oil
two 1-inch-thick rib pork chops
1 small onion,
    chopped
½ cup chopped green bell pepper
1 garlic clove, minced
a 14- to 16-ounce can tomatoes including
    the juice
cooked rice as an accompaniment

In a heavy skillet heat the oil over moderately high heat until it is hot but not smoking, in it brown the pork chops, patted dry, and transfer them to a plate. Add to the skillet the onion and the bell pepper and cook the mixture, stirring, until the onion is golden. Add the garlic and cook the mixture, stirring, for 1 minute. Add ¼ cup water and the tomatoes with the juice and cook the mixture, breaking up the tomatoes and stirring occasionally, for 15 minutes. Add the chops and any juices that have accumulated on the plate and salt and black pepper to taste and simmer the chops for 8 to 10 minutes, or until they are just tender and no longer pink. Divide the chops between 2 plates with the rice and spoon the sauce over the rice. Serves 2.

Braised Pork Chops with Dill Sauce

1 tablespoon vegetable oil
two 1-inch-thick pork chops
1 cup milk
2 teaspoons cornstarch dissolved in
    1 tablespoon cold water
1 tablespoon minced fresh dill, or
    to taste

In a skillet heat the oil over moderately high heat until it is hot but not smoking, in it brown the pork chops, patted dry and seasoned with salt and pepper, and pour off the excess fat. Add the milk to the skillet, bring it to a simmer, and braise the chops, covered, over moderately low heat for 25 minutes, or until they are tender. (The milk will appear curdled.) Transfer the chops to a plate and keep them warm, covered. Stir the cornstarch mixture, stir it into the milk, and bring the sauce to a boil, stirring. In a blender blend the sauce until it is smooth and stir in the dill. Transfer the pork chops to 2 plates and pour the sauce over them. Serves 2.

*Pork and Pineapple Kebabs with
Sweet-and-Sour Sauce*

2 tablespoons red-wine vinegar
1 garlic clove, minced and mashed to a paste
    with ½ teaspoon salt
1 tablespoon dried hot red pepper flakes
¼ cup vegetable oil
1½ pounds boneless trimmed pork shoulder or
    pork loin, cut into forty 1-inch pieces
¼ cup ketchup
2 tablespoons distilled vinegar
2 tablespoons sugar
2 teaspoons soy sauce
½ teaspoon salt
¼ teaspoon Oriental sesame oil
a 4-pound pineapple, peeled, cored, and cut
    into thirty ¾-inch-thick wedges
ten 10-inch wooden skewers, soaked in water
    for 30 minutes

In a large bowl whisk together the red-wine vinegar, the garlic paste, and the red pepper flakes, add the vegetable oil in a stream, whisking, and whisk the marinade until it is emulsified. Add the pork, stirring to coat it with the marinade, and let it marinate, covered and chilled, for at least 6 hours or overnight.

In a bowl whisk together the ketchup, the distilled vinegar, the sugar, the soy sauce, the salt, and the Oriental sesame oil, until the sugar is dissolved and reserve the sauce.

Drain the pork, reserving the marinade, and thread it and the pineapple, alternating them, onto the skewers, using 4 pieces of pork and 3 pieces of pineapple on each skewer. Brush the kebabs with some of the reserved marinade and grill them on a rack set 5 to 6 inches over glowing coals, basting them for the first 10 minutes with the reserved marinade and turning them, for 20 to 25 minutes, or until the pork is just cooked through but still juicy. Brush the kebabs with the reserved sweet-and-sour sauce and grill them, turning them, for 2 minutes more. (Discard any remaining marinade; do not serve it as an accompaniment.) Serves 4 to 6.

Pork and Pumpkin Stew

¼ cup vegetable oil
2 pounds boneless pork shoulder, cut into
   1½-inch pieces
2 onions, chopped
3 garlic cloves, minced
a 14- to 16-ounce can tomatoes, including
   the juice
1½ cups water
1 pound turnips, cut into 1-inch pieces
4 cups chopped washed turnip greens or kale
a 2-pound pumpkin (preferably a sugar
   pumpkin), seeded, reserving the seeds for
   toasting (procedure on page 117) if desired,
   peeled, and cut into 1-inch pieces
steamed rice (recipe follows) as an
   accompaniment

In a heavy kettle heat the oil over moderately high heat until it is hot but not smoking and in it brown the pork, patted dry, in batches, transferring it with a slotted spoon to a bowl as it is browned. Add the onions to the kettle, cook them, stirring occasionally, until they are golden, and stir in the garlic. Add the tomatoes with their juice, breaking them up, the water, and the pork with any juices that have accumulated in the bowl, bring the mixture to a boil, and braise the stew, covered, in the middle of a preheated 350° F. oven for 1 hour. Stir in the turnips and braise the stew, covered, for 20 minutes. Stir in the greens and the pumpkin and braise the stew, covered, for 25 to 30 minutes, or until the pumpkin is tender. Season the stew with salt and pepper and serve it with the rice. Serves 6 to 8.

Steamed Rice

1 tablespoon salt
2 cups long-grain rice

In a large saucepan bring 5 quarts water to a boil with the salt. Sprinkle in the rice, stirring until the water returns to a boil, and boil it for 10 minutes. Drain the rice in a large colander and rinse it. Set the colander over a large saucepan of boiling water and steam the rice, covered with a kitchen towel and the lid, for 15 minutes, or until it is fluffy and dry. Makes about 6 cups.

Kielbasa with Smothered Cabbage
and Mashed Potatoes

1 tablespoon vegetable oil
¾ pound *kielbasa* (Polish sausage), cut into
   1-inch pieces
4 cups chopped cabbage
1 onion, sliced thin
¾ pound yellow-fleshed or russet
   (baking) potatoes
¼ cup milk
1 tablespoon unsalted butter,
   cut into bits

In a large heavy skillet heat the oil over moderate heat until it is hot but not smoking and in it brown the *kielbasa*. Add the cabbage and the onion and cook the mixture, stirring occasionally, until the cabbage is browned. Add 1½ cups water and simmer the mixture, covered partially, for 15 to 20 minutes, or until the cabbage is tender.

While the mixture is simmering, in a steamer set over boiling water steam the potatoes, peeled and cut into ¾-inch pieces, covered, for 12 minutes, or until they are very tender, transfer them to a bowl, and mash them with a potato masher. Add the milk, scalded, 3 tablespoons hot water, the butter, and salt and pepper to taste and stir the potato mixture until the butter is melted. Serve the *kielbasa* mixture on the mashed potatoes. Serves 2.

Spicy Sausage Patties

2 pounds coarsely ground fresh pork butt, chilled
½ pound coarsely ground fresh pork fat
    (available at butcher shops), chilled
2 large garlic cloves, minced and mashed to a
    paste with 2 teaspoons salt
2 teaspoons black pepper
1 tablespoon dried sage, crumbled
3 tablespoons minced fresh thyme leaves or
    1 tablespoon dried, crumbled, plus, if
    desired, fresh thyme sprigs for garnish
½ teaspoon cayenne, or to taste
2 tablespoons vegetable oil

In a bowl combine well the pork butt, the pork fat, the garlic paste, the pepper, the sage, the thyme leaves, and the cayenne and chill the mixture, covered, overnight. Divide the mixture into 16 balls and flatten each ball into a ⅓-inch-thick patty. In a large skillet heat the oil over moderate heat until it is hot but not smoking, in it fry the patties in batches for 4 minutes on each side, or until they are golden and no longer pink within, and drain them on paper towels. Transfer the patties to a serving plate and garnish them with the thyme sprigs. Serves 8.

PHOTO ON PAGE 21

Sausage, Bell Pepper, and Onion Focaccia Sandwiches

3 bell peppers of assorted colors, sliced thin
2 onions, sliced thin
2 large garlic cloves, minced and mashed to
    a paste with a pinch of salt
¼ teaspoon fennel seeds
¼ cup olive oil
1½ pounds fresh hot Italian sausages, cut
    into 4-inch lengths
six 4-inch squares of thick *focaccia*
    (page 98)

In a large skillet sauté the bell peppers, the onions, the garlic paste, and the fennel seeds in the oil over moderately high heat, stirring, until the vegetables are browned lightly, cook the mixture over moderate heat, stirring, for 5 minutes, or until the vegetables are softened, and season the mixture with salt and pepper. While the vegetables are cooking, in a well-seasoned ridged grill pan or large skillet grill the sausage lengths over moderately high heat, turning them once, for 6 to 10 minutes, or until they are cooked through, and halve them lengthwise.

Halve the *focaccia* squares horizontally, leaving one edge uncut to form a hinge, and fill them with the pepper mixture and the sausage. Serves 6.

Pinto Bean, Sausage, and Fennel Gratin

1 pound dried pinto or red kidney beans,
    soaked in enough cold water to cover them
    by 2 inches overnight or quick-soaked
    (procedure on page 143)
1 pound Italian sausage, casings discarded
    and the meat chopped
1 tablespoon olive oil
2 cups finely chopped onion
3 cups thinly sliced fennel bulb
    (about 1 large bulb)
1 large red bell pepper, cut into thin strips
1 teaspoon dried basil, crumbled
1 teaspoon dried thyme, crumbled
½ cup chicken broth
a 10-ounce can artichoke hearts, rinsed,
    drained well, and each heart cut into
    8 pieces
½ cup minced fresh parsley leaves
1 cup fresh bread crumbs
1 cup freshly grated Parmesan
1 tablespoon unsalted butter, cut into bits

In a kettle combine the beans with enough cold water to cover them by 2 inches and simmer them, covered, for 1 to 1½ hours, or until they are tender. Drain the beans in a colander set over a large bowl and reserve the cooking liquid. In a large heavy skillet cook the sausage over moderate heat, stirring and breaking up any lumps, until it is cooked through and transfer it with a slotted spoon to a bowl. To the fat remaining in the skillet add the oil and in the fat cook the onion, the fennel, the bell pepper, the basil, the thyme, and salt and pepper to taste over moderate heat, stirring, until the vegetables are softened. Add the broth and simmer the mixture, covered, for 5 to 10 minutes, or until the vegetables are tender. In a blender or food processor purée 1½ cups of the cooked beans with 1 cup of the reserved cooking liquid. Add the purée to the vegetable mixture with the remaining cooked beans, the sausage, the artichoke hearts, the parsley, and salt and pepper to taste and transfer the mixture to a buttered 4-quart gratin dish, 15 by 10 by 2 inches. In a small bowl stir together the bread crumbs and the Parmesan and sprinkle the mixture evenly over the gratin. Dot the gratin with the butter and bake it in the middle of a preheated 350° F. oven for 45 to 50 minutes, or until it is golden. Serves 6 to 8.

Individual Sausage, Tomato, and Artichoke-Heart Pizzas

For the crust

1½ cups unbleached all-purpose flour
1¼ teaspoons (half of a ¼-ounce package) fast-acting yeast
½ cup hot water (130° F.)
1 tablespoon olive oil
1 teaspoon sugar
½ teaspoon salt

½ pound hot Italian sausage, casings discarded and the sausage chopped
½ cup finely chopped onion
1 large garlic clove, minced
½ teaspoon dried orégano, crumbled
½ teaspoon dried basil, crumbled
yellow cornmeal for sprinkling the baking sheet
a 14-ounce can Italian tomatoes, drained, chopped fine, and drained well again in a colander
a 6-ounce jar marinated artichoke hearts, drained, rinsed, and patted dry
½ cup coarsely grated mozzarella
⅓ cup freshly grated Parmesan

Make the crust: In a food processor combine ½ cup of the flour and the yeast, with the motor running add the water, and turn the motor off. Add the oil, the sugar, the salt, and the remaining 1 cup flour, blend the mixture until it forms a ball, and turn it out onto a lightly floured surface. Knead the dough 8 to 10 times, form it into a ball, and let it rest while making the sausage mixture.

In a small heavy skillet cook the sausage over moderate heat, stirring, until it is cooked through, transfer the sausage with a slotted spoon to a bowl, and discard all but 1 tablespoon of the fat remaining in the skillet. In the fat cook the onion, the garlic, the orégano, the basil, and salt and pepper to taste over moderately low heat, stirring, until the onion is soft and transfer the onion mixture to the bowl.

Halve the dough, form each half into a ball, and stretch each ball into a 7-inch round, making the rounds slightly thicker around the edges. Transfer the rounds to a baking sheet (preferably black steel, for a crisper crust), oiled and sprinkled lightly with the cornmeal, top the rounds evenly with the sausage mixture, the tomatoes, the artichoke hearts, the mozzarella, the Parmesan, and salt and pepper to taste, and bake the pizzas on the bottom rack of a preheated 500° F. oven for 10 to 12 minutes, or until the crusts are golden. Serves 2.

LAMB

Lamb Chops with Onion and Mint Sauce

two 1¼-inch-thick loin lamb chops, patted
    dry and the fat trimmed and slashed at
    1-inch intervals
2 tablespoons plus 1 teaspoon olive oil
1 garlic clove, minced
1 onion, sliced thin
½ teaspoon dried mint, or to taste, crumbled
¼ teaspoon dried marjoram, crumbled
2 tablespoons white-wine vinegar
½ cup beef broth
¼ cup peeled, seeded, and finely
    chopped tomato
1 teaspoon finely chopped fresh parsley leaves

Brush the chops lightly with 1 teaspoon of the oil and
season them with pepper. In a large skillet sauté the
chops over moderately high heat for 4 minutes. Turn the
chops and sauté them for 4 minutes more, or until they
are browned well but still rare. Transfer the chops with
tongs to a plate and keep them warm. To the fat remaining in the skillet add the remaining 2 tablespoons oil, in
the fat cook the garlic and the onion over moderately
low heat, stirring occasionally, until they are softened,
and stir in the mint and the marjoram. Cook the mixture
over moderate heat until the onion is golden, add the
vinegar and the broth, and boil the mixture, scraping up
the brown bits, until it is thickened. Add the tomato, the
chops with any juices that have accumulated on the
plate, the parsley, and salt and pepper to taste and simmer the chops for 2 minutes, or until the meat is just
pink. Divide the onion sauce between 2 heated plates
and arrange the chops on it. Serves 2.

Poached Loin of Lamb

a 4-pound lamb loin, fully boned and trimmed
    of fat and membrane, reserving the bones
    and scraps for the stock and separating the
    eye of the loin and the tenderloin
2 garlic cloves, or to taste, sliced thin
1 tablespoon salt
coriander, mint, and chili chutney
    (recipe follows) as an accompaniment

On a work surface tie together with string the eye of
the loin and the tenderloin at 1-inch intervals and tie the
length of the meat with string, leaving enough string at
the ends to reach the handles of a kettle. Make several
slits in the meat, insert the garlic, and chill the meat,
covered, while making the stock.

In the kettle combine the reserved bones and scraps,
the salt, and 12 cups cold water, bring the water to a
boil, skimming the froth, and simmer the mixture for 1
hour. Strain the stock through a fine sieve into a bowl,
discarding the solids, return it to the kettle, cleaned, and
bring it to a simmer over moderately high heat. Lower
the lamb into the stock without letting it touch the side or
the bottom of the kettle, tie the string to the handles, and
simmer the lamb for 10 to 12 minutes for medium-rare
meat. Remove the lamb from the kettle, discard the
strings, and let the lamb stand on a cutting board for
3 minutes. Cut the lamb diagonally into ½-inch-thick
slices, divide it among 4 plates, and spoon the chutney
onto the plates. Serves 4.

PHOTO ON PAGE 45

Coriander, Mint, and Chili Chutney

1 cup packed chopped fresh coriander
⅓ cup packed chopped fresh mint leaves
1 tablespoon finely chopped fresh *jalapeño*
    pepper, not seeded, or to taste
    (wear rubber gloves)
½ teaspoon minced garlic
1 teaspoon minced peeled fresh gingerroot
2 tablespoons fresh lemon juice
⅛ teaspoon ground cumin
1 teaspoon honey or sugar, or to taste
¼ cup plain yogurt

In a food processor purée the coriander, the mint, the
jalapeño pepper, the garlic, the gingerroot, the lemon

juice, the cumin, the honey, and salt and pepper to taste, scraping down the side of the bowl occasionally. Transfer the chutney to a bowl, and whisk in the yogurt. *The chutney may be made 3 hours in advance and kept covered and chilled.* Makes about ¾ cup.

PHOTO ON PAGE 45

Braised Lamb with Spinach

8 garlic cloves
a 1½-inch cube of peeled fresh gingerroot
6 tablespoons vegetable oil
3 pounds boneless lamb shoulder, trimmed
    and cut into 1½-inch pieces
a 3-inch cinnamon stick
7 whole cloves
1 bay leaf
3 onions, chopped fine
1 tablespoon ground cumin
1 tablespoon ground coriander seeds
¼ teaspoon cayenne
1 cup chopped drained canned tomatoes
½ cup plain yogurt
1 teaspoon salt
1¼ pounds fresh spinach, coarse stems
    discarded and the leaves washed well
    and drained
1 teaspoon fresh lemon juice, or to taste
1 tablespoon pine nuts, toasted lightly

In a blender purée the garlic and the gingerroot with ⅓ cup water. In a heavy kettle heat 3 tablespoons of the oil over moderately high heat until it is hot but not smoking and in it brown the lamb, patted dry, in batches, transferring it as it is browned with tongs to a bowl. To the skillet add the remaining 3 tablespoons oil, heat it until it is hot but not smoking, and in it fry the cinnamon stick, the cloves, and the bay leaf, stirring, for 30 seconds, or until the cloves are puffed slightly. Add the onions and cook the mixture over moderate heat, stirring occasionally, until the onions are golden. Add the garlic purée and cook the mixture, stirring, for 2 minutes, or until the liquid is evaporated. Add the cumin, the coriander, and the cayenne and cook the mixture, stirring, for 1 minute. Add the tomatoes and the yogurt, simmer the mixture, stirring, for 1 minute, and add the lamb, the salt, and 1 cup water. Bring the mixture to a boil and braise it, covered, in a preheated 350° F. oven for 1 to 1¼ hours, or until the lamb is tender. *The lamb mixture may be prepared up to this point 2 days in advance. Let the lamb cool, uncovered, and chill it, covered. Reheat the lamb mixture.*

In a large saucepan bring 1 inch water to a boil, add the spinach, and steam it, covered, for 2 minutes, or until it is wilted. Drain the spinach in a colander.

Spoon off any excess fat from the lamb mixture and add the lemon juice and salt and pepper to taste. Distribute the spinach over the stew and stir it in gently. Transfer the stew to a heated serving dish and sprinkle it with the pine nuts. Serves 6.

PHOTO ON PAGE 27

Lamb and Parsley Patties

1 pound ground lamb (not too lean)
¼ cup minced fresh parsley leaves
1 tablespoon minced fresh coriander
1 tablespoon minced fresh mint leaves or
    1 teaspoon dried, crumbled, or to taste
2 tablespoons grated onion
a pinch of cinnamon
⅛ teaspoon ground cumin
For the sauce
½ cup plain yogurt
1 teaspoon minced fresh mint leaves, or to
    taste, if desired

romaine, rinsed and spun dry, for lining
    the plates
pita loaves, halved, as an accompaniment
    if desired

In a bowl combine the lamb, the parsley, the coriander, the mint, the onion, the cinnamon, the cumin, and salt and pepper to taste, knead the mixture with your hands until it is combined well, and chill it, covered, for 15 minutes. With moistened hands form the mixture into eight 3-inch oval patties, about 1½ inches thick. On the lightly oiled rack of a broiler pan broil the patties under a preheated broiler about 4 inches from the heat for 4 to 5 minutes on each side, or until the lamb is just cooked through.

Make the sauce while the lamb is broiling: In a bowl whisk together the yogurt, the mint, and salt and pepper to taste.

Divide the patties between 2 plates lined with the romaine and serve them with the yogurt sauce and the *pita* loaves. Serves 2.

OTHER MEATS

Liver and Onions with Cider Gravy and Biscuits
For the biscuits
1 cup all-purpose flour
1½ teaspoons double-acting baking powder
½ teaspoon salt
2 tablespoons cold unsalted butter, cut
 into bits
½ cup milk

¾ pound ¼-inch-thick slices of calf's liver,
 cut into ¼-inch-wide strips
2 tablespoons all-purpose flour
2 tablespoons vegetable oil
1½ cups thinly sliced onion
¾ cup apple cider

Make the biscuits: In a bowl whisk together the flour, the baking powder, and the salt, add the butter, and blend the mixture until it resembles coarse meal. Add the milk and stir the mixture until it is just combined. Knead the dough gently on a floured surface for 30 seconds, pat or roll it out ¼ inch thick, and with a floured 3-inch cutter cut out 4 rounds. Bake the biscuits on a buttered baking sheet in the middle of a preheated 450° F. oven for 12 to 15 minutes, or until they are golden.

While the biscuits are baking, in a bowl toss the liver with the flour and salt and pepper to taste. In a large heavy skillet heat 1 tablespoon of the oil over moderately high heat until it is hot but not smoking, in it brown the liver, and transfer the liver to another bowl. Add to the skillet the remaining 1 tablespoon oil and the onion and cook the onion over moderate heat, stirring occasionally and scraping up the brown bits, until it is gold-

en. Add the cider, ¼ cup water, and the liver with any juices that have accumulated in the bowl, simmer the mixture, stirring occasionally, for 8 to 10 minutes, or until the liver is cooked through, and season it with salt and pepper.

Split the biscuits and spoon the liver and onion mixture over them. Serves 2.

Barbecue-Braised Oxtails with Red Chili Beans
 6 pounds oxtails, trimmed
 seasoned flour for dredging the oxtails
 6 tablespoons vegetable oil
 3 cups finely chopped onion
 3 large garlic cloves, minced
 1 tablespoon grated peeled fresh gingerroot
 ⅔ cup firmly packed light brown sugar
 1½ cups ketchup
 3 tablespoons Dijon-style mustard
 1 cup cider vinegar
 ¼ cup Worcestershire sauce
 ¼ cup lemon juice
 Tabasco to taste
 cayenne to taste
 a 28-ounce can Italian tomatoes, drained and
 chopped, reserving the juice
 1 pound dried small red chili beans, soaked
 in enough cold water to cover them by
 2 inches overnight or quick-soaked
 (procedure follows) and drained

Dredge the oxtails in the flour, shaking off the excess. In a heavy kettle heat 4 tablespoons of the oil over moderately high heat until it is hot but not smoking and in it brown the oxtails in batches, transferring them with a slotted spoon as they are browned to a plate. To the kettle add the remaining 2 tablespoons oil, in it cook the onion, the garlic, and the gingerroot over moderately low heat, stirring, until the onion is softened, and stir in the brown sugar, the ketchup, the mustard, the vinegar, the Worcestershire sauce, the lemon juice, the Tabasco, the cayenne, the tomatoes with the reserved juice, and salt and pepper to taste. Simmer the sauce, stirring occasionally, for 5 minutes, add the oxtails, and simmer the mixture, covered, stirring occasionally, for 2½ hours.

While the oxtails are cooking, in a large saucepan combine the beans with enough cold water to cover them by 2 inches, bring the liquid to a boil, and simmer

the beans, covered, for 1 hour, or until they are tender. Drain the beans well, stir them into the oxtail mixture, and simmer the mixture, uncovered, stirring occasionally, for 30 minutes to 1 hour, or until the meat is very tender. Serves 6 to 8.

To Quick-Soak Dried Beans

½ to 1 pound dried beans, picked over

In a colander rinse the beans under cold water and discard any discolored ones. In a kettle combine the beans with enough cold water to cover them by 2 inches, bring the water to a boil, and boil the beans for 2 minutes. Remove the kettle from the heat and let the beans soak, covered, for 1 hour.

Braised Oxtails with Rutabaga

2 tablespoons vegetable oil
4 pounds oxtails, trimmed
3 garlic cloves, minced
½ teaspoon dried hot red pepper flakes
3 cups beef broth
¼ cup soy sauce
3 tablespoons Scotch
five 4- by 1-inch strips of fresh orange zest, removed with a vegetable peeler
1 star anise (available at Oriental markets, specialty shops, and many supermarkets)
2 tablespoons sugar
½ teaspoon salt
1½ pounds rutabaga, peeled and cut into 1-inch pieces
1 tablespoon cornstarch dissolved in 3 tablespoons cold water
3 tablespoons chopped fresh coriander, or to taste

In a large kettle heat the oil over moderately high heat until it is hot but not smoking and in it brown the oxtails, patted dry and seasoned with salt and pepper, in batches, transferring them as they are browned with tongs to a bowl. If necessary pour off all but 1 tablespoon of the fat, add the garlic and the red pepper flakes, and cook the mixture, stirring, for 30 seconds. Return the oxtails to the kettle with the broth, 2 cups water, the soy sauce, the Scotch, the zest, the star anise, the sugar, and the salt, bring the mixture to a boil, and braise the oxtails, covered, in a preheated 350° F. oven for 2 hours. Stir in the rutabaga and braise the mixture, covered, for 30 to 45 minutes, or until the rutabaga is tender. Skim any fat from the cooking liquid and bring the mixture to a boil. Stir the cornstarch mixture, add it to the oxtail mixture, stirring, and simmer the mixture, stirring, for 1 minute. Transfer the mixture to a large serving dish and sprinkle it with the coriander. Serves 4 to 6.

POULTRY

CHICKEN

*Braised Chicken with Artichoke Hearts,
Mushrooms, and Peppers*

1½ tablespoons olive oil
1 whole chicken breast, halved
½ cup finely chopped onion
1 tablespoon minced garlic
2 tablespoons minced *peperoncini*
    (pickled Tuscan peppers)
1 red bell pepper, cut into julienne strips
½ pound mushrooms, sliced
½ cup dry white wine
½ cup chicken broth
a 14-ounce can artichoke hearts, rinsed,
    drained, and quartered
a *beurre manié* made by kneading together
    1 tablespoon softened unsalted butter and
    1 tablespoon all-purpose flour
3 tablespoons minced fresh parsley leaves

In a heavy skillet heat the oil over moderately high heat until it is hot but not smoking, in it brown the chicken, patted dry, and transfer the chicken to a plate. In the fat remaining in the skillet cook the onion, the garlic, and the *peperoncini* over moderately low heat, stirring, until the onion is softened. Add the bell pepper, the mushrooms, and salt and pepper to taste and cook the mixture over moderate heat, stirring, until the bell pepper is softened. Add the wine, the broth, the artichoke hearts, and the chicken, bring the liquid to a boil, and simmer the mixture, covered, for 15 to 20 minutes, or until the chicken is cooked through. Transfer the chicken to a platter and keep it warm. Whisk the *beurre manié* into the pepper mixture and simmer the sauce, whisking, for 2 to 3 minutes, or until it is thickened. Stir in the parsley and pour the sauce over the chicken. Serves 2.

Poulet au Vinaigre à l'Estragon
(Braised Chicken with Vinegar and Tarragon)

a 10-ounce container fresh pearl onions (about
    2½ cups), blanched in boiling water for
    1 minute, drained, and peeled
2 tablespoons vegetable oil
1 tablespoon unsalted butter
3½ pounds chicken pieces
1 cup tarragon white-wine vinegar
½ cup dry white wine
1½ cups chicken broth
1 cup chopped and drained canned
    whole tomatoes
2 tablespoons finely chopped fresh tarragon or
    1 teaspoon dried, crumbled, plus, if
    desired, fresh tarragon sprigs for garnish
4 teaspoons arrowroot or 1½ tablespoons
    cornstarch, either dissolved in
    2 tablespoons cold water

In a saucepan of boiling salted water boil the onions for 10 minutes, or until they are just tender, and drain them well. In a heavy kettle heat the oil and the butter over moderately high heat until the mixture is hot but not smoking and in the fat brown well the chicken, patted dry and seasoned with salt and pepper, in batches, transferring it as it is browned with tongs to a platter. Pour the fat from the kettle, add the onions, and sauté them, stirring, for 1 minute. Add the vinegar and the wine and boil the liquid, scraping up the brown bits, until it is reduced by half. Add the broth, the tomatoes, the dried tarragon, if using, and the chicken, bring the mixture to a boil, and simmer it, covered, for 20 to 25 minutes, or until the chicken is cooked through. *The chicken may be prepared up to this point 1 day in advance: Let the mixture cool, uncovered, and chill it, covered. Reheat the mixture before proceeding.*

Transfer the chicken and the onions with a slotted spoon to a heated platter and keep them warm, covered with foil. Stir the arrowroot or cornstarch mixture, add it to the simmering cooking liquid with half the chopped fresh tarragon, if using, and simmer the sauce, stirring, for 1 minute. Spoon the sauce over the chicken, sprinkle the chicken with the remaining chopped fresh tarragon, if using, and garnish it with the tarragon sprigs. Serves 6.

PHOTO ON PAGE 36

Southern California Crêpes
(Spicy Chicken Crêpes)

For the filling:
1¼ cups sour cream
⅔ cup mayonnaise
3 tablespoons fresh lime juice
1 to 2 drained bottled pickled *jalapeño*
    chilies, or to taste, seeded and minced
    (wear rubber gloves)
4⅔ cups chopped cooked chicken
4 plum tomatoes, seeded and chopped
2 cups chopped scallion
¼ cup chopped coriander

chili corn crêpe batter (recipe follows)
melted butter for brushing the crêpes
sour cream, avocado slices, coriander sprigs,
    and lime slices for garnish

Make the filling: In a bowl stir together the sour cream, the mayonnaise, the lime juice, and the chilies until the mixture is smooth and stir in the chicken, the tomatoes, the scallion, the chopped coriander, and salt and pepper to taste. *The filling may be made 1 day in advance and kept covered and chilled.*

Make 12 crêpes (procedure on page 235) with the chili corn crêpe batter. Mound about ½ cup of the filling on half of each crêpe, fold the crêpes gently over the filling, and transfer them to a buttered baking sheet. Brush the top of each crêpe with the butter and bake the crêpes in a preheated 400° F. oven for 10 minutes, or until they are heated through. With a long spatula transfer the crêpes to serving plates and garnish them with the sour cream, the avocado slices, the coriander sprigs, and the lime slices. Makes 12 filled crêpes, serving 6 to 12.

Chili Corn Crêpe Batter

¾ cup all-purpose flour
⅓ cup yellow cornmeal
½ teaspoon salt
4 teaspoons chili powder
¾ cup plus 2 teaspoons chicken broth
3 large eggs
1 tablespoon unsalted butter, melted
    and cooled

In a blender or food processor blend the flour, the cornmeal, the salt, the chili powder, the broth, the eggs, and the butter for 5 seconds. Turn off the motor, with a rubber spatula scrape down the sides of the container, and blend the batter for 20 seconds more. Transfer the batter to a bowl and let it stand, covered, for 1 hour. *The batter may be made 1 day in advance and kept covered and chilled.* Makes enough batter for about 18 crêpes.

145

Chicken Curry with Pineapple

¼ cup vegetable oil
a 3½-pound chicken, cut into serving pieces
1 onion, chopped
1 large garlic clove, minced
1½ teaspoons turmeric
1½ teaspoons ground coriander
1½ teaspoons ground cumin
½ teaspoon cinnamon
½ teaspoon ground ginger
3 carrots, chopped coarse
a 14- to 16-ounce can whole tomatoes
   including the juice
1 cup chicken broth
1½ cups chopped fresh pineapple
cayenne to taste
2 tablespoons minced fresh parsley leaves
cooked rice as an accompaniment

In a heavy kettle heat the oil over moderately high heat until it is hot but not smoking and in it brown the chicken, patted dry, in batches, transferring it as it is browned to a bowl. Pour off all but 2 tablespoons of the fat and in the remaining fat cook the onion over moderate heat, stirring, until it is golden. Add the garlic, the turmeric, the coriander, the cumin, the cinnamon, and the ginger and cook the mixture, stirring, for 1 minute. Add the carrots, the tomatoes with the juice, the broth, and the chicken including any juices that have accumulated in the bowl and simmer the mixture, covered, for 30 minutes, or until the chicken is no longer pink. Transfer the chicken to a plate, boil the sauce until it is thickened slightly, and stir in the pineapple, the cayenne, and salt to taste. Simmer the mixture for 1 minute, stir in the chicken and the parsley, and serve the curry over the rice. Serves 4 to 6.

Grilled Lemon-Lime Chicken

the grated zest (about 2 teaspoons) and juice
   (about ¾ cup) of 2 lemons
the grated zest (about 2½ teaspoons) and juice
   (about ¾ cup) of 3 limes
1½ tablespoons sugar
1 teaspoon finely chopped garlic
¼ teaspoon cayenne
¼ cup vegetable oil
8 whole chicken legs
   (about 4 pounds)

In a saucepan whisk together the zests, the juices, the sugar, the garlic, the cayenne, and salt and pepper to taste and simmer the mixture, stirring, for 5 minutes, or until the sugar is dissolved. Whisk in the oil and let the marinade cool.

In a large shallow dish arrange the chicken, pricked in several places with a fork, in one layer, pour the marinade over it, and let the chicken marinate, covered and chilled, turning it once, for 1 to 3 hours. Transfer the chicken with tongs to an oiled grill set about 6 inches over glowing coals or to an oiled ridged grill pan set over moderately high heat and grill it, basting it with the marinade for the first 20 minutes (discard any remaining marinade). Turn the chicken over and grill it for 20 minutes more or until it is cooked through. Serves 4 to 8.

Japanese Chicken, Water Chestnut, and Scallion Yakitori

½ cup soy sauce (preferably dark
   Japanese style)
½ cup dry Sherry
2 tablespoons sugar
1 tablespoon minced peeled fresh gingerroot
1 garlic clove, minced
¼ teaspoon salt

12 wooden skewers for skewering the chicken
   and vegetables
8 skinless boneless chicken thighs, cut into
   thirty-six 1½-inch pieces
2 bunches of scallions (about 10), the white
   and pale green parts cut into twenty-four
   1½-inch lengths
24 canned whole water chestnuts, rinsed and
   drained

Make the marinade: In a saucepan whisk together the soy sauce, the Sherry, the sugar, the gingerroot, the garlic, the salt, and pepper to taste and bring the mixture to a boil over moderate heat. Simmer the mixture for 5 minutes, or until the sugar is dissolved, and let the marinade cool.

On each skewer alternate 3 pieces of chicken with 2 scallion lengths and 2 water chestnuts, skewering the water chestnuts carefully so that they do not split and beginning and ending with the chicken. In a large shallow baking dish arrange the kebabs in one layer, pour the marinade over them, and let the chicken marinate, covered and chilled, turning the kebabs once, for 30 minutes. Arrange the kebabs, reserving the marinade, in one layer on an oiled rack of a broiler pan and broil them under a preheated broiler about 4 inches from the heat, basting them with the marinade for the first 6 minutes, for 10 to 15 minutes, or until the chicken is cooked through. Discard any remaining marinade. Makes 12 *yakitori*, serving 4 to 6.

Mexican Chicken and Vegetable Casserole

1 teaspoon ground cumin
1 teaspoon chili powder
½ teaspoon cinnamon
2 teaspoons white-wine vinegar
3 garlic cloves
3 tablespoons vegetable oil
8 chicken thighs (about 2 pounds)
1 large onion, sliced thin
2 tomatoes, chopped coarse
4 zucchini (about 1½ pounds), scrubbed, quartered lengthwise, and cut crosswise into ¾-inch pieces
¼ cup chicken broth
1 to 2 tablespoons drained, minced, pickled green *jalapeño* pepper (use rubber gloves)
1 red bell pepper, cut into ½-inch pieces
1 cup fresh or thawed frozen corn
¼ teaspoon dried orégano, crumbled
½ cup coarsely grated Monterey Jack

In a small bowl whisk together the cumin, the chili powder, the cinnamon, the vinegar, 1 of the garlic cloves, minced and mashed to a paste with a pinch of salt, 1 tablespoon of the oil, and salt and pepper to taste, coat the chicken with the spice paste, and grill it on an oiled grill set over glowing coals or in an oiled ridged grill pan set over moderately high heat, turning it once, for 12 to 15 minutes on each side, or until it is cooked through.

While the chicken is cooking, in a skillet cook the onion in the remaining 2 tablespoons oil over moderate heat, stirring occasionally, until it is lightly golden, add the remaining 2 garlic cloves, minced, and the tomatoes, and cook the mixture over moderately low heat, stirring occasionally, for 5 minutes. Add the zucchini, the broth, the *jalapeño*, the bell pepper, the corn, the orégano, and salt and pepper to taste and simmer the mixture, stirring occasionally, for 20 minutes, or until the zucchini and the bell pepper is tender.

In a large flameproof shallow casserole combine the zucchini mixture and the chicken, sprinkle the Monterey Jack over the top, and broil the mixture under a preheated broiler about 6 inches from the heat for 1 minute, or until the cheese is bubbling. Serves 4 to 8.

PHOTO ON PAGE 82

Chicken Piccata with Capers

a ¾-pound whole skinless boneless chicken breast, halved lengthwise
2 tablespoons unsalted butter
1 tablespoon vegetable oil
2 tablespoons dry white wine
1 tablespoon fresh lemon juice
1 tablespoon drained bottled capers, chopped
3 tablespoons minced fresh parsley leaves

Halve the chicken pieces horizontally with a sharp knife and flatten them slightly between sheets of plastic wrap. In a large heavy skillet heat 1 tablespoon of the butter and the oil over moderately high heat until the foam subsides and in the fat sauté the chicken pieces, seasoned with salt and pepper, for 1 minute on each side, or until they are cooked through. Transfer the chicken with tongs to a platter and keep it warm, covered loosely. Pour off the fat in the skillet, to the skillet add the remaining 1 tablespoon butter, the wine, and the lemon juice, and bring the mixture to a boil. Stir in the capers, the parsley, and salt and pepper to taste and spoon the sauce over the chicken. Serves 2.

Middle-Eastern Grilled Chicken Pita Sandwiches with Yogurt Mint Sauce

For the marinade
1 cup plain yogurt
½ cup fresh lemon juice
1 garlic clove, minced and mashed to
    a paste with a pinch of salt
½ teaspoon dried thyme, crumbled

8 skinless boneless chicken thighs
    (about 1½ pounds)
For the sauce
⅓ cup plain yogurt
1 garlic clove, minced and mashed to
    a paste with ¼ teaspoon salt
2 teaspoons fresh lemon juice, or to taste
1 tablespoon finely chopped fresh
    parsley leaves
2 teaspoons finely chopped fresh mint leaves,
    or to taste

1 small red onion, sliced thin
1½ tablespoons olive oil
1 tomato, minced
1 tablespoon sesame seeds, toasted lightly
6 whole-wheat *pita* loaves

Make the marinade: In a bowl whisk together the yogurt, the lemon juice, the garlic paste, the thyme, and pepper to taste.

Arrange the chicken, pricked in several places with a fork, in one layer in a large shallow dish, pour the marinade over it, and let the chicken marinate, covered and chilled, turning it once, for at least 3 hours or, preferably, overnight.

Make the sauce: In a bowl whisk together the yogurt, the garlic paste, the lemon juice, the parsley, the mint, and salt and pepper to taste.

On an oiled grill set about 6 inches over glowing coals or in an oiled ridged grill pan set over moderately high heat grill the chicken (discard the marinade) turning it, for 12 to 15 minutes on each side, or until it is cooked through. While the chicken is cooking, in a skillet cook the onion in the oil over moderate heat, stirring, until it is softened and lightly golden. Remove the skillet from the heat, add the tomato and the sesame seeds, and season the mixture with salt and pepper. Transfer the chicken to a cutting board and cut it diagonally into thin slices. Cut off a small piece of each *pita* loaf to form an opening and heat the *pita* loaves on the grill, turning them once, for several seconds, or until they are just softened. Divide the chicken, the onion mixture, and the sauce among the *pita* loaves. Serves 6.

Poached Chicken with Vegetables, Coriander, and Saffron Couscous

For the chicken
¾ pound skinless chicken breast, halved
¼ teaspoon ground cumin
¼ teaspoon ground ginger
¼ teaspoon salt
1 garlic clove, minced
1 tablespoon olive oil

1 onion, chopped
2 garlic cloves, minced
3 tablespoons olive oil
½ teaspoon ground ginger
¼ teaspoon crumbled saffron threads
2 cups chicken broth
3 tablespoons chopped fresh coriander
3 tablespoons chopped fresh-flat leafed
    parsley leaves
1 carrot, cut crosswise into ¼-inch slices
1 zucchini, halved lengthwise and cut
    crosswise into ⅓-inch slices
1 tablespoon Niçoise olives
saffron couscous (recipe follows)

Prepare the chicken: In a shallow dish sprinkle the chicken with the cumin, the ginger, the salt, and the garlic, drizzle it with the oil, and rub it all over to coat it well. Chill the chicken, covered, for at least 1 hour or overnight.

In a heavy saucepan cook the onion and the garlic in the oil over moderately low heat, stirring, until they are softened, stir in the ginger and the saffron, and cook the mixture for 30 seconds. Add the broth and 2 tablespoons each of the coriander and the parsley, bring the mixture to a boil, and simmer it for 10 minutes. Add the chicken and the carrot and poach the chicken, covered, for 10 minutes. Turn the chicken, add the zucchini, and cook the mixture, covered, for 10 minutes, or until the chicken is cooked through. Transfer the chicken with tongs to a cutting board and let it stand for 5 minutes. While the chicken is standing, add the olives and the remaining 1 tablespoon each of the coriander and the parsley to the pan, bring the liquid to a boil, and boil the mixture for 2 minutes. Slice the chicken, divide it between 2 plates with the couscous, and spoon the vegetable mixture over it. Serves 2.

PHOTO ON PAGE 17

Saffron Couscous

¼ teaspoon crumbled saffron threads
¾ cup chicken broth
1 tablespoon olive oil
½ cup couscous

Put the saffron in a small dish, set the dish on a rack set over a saucepan of the broth and ¾ cup water, and bring the liquid to a boil. Heat the saffron for 1 minute, crumble it into the broth, and add the oil. Stir in the couscous, remove the pan from the heat, and let the couscous stand, covered, for 5 minutes. Fluff the couscous with a fork before serving. Serves 2.

B. Charlton

Red-Wine Marinated Fried Chicken with Onions

For the marinade

1 cup dry red wine
½ cup red-wine vinegar
3 garlic cloves, minced and mashed to
    a paste with a pinch of salt
1 tablespoon Dijon-style mustard

8 chicken thighs or drumsticks
    (about 2 pounds)
1 large egg
1 cup all-purpose flour
1 teaspoon salt
½ teaspoon dried thyme,
    crumbled
vegetable oil for frying the chicken
2 large onions, sliced thin

Make the marinade: In a large shallow dish whisk together the wine, the vinegar, the garlic paste, the mustard, and pepper to taste.

Arrange the chicken, pricked in several places with a fork, in one layer in the dish, let it marinate, covered and chilled, turning it once, for at least 3 hours or, preferably, overnight, and drain it, reserving ½ cup of the marinade and discarding the rest.

In a shallow dish whisk together the egg and the reserved marinade. In another shallow dish stir together the flour, the salt, the thyme, and pepper to taste. Dip the chicken in the egg mixture, letting the excess drip off, and dredge it twice in the flour mixture to make a thicker coating, shaking off the excess each time. Reserve the remaining flour mixture. Let the chicken stand in one layer on a wire rack for 15 minutes.

In a large skillet, preferably cast-iron, heat 1 inch of the oil to 375° F. and in it fry half the chicken for 1 minute on each side. Reduce the heat to moderate so that the temperature of the oil is reduced to 300° F., fry the chicken, uncovered, for 20 to 25 minutes, or until it is cooked through, and transfer it with tongs to paper towels to drain. Keep the chicken warm while frying the remaining chicken in the same manner. Dredge the onions in the reserved flour mixture, shaking off the excess, and in the skillet fry them in 375° F. oil, turning them carefully, for 5 minutes, or until they are lightly golden. Transfer the onions with a slotted spoon to paper towels to drain and sprinkle them with salt to taste. Mound the onions in the middle of a large platter and arrange the chicken around them. Serves 4 to 8.

Roasted Poussins with Fennel

six 1-pound *poussins* (baby chickens,
    available at specialty butcher shops) or
    six 1¼-pound Cornish hens
1½ pounds fennel bulbs (about 3), trimmed,
    reserving the ribs for stuffing the chickens,
    and the bulbs sliced thin
2 tablespoons unsalted butter
1 tablespoon vegetable oil
½ cup dry white wine
½ to ¾ cup water
2 tablespoons Pernod or other anise-flavored
    liqueur
6 parsley sprigs for garnish

Stuff the chicken cavities with the reserved fennel ribs, chopped, and truss the chickens. In a large heavy skillet heat the butter and the oil over moderately high heat until the foam subsides and in the fat brown the chickens, patted dry and seasoned with salt and pepper, in batches, transferring them as they are browned to a flameproof roasting pan. Pour off all but 1 tablespoon of the fat and in the fat remaining in the skillet cook the sliced fennel over moderate heat, stirring, until it is golden and softened. Spoon the fennel around the chickens and add the wine and ½ cup of the water. Roast the chickens in the middle of a preheated 400° F. oven, basting them every 15 minutes and adding enough of the remaining ¼ cup water as necessary to maintain about 1 cup pan juices, for 40 to 50 minutes, or until a meat thermometer inserted in the fleshy part of a thigh registers 180° F. and the juices run clear when the thigh is pierced with a skewer.

Transfer the pan to the stove top. In a small saucepan heat the Pernod over moderately low heat until it is warm, ignite it, and pour it carefully over the chickens, letting the flames go out. Transfer the chickens to plates, transfer the fennel with a slotted spoon to the plates, and garnish each serving with a parsley sprig. Boil the pan juices until they are reduced to about ⅔ cup, season the gravy with salt and pepper, and transfer it to a gravy boat. Serves 6.

PHOTO ON PAGE 81

Spicy Stir-Fried Orange Chicken

2 teaspoons cornstarch
3 tablespoons soy sauce
½ cup chicken broth
⅓ cup fresh orange juice
2 teaspoons sugar
2 teaspoons white-wine vinegar
1 teaspoon Oriental sesame oil
2 tablespoons vegetable oil
1 whole skinless boneless chicken breast, cut
    into ¼-inch-thick slices
six 2-inch strips of orange zest removed
    with a vegetable peeler, cut into fine
    julienne strips
1 garlic clove, minced
¼ teaspoon dried hot red pepper flakes
1 red bell pepper,
    cut into thin strips
1 cup snow peas,
    trimmed
cooked rice as an accompaniment

In a small bowl stir together the cornstarch, the soy sauce, the broth, ¼ cup water, the orange juice, the sugar, the vinegar, and the sesame oil until the mixture is combined well. In a large skillet heat the vegetable oil over moderately high heat until it is hot but not smoking, in it stir-fry the chicken for 3 minutes, or until it is just cooked through, and transfer the chicken with tongs to a bowl. Reduce the heat to moderate and in the oil remaining in the skillet cook the zest, stirring, for 1 minute. Add the garlic and the red pepper flakes and cook the mixture, stirring, until the garlic is golden. Add the bell pepper and the snow peas, stir the soy sauce mixture, and add it to the vegetables. Simmer the mixture, stirring, for 3 minutes, add the chicken, and simmer the mixture, stirring, for 2 minutes. Serve the chicken mixture over the rice. Serves 2.

Tacos de Pollo con Guacamole
(Chicken Tacos with Guacamole)

3 cups shredded cooked chicken
2 cups *jalapeño* sauce (recipe follows)
12 taco shells (recipe follows)
guacamole (recipe follows)
diced red and green bell peppers
    for garnish

In a bowl combine the chicken with the *jalapeño* sauce and fill the taco shells one half full with the chicken mixture. Top the chicken mixture with some of the *guacamole* and the bell peppers. Makes 12 tacos.

Jalapeño Sauce

1 small onion, chopped fine
1 garlic clove, minced
¼ cup vegetable oil
4 cups peeled, seeded, and chopped tomato
   (about 5 tomatoes)
1 cup chicken broth
minced seeded fresh *jalapeño* chilies to taste
   (wear rubber gloves)
1 teaspoon dried orégano, crumbled

In a skillet cook the onion and the garlic in the oil over moderately low heat, stirring, until the onion is softened, add the tomato, and bring the mixture to a boil. Add the broth and simmer the mixture for 5 minutes, or until it is thickened. Add the chilies, the orégano, and salt to taste and combine the sauce well. Makes about 3 cups.

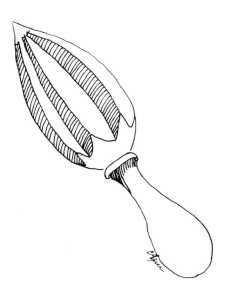

Taco Shells

vegetable oil for frying the tortillas
twelve 7-inch corn tortillas

In a skillet heat ½ inch of the oil over moderately high heat until it is hot but not smoking, in it fry the tortillas, 1 at a time, folding them almost in half with tongs to form taco shells, for 1 minute, or until they are crisp and golden, and transfer them with the tongs as they are fried to paper towels to drain. Makes 12 taco shells.

Guacamole

3 ripe avocados (preferably California)
2 cups seeded and chopped tomato
1 red onion, chopped fine
¼ cup finely chopped fresh coriander,
   or to taste
⅓ cup fresh lemon juice
cayenne to taste if desired

Halve and pit the avocados, scoop the flesh into a bowl, and mash it coarse with a fork. Stir in the tomato, the onion, the coriander, the lemon juice, the cayenne, and salt to taste. *The guacamole may be made 2 hours in advance and kept, its surface covered with plastic wrap, chilled.* Makes about 2½ cups.

Filipino ''Adobo''-Style Chicken
(Tangy Soy Chicken)

8 whole chicken legs (about 4 pounds), cut
   into drumstick and thigh sections
1½ cups distilled white vinegar
3 garlic cloves, crushed
2 bay leaves
½ tablespoon whole black peppercorns,
   crushed lightly
¾ cup soy sauce
3 tablespoons vegetable oil
cooked rice as an accompaniment

In a large kettle combine the chicken, the vinegar, the garlic, the bay leaves, the peppercorns, and 1 cup water, bring the mixture to a boil, and simmer it, covered, for 20 minutes. Add the soy sauce and simmer the mixture, covered, for 20 minutes. Transfer the chicken with tongs to a plate and boil the liquid for 10 minutes, or until it is reduced to about 1 cup. Let the sauce cool, remove the bay leaves, and skim the fat from the surface.

In a large skillet heat the oil over high heat until it is hot but not smoking and in it sauté the chicken, patted dry, in batches, turning it, for 5 minutes, or until it is browned well. Transfer the chicken to a rimmed platter, pour the sauce, heated, over it, and serve the chicken with the rice. Serves 4 to 8.

Chicken Tetrazzini

a 4-pound chicken, cut into 8 pieces
½ pound mushrooms, sliced thin
5 tablespoons unsalted butter
½ pound spaghetti
2 tablespoons all-purpose flour
1 cup heavy cream
3 tablespoons medium-dry Sherry
freshly grated nutmeg to taste
½ cup freshly grated Parmesan

In a kettle combine the chicken with enough salted water to cover it by 2 inches, bring the water to a boil, and simmer the chicken for 20 minutes, or until it is tender. Let the chicken cool in the broth, separate the meat from the skin and bones, returning the skin and bones to the broth, and cut the meat into strips, reserving it. Simmer the broth until it is reduced by half, strain it through a fine sieve, discarding the solids and skimming the fat, and boil it until it is reduced to about 2 cups.

While the broth is reducing, in a large saucepan cook the mushrooms in 2 tablespoons of the butter over moderately low heat, stirring, until they are softened. In a kettle of boiling salted water boil the spaghetti until it is *al dente* and drain it well. In a saucepan melt the remaining 3 tablespoons butter over moderately low heat, add the flour, and cook the *roux*, stirring, for 3 minutes. Whisk in the reduced broth, the cream, and the Sherry, bring the sauce to a boil, whisking, and simmer it for 5 minutes. Season the sauce with the nutmeg and salt and pepper. Stir half the sauce into the mushrooms with the spaghetti and transfer the mixture to a well-buttered 2½-quart baking dish, making a well in the center. Add the reserved chicken to the remaining sauce, combine the mixture well, and transfer it to the center of the spaghetti mixture. Sprinkle the mixture with the Parmesan and bake it in the middle of a preheated 350° F. oven for 25 to 30 minutes, or until it is pale golden. Serves 4.

Thai-Style Chicken in Coconut Sauce

2 tablespoons vegetable oil
6 whole chicken legs (about 3 pounds), cut
    into drumstick and thigh sections
2 teaspoons minced peeled fresh gingerroot
2 teaspoons finely chopped garlic
1½ tablespoons all-purpose flour
½ teaspoon curry powder
2 tablespoons dry Sherry
an 8½-ounce can cream of coconut
1½ cups chicken broth
½ teaspoon black pepper
¼ cup finely chopped fresh coriander plus, if
    desired, coriander sprigs for garnish
¼ cup soy sauce
2½ teaspoons minced seeded fresh *jalapeño*
    pepper, or to taste (wear rubber gloves)
2 red bell peppers, chopped
1 tablespoon fresh lime juice, or to taste
cooked rice as an accompaniment

In a large kettle heat the oil over moderately high heat until it is hot but not smoking and in it brown the chicken, patted dry, in batches, transferring it as it is browned to a plate. To the kettle add the gingerroot and the garlic and cook the mixture for 1 minute. Add the flour and the curry powder and cook the mixture, stirring, for 1 minute. Whisk in the Sherry, the coconut cream, and the broth and bring the mixture to a boil, whisking. Add the black pepper, the chopped coriander, the soy sauce, the *jalapeño*, the chicken, and any juices that have accumulated on the plate and simmer the mixture, covered, for 10 minutes. Add the bell peppers and simmer the mixture, covered, for 20 to 25 minutes, or until the chicken is cooked through. Transfer the chicken with a slotted spoon to a serving dish and keep it warm. Boil the liquid until it is thickened and reduced to about 2 cups, skim off the fat, and season the sauce with salt and pepper and the lime juice. Nap the chicken with some of the sauce, garnish it with the coriander sprigs, and serve it with the rice. Serves 6.

Baked Chicken Breasts with
Coarse-Grained Mustard and Tarragon Sauce

1¼ cups fresh bread crumbs
1 teaspoon minced fresh tarragon, or dried,
    crumbled, or to taste
1½ teaspoons minced fresh parsley leaves
2 teaspoons coarse-grained Dijon-style
    mustard
1 tablespoon unsalted butter, melted and
    cooled
1 whole skinless boneless chicken breast
    (¾ pound), halved
¼ cup dry white wine
½ cup chicken broth

In a shallow dish stir together the bread crumbs, ½ teaspoon of the tarragon, the parsley, and salt and pepper to taste. In a small bowl whisk together 1½ teaspoons of the mustard and the butter, coat the chicken with the mustard mixture, and dredge it in the bread crumb mixture, patting the mixture to help it adhere. Arrange the chicken on the rack of a broiler pan and bake it in the middle of a preheated 475° F. oven for 6 to 8 minutes on each side, or until it is cooked through. Divide the chicken between 2 plates, keeping it warm, and put the broiler pan over high heat. Stir in the wine, scraping up the brown bits, and boil it for 1 minute. Add the broth, the remaining ½ teaspoon mustard, the remaining ½ teaspoon tarragon, and pepper to taste and boil the mixture, whisking, until it is reduced to about ½ cup. Strain the sauce if desired and pour it around the chicken. Serves 2.

Chicken Breasts Stuffed with Zucchini, Roasted Red Pepper, and Goat Cheese

¼ cup minced onion
2 tablespoons olive oil
½ cup firmly packed coarsely grated unpeeled scrubbed zucchini, squeezed dry in a paper towel
2 tablespoons minced drained bottled roasted red pepper or pimiento
1 ounce soft mild goat cheese, crumbled
1 whole boneless chicken breast (with skin), halved
½ cup chicken broth

In a skillet cook the onion in 1 tablespoon of the oil over moderately low heat until it is softened, add the zucchini, and cook the mixture, stirring, for 1 minute, or until the zucchini is tender. Stir in the red pepper, the goat cheese, and salt and pepper to taste and cook the mixture, stirring, until the cheese is melted. Transfer the mixture to a small bowl and let it cool slightly.

With your fingers make a pocket for the filling in each chicken breast half by separating the skin from the meat, being careful not to tear the skin and keeping the skin attached along most of the edge. Stuff each pocket with half the filling with a small spoon, packing it and pulling the skin to cover the filling completely, and secure the pockets with wooden picks if desired. In a large skillet heat the remaining 1 tablespoon oil over moderately high heat until it is hot but not smoking and in it sauté the chicken, beginning with the skin side up, for 2 minutes on each side. Reduce the heat to moderate, cook the chicken for 9 minutes on each side, or until it is cooked through, and divide it between 2 plates. Pour off the fat from the skillet, to the skillet add the broth, and boil the broth, scraping up the brown bits, for 30 seconds. Strain the sauce and pour it around the chicken. Serves 2.

Beverly Charlton

Roasted Chicken Legs with Plum Chili Salsa

For the marinade

4 large ripe purple or red plums
    (about 1 pound), chopped
2 garlic cloves, minced and mashed to
    a paste with 1 teaspoon salt
1 tablespoon Oriental sesame oil
¼ cup soy sauce
½ cup fresh orange juice
¼ cup white-wine vinegar
3 tablespoons sugar
1 tablespoon minced seeded fresh *jalapeño*
    pepper (wear rubber gloves)
1 tablespoon minced peeled fresh gingerroot
½ teaspoon dry mustard

8 whole chicken legs (about 4 pounds)
For the salsa
1 pound ripe purple or red plums
    (about 4 large), diced (about 3 cups)
⅓ cup minced red onion
½ cup finely chopped fresh coriander
¼ cup finely chopped fresh mint leaves
1 teaspoon minced seeded fresh *jalapeño*
    pepper (wear rubber gloves)
1 tablespoon fresh lime juice
2 teaspoons sugar, or to taste

For garnish
ripe plum wedges
lime wedges
whole fresh mint leaves

Make the marinade: In a food processor purée the plums, the garlic paste, the oil, the soy sauce, the orange juice, the vinegar, the sugar, the *jalapeño*, the gingerroot, the mustard, and black pepper to taste until the mixture is smooth. In a large saucepan bring the marinade to a boil, simmer it, stirring occasionally, for 10 minutes, or until it is reduced to 2 cups, and let it cool. In a large shallow dish arrange the chicken, pricked in several places with a fork, in one layer, pour the marinade over it, reserving ¼ cup for the *salsa*, and let the chicken marinate, covered and chilled, turning it once, for at least 1 hour or, preferably, overnight. Transfer the chicken to an oiled rack set over a foil-lined roasting pan, spoon the marinade over it, and roast the chicken in the upper third of a preheated 450° F. oven for 30 to 35 minutes, or until it is cooked through.

Make the *salsa* while the chicken is roasting: In a bowl stir together the plums, the onion, the coriander, the mint, the *jalapeño*, the lime juice, the sugar, some of the reserved marinade to taste, and salt and pepper to taste.

Arrange the chicken on a heated platter, garnish it with the plum wedges, the lime wedges, and the mint leaves, and serve it hot or at room temperature with the *salsa*. Serves 4 to 8.

PHOTO ON PAGE 82

Jamaican "Jerk" Chicken Wings
(Spicy Baked Chicken Wings)

For the marinade
1 onion, chopped
⅔ cup finely chopped scallion
2 garlic cloves
½ teaspoon dried thyme, crumbled
1½ teaspoons salt
1½ teaspoons ground allspice
¼ teaspoon freshly grated nutmeg
½ teaspoon cinnamon
¼ cup minced pickled *jalapeño* pepper, or to
    taste (wear rubber gloves)
1 teaspoon black pepper
6 drops of Tabasco, or to taste
2 tablespoons soy sauce
¼ cup vegetable oil

18 chicken wings (about 3¼ pounds), the
    wing tips cut off, reserved for another use

Make the marinade: In a food processor or blender purée the onion, the scallion, the garlic, the thyme, the salt, the allspice, the nutmeg, the cinnamon, the *jalapeño*, the black pepper, the Tabasco, the soy sauce, and the oil.

In a large shallow dish arrange the wings in one layer and spoon the marinade over them, rubbing it in (use rubber gloves). Let the wings marinate, covered and chilled, turning them once, for at least 1 hour or, preferably, overnight.

Arrange the wings in one layer on an oiled rack set over a foil-lined roasting pan, spoon the marinade over them, and bake the wings in the upper third of a preheated 450° F. oven for 30 to 35 minutes, or until they are cooked through. Serves 4 to 6.

ASSORTED FOWL

Crispy Braised Duck with Turnips and Olives
a 4½- to 5-pound duck, cut into serving pieces
  (2 breasts, 2 whole legs, and 2 wings),
  trimmed of as much fat as possible,
  and the skin pricked well with the point
  of a sharp knife
1 tablespoon vegetable oil
1 onion, chopped
3 garlic cloves, minced
¼ teaspoon dried thyme, crumbled
¾ cup dry white wine
¾ cup chicken broth
¾ pound turnips, peeled and cut into
  1-inch-thick wedges
1 teaspoon cornstarch dissolved in
  1 tablespoon cold water
½ cup Kalamata or other brine-cured
  black olives
2 teaspoons fresh lemon juice, or to taste
3 tablespoons minced fresh parsley leaves

Pat the duck dry and season it with salt and pepper. In a wide heavy flameproof casserole heat the oil over moderately high heat until it is hot but not smoking and in it brown the duck well, in batches if necessary, transferring it as it is browned with tongs to a plate. Pour off all but ½ tablespoon of the fat, add the onion, and cook it over moderately low heat, stirring, until it is softened. Add the garlic and the thyme and cook the mixture, stirring, for 1 minute. Add the wine and the broth and bring the mixture to a boil. Return the duck to the casserole, skin sides up, in 1 layer and braise it, covered, in the middle of a preheated 350° F. oven for 15 minutes. Stir in the turnips and braise the mixture, covered, for 45 minutes, or until the duck and the turnips are tender. Transfer the duck, skin sides up, to a flameproof platter, skim any fat from the cooking liquid, and bring the liquid to a boil over moderately high heat. Stir the cornstarch mixture, add it to the sauce and turnips, stirring, and stir in the olives and the lemon juice. Simmer the sauce and turnip mixture for 2 minutes, season it with salt and pepper, and keep it warm. Broil the duck under a preheated broiler about 4 inches from the heat for 1 to 2 minutes, or until the skin is crisp. Spoon the sauce and turnips around the duck and sprinkle the dish with the parsley. Serves 4.

Spiced Broiled Chicken Wings
1 large garlic clove, chopped
2 tablespoons unsalted butter
1½ pounds chicken wings
¼ teaspoon cinnamon
⅛ teaspoon ground cardamom
a pinch of ground cloves

In a small saucepan combine the garlic and the butter, heat the mixture over moderately low heat until the butter is melted, and let it stand off the heat for 5 minutes. Strain the mixture through a sieve into a large bowl, pressing on the garlic, add the chicken wings to the bowl, and toss them to coat them well. Broil the wings on the rack of a broiler pan under a preheated boiler about 4 inches from the heat, turning them, for 20 minutes, or until they are golden. In a large bowl stir together the cinnamon, the cardamom, the cloves, and salt and pepper to taste, add the wings, and toss them with the mixture until they are coated well. Return the wings to the broiler rack and broil the wings, turning them, for 1 minute. Serves 2.

Breast of Duck with Port Sauce

For the marinade

1¼ cups dry red wine
¼ cup balsamic vinegar
3 tablespoons soy sauce
¼ cup fresh lemon juice
3 garlic cloves, crushed
1½ tablespoons grated fresh gingerroot
¼ cup olive oil

two 2-pound whole boneless duck breasts
    with skin*
3 tablespoons sugar
3 tablespoons water
2 tablespoons white-wine vinegar
3 tablespoons balsamic vinegar
¼ cup minced shallot
1 large garlic clove, minced
1½ cups dry red wine
¾ cup beef broth
⅓ cup heavy cream
¼ cup Tawny Port
a *beurre manié* made by kneading together
    3 tablespoons softened unsalted butter and
    2 tablespoons all-purpose flour
dried cherry and shallot *confit* (recipe follows)
    as an accompaniment

*Whole boneless duck breasts are available at
    many butcher shops and specialty foods
    shops. They can be ordered directly
    from D'Artagnan by calling
    (800) D'ARTAGNAN or in New Jersey
    (201) 792-0748.

Make the marinade: In a bowl whisk together the wine, the balsamic vinegar, the soy sauce, the lemon juice, the garlic, the gingerroot, the oil, and salt and pepper to taste.

Put the duck breasts in a large resealable plastic bag, pour the marinade over them, and seal the bag. Put the plastic bag in a large bowl and let the duck marinate, chilled, overnight. Remove the duck from the marinade and pat it dry between layers of paper towels. Score the skin of each duck breast in a crosshatch pattern with a sharp knife and sprinkle both sides of the duck with salt and pepper to taste. Heat 2 heavy skillets over moderately high heat until they are hot and in each skillet cook 1 of the duck breasts, skin side down, for 10 minutes.

Turn the duck and cook it for 2 minutes more, transfer the skillets to the middle of a preheated 450° F. oven (wrap the skillet handles with a double thickness of foil if the handles are not ovenproof), and roast the duck for 5 to 7 minutes, or until a meat thermometer registers 145° to 150° F. for medium meat.

While the duck is roasting, in a small heavy saucepan combine the sugar and the water, bring the mixture to a boil, stirring until the sugar is dissolved, and boil it, swirling the pan, until the mixture is a golden caramel. Add the vinegars carefully, swirling the pan until the caramel is dissolved, and reserve the mixture.

Transfer the duck to a cutting board and let it stand, covered loosely with foil, for 5 minutes. Pour off all but 2 tablespoons of the fat from 1 of the skillets and in the fat remaining in the skillet cook the shallot and the garlic over moderately low heat, stirring, until the shallot is softened. Add the dry red wine and boil the mixture until it is reduced by half. Add the broth, boil the mixture until it is reduced by one third, and pour the mixture through a fine sieve set over the reserved vinegar mixture, pressing hard on the solids. Whisk in the cream and the Port, simmer the mixture for 1 minute, and add the *beurre manié*, a little at a time, whisking until the sauce is smooth. Simmer the sauce, whisking occasionally, for 2 minutes, whisk into the sauce any juices that have accumulated on the cutting board, and season the sauce with salt and pepper.

Cut the duck diagonally across the grain into thin slices, divide the duck slices among 8 plates, and spoon the sauce over the duck. Serve the duck with the dried cherry and shallot *confit*. Serves 8.

PHOTO ON PAGE 67

Dried Cherry and Shallot Confit

1½ cups dried sour cherries*
    (about ½ pound)
½ cup white-wine vinegar
¼ cup balsamic vinegar
2 cups thinly sliced shallot (about ½ pound)
1 cup finely chopped onion
2 tablespoons unsalted butter
3 tablespoons sugar

*Dried sour cherries are available at many
    specialty foods shops. They can be ordered
    directly from American Spoon Foods by
    calling (800) 222-5886.

In a bowl let the cherries soak in the vinegars for 30 minutes. While the cherries are soaking, in a heavy skillet cook the shallot and the onion in the butter, covered, over moderately low heat, stirring occasionally, for 10 minutes, or until the shallot is soft. Sprinkle the mixture with the sugar and cook the mixture, covered, stirring occasionally, for 10 minutes. Add the cherries with the soaking liquid, simmer the mixture, uncovered, for 10 to 15 minutes, or until almost all the liquid is evaporated, and season the *confit* with salt and pepper. *The confit may be made 1 day in advance, kept covered and chilled, and reheated.* Makes about 2 cups.

PHOTO ON PAGE 67

Grilled Sausages

12 precooked sausages such as pheasant
    sausages or *Weisswurst*
vegetable oil for brushing the sausages
honey and tarragon coarse mustard
    (recipe follows) as an accompaniment

Brush the sausages with the oil and grill them on an oiled rack set 4 to 6 inches over glowing coals, turning them, for 8 to 10 minutes, or until they are browned and heated through. Serve the sausages with the mustard. Serves 6.

PHOTO ON PAGE 63

Honey and Tarragon Coarse Mustard

⅓ cup black mustard seeds (available at
    East Indian markets and some
    specialty foods shops)
⅓ cup yellow mustard seeds
⅔ cup cider vinegar
1 garlic clove
3 tablespoons honey
1 teaspoon chopped fresh tarragon leaves,
    or to taste
½ teaspoon salt, or to taste
¼ teaspoon cinnamon

In a small bowl combine the mustard seeds, the vinegar, and the garlic and chill the mixture, covered, for 36 hours. Discard the garlic and in a food processor purée the mixture coarse with the honey, the tarragon, the salt, and the cinnamon. Spoon the mustard into a sterilized jar with a tight-fitting lid (sterilizing procedure fol-

lows) and seal the jar with the lid. The mustard keeps, covered and chilled, indefinitely. Makes about 1⅓ cups.

PHOTO ON PAGE 63

To Sterilize Jars and Glasses for Pickling and Preserving

Wash the jars in hot suds and rinse them in scalding water. Put the jars in a kettle and cover them with hot water. Bring the water to a boil, covered, and boil the jars for 15 minutes from the time that steam emerges from the kettle. Turn off the heat and let the jars stand in the hot water. Just before they are to be filled invert the jars onto a towel to dry. (The jars should be filled while they are still hot.) Sterilize the jar lids for 5 minutes, or according to the manufacturer's instructions, and keep them in the hot water until sealing the jars.

Roast Turkey with Country Ham Stuffing and Giblet Gravy

For the stuffing

3 cups ½-inch cubes of day-old
    homemade-type white bread
3 cups ½-inch cubes of day-old
    whole-wheat bread
¾ pound boneless cooked or uncooked
    Smithfield or other country ham*, cut into
    ¼-inch dice
1 stick (½ cup) unsalted butter
2 onions, chopped
4 ribs of celery,
    chopped
2½ tablespoons minced fresh sage
    leaves or 2½ teaspoons dried,
    crumbled
1½ teaspoons dried thyme,
    crumbled

a 12- to 14-pound turkey, the neck and giblets
    (excluding the liver) reserved for making
    turkey giblet stock (recipe follows)
1½ sticks (¾ cup) unsalted butter, softened
2 cups water
1 cup turkey giblet stock
    or chicken broth

For the gravy

1 cup dry white wine
6 tablespoons all-purpose flour
4 cups turkey giblet stock, including the
    reserved cooked neck and giblets

fresh sage leaves for garnish

*country ham steaks are available by mail
    from Smithfield Collection, Smithfield,
    VA, Tel. (800) 628-2242 or (804) 357-
    2121, and from Burgers' Ozark Country
    Cured Hams, California, MO, Tel. (800)
    624-5426 or (314) 796-4111

Make the stuffing: In a shallow baking pan arrange the bread cubes in one layer, bake them in a preheated 325° F. oven, stirring occasionally, for 10 to 15 minutes, or until they are golden, and transfer them to a large bowl. In a large skillet sauté the ham in the butter over moderately high heat, stirring occasionally, for 5 to 10 minutes, or until it is deep red and the edges are crisp, and transfer it with a slotted spoon to the bowl. To the fat remaining in the skillet add the onions, the celery, the sage, and the thyme, cook the mixture over moderate heat, stirring, until the onions are softened, and transfer it to the bowl. Toss the stuffing well, season it with salt and pepper, and let it cool completely. *The stuffing may be made 1 day in advance and kept covered and chilled. (To prevent bacterial growth do not stuff the turkey cavities in advance.)*

Rinse the turkey, pat it dry, and season it inside and out with salt and pepper. Pack the neck cavity loosely with some of the stuffing, fold the neck skin under the body, and fasten it with a skewer. Pack the body cavity loosely with some of the remaining stuffing and truss the turkey. Transfer the remaining stuffing to a buttered 2-quart baking dish and reserve it, covered and chilled.

Spread the turkey with ½ stick of the butter and roast it on a rack in a roasting pan in a preheated 425° F. oven for 30 minutes. Reduce the oven temperature to 325° F., baste the turkey with the pan juices, and drape it with a piece of cheesecloth, soaked in the remaining 1 stick butter, melted and cooled. Add the water to the pan and roast the turkey, basting it every 20 minutes, for 2½ to 3 hours more, or until a meat thermometer inserted in the fleshy part of a thigh registers 180° F. and the juices run clear when the thigh is pierced with a skewer. During the last 1½ hours of roasting, drizzle the reserved stuffing with the stock, bake it, covered, in the 325° F. oven for 1 hour, and bake it, uncovered, for ½ hour more. Discard the cheesecloth and string from the turkey, transfer the turkey to a heated platter, reserving the juices in the roasting pan, and keep it warm, covered loosely with foil.

Make the gravy: Skim all of the fat from the roasting pan juices, reserving ⅓ cup of the fat, add the wine to the pan, and deglaze the pan over moderately high heat, scraping up the brown bits. Boil the mixture until it is reduced by half. In a saucepan combine the reserved fat and the flour and cook the *roux* over moderately low heat, whisking, for 3 minutes. Add the stock and the wine mixture in a stream, whisking, bring the mixture to a boil, whisking, and simmer the gravy, stirring occasionally, for 10 minutes. Add the reserved cooked giblets and neck meat, chopped, and salt and pepper to taste, simmer the gravy for 2 minutes, and transfer it to a heated sauceboat.

Garnish the turkey with the sage leaves and serve it with the gravy and the stuffing.

PHOTO ON PAGES 72 AND 73

Turkey Giblet Stock

the neck and giblets (excluding the liver)
   from a 12- to 14-pound turkey
5 cups chicken broth
5 cups water
1 rib of celery, chopped
1 carrot, chopped
1 onion, quartered
1 bay leaf
½ teaspoon dried thyme, crumbled
1 teaspoon black peppercorns

In a large saucepan combine the neck and the giblets, the broth, the water, the celery, the carrot, and the onion and bring the liquid to a boil, skimming the froth. Add the bay leaf, the thyme, and the peppercorns, cook the mixture at a bare simmer for 2 hours, or until it is reduced to about 5 cups, and strain the stock through a fine sieve into a bowl, reserving the neck meat and the giblets for the gravy. Makes about 5 cups.

Turkey Chow Mein with Almonds

2 tablespoons vegetable oil
½ onion, sliced
4 cups sliced Napa cabbage
1 cup sliced celery
½ teaspoon sugar
¾ cup chicken broth
¼ cup water
1 tablespoon soy sauce
1 teaspoon Oriental sesame oil
1 tablespoon cornstarch dissolved
   in 2 tablespoons cold water
2 cups diced cooked turkey
cooked rice as
   an accompaniment
¼ cup slivered almonds,
   toasted lightly

In a large heavy skillet heat the vegetable oil until it is hot but not smoking and in it stir-fry the onion, the cabbage, and the celery for 3 minutes, or until the cabbage is wilted. Add the sugar, the broth, the water, the soy sauce, and the sesame oil and simmer the mixture, covered, for 3 minutes. Stir the cornstarch mixture, stir it into the vegetable mixture, and bring the liquid to a boil. Stir in the turkey and simmer the chow mein until it is heated through. Serve the chow mein over the rice and sprinkle with the almonds. Serves 2.

CHEESE, EGGS, AND BREAKFAST ITEMS

CHEESE

Croques-Monsieurs with Tomato and Thyme
(Grilled Ham and Gruyère Sandwiches)

½ cup plus 2 tablespoons finely grated
    Gruyère or other Swiss cheese
1½ tablespoons mayonnaise
¼ teaspoon Dijon-style mustard
a pinch of dried thyme, crumbled
4 slices of homemade-type white bread
4 thin slices of cooked ham
2 slices of fresh tomato
1½ tablespoons unsalted butter, softened

In a bowl stir together ½ cup of the Gruyère, the mayonnaise, the mustard, the thyme, and salt and pepper to taste and spread the mixture, dividing it evenly, onto the bread slices, avoiding the crusts. Sandwich the ham and the tomato between the bread slices to form 2 sandwiches. Remove the crusts with a sharp knife and spread the tops of the sandwiches with half the butter. Invert the sandwiches into a large non-stick skillet, spread the tops with the remaining butter, and cook the sandwiches over moderate heat for 2 to 3 minutes on each side, or until they are golden brown and the Gruyère is melted.

Transfer the sandwiches with a metal spatula to a baking sheet, sprinkle them with the remaining 2 tablespoons Gruyère, and broil them under a preheated broiler about 4 inches from the heat for 2 to 3 minutes, or until the Gruyère topping is melted. Serves 2.

Swiss Fondue

½ garlic clove
1⅔ cups dry white wine
1 pound Gruyère, grated coarse
2 teaspoons cornstarch
¼ cup kirsch plus additional for thinning the
    fondue if necessary
freshly grated nutmeg to taste
2 loaves of crusty French bread, cut into
    1-inch cubes

Rub the inside of a heavy saucepan with the garlic, add the wine, and heat it over moderately low heat until it is hot. Add the Gruyère by handfuls, stirring, cook the mixture, stirring, until the cheese is melted and the mixture is blended well, and keep the mixture just below the simmering point. In a small bowl stir together well the cornstarch and ¼ cup of the kirsch, add the mixture to the Gruyère mixture with the nutmeg and pepper to taste, and heat the fondue, stirring constantly, until it just begins to bubble, but do not let it boil. Transfer the fondue to a heated fondue pot and keep it hot over a low flame. If the fondue becomes too thick, add some of the additional kirsch. Spear the bread cubes with long-handled forks and dip them into the fondue. Serves 4 to 6.

Savory Mascarpone Cheesecake with
Sun-Dried Tomato Pesto

For the crust
1 cup finely ground Wheat Thins or other
    wheat crackers
½ cup finely chopped walnuts
1 tablespoon unsalted butter, melted
    and cooled
For the pesto
1½ cups packed fresh basil leaves
6 ounces sun-dried tomatoes in oil, drained,
    reserving 2 tablespoons of the oil
1 garlic clove, minced
¼ cup freshly grated Parmesan
3 tablespoons pine nuts

For the filling

1 pound *mascarpone* (available at specialty
    foods shops and cheese shops)
8 ounces cream cheese, cut into bits
    and softened
3 large eggs, beaten lightly
1 tablespoon all-purpose flour

8 ounces sour cream
1 teaspoon all-purpose flour
sun-dried tomato slices for garnish
basil sprigs for garnish
assorted greens with vinaigrette

Make the crust: In a bowl blend together the cracker crumbs, the walnuts, the butter, and salt and pepper to taste. Press the mixture onto the bottom of a buttered 10-inch springform pan and bake the crust in the middle of a preheated 325° F. oven for 10 minutes.

Make the *pesto*: In a food processor purée the basil, the sun-dried tomatoes with the reserved oil, the garlic, the Parmesan, the pine nuts, and salt and pepper to taste until the mixture is smooth.

Make the filling: In the bowl of an electric mixer blend together the *mascarpone*, the cream cheese, the eggs, and the flour until the mixture is very smooth.

Pour half the filling into the crust, spoon the *pesto* over it, spreading the *pesto* carefully with the back of a spoon, and spread the remaining filling over the *pesto*. Bake the cheesecake in the middle of a preheated 325° F. oven for 1 hour.

In a bowl blend together the sour cream and the flour, spread the sour cream topping on the cheesecake, and bake the cheesecake for 5 to 10 minutes more, or until it is set. Let the cheesecake cool in the pan on a rack and chill it, covered loosely, for at least 3 hours or over-night. Remove the side of the pan, garnish the cheese-cake with the sun-dried tomato slices and the basil, and serve it with the greens.

PHOTO ON PAGE 60

*Herbed Crêpes with Ricotta, Green Bell Pepper, and
Spring Tomato Sauce*

1 large green bell pepper, minced
¼ cup olive oil
1 garlic clove, minced
1 pound ricotta cheese
½ cup freshly grated Parmesan
herbed crêpe batter (page 162) made with
    parsley or chives
melted butter for brushing the crêpes
1¼ cups spring tomato sauce
    (page 162)

In a skillet cook the bell pepper in the oil over moderately low heat, stirring, until it is softened, add the garlic, and cook the mixture, stirring, for 1 minute. In a bowl stir together the bell pepper mixture, the ricotta, and ⅓ cup of the Parmesan with salt and pepper to taste and let the filling cool.

Make 12 crêpes (procedure on page 235) with the herbed crêpe batter. Spread about 2 tablespoons of the filling on each crêpe and roll the crêpes up jelly-roll fashion. Arrange the crêpes, seam sides down, in a buttered shallow baking dish just large enough to hold them in one layer, brush them lightly with the butter, and sprinkle them with the remaining Parmesan. Bake the crêpes in the middle of a preheated 400° F. oven for 20 minutes and serve them with the sauce. Makes 12 filled crêpes, serving 4 to 6.

Beverly Charlton

Herbed Crêpe Batter

1 cup all-purpose flour
1 cup plus 2 tablespoons chicken or beef broth
3 large eggs
2 tablespoons unsalted butter, melted
    and cooled
½ tablespoon salt
⅓ cup minced fresh parsley leaves or a
    mixture of other minced fresh herbs, such
    as chives, coriander, or tarragon

In a blender or food processor blend the flour, the broth, the eggs, the butter, and the salt for 5 seconds. Turn off the motor, with a rubber spatula scrape down the sides of the container, and blend the batter for 20 seconds more. Transfer the batter to a bowl, stir in the herbs, and let the batter stand, covered, for 1 hour. *The batter may be made 1 day in advance and kept covered and chilled.* Makes enough batter for about 16 crêpes.

Spring Tomato Sauce

a 14- to 16-ounce can plum tomatoes
    including the juice
½ teaspoon salt, or to taste
¼ teaspoon sugar
2 tablespoons tomato paste
½ teaspoon dried basil, crumbled
⅛ teaspoon cayenne, or to taste
¾ cup peeled, seeded, and diced
    fresh tomatoes

Force the canned tomatoes with the juice through a food mill into a saucepan. Stir in the salt, the sugar, the tomato paste, the basil, and the cayenne, bring the mixture to a boil, and simmer it, stirring, for 20 minutes. Add the fresh tomatoes and cook the mixture for 5 minutes. Serve the sauce warm. Makes about 1¼ cups.

Four-Cheese Vegetable Calzoni

For the dough
a ¼-ounce package (2½ teaspoons)
    active dry yeast
1 tablespoon sugar
3 cups all-purpose flour
1 teaspoon salt
¼ cup olive oil

For the filling
2 garlic cloves, minced
2 cups thinly sliced onion
¼ teaspoon dried hot red pepper flakes,
    or to taste
2 tablespoons olive oil
2 cups thinly sliced fennel bulb
1 green bell pepper, sliced thin
1 red bell pepper, sliced thin
4 plum tomatoes, chopped
⅓ cup minced fresh parsley leaves
1 cup freshly grated Parmesan
    (about 3 ounces)
1 cup coarsely grated mozzarella
    (about ¼ pound)
1 cup coarsely grated provolone
    (about ¼ pound)
1 cup crumbled Gorgonzola (about ¼ pound)

Make the dough: In a large bowl proof the yeast with the sugar in 1 cup warm water for 5 minutes, or until it is foamy. In a food processor blend the flour and the salt, with the motor running add the yeast mixture and the oil, and blend the mixture until it forms a ball. Knead the dough on a lightly floured surface 8 to 10 times and transfer it to a lightly oiled bowl. Turn the dough to coat it with the oil and let it rise, covered with plastic wrap, in a warm place for 1 hour, or until it is double in bulk.

Make the filling: In a large heavy skillet cook the garlic, the onion, and the red pepper flakes in the oil over moderately low heat, stirring, until the onion is softened. Add the fennel, the bell peppers, and salt and pepper to taste and cook the mixture, covered, stirring occasionally, for 10 minutes, or until the vegetables are tender. Add the tomatoes and cook the mixture, covered, for 5 minutes. Remove the lid, cook the mixture, stirring, until most of the liquid is evaporated, and stir in the parsley. In a bowl stir together the cheeses.

Punch down the dough, turn it out onto a lightly floured surface, and divide it into 6 equal pieces. Roll 1 piece of the dough into a 7- to 8-inch round, spoon about ½ cup of the vegetable mixture onto one half of the round, and top it with about ⅔ cup of the cheeses. Fold the other half of the dough over the filling, stretching the dough to enclose the filling, pinch the edges of the dough together, and fold the bottom edge of the dough up over the top edge. Crimp the edge to seal the *calzone*, transfer the *calzone* with a lightly floured spatula to a lightly oiled baking sheet, and make 5 more *calzoni* in the same manner. Bake the *calzoni* on the bottom rack of a preheated 450° F. oven for 20 to 25 minutes, or until they are golden, transfer them to a rack, and let them stand for 5 minutes. Makes 6 *calzoni*.

Vegetable and Cheese Strata

1½ cups finely chopped onion
1 cup finely chopped scallion
¾ pound mushrooms,
   sliced thin
3 tablespoons olive oil
2 red bell peppers, cut into thin strips
   (about 2 cups)
2 green bell peppers, cut into thin strips
   (about 2 cups)
enough Italian bread cut into
   1-inch cubes to measure 9 cups
   (about 1½ loaves)
2½ cups coarsely grated extra-sharp Cheddar
   (about 10 ounces)
1 cup freshly grated Parmesan
12 large eggs
3½ cups milk
3 tablespoons Dijon-style mustard
Tabasco to taste

In a large skillet cook the onion, the scallion, and the mushrooms in the oil over moderately low heat, stirring, until the onion is softened, add the bell peppers and salt and pepper to taste, and cook the mixture over moderate heat, stirring, for 10 to 15 minutes, or until all the liquid the mushrooms give off is evaporated and the peppers are tender. Arrange half the bread cubes in a buttered large shallow (4½-quart) baking dish, spread half the vegetable mixture over them, and sprinkle half the Cheddar and half the Parmesan over the vegetables. Arrange the remaining bread cubes over the cheeses, top them with the remaining vegetables, and sprinkle the remaining cheeses over the top. In a bowl whisk together the eggs, the milk, the mustard, the Tabasco, and salt and pepper to taste, pour the egg mixture evenly over the *strata*, and chill the *strata*, covered, overnight. Let the *strata* stand at room temperature for 15 minutes and bake it in the middle of a preheated 350° F. oven for 50 minutes to 1 hour, or until it is puffed and golden and cooked through. Serves 8.

PHOTO ON PAGE 21

JEANNE

EGGS

Curried Egg Salad

¼ cup bottled mayonnaise
¾ teaspoon curry powder
⅛ teaspoon celery salt
3 to 4 drops of Tabasco, or to taste
¾ teaspoon ground cumin
1 teaspoon Dijon-style mustard
1 tablespoon fresh lemon juice, or to taste
1½ tablespoons bottled mango chutney,
   chopped
6 hard-boiled large eggs, chopped
¼ cup finely chopped celery
3 scallions, chopped

In a bowl stir together the mayonnaise, the curry powder, the celery salt, the Tabasco, the cumin, the mustard, the lemon juice, and the chutney. Stir in the eggs, the celery, and the scallions and season the salad with salt and pepper. Serves 4 to 6.

Scotch Eggs

1¼ pounds bulk country-style or
   herbed sausage
1 teaspoon dried sage, crumbled
½ teaspoon dried thyme, crumbled
¼ teaspoon cayenne
4 hard-boiled large eggs
½ cup all-purpose flour
2 raw large eggs, beaten lightly
1 cup fresh bread crumbs
vegetable oil for deep-frying the eggs

In a large bowl combine well the sausage, the sage, the thyme, and the cayenne, divide the mixture into 4 equal portions, and flatten each portion into a thin round. Enclose each hard-boiled egg completely in 1 of the sausage rounds, patting the sausage into place. Dredge the sausage-coated eggs in the flour, shaking off the excess, dip them in the raw eggs, letting the excess drip off, and roll them gently in the bread crumbs, coating them well. In a deep fryer heat 2½ inches of the oil to 350° F. and in it fry the Scotch eggs, 2 at a time, turning them and transferring them to paper towels to drain with a slotted spoon as they are done, for 10 minutes. Makes 4 Scotch eggs, serving 4.

Scrambled Eggs with Cream Cheese and Scallions

4 scallions, chopped fine
1 tablespoon unsalted butter
4 large eggs
2 ounces cream cheese, cut into bits
   and softened

In a small non-stick skillet cook the scallions in the butter over moderately low heat, stirring, until they are soft. In a bowl whisk together the eggs, the cream cheese, and salt and pepper to taste, pour the egg mixture into the skillet, and cook the mixture over moderate heat, stirring, for 3 to 4 minutes, or until it is cooked through. Serves 2.

Ham and Swiss Cheese Frittata

⅓ cup finely chopped onion
⅓ cup finely chopped green bell pepper
1½ tablespoons olive oil
4 large eggs

⅔ cup (about 3 ounces) chopped cooked ham
⅔ cup (about 3 ounces) grated Swiss cheese

In a 9-inch non-stick skillet cook the onion and the bell pepper with salt and pepper to taste in 1 tablespoon of the oil over moderately low heat, stirring, until the bell pepper is tender. In a bowl whisk together the eggs, the ham, ⅓ cup of the Swiss cheese, and salt and pepper to taste, add the bell pepper mixture, and stir the mixture until it is combined well. In the skillet heat the remaining ½ tablespoon oil over moderate heat until it is hot but not smoking, pour in the mixture, distributing the ham and bell pepper evenly, and cook the *frittata*, without stirring, for 8 to 10 minutes, or until the edge is set but the center is still soft. Sprinkle the remaining ⅓ cup Swiss cheese over the top. (If the skillet handle is plastic, wrap it in a double thickness of foil.) Broil the *frittata* under a preheated broiler about 4 inches from the heat for 2 to 3 minutes, or until the cheese is golden, and let it cool in the skillet for 5 minutes. Slide the *frittata* onto a serving plate, cut it into wedges, and serve it warm or at room temperature. Serves 2.

Cheddar, Bacon, and Scallion Soufflé

½ cup finely chopped scallion
2 tablespoons unsalted butter
6 slices of lean bacon, cooked, drained,
   reserving 2 tablespoons of the fat,
   and crumbled

⅓ cup all-purpose flour
1⅓ cups milk
cayenne to taste
1½ cups coarsely grated Cheddar
   (about 6 ounces)
4 large eggs, separated

In a small heavy saucepan cook the scallion in the butter and the reserved bacon fat over moderately low heat, stirring, until the scallion is softened, stir in the flour, and cook the *roux*, stirring, for 3 minutes. Add the milk in a stream, whisking, and boil the mixture, whisking, for 2 minutes. Remove the pan from the heat and whisk in the cayenne, the Cheddar, and salt and pepper to taste, whisking until the cheese is melted. Add the egg yolks, 1 at a time, whisking well after each addition, and whisk in the bacon. In a bowl with an electric mixer beat the egg whites with a pinch of salt until they hold stiff peaks, whisk about one fourth of them into the cheese mixture, and fold in the remaining whites gently but thoroughly. Pour the mixture into a buttered 1½-quart soufflé dish and bake the soufflé in the middle of a preheated 375° F. oven for 30 to 40 minutes, or until it is puffed and golden. Serve the soufflé immediately. Serves 4 to 6.

Cheese and Tomato Soufflés

2 tablespoons unsalted butter
¼ cup all-purpose flour
1½ cups milk
3 tablespoons tomato paste
1 cup grated Swiss cheese
3 tablespoons freshly grated Parmesan
cayenne to taste
3 large eggs, separated
1 tablespoon medium-dry Sherry

In a saucepan melt the butter over low heat, stir in the flour, and cook the *roux*, stirring, for 3 minutes. Remove the pan from the heat and add the milk, scalded, in a stream, whisking vigorously until the mixture is thick and smooth. Simmer the sauce for 3 to 4 minutes, or until it is thickened, and whisk in the tomato paste, the Swiss cheese, the Parmesan, the cayenne, and salt to taste, whisking until the cheeses are melted. Remove the pan from the heat and whisk in the yolks, 1 at a time, beating well after each addition. Transfer the mixture to

a bowl and let it cool. In a bowl with an electric mixer beat the whites with a pinch of salt until they hold soft peaks, add the Sherry, and beat the egg-white mixture until it just holds stiff peaks. Fold the egg-white mixture into the cheese mixture gently but thoroughly, transfer the mixture to 6 buttered ⅔-cup ramekins, and bake the soufflés on a jelly-roll pan in the middle of a preheated 400° F. oven for 25 to 30 minutes, or until they are cooked through. Serve the soufflés immediately. Serves 6.

Rutabaga and Cheddar Soufflé

dry bread crumbs for dusting the soufflé dish
1 pound rutabaga, peeled and cut into
   ½-inch pieces
½ stick (¼ cup) unsalted butter
¼ cup all-purpose flour
6 large eggs, separated
¼ teaspoon salt
¼ teaspoon cream of tartar
1¾ cups (about 6 ounces) grated
   sharp Cheddar

Fit a 1½-quart buttered soufflé dish with a 6-inch-wide doubled band of foil to form a collar extending about 3 inches above the rim, butter the foil, and dust the soufflé dish with the bread crumbs, knocking out the excess.

In a large saucepan combine the rutabaga with salted water to cover, bring the water to a boil, and simmer the rutabaga, covered, for 25 to 30 minutes, or until it is tender. Drain the rutabaga in a sieve set over a bowl and reserve the liquid. In the pan, cleaned, melt the butter over moderately low heat, add the flour, and cook the *roux*, stirring, for 3 minutes. Add 1½ cups of the reserved cooking liquid, whisking, bring the mixture to a boil, whisking, and simmer the sauce, stirring occasionally, for 5 minutes. In a food processor or blender purée the rutabaga with the sauce and season the mixture with salt and pepper. Transfer the mixture to a large bowl and whisk in the egg yolks. In another large bowl with an electric mixer beat the egg whites with the salt and the cream of tartar until they just hold stiff peaks. Stir one fourth of the whites into the rutabaga mixture and fold in the remaining whites with the Cheddar. Pour the mixture into the prepared soufflé dish and bake the soufflé in the middle of a preheated 400° F. oven for 50 minutes, or until it is puffed and golden. Serves 6.

BREAKFAST ITEMS

Cheddar French Toast with Dried Fruit in Syrup

¾ cup maple syrup
¼ cup thinly sliced dried apricots
¼ cup golden raisins
¼ cup dried cherries (available at specialty
 foods shops)
¼ cup coarsely chopped walnuts
twelve 1-inch-thick diagonal slices of Italian
 bread (about one 14-inch-long loaf)
6 ounces sharp Cheddar, sliced very thin
4 large eggs
2 cups milk
2 tablespoons unsalted butter

In a small bowl stir together the syrup, the apricots, the raisins, the cherries, and the walnuts. *The syrup mixture may be made 1 day in advance and kept covered at room temperature.*

Cut a pocket down the length of the crust, of each piece of bread with a small, pointed serrated knife, and stuff each bread slice with some of the Cheddar. In a bowl whisk together the eggs, the milk, and salt and pepper to taste, dip the stuffed bread slices, 1 at a time, in the egg mixture, soaking them thoroughly and letting the excess drip off, and transfer them to a tray.

In a large skillet heat 1 tablespoon of the butter over moderately high heat until the foam subsides and in it sauté the bread slices in batches, adding the remaining 1 tablespoon butter as necessary, for 3 minutes on each side, or until they are golden. Transfer the French toast as it is cooked to a baking sheet and keep it warm in a preheated 250° F. oven. Serve the French toast with the syrup mixture, heated. Serves 6.

PHOTO ON PAGE 69

Lemon Ricotta Pancakes with Sautéed Apples

For the sautéed apples
4 large Granny Smith apples, peeled, cored,
 and sliced
2 tablespoons unsalted butter
3 tablespoons sugar
½ teaspoon cinnamon
fresh lemon juice to taste
For the pancakes
4 large eggs, separated

1⅓ cups ricotta
1½ tablespoons sugar
1½ tablespoons freshly grated lemon zest
½ cup all-purpose flour
melted butter for brushing the griddle

maple syrup as an accompaniment

Prepare the sautéed apples: In a large heavy skillet sauté the apples in the butter over moderately high heat, stirring occasionally, for 5 minutes, or until they are softened, sprinkle them with the sugar and the cinnamon, and cook them over moderate heat, stirring occasionally, for 5 to 10 minutes, or until they are tender. Stir in the lemon juice and keep the mixture warm.

Make the pancakes: In a bowl whisk together the egg yolks, the ricotta, the sugar, and the zest, add the flour, and stir the mixture until it is just combined. In a bowl with an electric mixer beat the egg whites with a pinch of salt until they hold stiff peaks, whisk about one fourth of them into the ricotta mixture, and fold in the remaining whites gently but thoroughly. Heat a griddle over moderately high heat until it is hot enough to make drops of water scatter over its surface and brush it with some of the melted butter. Working in batches, pour the batter onto the griddle by ¼-cup measures and cook the pancakes for 1 to 2 minutes on each side, or until they are golden, brushing the griddle with some of the melted butter as necessary. Transfer the pancakes as they are cooked to a heatproof platter and keep them warm in a preheated 200° F. oven.

Serve the pancakes with the sautéed apples and the maple syrup. Makes about twelve 3- to 4-inch pancakes.

Cornmeal Porridge with Dried Fruit

2 tablespoons golden raisins
½ cup yellow cornmeal
¼ teaspoon salt
½ cup milk plus additional
 as an accompaniment
1 tablespoon unsalted butter, halved
8 dried apricots, cut into pieces
light brown sugar or maple syrup as an
 accompaniment

In a small bowl cover the raisins with cold water and let them stand for 10 minutes. In a saucepan whisk together the cornmeal, ½ cup cold water, and the salt until the mixture is smooth and add 1½ cups boiling water and ½ cup of the milk in a slow stream, whisking. Cook the mixture in a double boiler set over a pan of simmering water, stirring often, for 10 to 15 minutes, or until the liquid is absorbed and the porridge is thickened. Divide the porridge between 2 bowls and top it with the butter, the apricots, and the raisins, drained well. Serve the porridge with the sugar or the syrup and the additional milk. Serves 2.

Cinnamon-Raisin Waffles

1 cup all-purpose flour
2 tablespoons sugar
2 teaspoons double-acting
   baking powder
¼ teaspoon salt
1 large egg
2 tablespoons unsalted butter, melted,
   plus additional melted butter
   as an accompaniment
⅓ cup raisins
1½ teaspoons cinnamon
vegetable oil for brushing the waffle iron
maple syrup as an accompaniment

In a small bowl whisk together the flour, the sugar, the baking powder, and the salt. In a bowl whisk together the egg, 2 tablespoons of the butter, ½ cup water, the raisins, and the cinnamon, add the flour mixture, and stir the batter until it is just combined. Heat a waffle iron until it is hot, brush it with the oil, and pour half the batter onto it. Cook the waffle according to the manufacturer's instructions, transfer it to a baking sheet, and keep it warm, uncovered, in a warm oven. Make another waffle with the remaining batter in the same manner. Serve the waffles with the syrup and the additional butter. Serves 2.

PASTA AND GRAINS

PASTA

Fusilli with Carrots, Peas, and Mint

¾ cup fresh bread crumbs
2 tablespoons olive oil
½ cup finely chopped shallot
1 cup cooked fresh or thawed frozen peas
¾ cup chicken broth
1¼ cups coarsely grated (preferably in a food
  processor) carrots
¼ cup heavy cream
½ pound *fusilli* (twisted spaghetti) or
  fettuccine
¼ cup minced fresh mint leaves

In a skillet cook the bread crumbs in 1 tablespoon of the oil over moderate heat, stirring, until they are golden and crisp and transfer them to a small bowl. In the skillet cook the shallot in the remaining 1 tablespoon oil over moderately low heat, stirring, until it is softened, add the peas and the broth, and simmer the mixture, stirring, for 3 minutes. Stir in the carrots, simmer the mixture, stirring, for 2 minutes, or until the carrots are just tender, and stir in the cream and salt and pepper to taste. Simmer the mixture until the liquid is reduced by about one fourth, remove the sauce from the heat, and keep it warm. In a kettle of boiling salted water cook the *fusilli* until it is *al dente*, drain it well, and in a bowl toss it with the sauce, half of the bread crumbs, and the mint. Divide the *fusilli* between 2 soup bowls and top it with the remaining bread crumbs. Serves 2.

Chilled Japanese Noodles
with Grilled Chicken and Vegetables

For the sauce
½ cup soy sauce
⅓ cup *mirin* (sweet rice wine, available at
  Asian markets and some supermarkets)
⅓ cup chicken broth
2 tablespoons *sake*
½ teaspoon sugar
2 tablespoons thinly sliced scallion green

2 whole skinless boneless chicken breasts
  (about 1½ pounds), halved
10 ounces dried thin *somen* (wheat noodles,
  available at Asian markets, some
  supermarkets, and some health foods
  stores)
¾ cup finely shredded carrot
¾ cup finely shredded radish
¾ cup very thinly sliced cucumber
¾ cup snow peas, blanched for 1 minute in
  boiling water and cut into ½-inch pieces

Make the sauce: In a small saucepan combine ⅓ cup water, the soy sauce, the *mirin*, the broth, the *sake*, the sugar, and a pinch of salt, bring the liquid to a boil, and add the scallion green. Chill the sauce until it is cold.

On an oiled rack set about 4 inches over glowing coals or in an oiled ridged grill pan heated over moderately high heat grill the chicken breasts, seasoned with salt and pepper, for 8 minutes on each side, or until they are cooked through. Transfer the chicken to a cutting board and let it cool. In a kettle of boiling water boil the *somen* for 3 minutes, or until they are *al dente*, drain them, and rinse them under cold water until they are cold. Divide the noodles among 4 plates, forming bunches of the noodles by wrapping them around the hand and overlapping them on each plate. Surround the noodles with mounds of the carrot, the radish, the cucumber, and the snow peas. Cut the chicken into thin slices and divide it among the plates, fanning out the slices. Serve the noodles with the sauce for dipping or pouring over them. Serves 4.

PHOTO ON PAGE 51

Spicy Macaroni and Cheese

1½ cups finely chopped onion
2 large garlic cloves, minced
1½ tablespoons minced pickled *jalapeño*
    chilies, or to taste
1 teaspoon ground coriander
1½ teaspoons ground cumin
½ stick (¼ cup) unsalted butter
¼ cup all-purpose flour
4 cups milk
a 28-ounce can plum tomatoes, the juice
    discarded and the tomatoes chopped and
    drained well
cayenne to taste if desired
1 pound elbow macaroni
1½ cups coarsely grated Monterey Jack
    (about 6 ounces)
1½ cups coarsely grated extra-sharp Cheddar
    (about 6 ounces)
1½ cups fresh bread crumbs
1⅓ cups freshly grated Parmesan
    (about ¼ pound)

In a large heavy saucepan cook the onion, the garlic, the *jalapeños*, the coriander, and the cumin in the butter over moderately low heat, stirring, until the onion is softened, stir in the flour, and cook the mixture, stirring, for 3 minutes. Add the milk in a stream, whisking, bring the liquid to a boil, whisking, and whisk in the tomatoes. Simmer the mixture for 2 minutes and add the cayenne and salt and pepper to taste.

In a kettle of boiling salted water cook the macaroni for 6 to 7 minutes, or until it is barely *al dente*, drain it well, and in a large bowl combine it with the tomato mixture. Stir in the Monterey Jack and the Cheddar and transfer the mixture to a buttered 13- to 14- by 9-inch shallow baking dish or 3-quart gratin dish. In a bowl stir together the bread crumbs and the Parmesan, sprinkle the mixture evenly over the macaroni mixture, and bake the macaroni and cheese in the middle of a preheated 375° F. oven for 20 to 25 minutes, or until it is golden and bubbling. Serves 6 to 8.

Orzo with Dried Cherries and Almonds

1 cup *orzo* (rice-shaped pasta, available at
    specialty foods shops and many
    supermarkets)
¼ teaspoon crumbled saffron threads
2 teaspoons freshly grated orange zest
2 tablespoons fresh orange juice
3 tablespoons olive oil
⅓ cup dried cherries (available at specialty
    foods shops)
2 tablespoons slivered almonds, toasted
    lightly
1 scallion, sliced thin diagonally

In a saucepan boil the *orzo* in 6 cups boiling water with the saffron for 8 minutes, or until it is *al dente*, drain it, and refresh it under cold water. In a bowl stir together the zest, the orange juice, and salt to taste, add the oil in a stream, whisking, and whisk the dressing until it is emulsified. In a bowl toss the *orzo*, drained well, with the dressing and stir in the cherries, the almonds, and the scallion. Serve the *orzo* at room temperature. Serves 4.

PHOTO ON PAGE 54

Pasta with Cheddar Sauce and Sunflower Seeds

1 tablespoon unsalted butter
1 tablespoon all-purpose flour
¾ cup milk
1 garlic clove, minced and mashed to a paste
   with ¼ teaspoon salt
¾ cup grated sharp Cheddar
¼ pound *rotini* or other corkscrew-shaped pasta
freshly grated nutmeg to taste
¼ cup hulled sunflower seeds, toasted lightly
⅓ cup minced fresh parsley leaves

In a small heavy saucepan melt the butter over moderately low heat, add the flour, and cook the *roux*, stirring, for 3 minutes. Whisk in the milk and the garlic paste and simmer the mixture, whisking frequently, for 8 minutes. Whisk in the Cheddar, whisking until the sauce is smooth, and keep the sauce warm, covered.

In a large saucepan of boiling salted water cook the pasta until it is *al dente*, reserve 2 tablespoons of the cooking water, and drain the pasta well. Whisk the reserved cooking water, the nutmeg, and salt and pepper to taste into the Cheddar sauce and in a bowl toss the pasta with the sauce, the sunflower seeds, and the parsley. Serves 2.

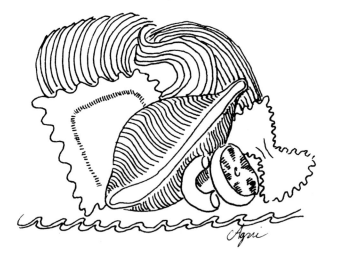

Pasta with Spring Vegetables and Prosciutto

3 garlic cloves, minced
½ teaspoon dried hot red pepper flakes, or
   to taste
3 tablespoons olive oil
a 35-ounce can plum tomatoes, drained and
   chopped coarse (about 3 cups)
¼ cup chopped fresh basil leaves or
   1 teaspoon dried basil, crumbled, plus fresh
   whole basil leaves for garnish if desired
2 tablespoons unsalted butter
½ cup heavy cream
½ cup chicken broth
1 cup freshly grated Parmesan
8 asparagus stalks, trimmed and cut into
   1-inch pieces (about 2 cups)
1 bunch of broccoli, the flowerets cut into
   1-inch pieces (about 2 cups) and the stems
   reserved for another use
2 small zucchini, trimmed, quartered, and cut
   into 1-inch pieces (about 2 cups)
1 cup shelled fresh or frozen *petits pois*
   (tiny peas)
1 cup snow peas (about 3 ounces), trimmed
   and cut diagonally into 1-inch pieces
1 pound dried pasta such as *trenette*
   (fettuccine with one ruffled edge, available
   by mail from Grace's Marketplace,
   1237 Third Avenue, New York, NY 10021.
   Tel. (212) 737-0600 ext. 216) or spaghetti
¼ pound prosciutto, cut into thin strips

In a kettle cook the garlic and the red pepper flakes in the oil over moderately low heat, stirring occasionally, until the garlic is softened, add the tomatoes, and boil the mixture, stirring occasionally, for 5 minutes, or until it is thickened and the liquid is reduced to a thick purée. Stir in the chopped basil and salt and pepper to taste.

In a saucepan combine the butter, the cream, and the broth, bring the mixture to a boil, and simmer it, stirring occasionally, until it is reduced to ½ cup. Whisk in the Parmesan, whisking until the mixture is smooth, whisk the mixture into the tomato mixture, whisking until the sauce is combined well, and keep the sauce warm.

In a kettle of boiling salted water cook the asparagus for 2 minutes, add the broccoli and the zucchini, and cook the vegetables for 2 minutes. Add the peas, cook the vegetables for 1 minute, and add the snow peas.

Cook the vegetables for 30 seconds, or until they are all just tender, transfer them with a slotted spoon or sieve to the sauce, and toss them gently into the sauce.

Return the cooking liquid in the kettle to a boil, in it cook the pasta until it is *al dente*, and drain it well. In the kettle combine the pasta with the vegetable mixture, the prosciutto, and salt and pepper to taste. Divide the pasta mixture among 6 heated plates and garnish it with the basil leaves. Serves 6.

PHOTO ON PAGE 33

Pasta with Sun-Dried Tomatoes, Olives, and Goat Cheese

2 large garlic cloves, minced
¾ cup finely chopped onion
2 tablespoons olive oil
⅔ cup chopped drained sun-dried tomatoes packed in oil (about ¼ pound)
½ cup chicken broth
¼ cup sliced pitted Kalamata or other brine-cured black olives
⅓ cup finely chopped fresh parsley leaves
½ pound medium-sized pasta shells
3 ounces mild goat cheese such as Montrachet, crumbled (about 1 cup), plus additional for sprinkling over the pasta if desired

In a small skillet cook the garlic, the onion, and salt and pepper to taste in the oil over moderately low heat, stirring, until the onion is soft, add the tomatoes and the broth, and simmer the mixture until the liquid is reduced by about one third. Stir in the olives, the parsley, and salt and pepper to taste and keep the mixture warm. In a kettle of boiling salted water cook the pasta until it is *al dente* and drain it well, reserving ⅓ cup of the cooking water. In a serving bowl whisk 3 ounces of the goat cheese with the reserved cooking water until the cheese is melted and the mixture is smooth, add the pasta and the tomato mixture, and toss the mixture well. Sprinkle the pasta with the additional goat cheese. Serves 2.

Baked Pasta with Tomatoes, Shiitake Mushrooms, and Prosciutto

2 cups finely chopped onion
2 large garlic cloves, minced

¼ teaspoon dried hot red pepper flakes, or to taste
1 teaspoon dried basil, crumbled
1 teaspoon dried orégano, crumbled
2 tablespoons olive oil
1 pound fresh *shiitake* mushrooms, stems discarded and the caps sliced
½ stick (¼ cup) unsalted butter
3 tablespoons all-purpose flour
2 cups milk
two 28-ounce cans Italian tomatoes, drained well and chopped
¼ pound thinly sliced prosciutto, cut into strips
¼ pound Italian Fontina, grated (about 1 cup)
¼ pound Gorgonzola, crumbled (about 1 cup)
1½ cups freshly grated Parmesan
⅔ cup minced fresh parsley leaves
1 pound *farfalle* (large bow-tie-shaped pasta) or *penne* (quill-shaped macaroni)

In a large skillet cook the onion, the garlic, the red pepper flakes, the basil, and the orégano in the oil over moderately low heat, stirring, until the onion is softened. Add the mushrooms, cook the mixture over moderate heat, stirring, for 10 to 15 minutes, or until the mushrooms are tender, and transfer the mushroom mixture to a large bowl. In the skillet melt 3 tablespoons of the butter over moderately low heat, whisk in the flour, and cook the *roux*, stirring, for 3 minutes. Add the milk in a stream, whisking, and simmer the mixture, whisking, for 2 minutes, or until it is thickened. Pour the sauce over the mushroom mixture and add the tomatoes, the prosciutto, the Fontina, the Gorgonzola, 1¼ cups of the Parmesan, and the parsley.

In a kettle of boiling salted water cook the pasta for 5 minutes (the pasta will not be tender) and drain it well. Add the pasta and salt and pepper to taste to the mushroom mixture, toss the mixture until it is combined well, and transfer it to a buttered 3- to 4-quart baking dish. *The pasta may be prepared up to this point and kept covered and chilled overnight. Bring the pasta to room temperature before continuing with the recipe.* Sprinkle the pasta with the remaining ¼ cup Parmesan, dot it with the remaining 1 tablespoon butter, cut into bits, and bake it in the middle of a preheated 450° F. oven for 25 to 30 minutes, or until the top is golden and the pasta is tender. Serves 6 to 8.

PHOTO ON PAGE 75

Pasta with White Beans, Tomatoes, and Escarole

1 pound dried white beans such as Great
    Northern, soaked in enough cold water to
    cover them by 2 inches overnight or quick-
    soaked (procedure on page 143) and
    drained
2 cups finely chopped onion
1½ tablespoons minced garlic
1 teaspoon dried sage, crumbled
¾ teaspoon dried rosemary, crumbled
½ teaspoon dried thyme, crumbled
¼ teaspoon dried hot red pepper flakes, or
    to taste
¼ cup olive oil
12 cups packed coarsely shredded escarole
½ cup dry white wine
a 28-ounce can Italian tomatoes, drained and
    chopped, reserving the juice
½ cup minced fresh parsley leaves
    (preferably flat-leafed)
1 pound *fusilli* (corkscrew-shaped pasta)
freshly grated Parmesan to taste

In a kettle combine the beans with enough cold water to cover them by 2 inches and simmer them, covered, for 1 to 1½ hours, or until they are tender. Drain the beans in a colander set over a bowl and reserve the cooking liquid. In a large deep skillet cook the onion, the garlic, the sage, the rosemary, the thyme, the red pepper flakes, and salt and pepper to taste in the oil over moderately low heat, stirring, until the onion is softened, add the escarole in 2 batches, and cook each batch, stirring, for 2 minutes, or until the escarole is wilted. Add the wine and simmer the mixture for 3 minutes. In a blender or food processor purée 1½ cups of the cooked beans with 2 cups of the reserved cooking liquid and add the purée to the skillet with the remaining beans, the tomatoes with the reserved juice, and salt and pepper to taste. Simmer the sauce, uncovered, stirring occasionally, for 10 minutes, or until it is thickened slightly, and stir in the parsley. In a kettle of boiling salted water cook the *fusilli* until it is *al dente*, drain it well, and in a large bowl toss it with the sauce and the Parmesan. Serves 8.

Penne with Swiss Chard and Garlic

1 pound Swiss chard, stems cut from the
    leaves and the stems and leaves chopped
    separately

⅛ teaspoon dried hot red pepper flakes,
    or to taste
3 large garlic cloves, sliced thin
2 tablespoons olive oil
½ cup water
1 cup drained canned tomatoes, chopped
½ pound *penne* or other tubular pasta
¼ cup freshly grated Parmesan plus additional
    as an accompaniment

Rinse and drain separately the Swiss chard stems and leaves. In a large heavy skillet cook the red pepper flakes and the garlic in the oil over moderate heat, stirring, until the garlic is pale golden, add the stems and ¼ cup of the water, and cook the mixture, covered, for 5 minutes, or until the stems are just tender. Add the leaves with the remaining ¼ cup water and salt and pepper to taste and cook the mixture, covered, for 5 minutes. Stir in the tomatoes and cook the mixture, covered, for 3 minutes, or until the leaves are tender. While the chard is cooking, in a kettle of salted boiling water boil the *penne* until it is *al dente* and drain it in a colander. In a large bowl toss the *penne* with the chard mixture and ¼ cup of the Parmesan and serve it with the additional Parmesan. Serves 2.

*Cheese Won Ton Ravioli Triangles with
Tomato Sauce and Confetti Vegetables*

For the filling
4 cups plain yogurt
¼ cup finely chopped shallot
2 tablespoons unsalted butter
½ cup finely grated mozzarella
½ cup freshly grated Parmesan
1 large egg, lightly beaten
1 tablespoon finely chopped fresh
    parsley leaves
freshly grated nutmeg to taste

For the sauce
1 garlic clove, minced
2 tablespoons olive oil
a 35-ounce can plum tomatoes
¼ cup shredded fresh basil leaves if desired,
    plus additional sprigs for garnish

For the confetti vegetable topping
3 tablespoons minced peeled carrots

1 teaspoon olive oil
3 tablespoons minced yellow bell pepper
3 tablespoons minced red bell pepper
3 tablespoons minced zucchini

about 36 won ton wrappers (available at
    Oriental markets, specialty food shops, and
    some supermarkets), thawed if frozen

Make the filling: In a large fine sieve set over a bowl drain the yogurt with a pinch of salt and chill it for at least 3 hours or overnight. Discard the residue in the bowl and measure 1 cup of the yogurt cheese from the sieve, reserving any remaining yogurt cheese for another use. In a skillet cook the shallot in the butter over moderately low heat, stirring, until it is softened and let it cool. In a bowl stir together the shallot mixture, the 1 cup yogurt cheese, the mozzarella, the Parmesan, the egg, the parsley, the nutmeg, and salt and pepper to taste and chill the filling, covered, for 1 hour, or until it is cold.

Make the sauce: In a saucepan cook the garlic in the oil over moderately low heat, stirring, until it is softened. Add the tomatoes and bring the mixture to a boil. Simmer the mixture, stirring occasionally, for 10 minutes, or until it is thickened and slightly chunky. Add the basil and salt and pepper to taste. Remove the sauce from the heat, and keep it covered while preparing the ravioli.

Make the confetti vegetable topping: In a skillet cook the carrot in the oil, stirring, for 1 minute. Stir in the bell peppers and the zucchini, and cook the mixture, stirring, for 1 minute, or until the vegetables are crisp-tender. Season the mixture with salt and pepper to taste.

Put 1 won ton wrapper on a slightly floured surface, mound about 1½ teaspoons of the filling in the center of the wrapper, and brush the edges with water. Fold one corner of the won ton over the filling to form a triangle, pressing down around the filling carefully to force out any air. Seal the edges well and trim the excess dough around the filling with a sharp knife. Make more won ton ravioli in the same manner with the remaining wrappers and filling. Transfer the ravioli as they are formed to a dry kitchen towel and turn them occasionally to let them dry slightly.

Reheat the sauce and keep it warm over moderately low heat while the ravioli are cooking.

Bring a kettle of boiling salted water to a gentle boil and in it cook the ravioli in batches for 2 minutes, or until they rise to the surface and are tender. (Do not let the water boil vigorously after the ravioli have been added.) Transfer the ravioli with a slotted spoon as they are cooked to a dry kitchen towel to drain.

Spoon the sauce onto 6 plates and arrange 6 ravioli on each plate. Garnish each serving with 2 tablespoons of the confetti vegetables and a basil sprig. Makes 36 ravioli, serving 6.

PHOTO ON FRONT JACKET

Rigatoni with Shrimp in Tomato and Feta Sauce

½ cup finely chopped onion
1 garlic clove, minced
6 tablespoons olive oil
½ cup dry white wine
three 14- to 16-ounce cans plum tomatoes
    including the juice, chopped coarse
2 tablespoons finely chopped fresh parsley
    leaves (preferably flat-leafed)
½ teaspoon dried basil, crumbled
½ teaspoon dried orégano, crumbled
¾ teaspoon salt
dried hot red pepper flakes to taste
    if desired
1½ pounds medium shrimp (about 34),
    shelled, deveined if desired, and rinsed
1 pound dried rigatoni or other tubular pasta
½ pound Feta, crumbled

In a kettle cook the onion and the garlic in the oil over moderately low heat, stirring occasionally, until they are softened, add the wine, and boil the mixture for 1 minute. Stir in the tomatoes with the juice, 1 tablespoon of the parsley, the basil, the orégano, the salt, and the red pepper flakes and boil the mixture, stirring occasionally, for 5 minutes, or until it is thickened. Add the shrimp and cook the mixture over moderate heat, stirring, for 4 to 5 minutes, or until the shrimp are just firm.

In a large kettle of boiling salted water cook the rigatoni until it is just *al dente*, drain it well, and stir it into the shrimp mixture. Stir in 6 ounces of the Feta and salt and pepper to taste, transfer the mixture to a lightly oiled 4-quart shallow glass baking dish, and sprinkle the top with the remaining 1 tablespoon parsley and the remaining 2 ounces Feta. Bake the pasta in the middle of a preheated 450° F. oven for 20 minutes, or until the Feta is bubbling and the top is slightly crusty. Serves 6.

*Rigatoni with Southwestern-Style
Ground-Turkey Sauce*

½ cup minced red onion
2 tablespoons olive oil
1 garlic clove, minced
1 small red bell pepper, cut into ¼-inch dice
½ teaspoon chili powder
¼ teaspoon ground cumin
⅛ teaspoon cayenne
¾ pound ground turkey

a 14-ounce can plum tomatoes including
    the juice
a pinch of dried hot red pepper flakes
¼ cup finely chopped fresh coriander plus
    coriander sprigs for garnish if desired
¼ pound rigatoni
coarsely grated Monterey Jack for sprinkling
    the pasta

In a large skillet cook the onion in the oil over moderately low heat, stirring occasionally, until it is softened, add the garlic, the bell pepper, the chili powder, the cumin, and the cayenne, and cook the mixture, stirring, for 1 minute. Add the turkey and cook the mixture over moderately high heat, stirring and breaking up the turkey with a wooden spoon, for 3 to 4 minutes, or until the turkey is no longer pink. Stir in the tomatoes with the juice, breaking them up, the red pepper flakes, the chopped coriander, and salt and pepper to taste and simmer the sauce, stirring occasionally, for 10 minutes, or until it is thickened.

While the sauce is simmering, in a kettle of boiling salted water cook the rigatoni until it is *al dente*, drain it well, and divide it between 2 bowls. Divide the sauce between the bowls, sprinkle it with the Monterey Jack, and garnish each serving with a coriander sprig. Serves 2.

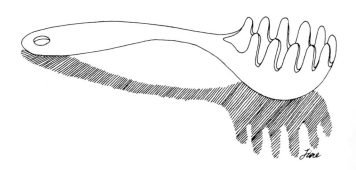

Cold Sesame Noodles

3 tablespoons soy sauce
2 tablespoons rice vinegar or white-wine vinegar
½ teaspoon dried hot red pepper flakes, or
    to taste
2 tablespoons firmly packed brown sugar or
    granulated sugar, or to taste
½ cup creamy peanut butter
1 tablespoon Oriental sesame oil

1 teaspoon grated peeled fresh gingerroot
½ cup chicken broth
1 pound *linguine* or *lo mein* noodles
chopped scallion and cucumber strips for
  garnish

In a saucepan combine the soy sauce, the vinegar, the red pepper flakes, the brown sugar, the peanut butter, the oil, the gingerroot, and the broth, simmer the mixture, stirring, until it is thickened and smooth, and let it cool slightly. In a kettle of boiling salted water cook the noodles until they are *al dente*, drain them in a colander, and rinse them under cold water. Drain the noodles well, transfer them to a bowl, and toss them with the sauce. Serve the noodles at room temperature and garnish them with the scallion and the cucumber. Serves 4 to 6.

Spaghetti with Chicken, Sausage, and Pepper Sauce
  1 onion, sliced thin
  1 garlic clove, minced
  1 green bell pepper, cut into strips
  1 tablespoon olive oil
  ½ pound skinless boneless chicken breast,
    cut into ½-inch-wide strips
  ½ pound sweet or hot Italian sausage links,
    cut crosswise into ½-inch-thick pieces
  a 14- to 16-ounce can tomatoes, chopped,
    including the juice
  ¼ cup dry red wine
  ½ teaspoon dried orégano, crumbled
  ¼ teaspoon dried basil, crumbled
  ¼ teaspoon sugar
  ¾ pound spaghetti
  ¼ cup heavy cream

In a large saucepan sauté the onion, the garlic, and the bell pepper in the oil over moderately high heat, stirring, until the vegetables begin to brown. Add the chicken, the sausage, the tomatoes with the juice, the wine, the orégano, the basil, and the sugar and boil the mixture gently, stirring occasionally, for 10 minutes. While the mixture is boiling, in a kettle of boiling salted water boil the spaghetti until it is *al dente* and drain it well. To the tomato mixture add the cream and salt and pepper to taste and simmer the sauce for 3 minutes, or until it is thickened slightly. Divide the spaghetti between 2 plates and spoon the sauce over it. Serves 2.

Spaghettini with Meat Sauce and Chicken Livers
  1 pound ground round
  4 tablespoons olive oil
  a 28- to 32-ounce can tomatoes, chopped,
    including the juice
  a 6-ounce can tomato paste
  ½ ounce dried Italian mushrooms, soaked in
    ½ cup hot water for 1 hour
  2 onions, chopped
  2 green bell peppers, chopped
  1 teaspoon salt
  1 teaspoon dried rosemary, crumbled
  1 teaspoon dried basil, crumbled
  ½ teaspoon dried thyme, crumbled
  ½ teaspoon dried sage, crumbled
  ¼ teaspoon cayenne
  2 garlic cloves, or to taste, minced
  ½ cup minced fresh parsley leaves
  ½ pound chicken livers, trimmed
  2 tablespoons all-purpose flour
  1 pound *spaghettini* or
    other thin spaghetti
  freshly grated Parmesan to taste

Form the meat into 6 patties and season the patties with salt and black pepper. In a skillet heat 2 tablespoons of the oil over moderately high heat until it is hot but not smoking and in it brown the patties well on both sides. Transfer the patties and the fat to a heavy kettle, break up the meat with a fork, and add the tomatoes with the juice, the tomato paste, 1 cup water, the mushrooms with the soaking liquid, the onions, the bell peppers, the salt, the rosemary, the basil, the thyme, the sage, the cayenne, and the garlic. Simmer the mixture, covered, stirring occasionally, for 2 hours, stir in the parsley, and simmer the sauce for 5 minutes.

While the sauce is cooking, dredge the chicken livers in the flour, shaking off the excess, in a skillet heat the remaining 2 tablespoons oil over moderately high heat until it is hot but not smoking, and in it sauté the chicken livers, stirring, until they are browned on the outside but still barely pink within. Transfer the chicken livers to a cutting board. Let the chicken livers cool and cut them into small pieces.

In a kettle of boiling salted water cook the pasta until it is *al dente*, drain it well, and transfer it to a large serving bowl. Spoon the meat sauce over the pasta, top it with the chicken livers, and sprinkle the mixture with the Parmesan. Serves 8.

GRAINS

Barley with Havarti and Endive

1 tablespoon vegetable oil
1 small onion, chopped fine
½ cup medium pearl barley
¾ cup plus 2 tablespoons chicken broth
½ cup grated Havarti
⅔ cup chopped Belgian endive

In a 9-inch round glass baking dish stir together the oil and the onion and microwave the mixture at high power (100%) for 3 minutes. Stir in the barley and ¾ cup of the broth, microwave the mixture, covered, at high power (100%) for 5 minutes, or until the liquid is boiling, and microwave it, covered, at medium power (50%) for 8 to 10 minutes more, or until the liquid is absorbed and the barley is tender. Stir in the Havarti, the endive, the remaining 2 tablespoons broth, and salt and pepper to taste, microwave the mixture, covered, at medium power (50%) for 1 minute, and let it stand, covered, for 5 minutes. Serves 2.

Lemon Bulgur Timbales with Chives

1¼ cups thinly sliced scallion
1 stick (½ cup) unsalted butter
4½ cups *bulgur* (available at natural foods
    stores, specialty food shops, and some
    supermarkets)
the zest of 3 lemons removed with a vegetable
    peeler, making sure no white pith is
    included, and minced fine
6¾ cups chicken broth
1 cup thinly sliced fresh chives plus chive
    blades for garnish
thin slices of lemon for garnish

In a kettle cook the scallion in the butter in a moderately low heat, stirring, until it is softened, add the *bulgur* and the zest, and cook the mixture, stirring, for 1 minute. Add the broth, bring it to a boil, and simmer the mixture, covered, for 10 minutes, or until the liquid is absorbed. Fluff the *bulgur* with a fork, stir in the sliced chives, and let the mixture stand, covered, off the heat for 5 minutes. Season the *bulgur* mixture with salt and pepper. Using an oiled ⅔ cup timbale mold and forming 1 timbale at a time, pack the *bulgur* mixture into the

mold and invert it onto the dinner plates. Garnish the timbales with the chive blades and the lemon slices. Serves 18.

PHOTO ON PAGE 14

Curried Couscous

the white part of 3 scallions, chopped fine,
    plus 1 tablespoon minced scallion green
1 tablespoon unsalted butter
1½ teaspoons curry powder
¾ cup chicken broth
½ cup couscous

In a heavy saucepan cook the white part of scallion in the butter over moderately low heat, stirring, for 1 minute, add the curry powder, and cook the mixture, stirring, for 1 minute. Add the broth, bring it to a boil, and stir in the couscous. Remove the pan from the heat, let the couscous stand, covered, for 5 minutes, and stir in the scallion green and salt and pepper to taste. Serves 2.

Couscous with Pine Nuts and Parsley

1½ tablespoons unsalted butter
½ teaspoon salt
1 cup couscous
⅓ cup pine nuts, toasted lightly
¼ cup minced fresh parsley leaves
⅓ cup thinly sliced scallion
1 tablespoon white-wine vinegar

In a saucepan combine the butter, the salt, and 1½ cups water, bring the liquid to a boil, and stir in the couscous. Let the couscous stand, covered, off the heat for 5 minutes, fluff it with a fork, and stir in the pine nuts, the parsley, the scallion, and the vinegar. *The couscous may be made 6 hours in advance and kept covered and chilled.* Serves 4.

PHOTO ON PAGE 57

Couscous Timbales with Pistachios, Scallions, and Currants

1 tablespoon unsalted butter
¾ cup chicken broth
½ cup couscous
¼ cup dried currants, soaked in hot water for
    15 minutes and drained

⅓ cup thinly sliced scallion

¼ cup shelled pistachio nuts, toasted lightly
and chopped fine

1 tablespoon minced fresh parsley leaves

1½ tablespoons fresh lemon juice

a pinch of cinnamon

3 tablespoons olive oil

In a saucepan combine the butter and the broth, bring
the liquid to a boil, and stir in the couscous. Remove the
pan from the heat, let the mixture stand, covered, for 5
minutes, and transfer it to a bowl. Break up any lumps
with a fork and stir in the currants, the scallion, the pistachios, the parsley, and salt and pepper to taste. In a
small bowl whisk together the lemon juice, the cinnamon, and the oil. Toss the couscous mixture with the
dressing and season it with salt and pepper. Pack the
mixture into two ¾-cup timbales and unmold the timbales onto 2 plates. Serves 2.

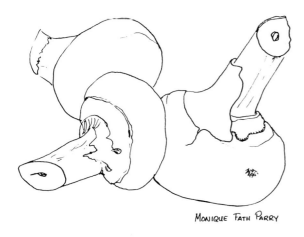

MONIQUE FATH PARRY

Grilled Polenta with Wild Mushrooms

3½ cups water

4 cups chicken broth

1½ teaspoons salt

3 cups (about 17 ounces) instant polenta
(available at specialty foods shops)

1½ cups freshly grated Parmesan plus
additional for sprinkling the mushrooms

3 large garlic cloves, minced

1 cup finely chopped onion

3 tablespoons olive oil plus additional for
brushing the polenta

1½ pounds assorted fresh wild mushrooms
such as *porcini*, chanterelles, *shiitake*, and
portobello (available at specialty produce
markets and some supermarkets), trimmed
and sliced

½ pound fresh white mushrooms, trimmed
and sliced

¼ cup dry Marsala

1½ tablespoons minced fresh sage leaves
plus, if desired, fresh whole sage leaves
for garnish

¼ cup minced fresh parsley leaves

In a large heavy saucepan combine the water and the
broth and bring the mixture to a boil. Add the salt and
the polenta in a stream, stirring with a long-handled
spoon until the mixture is smooth, and simmer the mixture, stirring, for 4 to 5 minutes, or until it is thick. (The
polenta will splatter.) Stir in 1½ cups of the Parmesan,
working quickly spread the polenta evenly in a 15½- by
10½-inch jelly-roll pan, and let it cool completely. *The
polenta may be prepared up to this point 1 day in advance and kept covered and chilled.* Invert the polenta
onto a cutting board, cut out 8 rounds of polenta with a
3- to 4-inch round cutter, and cut each round in half.

In a large heavy skillet cook the garlic and the onion
in 3 tablespoons of the oil over moderately low heat,
stirring, until the onion is softened, add the wild mushrooms, the white mushrooms, and salt and pepper to
taste, and cook the mixture over moderate heat, stirring,
for 10 to 15 minutes, or until most of the liquid the
mushrooms give off is evaporated. Add the Marsala and
simmer the mixture, stirring occasionally, until most of
the Marsala is evaporated. Stir in the minced sage and
the parsley and keep the mixture warm.

Brush the polenta on both sides with the additional oil
and grill it on an oiled rack set about 4 inches over glowing coals or in batches in a well-seasoned ridged grill
pan over moderately high heat for 3 to 4 minutes on each
side, or until it is golden and heated through.

Arrange 2 pieces of polenta decoratively on each of 8
plates and divide the mushroom mixture among the
plates. Sprinkle each serving with some of the additional Parmesan and garnish each plate with some of the
whole sage leaves. Serves 8.

PHOTO ON PAGE 66

Cumin-Scented Rice Timbales

½ cup minced onion
1 teaspoon cuminseed, plus additional,
   toasted lightly, for garnish
⅛ teaspoon dried hot red pepper flakes
2 tablespoons olive oil
1 cup converted rice
1 cup chicken broth
¼ teaspoon salt
1 tablespoon minced fresh parsley leaves

In a heavy saucepan cook the onion, 1 teaspoon of the cuminseed, and the red pepper flakes in the oil over moderately low heat, stirring, until the onion is softened, add the rice, and cook the mixture, stirring, for 1 minute. Stir in the broth, 1 cup water, and the salt, bring the liquid to a boil, and cook the mixture, covered, over low heat for 18 to 20 minutes, or until the liquid is absorbed. Fluff the rice with a fork, stir in the parsley, and let the rice stand, covered, off the heat for 5 minutes. Pack the rice into 4 lightly oiled ¾-cup timbale molds, unmold the timbales, and sprinkle the additional cuminseed on top of them. Serves 4.

PHOTO ON PAGE 45

Spiced Saffron Rice

1½ cups long-grain rice
2 tablespoons vegetable oil
a 3-inch cinnamon stick
7 whole cloves
5 cardamom pods if desired
1 teaspoon salt
¼ teaspoon crumbled saffron threads
2 tablespoons milk

In a large bowl wash the rice in several changes of cold water until the water runs clear and drain it in a fine sieve. In a large heavy saucepan heat the oil over moderately high heat until it is hot but not smoking, add the cinnamon stick, the cloves, and the cardamom pods, if using, and fry the spices, stirring, for 30 seconds, or until the cloves are puffed slightly. Add the rice and cook the mixture, stirring, for 1 minute, or until the rice is opaque. Add 2¼ cups water and the salt, bring the mixture to a boil, and cook the rice, covered, over low heat for 15 minutes.

While the rice is cooking, in a heatproof bowl set over a small pan of simmering water heat the saffron for 3 to 4 minutes, or until it is brittle. Add the milk, heat the mixture, stirring occasionally, until it is hot, and remove the pan from the heat. Drizzle the saffron mixture over the rice and continue to cook the rice, covered, for 5 minutes. Remove the pan from the heat and let the rice stand, covered, for 5 minutes, Serves 6.

PHOTO ON PAGE 27

Asian-Style Shrimp and Pineapple Fried Rice

a 4-pound pineapple
½ cup julienne red bell pepper
3 scallions, sliced thin
2 teaspoons minced fresh *jalapeño* pepper,
   including the seeds (wear rubber gloves),
   or to taste
1½ tablespoons soy sauce
1½ teaspoons sugar
1 teaspoon anchovy paste
½ teaspoon turmeric
2 tablespoons vegetable oil
1 pound small shrimp, shelled and deveined
2 garlic cloves, minced
5 cups cooked rice
¼ cup finely chopped fresh coriander

Halve the pineapple lengthwise, cut out the flesh, leaving ½-inch-thick shells, and reserve the shells. Discard the core and cut enough of the pineapple into ½-inch pieces to measure 1½ cups, reserving the remaining pineapple for another use. In a bowl combine the pineapple pieces, the bell pepper, the scallions, and the *jalapeño* pepper. In a small bowl whisk together the soy sauce, the sugar, the anchovy paste, the turmeric, and 1 tablespoon water.

In a wok or heavy skillet heat 1 tablespoon of the oil over moderately high heat until it is hot but not smoking, in it stir-fry the shrimp for 1½ minutes, or until they are just firm, and transfer them to a bowl. Heat the remaining 1 tablespoon oil over moderately high heat until it is hot but not smoking and in the oil stir fry the garlic for 5 seconds, or until it is golden. Add the rice and stir-fry the mixture for 30 seconds, or until the rice is hot. Add the soy mixture and stir-fry the mixture for 1 minute. Add the pineapple mixture and the shrimp, stir-fry the mixture for 1 minute, or until it is hot, and stir in the coriander. Serve the fried rice in the reserved pineapple shells if desired. (There will be extra fried rice.) Serves 6.

Fried Rice with Vegetables and Basil

½ cup long-grain rice
¼ teaspoon salt
1½ tablespoons vegetable oil
1½ teaspoons grated peeled fresh gingerroot
⅓ cup thawed frozen peas
⅓ cup thawed frozen corn
¼ cup coarsely grated carrot
2 scallions, sliced thin
½ teaspoon Worcestershire sauce
2 teaspoons white-wine vinegar or distilled
    white vinegar
¼ cup finely chopped fresh basil leaves

In a bowl wash the rice well in several changes of cold water and drain it in a sieve. In a small saucepan combine the rice, the salt, and ¾ cup water and simmer the mixture, covered, for 18 minutes, or until the water is absorbed. Transfer the rice to a large bowl and let it cool for 10 minutes.

In a wok or heavy skillet heat the oil over high heat until it is hot but not smoking and in it stir-fry the gingerroot for 10 seconds, or until it is fragrant. Add the rice, the peas, the corn, the carrot, and the scallions and stir-fry the mixture for 1 minute. Add the Worcestershire sauce and the vinegar and stir-fry the mixture for 1 minute, or until it is hot. Stir in the basil and salt and pepper to taste. Serves 2.

Spicy Peanut and Scallion Pilaf

1 small garlic clove, minced
⅛ teaspoon dried hot red pepper flakes
2 teaspoons olive oil
½ cup converted rice
¼ teaspoon salt
¼ cup salted roasted peanuts, chopped
¼ cup thinly sliced scallion
1 teaspoon fresh lime juice

In a small heavy saucepan cook the garlic and the red pepper flakes in the oil over moderately low heat for 1 minute, add the rice, and cook the mixture over moderate heat, stirring, for 1 minute. Stir in 1 cup water and the salt, bring the liquid to a boil, and cook the rice, covered, over low heat for 18 to 20 minutes, or until the liquid is absorbed. Fluff the rice with a fork, let it stand, covered, off the heat for 5 minutes, and stir in the peanuts, the scallion, and the lime juice. Serves 2.

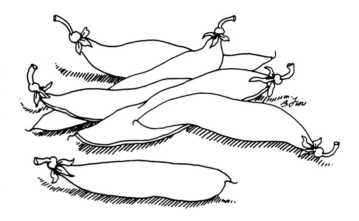

Snow Pea and Sesame Rice Pilaf

1 tablespoon Oriental sesame oil
½ tablespoon unsalted butter
⅓ cup finely chopped onion
3 scallions, sliced thin
1 teaspoon grated peeled fresh gingerroot
⅓ cup long-grain rice
1 cup chicken broth
¼ pound snow peas, trimmed and cut into
½-inch pieces (about ⅔ cup)
2 teaspoons sesame seeds, toasted lightly

In a microwave-safe bowl combine the oil, the butter, the onion, the scallions, and the gingerroot and microwave the mixture at high power (100%) for 2 minutes, or until the onion is softened. Stir in the rice, stirring until it is coated with the oil mixture, add the broth, and microwave the mixture, covered with microwave-safe plastic wrap, at high power (100%) for 5 minutes. Microwave the mixture at medium power (50%) for 12 to 15 minutes, or until all the liquid is absorbed and the rice is tender. Uncover the pilaf carefully and stir in the snow peas. Let the pilaf stand, covered, for 5 minutes and stir in the toasted sesame seeds. Serves 2.

Wild Rice Amandine en Casserole

2 tablespoons chopped onion
2 tablespoons finely chopped fresh chives
1 teaspoon finely chopped shallot
3 tablespoons finely chopped green
    bell pepper
¼ cup olive oil or ½ stick (¼ cup)
    unsalted butter
2 cups wild rice (about 12 ounces), rinsed
    well in several changes of cold water
    and drained
4½ cups chicken broth, heated
¾ cup blanched slivered almonds

In a large saucepan cook the onion, the chives, the shallot, and the bell pepper in the oil over moderately low heat, stirring occasionally, until the vegetables are softened, add the rice, and cook the mixture, stirring constantly, for 1 minute. Stir in the broth, season the mixture with salt and pepper, and add the almonds. Transfer the mixture to a 4-quart casserole and bake it, covered, in the middle of a 325° F. oven, stirring once halfway through the cooking time, for 1 hour and 15 minutes, or until the rice is tender. Serves 6 to 8.

Wild Rice Pancakes

1 cup wild rice
2⅔ cups water
1 teaspoon salt
¾ cup finely diced carrot
¾ cup finely diced celery
1 cup finely chopped onion
⅓ cup finely chopped scallion green
¾ teaspoon dried thyme, crumbled
3 tablespoons unsalted butter
2 large eggs
¾ cup milk
1 cup all-purpose flour
vegetable oil for brushing the griddle

In a heavy saucepan combine the rice, the water, and the salt and simmer the mixture, covered, for 45 to 50 minutes, or until the rice is tender and all the water is absorbed. Transfer the rice to a large bowl and let it cool. In a heavy skillet cook the carrot, the celery, the onion, the scallion green, and the thyme in the butter over moderate heat, stirring, for 10 minutes, or until the carrot is just tender, and transfer the mixture to the bowl. In a small bowl whisk together the eggs and the milk, stir the egg mixture into the rice mixture, and stir in the flour and salt and pepper to taste.

Heat the griddle over moderately high heat until it is hot enough so that drops of water scatter over its surface and brush it with some of the oil. Working in batches, scoop the batter onto the griddle by ¼-cup measures, flatten the pancakes slightly, and cook them for 2 to 3 minutes on each side, or until they are golden. Transfer the pancakes as they are cooked to a heatproof platter and keep them warm in a preheated 200° F. oven. Makes about eighteen 3-inch pancakes.

Risotto with Artichoke Hearts, Prosciutto, and Red Bell Pepper

2 cups chicken broth
½ small red bell pepper, cut into julienne strips
½ cup frozen artichoke hearts, cooked
    according to package directions and drained
3 tablespoons olive oil
1 onion, minced
a ¼-inch-thick slice of prosciutto, cut into
    ¼-inch dice (about ¼ cup)
1 cup Arborio rice (Italian short-grain rice,
    available at specialty foods shops and
    some supermarkets)
⅓ cup dry wine
¼ cup freshly grated Parmesan
1 tablespoon minced fresh parsley leaves
white pepper to taste

In a small saucepan dilute the broth with 2 cups water, bring it to a boil, and keep the broth at a bare simmer. In a heavy saucepan cook the bell pepper and the artichoke hearts in 1 tablespoon of the oil over moderate heat, stirring, for 2 minutes and transfer them with a slotted spoon to a bowl. In the heavy pan cook the onion in the remaining 2 tablespoons oil over moderately low heat, stirring, until it is softened, stir in the prosciutto and the rice with a wooden spatula, and cook the mixture over moderate heat, stirring, for 1 minute, or until the rice is coated well with oil. Add the wine and cook the mixture over moderately high heat, stirring, for 1 to 3 minutes, or until the wine is absorbed, add ½ cup of the simmering broth, and cook the mixture at a vigorous simmer, stirring, for 3 to 5 minutes, or until the liquid is absorbed. Continue adding the broth, about ½ cup at a time, stirring constantly and letting each portion be absorbed before adding the next, until only ½ cup of the broth remains. Stir in the vegetables and ⅓ cup of the remaining broth and simmer the mixture, stirring, for 1 minute, or until the liquid is absorbed. (The risotto should be creamy, but the rice grains should be *al dente*.) If necessary add the remaining broth and cook the risotto in the same manner until the rice is *al dente*. Remove the pan from the heat and stir in the Parmesan, the parsley, and the white pepper. Serves 2.

PHOTO ON PAGE 18

Lemon Broccoli Risotto

4 cups chicken broth
2 cups water
1 pound broccoli, cut into flowerets, quartered if large, and stems cut into ½-inch dice
1 teaspoon freshly grated lemon zest
1 tablespoon fresh lemon juice
1 small onion, chopped fine
1 small garlic clove, minced
2 tablespoons olive oil
1½ cups rice (short, medium, or long grain)
½ cup freshly grated Parmesan

In a large saucepan bring the broth and the water to a boil and in the broth simmer the broccoli flowerets for 3 minutes, or until they are just tender. Transfer the flowerets with a skimmer to a bowl and reserve them. To the simmering broth add the broccoli stems, the zest, and the lemon juice and simmer the mixture for 5 minutes. While the stems are cooking, in a large heavy saucepan cook the onion and the garlic in the oil over moderately low heat, stirring, until the onion is softened and stir in the rice, stirring until each grain is coated with the oil. Add ½ cup of the simmering broth, stems included, and cook the mixture over moderately high heat, stirring constantly, until the broth is absorbed. Continue adding the broth mixture, ½ cup at a time, stirring constantly and letting each portion be absorbed before adding the next, until the rice is tender but still *al dente*. (The rice should take about 20 minutes to become *al dente*.) Stir in the reserved broccoli flowerets and simmer the risotto, stirring, until the flowerets are heated through. Remove the pan from the heat and stir in the Parmesan and salt and pepper to taste. Serves 2.

VEGETABLES

Artichokes with Garlic Pimiento Vinaigrette

6 artichokes (about ½ pound each)
¼ cup fresh lemon juice
6 tablespoons extra-virgin olive oil
3 tablespoons white-wine vinegar
1 large garlic clove, minced and mashed to a
    paste with ½ teaspoon salt
3 tablespoons finely chopped drained
    bottled pimiento
2 tablespoons minced fresh parsley

Cut off and discard the stems of the artichokes with a serrated knife and rub the artichoke bottoms with some of the lemon juice. To a kettle of boiling salted water add the remaining lemon juice and the artichokes, boil the artichokes for 15 to 20 minutes, or until the bottoms are tender when pierced with a knife, and plunge them into a bowl of ice and cold water to stop the cooking. Drain the artichokes well, pull off the leaves, reserving 36 tender ones, and scrape out the chokes from the bottoms. Trim the artichoke bottoms and cut them into julienne strips.

In a small bowl whisk together the oil, the vinegar, the garlic paste, the pimiento, and pepper to taste, add the artichoke strips, and toss the mixture well. *The artichoke mixture and leaves may be prepared 1 day in advance and kept covered and chilled.* Divide the artichoke mixture among 6 salad plates with a slotted spoon, arrange the reserved leaves around it, and spoon the dressing remaining in the bowl onto the leaves. Sprinkle the artichokes with the parsley. Serves 6.

PHOTO ON PAGE 30

Artichoke Croustades

18 slices of very soft white bread, the crusts
    removed and reserved for another use
3 tablespoons unsalted butter, melted
½ cup finely chopped drained marinated
    artichoke hearts (a 6-ounce jar)
3 tablespoons mayonnaise
1 tablespoon finely chopped scallion plus
    finely chopped scallion green for garnish
¼ cup plus 1 tablespoon freshly grated Parmesan

Roll each bread slice flat with a rolling pin and trim it to form a 2½-inch square. Brush both sides of the squares lightly with the butter and fit the squares into ⅛-cup muffin tins (gem tins), pressing the bread against the sides of the tins. Bake the croustades in the middle of a preheated 350° F. oven for 12 to 14 minutes, or until the edges are pale golden. *The croustades may be made 2 days in advance and kept in an airtight container.*

In a bowl stir together the artichoke hearts, the mayonnaise, 1 tablespoon of the scallion, ¼ cup of the Parmesan, and salt and pepper to taste, divide the mixture by heaping teaspoons among the croustades, and sprinkle the remaining tablespoon Parmesan on top. Broil the croustades under a preheated broiler about 6 inches from the heat, being careful not to let the croustade edges burn, for 1 minute, or until the filling is bubbling. Garnish the croustades with the scallion green and arrange 3 of them on each of 6 heated small plates. Serves 6 as a first course.

Asparagus with Walnut-Chive Vinaigrette

4 pounds asparagus, trimmed and peeled
2 tablespoons Sherry vinegar*
½ teaspoon sugar
2 tablespoons walnut oil*
¼ cup olive oil
¼ cup thinly sliced fresh chives
coarse salt to taste

*available at specialty foods shops and some
    supermarkets

In a large deep skillet of boiling salted water cook the asparagus for 3 to 7 minutes, or until the stalks are tender but not limp, drain it well, and return it to the skillet. In a bowl whisk together the vinegar, the sugar, the oils, the chives, and salt and pepper to taste. Pour the dressing over the asparagus, shaking the skillet to coat the asparagus with it, and sprinkle the asparagus with the coarse salt. Serves 8.

PHOTO ON PAGE 24

Boston Baked Beans

2 cups dried navy or pea beans, picked over
¾ pound salt pork
½ cup molasses
½ teaspoon English-style dry mustard
¼ teaspoon paprika
1 teaspoon grated onion

In a bowl combine the beans with 4 cups cold water, let them soak overnight, and drain them, reserving any remaining liquid. Transfer the beans to a small heavy kettle, add fresh water to cover (about 3½ cups), and simmer the beans, covered, for 1 hour. Drain the beans in a colander, reserving the cooking water and combining it with the reserved soaking liquid, and reserve the liquid. To the kettle add a ¼-pound piece of the pork and the beans and bury the remaining piece of pork, well scored, in the center of the beans. In a small bowl stir together the molasses, ½ cup of the reserved bean water, the mustard, the paprika, and the onion and pour the mixture over the beans, lifting the beans with a spoon to allow the seasoning to penetrate to the bottom of the kettle. Bake the beans, covered, in the middle of a preheated 300° F. oven, adding some of the reserved bean water at hourly intervals to keep the mixture covered and lifting the beans to allow the liquid to penetrate to the bottom of the kettle, for 6 hours. (The surface of the liquid in the pot should just cover the beans.) Remove the lid for the last hour of cooking. Serves 6.

Spicy Black Beans and Rice

1 pound dried black beans, soaked in enough
    cold water to cover them by 2 inches
    overnight or quick-soaked (procedure on
    page 143) and drained
1 ham hock
2 large garlic cloves, minced
1 bay leaf
1½ teaspoons dried orégano, crumbled

3 cups coarsely chopped onion
2 green bell peppers, chopped
½ teaspoon dried hot red pepper flakes,
    or to taste
1 tablespoon chili powder
a 28-ounce can Italian tomatoes, drained
    and chopped
⅓ cup finely chopped fresh coriander,
    or to taste
red-wine vinegar to taste
cooked rice as an accompaniment
chopped radish or red onion as an
    accompaniment

In a kettle combine the beans, the ham hock, the garlic, the bay leaf, the orégano, the onion, the bell peppers, the red pepper flakes, the chili powder, and 8 cups water and simmer the mixture, covered, stirring occasionally, for 3 hours, or until the beans are tender. Stir in the tomatoes and salt to taste and simmer the mixture, uncovered, stirring occasionally, for 1 hour, or until the mixture is thickened. Discard the bay leaf, remove the ham hock from the mixture, and chop the meat. Stir the meat into the mixture with the coriander and the vinegar and serve the beans over the rice with the radish or onion. Serving 6 to 8.

Haricots Verts à la Vapeur
(Steamed Green Beans)

¾ pound *haricots verts* (French-style
    thin green beans, available at
    specialty produce markets) or
    green beans, trimmed

In a steamer set over a saucepan of boiling water
steam the beans, covered, for 3 to 6 minutes, or until
they are just tender. Serves 6.

PHOTO ON PAGE 36

Buttered Brussels Sprouts and Chestnuts

1½ pounds Brussels sprouts
    (about 2 pints), trimmed and
    an X cut into the
    base of each sprout
1½ tablespoons unsalted butter
5 vacuum-packed or rinsed
    drained canned whole chestnuts,
    chopped coarse

In a steamer set over boiling water steam the Brussels
sprouts, covered, for 7 to 8 minutes, or until they are
just tender. In a skillet heat the butter over moderately
high heat until it begins to color and in it sauté the chestnuts for 1 minute. Add the Brussels sprouts, season the
mixture with salt and pepper, and sauté it for 1 minute
more. Serves 6.

PHOTO ON PAGE 78

Lemon Soy Carrots

4 carrots, halved lengthwise and cut
    crosswise diagonally into ¼-inch-thick
    slices
1 tablespoon soy sauce
2 teaspoons fresh lemon juice
1 teaspoon sugar
½ tablespoon unsalted butter,
    cut into bits

In a 9-inch microwave-safe baking dish stir together
the carrots, the soy sauce, the lemon juice, the sugar,
and ¼ cup water and microwave the mixture at high
power (100%) for 8 to 10 minutes, or until the carrots
are just tender. Add the butter and pepper to taste and
toss the mixture until the butter is melted. Serves 2.

Moroccan-Style Carrots

½ pound carrots, cut diagonally into
    ¼-inch-thick slices
1 small garlic clove, minced
1½ tablespoons olive oil
¼ teaspoon ground cumin
⅛ teaspoon ground cinnamon
½ teaspoon sugar
a pinch of cayenne
2 teaspoons fresh lemon juice, or to taste

In a steamer set over boiling water steam the carrots,
covered, for 8 minutes, or until they are just tender. In a
skillet cook the garlic in the oil over moderately low
heat, stirring, for 1 minute, or until it is fragrant, add the
cumin, the cinnamon, the sugar, the cayenne, and the
carrots, and cook the mixture, stirring, for 1 minute, or
until the carrots are well-coated with the mixture. Stir in
the lemon juice and salt and pepper to taste, transfer the
carrots to a bowl, and let them cool to room temperature. Serves 2.

Cauliflower with Bacon and Dill

1 head of cauliflower, cut into 1-inch flowerets
2 slices of lean bacon, chopped fine
1 tablespoon minced fresh dill
½ teaspoon fresh lemon juice, or to taste

In a steamer set over boiling water steam the cauliflower, covered, for 5 minutes, or until it is just tender.
While the cauliflower is steaming, in a skillet cook the
bacon over moderate heat, stirring, until it is crisp and
transfer it with a slotted spoon to paper towels to drain.
Pour off all but 1 tablespoon of the fat, to the skillet add
the cauliflower, the dill, the lemon juice, and salt and
pepper to taste, and heat the mixture over moderately
low heat, stirring, until the cauliflower is coated well
with the dill mixture. Sprinkle the cauliflower with the
bacon bits. Serves 2.

Cauliflower with Ginger and Mustard Seeds

3 tablespoons vegetable oil
2 teaspoons black mustard seeds (available at
    East Indian markets and some specialty
    foods shops) or yellow mustard seeds
2 teaspoons grated peeled fresh gingerroot
½ teaspoon turmeric

1 large head of cauliflower
   (about 1¾ to 2 pounds), cut into small
   flowerets about 1 inch in diameter
1½ teaspoons fresh lemon juice, or to taste
3 tablespoons chopped fresh coriander
   if desired

In a large skillet heat the oil over moderate heat until it is hot but not smoking and in it cook the mustard seeds, covered, stirring occasionally, until the popping subsides. Add the gingerroot and the turmeric and cook the mixture, stirring, for 30 seconds. Add the cauliflower, stirring to coat it with the oil, and ½ cup water and steam the mixture, covered, adding more water a few tablespoons at a time if it evaporates, for 6 to 10 minutes, or until the cauliflower is just tender. Season the cauliflower mixture with the lemon juice and salt and pepper and stir in the coriander. Serves 6.

PHOTO ON PAGE 27

Baked Corn with Thyme

1½ cups fresh corn (cut from about 3 ears)
   or thawed frozen
⅓ cup heavy cream

½ teaspoon minced fresh thyme leaves
2 tablespoons fresh bread crumbs

In a bowl stir together the corn, the cream, the thyme, and salt and pepper to taste, spoon the mixture into a buttered 6-inch baking pan or gratin dish, and sprinkle the bread crumbs on top. Bake the corn mixture in the middle of a preheated 350° F. oven for 25 minutes, or until it is crusty around the edges. Broil the corn mixture under a preheated broiler about 4 inches from the heat for 2 minutes, or until the bread crumbs are toasted. Serves 2.

Brown Buttered Corn with Basil

1 tablespoon unsalted butter
1½ cups fresh corn
   (cut from about 3 ears)
½ cup finely shredded fresh basil leaves

In a skillet heat the butter over moderately high heat until the foam subsides and in it sauté the corn, stirring, for 4 minutes, or until it is browned partially. Remove the skillet from the heat and stir in the basil and salt and pepper to taste. Serves 2.

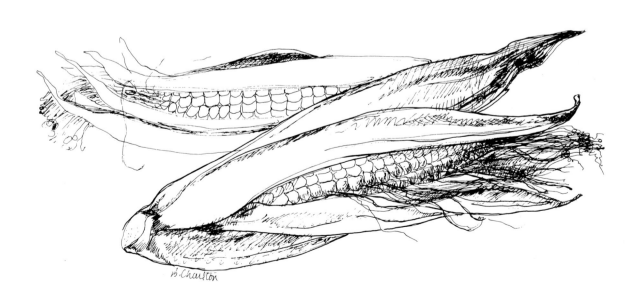

B. Charlton

Broiled Eggplant Rolls with Goat Cheese and Tomato

a 1-pound eggplant, cut lengthwise into
  ⅓-inch-thick slices
2 teaspoons salt
2 tablespoons olive oil
3 to 4 tablespoons (about 2 ounces)
  soft mild goat cheese, or
  to taste
1 tomato, seeded and diced
1½ tablespoons minced fresh parsley leaves

Working with 4 inner eggplant slices, reserving the remaining slices for another use, rub the salt into both sides of each slice and let the eggplant drain in a colander for 10 minutes. Rinse the eggplant and pat it dry. Brush both sides of each eggplant slice with the oil and on a baking sheet broil the eggplant under a preheated broiler about 3 inches from the heat for 3 to 4 minutes on each side, or until it is golden and tender. Spread the goat cheese on the eggplant, top it with the tomato, and sprinkle the tomato with the parsley. Beginning with a short side roll up the slices. Serves 2 as a first course.

Szechwan-Style Eggplant with Pita Wedges

¼ cup vegetable oil
a 1¼-pound eggplant, peeled if desired and
  cut into ½-inch cubes (about 6 cups)
1 teaspoon cornstarch
½ cup chicken broth
1 teaspoon minced garlic
1 tablespoon minced peeled fresh gingerroot
2 to 3 teaspoons Szechwan chili paste*,
  or to taste
1 teaspoon hoisin sauce*
1 tablespoon rice vinegar* or
  white-wine vinegar
1 tablespoon dry Sherry
3 scallions, sliced thin
2 tablespoons soy sauce
1 tablespoon firmly packed light brown sugar
1 red bell pepper, minced
½ teaspoon Oriental sesame oil, or
  to taste
white *pita* and whole-wheat *pita*, cut into
  wedges, as an accompaniment

*available at Oriental markets, specialty foods
  shops, and some supermarkets

In a wok or large skillet heat the vegetable oil over high heat until it is hot but not smoking and in it stir-fry the eggplant over moderately high heat for 3 to 5 minutes, or until it is tender and browned. Transfer the eggplant with a slotted spoon to paper towels to drain.

In a small bowl dissolve the cornstarch in the broth. To the wok add the garlic, the gingerroot, the chili paste, the hoisin sauce, the vinegar, and the Sherry and stir-fry the mixture for 30 seconds. Add the scallions and stir-fry the mixture for 30 seconds. Add the soy sauce, the brown sugar, the cornstarch mixture, stirred, the bell pepper, and the eggplant and stir-fry the mixture for 1 minute, or until the eggplant has absorbed most of the liquid. Remove the wok from the heat, add the sesame oil and salt and pepper to taste, and toss the mixture well. *The eggplant mixture may be made 1 day in advance and kept covered and chilled.* Transfer the eggplant mixture to a bowl and serve it with the *pita* wedges. Makes about 4 cups eggplant.

PHOTO ON PAGE 60

*Escarole with Olives, Raisins,
and Pine Nuts*

1 garlic clove, sliced
2 tablespoons olive oil
1 pound escarole, trimmed, cut into bite-size
  pieces, rinsed well, and spun dry
1 tablespoon sliced Kalamata or other
  brine-cured black olives
2 teaspoons golden raisins
2 teaspoons pine nuts, toasted lightly

In a large skillet sauté the garlic in the oil over moderately high heat, stirring, until it is golden and discard it. To the skillet add the escarole, the olives, the raisins, and salt and pepper to taste and sauté the mixture, stirring, for 1 minute. Cook the mixture, covered, over moderately low heat for 4 minutes, or until the escarole is tender, stir in the pine nuts, and boil the mixture for 1 minute, or until the liquid is evaporated. Serves 2.

Okra and Onion Pickle

1 pound small okra (available seasonally at
  specialty produce markets and many
  supermarkets)
3 tablespoons distilled white vinegar
1 teaspoon sugar

2 tablespoons vegetable oil
1 small onion, halved lengthwise and sliced
   thin crosswise

In a kettle of boiling salted water blanch the okra for 2 minutes, or until it is crisp-tender, drain it, and plunge it into a bowl of ice and cold water to stop the cooking. Drain the okra and pat it dry between layers of paper towels. In a bowl whisk together the vinegar and the sugar until the sugar is dissolved, whisk in the oil and salt and pepper to taste, and toss the okra and the onion with the dressing. *The okra and onion pickle may be made 1 hour in advance and kept covered and chilled. (Alternatively the okra and onion pickle may be made 1 day in advance and kept covered and chilled, but the okra will discolor.)* Serves 6.

PHOTO ON PAGE 31

Kale-Stuffed Onions

8 medium onions (about 3 pounds),
   the root ends trimmed so the onions
   can stand upright
¾ pound kale, stems discarded and the leaves
   rinsed well and shredded
3 garlic cloves, minced
2 tablespoons olive oil
⅛ teaspoon dried hot red pepper flakes
1½ cups water
1 tablespoon cornstarch dissolved in ⅔ cup
   chicken broth
3 tablespoons chopped drained
   bottled pimiento
3 tablespoons freshly grated Parmesan

Cut ⅓ inch off the top of each onion, peel the onions, and scoop out the centers with a melon-ball cutter, forming ⅓-inch-thick shells, with the bottoms slightly thicker, and reserving ½ cup of the scooped-out onion. In a steamer set over boiling water steam the onion shells, covered, for 10 to 15 minutes, or until they are tender.

Rinse and drain the kale and mince the reserved onion. In a large skillet cook the garlic in the oil over moderate heat, stirring, until it is pale golden, add the red pepper flakes and the minced onion, and cook the mixture, stirring, until the onion is softened. Add the kale, ½ cup of the water, and salt and pepper to taste and cook the mixture, covered, stirring occasionally and adding

½ cup of the remaining water every 5 minutes, for 15 minutes, or until the kale is just tender. (If there is excess liquid, boil the mixture, uncovered, until the liquid is evaporated.) Stir the cornstarch mixture, add it to the kale mixture with the pimiento, and simmer the mixture, stirring, for 1 minute, or until it is thickened. Remove the skillet from the heat, stir in the Parmesan and salt and pepper to taste, and fill the onion shells with the kale mixture. *The stuffed onions may be made 1 day in advance, kept covered and chilled, and reheated.* Serves 8.

PHOTO ON PAGE 72

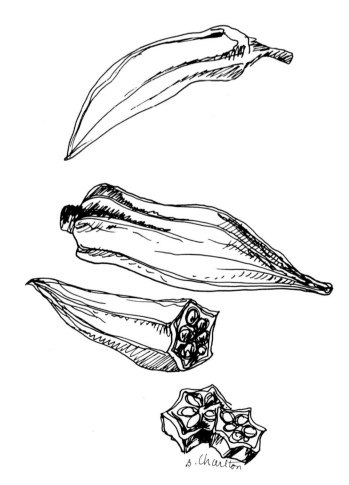

s. Charlton

Onion Tart with Sherry Peppers Sauce

For the shell

1¾ cups all-purpose flour
1 stick (½ cup) cold unsalted butter,
    cut into bits
2 tablespoons vegetable shortening
½ teaspoon salt
raw rice for weighting the shell

For the filling

3 pounds large onions, sliced thin
¼ cup olive oil
1 tablespoon all-purpose flour
2 cups half-and-half
4 large eggs
1½ tablespoons Sherry Peppers Sauce
    (available by mail and telephone order from
    Outerbridge Peppers, Ltd., P.O. Box FL
    85, Smith's Parish, FLBX Bermuda.
    Telephone: 809 293-0259, fax: 809 293-
    2810) or white-wine Worcestershire sauce
1½ teaspoons salt
1 teaspoon minced fresh thyme or
    ¼ teaspoon dried, crumbled

tomato basil *concassé* (recipe follows) as an
    accompaniment
basil sprigs for garnish

Make the shell: In a large bowl blend together the flour, the butter, the shortening, and the salt until the mixture resembles meal. Add 4 tablespoons ice water, toss the mixture until the water is incorporated, and form the dough into a ball. Chill the dough, wrapped well and flattened slightly, for 1 hour. Roll out the dough ⅛ inch thick on a lightly floured surface, fit it into an 11-inch tart pan with a removable fluted rim, leaving a 1-inch overhang, and fold the overhang inward, pressing it against the side of the shell so the dough stands slightly above the edge of the pan. Prick the bottom of the shell lightly with a fork and chill the shell for 30 minutes. Line the shell with foil, fill the foil with the rice, and bake the shell in the lower third of a preheated oven for 20 minutes. Remove the foil and rice, bake the shell for 5 to 7 minutes more, or until it is pale golden, and let it cool in the pan on a rack. *The shell may be made 1 day in advance and kept covered at room temperature.*

Make the filling: In a heavy kettle cook the onions in the oil, covered, over moderately high heat, stirring occasionally, for 15 minutes. Uncover the kettle and cook the onions over moderate heat, stirring occasionally, for 1 hour, or until they are golden. Add the flour, cook the mixture, stirring, for 1 minute, and remove the kettle from the heat. Stir in 1 cup of the half-and-half and combine the mixture well. In a large bowl whisk together the eggs, the remaining 1 cup half-and-half, the Sherry Peppers Sauce, the salt, and the thyme, add the onion mixture, and combine the filling well.

Put the shell on a baking sheet, pour the filling into it, and bake the tart in the middle of a preheated 375° F. oven for 30 to 35 minutes, or until it is set. Let the tart cool in the pan on a rack for 15 minutes. Serve the tart warm with the tomato basil *concassé* garnished with the basil sprigs. Serves 4 to 6.

PHOTO ON PAGE 39

Beverly Charlton

Tomato Basil Concassé

2 large tomatoes, seeded and chopped
2 teaspoons extra-virgin olive oil
1 teaspoon red-wine vinegar
⅓ cup finely chopped fresh basil leaves

In a bowl combine well the tomatoes, the oil, the vinegar, and salt and pepper to taste and stir in the basil. *The concassé may be made 2 hours in advance and kept covered and chilled.* Makes about 2½ cups.

PHOTO ON PAGE 39

Parsnip and Apple Purée

3 parsnips (about ¾ pound), peeled and
    chopped coarse
½ cup finely chopped onion

1 Granny Smith apple, peeled, cored, and
  sliced thin
1 tablespoon unsalted butter
2 tablespoons sour cream, or to taste
a pinch of ground allspice, or to taste

In a saucepan combine the parsnips with water to cover and simmer them, covered, for 15 minutes, or until they are very tender. While the parsnips are cooking, in a small skillet cook the onion and the apple in the butter with salt and pepper to taste over moderate heat, stirring, for 5 to 10 minutes, or until the apple is very tender. Drain the parsnips well, transfer them to a food processor, and add the apple mixture. Purée the mixture until it is smooth and with the motor running add the sour cream, the allspice, salt and pepper to taste, and enough hot water to thin the purée to the desired consistency if necessary. Serves 2.

Potato and Carrot Gratin Diamonds

1¼ pounds russet (baking) potatoes
6 tablespoons cornstarch
2¼ pounds carrots, grated coarse in a
  food processor
⅔ cup minced shallot
1 cup heavy cream
1 cup milk
2 large eggs

In a food processor fitted with the coarse grating disk grate the potatoes, peeled, and in a bowl toss them with 2 tablespoons of the cornstarch. In another bowl toss the carrots with the remaining 4 tablespoons cornstarch. In a buttered 13- by 9-inch baking dish spread half the carrot mixture, add the potato mixture, spreading it evenly, and sprinkle the shallot over the potatoes. Add the remaining carrot mixture, spreading it evenly, and tamp the mixture down with a rubber spatula. In a bowl whisk together the cream, the milk, the eggs, and salt and pepper to taste, pour the mixture over the carrot mixture, and bake the gratin in the middle of a preheated 375° F. oven for 45 minutes, or until the vegetables are tender and golden. Let the gratin cool and chill it, covered, overnight. Cut the gratin into diamonds, transfer the diamonds to a buttered baking sheet, and heat them in a preheated 350° F. oven for 15 minutes, or until they are heated through. Serves 6.

PHOTO ON PAGE 81

Potato Parsnip Purée

3 pounds russet (baking) potatoes
1½ pounds parsnips, peeled and cut into
  ¾-inch pieces
½ stick (¼ cup) unsalted butter,
  or to taste, softened
freshly ground white pepper to taste

In a large saucepan combine the potatoes, peeled and cut into 1½-inch pieces, and the parsnips with salted cold water to cover, bring the water to a boil, and simmer the vegetables, covered, for 20 to 25 minutes, or until they are very tender. Drain the vegetables, reserving 1 cup of the cooking liquid, and force them through the medium disk of a food mill or a ricer into a large bowl. Add the butter, stirring until it is melted, and stir in the white pepper, salt to taste, and enough of the reserved cooking liquid to achieve the desired consistency. *The purée may be made 2 days in advance, kept covered and chilled, and reheated.* Serves 8.

PHOTO ON PAGE 72

Herbed Home-Fried Potatoes

4 pounds boiling potatoes
3 cups finely chopped onion
½ cup olive oil
1 teaspoon dried rosemary, crumbled
¼ cup minced fresh parsley leaves

In a kettle combine the potatoes with enough cold water to cover them by 1 inch and simmer them for 15 to 20 minutes, or until they are just tender. Drain the potatoes and let them cool. *The potatoes may be prepared up to this point 1 day in advance and kept covered and chilled.* Cut the potatoes into 1-inch pieces and in a large bowl toss them with the onion, 2 tablespoons of the oil, the rosemary, and salt and pepper to taste. In a large non-stick skillet heat 3 tablespoons of the remaining oil over moderately high heat until it is hot but not smoking and in it sauté half the potato mixture, stirring, for 10 to 15 minutes, or until the potatoes are golden. Transfer the potatoes to a serving dish and keep them warm, covered. Cook the remaining potato mixture in the remaining 3 tablespoons oil in the same manner, transfer it to the serving dish, and toss the potatoes with the parsley and salt and pepper to taste. Serves 8.

PHOTO ON PAGE 21

Buttermilk Mashed Potatoes with Horseradish

2 russet (baking) potatoes
   (about ¾ pound each)
⅔ to ¾ cup buttermilk
1 tablespoon unsalted butter
2 tablespoons bottled horseradish

Scrub the potatoes and leave them wet. Prick each potato once with a fork and wrap it in a sheet of microwave-safe paper towel, tucking in the ends. Arrange the potatoes in the microwave, end to end and 1 inch apart with the tucked-in ends down, microwave them at high power (100%) for 8 to 10 minutes, or until they yield to gentle pressure, and let them stand, wrapped, for 5 minutes.

In a 1-quart microwave-safe bowl combine ⅔ cup of the buttermilk, the butter, the horseradish, and salt and pepper to taste and microwave the mixture, uncovered, at high power for 2 minutes. Peel the potatoes, while they are still hot force them through a ricer or the medium disk of a food mill into the buttermilk mixture, and combine the mixture well, adding some of the remaining buttermilk if necessary to reach the desired consistency. Serves 2.

Mashed Celery Potatoes

2 pounds russet potatoes (about 3), scrubbed
3 tablespoons unsalted butter
8 cups chopped celery including the leaves
3 garlic cloves, chopped
¾ to 1 cup milk, scalded

Prick the potatoes a few times with a fork and bake them in the middle of a preheated 375° F. oven for 1 hour. In a large skillet melt the butter over moderate heat, in it cook the celery and the garlic, covered, for 10 minutes, and cook the mixture, uncovered, stirring, for 10 minutes more, or until the celery is tender. Transfer the mixture to a food processor and purée it. Peel the baked potatoes and force them through a ricer into a bowl. (Alternatively, the potatoes may be mashed with a potato masher.) Stir in the celery purée, salt and pepper to taste, and enough of the milk to reach the desired consistency. *The mashed celery potatoes may be made 1 day in advance and kept covered and chilled.* Serves 6.

PHOTO ON PAGE 78

Goat Cheese Mashed Potatoes with Leeks and Chives

2½ pounds russet (baking) potatoes
1½ cups thinly sliced well-washed white and
   pale green part of leek
¾ cup finely chopped onion
2 garlic cloves, minced
3 tablespoons unsalted butter
⅔ cup milk
1½ cups crumbled mild goat cheese such as
   Montrachet (about 6 ounces)
¼ cup minced fresh chives

In a saucepan combine the potatoes, peeled and cut into 1-inch pieces, with enough cold water to cover them by 1 inch and simmer them for 10 to 15 minutes, or until they are tender. While the potatoes are cooking, in a heavy skillet cook the leek, the onion, and the garlic in 2 tablespoons of the butter, covered, over moderate heat, stirring occasionally, for 10 minutes, or until the vegetables are soft. Drain the potatoes, return them to the pan, and steam them over moderate heat, shaking the pan, for 30 seconds, or until any excess liquid is evaporated. Force the potatoes through a ricer or the medium disk of a food mill into a bowl and stir in the milk, the remaining 1 tablespoon butter, the leek mixture, half the goat cheese, the chives, and salt and pepper to taste. Spoon the mixture into a buttered 2-quart baking dish, sprinkle the remaining goat cheese over the top, and bake the mixture in the middle of a preheated 350° F. oven for 20 minutes. Serves 4 to 6.

Pommes Anna (Sliced Potato Cake)

½ stick (¼ cup) unsalted butter, melted
2 pounds russet (baking) or large
   yellow-fleshed potatoes

Brush the bottom of a 9-inch heavy ovenproof non-stick or well-seasoned cast-iron skillet with 1 tablespoon of the butter. Peel 1 potato, slice it thin, using a food processor fitted with the slicing blade, or a *mandoline*, or similar slicing device, and pat the slices dry quickly. Arrange the slices, overlapping them slightly, in layers in the skillet, brushing each layer with some of the remaining 3 tablespoons butter and seasoning it with salt and pepper. Peel, slice, pat dry, and arrange the remaining potatoes, 1 at a time, in the same manner.

Cover the layered potatoes with foil, weight them with an ovenproof saucepan, and cook them over moderate heat for 5 minutes from the time the butter sizzles. Transfer the skillet with the pan weight to the middle of a preheated 425° F. oven and bake the potatoes for 30 minutes. Remove the weight and the foil and bake the potatoes for 10 minutes more, or until they are tender. *The potatoes may be made 2 hours in advance and kept, covered loosely, at room temperature. Reheat the potatoes, covered with the foil, in a preheated 375° F. oven for 15 minutes.*

PHOTO ON PAGE 36

Pommes Soufflées
(*Soufléed Potatoes*)

russet (baking) potatoes, uniform in shape
vegetable oil for deep-frying the potatoes
coarse salt for sprinkling the potatoes
    if desired

Peel and trim the potatoes to an even, oval shape. Using a mandoline or similar slicing device, cut the potatoes lengthwise on a narrow side into long, narrow, and very even oval slices, slightly less than ⅛ inch thick and pat the slices dry with paper towels.

Half fill 2 large saucepans with the oil. Heat the oil in one saucepan to 350° F. on a deep-fat thermometer, heat the oil in the other saucepan to 400° F., and maintain these temperatures.

Drop several potato slices, 1 at a time, into the 350° F. oil, remove the pan from the heat, and shake it, constantly and very carefully, to keep the slices moving. (The potatoes will come to the surface and appear blistered.) When the oil temperature drops to 300° F., remove the potatoes with a large skimmer and plunge them into the pan containing the 400° F. oil. (The potatoes will puff immediately and bob around on the surface of the fat.) Turn the puffs constantly until they are browned well and cooked through, being careful not to pierce them, and transfer them with the skimmer to paper towels to drain. Sprinkle the puffs with the salt and keep them in a warm place until ready to serve. Make puffs with the remaining potato slices in the same manner.

If the *pommes soufflées* are not to be served immediately, transfer them from the 400° F. oil when they are well puffed and lightly golden to paper towels to drain, keeping them separated, and let them stand between pa-

per towels for several hours, or until just before serving. (The puffs will have deflated but will puff again when reheated.) Drop the puffs carefully into the 400° F. oil and turn them constantly until they are puffed and browned well on both sides. Drain the puffs, sprinkle them with the salt, and serve them immediately.

Steamed Potatoes

1¼ pounds red potatoes, quartered lengthwise
    and the ends trimmed
1 tablespoon unsalted butter, softened, or
    vegetable oil

In a steamer set over boiling water steam the potatoes, covered, for 10 to 12 minutes, or until they are just tender, and in a bowl toss them with the butter and salt and pepper to taste. Serves 6.

PHOTO ON PAGE 63

Candied Sweet Potatoes

3 pounds sweet potatoes, peeled and cut
    crosswise into ½-inch-thick slices
¾ cup firmly packed light brown sugar
2 tablespoons water
3 tablespoons unsalted butter, cut into pieces
1 teaspoon salt

In a steamer set over boiling water steam the potatoes, covered, for 10 to 15 minutes, or until they are just tender, and let them cool, uncovered. Arrange the potato slices in one layer, overlapping them slightly, in a buttered 2-quart shallow baking dish. In a small saucepan combine the brown sugar, the water, the butter, and the salt, bring the mixture to a boil, stirring, and cook it over moderate heat for 5 minutes. Drizzle the syrup evenly over the potatoes and bake the potatoes in the middle of a preheated 350° F. oven, basting them with the syrup mixture every 15 minutes, for 1½ hours, or until the syrup is thickened and the sweet potatoes have deepened in color. *The candied sweet potatoes may be made 1 day in advance, kept covered and chilled, and reheated.* Serves 8.

PHOTO ON PAGE 72

Sweet Potato Purée

5 pounds sweet potatoes
¾ cup fresh orange juice
3 tablespoons unsalted butter, cut into bits
1½ tablespoons sugar

In a shallow baking pan lined with foil bake the sweet potatoes, pricked in several places, in the middle of a preheated 350° F. oven for 1½ hours, or until they are very tender, let them cool until they can be handled, and peel them. Force the sweet potatoes through the medium disk of a food mill into a heavy saucepan and add the orange juice, the butter, and the sugar. *The sweet potato purée may be prepared up to this point 1 day in advance and kept covered and chilled.* Heat the sweet potato purée over moderately low heat, stirring, until it is heated through and the butter is melted and season it with salt and pepper. Serves 6.

PHOTO ON PAGE 31

Pumpkin Purée with Prune Swirl

a 4-pound pumpkin (preferably a sugar pumpkin)
3 tablespoons unsalted butter
⅓ cup pitted prunes
¼ cup sugar

Slice off the stem end of the pumpkin 2½ inches from the top, scrape out the seeds and the membranes, reserving the seeds for toasting (procedure on page 117) if desired, and brush the inside of the pumpkin with 1 tablespoon of the butter, melted. Bake the pumpkin in a shallow baking pan in the middle of a preheated 375° F. oven for 1 hour, or until the pulp is tender, let it cool in the pan until it can be handled, and reserve enough of the liquid that has accumulated in the shell to measure ¾ cup. (If necessary, add water to yield ¾ cup.)

In a small saucepan combine the prunes with the reserved pumpkin liquid, simmer the mixture for 15 to 20 minutes, or until the prunes are very tender and the liquid is reduced to about ½ cup, and let it cool slightly. In a blender purée the prune mixture, adding additional water if necessary to achieve the desired consistency, and transfer the prune purée to a small bowl.

Discard any remaining liquid from the pumpkin, scoop out the pulp, and force it through a sieve into a heavy saucepan. Simmer the pumpkin purée, stirring frequently, for 15 to 20 minutes, or until it is thickened,

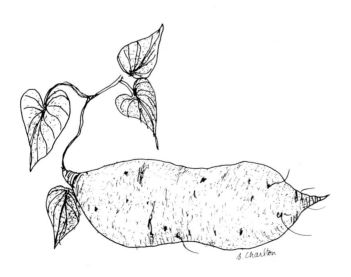

s. Charlton

add the sugar, a pinch of salt, and the remaining 2 tablespoons butter, and stir the mixture until the sugar is dissolved. Transfer the pumpkin purée to a serving bowl, drop spoonfuls of the prune purée onto the pumpkin purée, and with the blade of a knife make decorative swirls. Serves 6.

Daikon Radish Rémoulade

1 pound *daikon* radish (available at specialty
　　produce markets and many supermarkets),
　　peeled
3 tablespoons Dijon-style mustard
4 tablespoons olive oil
1 teaspoon wine vinegar
¼ cup minced fresh parsley leaves

Cut the *daikon* into 2-inch-long fine julienne strips or grate it coarse. Rinse a large bowl with hot water, dry it, and in it whisk the mustard with 3 tablespoons hot water. Add the oil in a slow stream, whisking until the dressing is emulsified, and whisk in the vinegar and salt and pepper to taste. Add the *daikon* strips and the parsley and toss the mixture well. Serves 6.

Glazed Radishes

1 pound radishes, trimmed
1 tablespoon unsalted butter
1 teaspoon sugar
½ teaspoon salt
2 tablespoons minced fresh parsley leaves

In a heavy saucepan wide enough to hold the radishes in one layer cook the radishes in the butter with the sugar and the salt over moderately low heat, stirring, for 1 minute. Add ½ cup water, simmer the radishes, covered, for 10 to 15 minutes, or until they are tender, and boil them, uncovered, shaking the pan occasionally, until the liquid has been reduced to a glaze. Cook the radishes over moderate heat, swirling them, until they are coated with the glaze and sprinkle them with the parsley. Serves 4.

Steamed Radishes with Lemon Dill Butter

1 pound radishes, trimmed and sliced thin
　　(about 4 cups)

2 tablespoons unsalted butter
2 teaspoons fresh lemon juice, or to taste
4 teaspoons finely chopped fresh dill

In a steamer set over boiling water steam the radishes, covered, for 5 minutes, or until they are just tender. In a large skillet melt the butter over moderately low heat, add the radishes, the lemon juice, the dill, and salt and pepper to taste, and heat the mixture, stirring, until the radishes are heated through. Serves 4.

Ratatouille

1 onion, sliced thin
2 garlic cloves, minced
5 tablespoons olive oil
a ¾-pound eggplant, cut into ½-inch pieces
　　(about 3 cups)
1 small zucchini, scrubbed, quartered
　　lengthwise, and cut into thin slices
1 red bell pepper, chopped
¾ pound small ripe tomatoes, chopped coarse
　　(about 1¼ cups)
¼ teaspoon dried orégano, crumbled
¼ teaspoon dried thyme, crumbled
⅛ teaspoon ground coriander
¼ teaspoon fennel seeds
¾ teaspoon salt
½ cup shredded fresh basil leaves

In a large skillet cook the onion and the garlic in 2 tablespoons of the oil over moderately low heat, stirring occasionally, until the onion is softened. Add the remaining 3 tablespoons oil and heat it over moderately high heat until it is hot but not smoking. Add the eggplant and cook the mixture, stirring occasionally, for 8 minutes, or until the eggplant is softened. Stir in the zucchini and the bell pepper and cook the mixture over moderate heat, stirring occasionally, for 12 minutes. Stir in the tomatoes and cook the mixture, stirring occasionally, for 5 to 7 minutes, or until the vegetables are tender. Stir in the orégano, the thyme, the coriander, the fennel seeds, the salt, and pepper to taste and cook the mixture, stirring, for 1 minute. Stir in the basil and combine the mixture well. *The ratatouille may be made 1 day in advance, kept covered and chilled, and reheated before serving.* Serves 4.

PHOTO ON PAGE 45

Rutabaga and Potato Gratin

1 pound rutabaga, peeled
1 pound boiling potatoes
1 garlic clove, minced
2 tablespoons all-purpose flour
1½ cups (about 6 ounces) coarsely grated
    Gruyère or Swiss cheese
2 large eggs
2¼ cups milk
2 tablespoons unsalted butter, cut into bits

Using a *mandoline* or similar slicing device, cut the
rutabaga into very thin slices (about ¹⁄₁₆ inch thick) and
steam the slices over boiling water, covered, for 8 minutes, or until they are just tender. While the rutabaga is
steaming, peel the potatoes and slice them very thin on
the *mandoline* or with a similar slicing device. Sprinkle
the garlic evenly over the bottom of a buttered 12- to
14-inch-long gratin dish and on it arrange overlapping
slices of the rutabaga and the potato in layers, sprinkling
each layer with some of the flour, salt and pepper to
taste, and some of the Gruyère, reserving ½ cup of the
Gruyère for the top. In a heatproof bowl whisk the eggs,
add the milk, scalded, in a stream, whisking, and pour
the custard evenly over the vegetables. Sprinkle the
reserved Gruyère over the top, dot the top with the butter, and bake the gratin in the middle of a preheated
375° F. oven for 45 minutes, or until the top is golden
and the vegetables are tender. Serves 6 to 8.

Sauerkraut with Apples and Caraway

two 1-pound packages or jars of sauerkraut,
    rinsed and drained well
2 Granny Smith apples
¾ cup dry white wine
1 cup chicken broth
3 tablespoons firmly packed brown sugar,
    or to taste
¾ teaspoon caraway seeds

In a large heavy saucepan combine the sauerkraut,
the apples, peeled and chopped, the wine, the broth, the
brown sugar, and the caraway seeds and simmer the
mixture, covered, stirring occasionally, for 1 hour. *The
sauerkraut may be made 1 day in advance, kept covered
and chilled, and reheated.* Serves 8.

PHOTO ON PAGE 73

Dilled Spinach Crêpes with Avgolemono Sauce
For the filling
1 onion, chopped
2 tablespoons unsalted butter
2 tablespoons all-purpose flour
1 cup milk
a pinch of freshly grated nutmeg
¼ cup minced fresh dill
two 10-ounce packages frozen chopped
    spinach, cooked according to package
    directions and drained

dill crêpe batter (recipe follows)
melted butter for brushing the crêpes
For the sauce
⅔ cup chicken broth
2 large eggs
¼ cup fresh lemon juice

Make the filling: In a saucepan cook the onion in the
butter over moderately low heat, stirring, until it is softened, add the flour, and cook the mixture, stirring, for
3 minutes. Add the milk in a stream, whisking, and

cook the mixture over moderate heat, whisking, until it is thick. Stir in the nutmeg, the dill, the spinach, and salt and pepper to taste and let the filling cool.

Make 12 crêpes (procedure on page 235) with the dill crêpe batter. Spread 2 scant tablespoons of the filling on each crêpe and roll the crêpes up jelly-roll fashion. Arrange the crêpes, seam sides down, in a buttered shallow baking dish just large enough to hold them in one layer. *The crêpes may be prepared up to this point 1 day in advance and kept covered and chilled.* Brush the crêpes lightly with the melted butter and bake them in the middle of a preheated 400° F. oven for 20 minutes.

Make the sauce: In a small saucepan bring the broth to a boil. In a bowl whisk together the eggs and the lemon juice. Add half the broth to the egg mixture in a stream, whisking, and whisk the mixture into the remaining broth. Heat the sauce, stirring, until it reaches 170° F. on a candy thermometer and is thickened slightly, but do not let it boil, and add salt and pepper to taste.

Divide the crêpes among plates and drizzle the sauce over them. Makes 12 filled crêpes, serving 4 to 6.

Dill Crêpe Batter

1 cup all-purpose flour
½ cup milk
3 large eggs
2 tablespoons unsalted butter, melted
  and cooled
½ teaspoon salt
3 tablespoons minced fresh dill

In a blender or food processor blend the flour, ½ cup plus 2 tablespoons water, the milk, the eggs, the butter, and the salt for 5 seconds. Turn off the motor, add the dill, and with a rubber spatula scrape down the sides of the container. Blend the batter for 20 seconds more, transfer it to a bowl, and let it stand, covered and chilled, for 1 hour. *The batter may be made 1 day in advance and kept covered and chilled.* Makes enough batter for about 13 crêpes.

Acorn Squash Purée

3 acorn squash, halved, the seeds and
  strings discarded
2 tablespoons unsalted butter
freshly grated nutmeg to taste

Sprinkle the cavities of the squash halves with salt and arrange the squash, inverted, in one layer in a buttered baking dish. Bake the squash, covered with foil, in the middle of a preheated 375° F. oven for 1 hour and let it cool until it can be handled. Scoop out the squash pulp, discarding the skin, and in a food processor purée it with the butter. Transfer the purée to a saucepan and simmer it, stirring occasionally, until the excess liquid is evaporated. Season the purée with the nutmeg and salt and pepper. *The purée may be made 1 day in advance and kept covered and chilled.* Serves 6.

PHOTO ON PAGE 78

Baked Breaded Acorn Squash

½ cup fine dry bread crumbs
½ teaspoon dried thyme, crumbled
2 tablespoons unsalted butter, melted
½ acorn squash, peeled, seeded, and cut
  lengthwise into ¼-inch-thick slices

On a plate combine well the bread crumbs, the thyme, and salt and pepper to taste and in a bowl have ready the butter. Dip the squash slices in the butter, coat them with the bread crumb mixture, and arrange them on a baking sheet. Bake the squash in the upper third of a preheated 375° F. oven for 15 to 20 minutes, or until it is golden. Serves 2.

Honey Orange Butternut Squash

a 1-pound butternut squash, peeled,
  halved lengthwise, seeded, and cut into
  ¾-inch pieces
1 tablespoon unsalted butter
2 teaspoons honey
¼ teaspoon freshly grated orange zest,
  or to taste
2 tablespoons fresh orange juice

In a steamer set over boiling water steam the squash, covered, for 5 to 6 minutes, or until it is just tender but not soft, and remove it from the steamer. In a skillet melt the butter with the honey, the zest, and the orange juice, stirring, add the squash and salt and pepper to taste, and cook the mixture over moderately low heat, stirring gently, for 1 to 2 minutes, or until the squash is coated well with the orange mixture. Serves 2.

Grilled Yellow Squash with Orégano

¾ pound yellow squash, cut diagonally into
    ¼-inch-thick slices
2½ tablespoons olive oil
1 teaspoon fresh lemon juice, or to taste
½ teaspoon dried orégano, crumbled
1 tablespoon minced fresh parsley leaves

Sprinkle both sides of the squash slices with salt and let the slices drain between paper towels for 10 minutes. Pat the slices dry and brush the top sides with some of the oil. Heat a well-seasoned ridged grill pan over moderate heat until it is hot and in it cook the squash slices, in batches if necessary, oiled-side down first and brushing the tops with some of the remaining oil before turning them, for 3 to 4 minutes on each side, or until they are just tender. Transfer the slices with a spatula to a small platter. In a small bowl whisk together the lemon juice, the orégano, the remaining oil, and salt and pepper to taste, drizzle the dressing over the squash, and sprinkle the squash with the parsley. Serves 2.

Baked Tomatoes Filled with Egg, Bacon, and Scallions

2 large tomatoes (about 1½ pounds), a ½-inch
    slice cut from the stem end of each and
    discarded and the pulp scooped out
4 slices of lean bacon
1 teaspoon unsalted butter, melted
3 large eggs, beaten lightly
¼ teaspoon Dijon-style mustard
2 scallions, sliced thin
1 tablespoon finely shredded fresh basil leaves
    plus basil sprigs for garnish
thin 2-inch strips of Monterey Jack

Arrange the tomatoes, cut sides down, on a rack to drain. On a microwave-safe plate lined with several layers of paper towel microwave the bacon at high power (100%) for 2 to 3 minutes, or until it is browned. Transfer the bacon to another paper towel to drain and when it is crisp crumble it coarse. Sprinkle the inside of the tomatoes with salt and pepper to taste, arrange them, cut sides up, in a microwave-safe shallow baking dish, and microwave them at medium power (50%) for 30 seconds to 1 minute, or until they are softened. (Do not overcook the tomatoes or they will collapse.)

In a shallow microwave-safe bowl melt the butter at high power (100%), whisk in the eggs, the mustard, the scallions, and salt and pepper to taste, and microwave the mixture at high power (100%), stirring every 30 seconds, for 1½ minutes, or until the eggs are in large chunks and almost set. Stir the mixture briskly to break up the chunks and stir in the bacon and the shredded basil. Divide the egg mixture between the tomatoes, top it with the Monterey Jack strips, forming Xs, and microwave the filled tomatoes at high power (100%) for 15 seconds, or until the cheese is melted. Serves 2.

Tomates Persillées
(Parsleyed Tomatoes with Pine Nuts)

6 ripe tomatoes (about 2¼ pounds), halved
    and seeded
salt for sprinkling the tomatoes
¼ cup plus 2 tablespoons olive oil
½ cup pine nuts
½ stick (¼ cup) unsalted butter
3 garlic cloves, minced
1 cup minced fresh parsley leaves

Sprinkle the cut sides of the tomatoes with the salt and let the tomatoes drain upside down on a rack for 30 minutes. In a skillet heat ¼ cup of the oil over moderately high heat until it is hot but not smoking and in it sauté the tomato halves for 3 to 4 minutes on each side, or until they are just softened but not browned. Transfer the tomatoes to a baking sheet and keep them warm, covered.

In a small skillet heat the remaining 2 tablespoons oil over moderately high heat until it is hot but not smoking, in it sauté the pine nuts, stirring, until they are golden, and transfer them to paper towels to drain. Add the butter to the skillet and in the fat cook the garlic over moderate heat, stirring, until it is light golden. Add the parsley and cook the mixture, stirring, for 1 minute. Season the mixture with salt and pepper, spoon it into the tomatoes, and top the tomatoes with the pine nuts. Serves 6.

Goat Cheese and Tomato Tart
For the crust
a ¼-ounce package (2½ teaspoons) active
    dry yeast
½ teaspoon sugar
2 tablespoons olive oil

1 cup yellow cornmeal

1½ to 1¾ cups all-purpose flour

¾ teaspoon salt

For the custard

1½ tablespoons minced scallion

7 ounces mild soft goat cheese, mashed

2 large eggs, beaten lightly

½ cup heavy cream

¼ cup minced fresh basil leaves

2 tablespoons olive oil

4 tomatoes (about 2 pounds), each cut
   into ⅓-inch-thick slices

1 garlic clove, minced

basil sprigs for garnish

Make the crust: In the bowl of an electric mixer stir together the yeast, the sugar, and ⅓ cup lukewarm water and proof the yeast mixture for 5 minutes, or until it is foamy. Stir in an additional ⅓ cup lukewarm water, the oil, the cornmeal, 1½ cups of the flour, and the salt and blend the mixture, adding more water, 1 teaspoon at a time, as necessary to form a dough. Knead the dough, incorporating as much of the remaining ¼ cup flour as necessary to form a smooth and elastic dough, for 3 to 5 minutes. Transfer the dough to an oiled bowl and turn it to coat it with the oil. Let the dough rise, covered with plastic wrap, for 1 hour, or until it is double in bulk, and punch it down. Roll out the dough ⅛ inch thick on a floured surface, fit it into a greased 15- by 10½-inch jelly-roll pan, crimping the edges decoratively, and bake the crust in the bottom third of a preheated 450° F. oven for 10 to 15 minutes, or until it is pale golden. Transfer the crust on the pan to a rack and let it cool for 10 minutes. *The crust may be made 1 day in advance and kept, covered tightly with plastic wrap, at room temperature.*

Make the custard: In a bowl whisk together the scallion, the goat cheese, the eggs, the cream, the minced basil, and salt and pepper to taste until the mixture is smooth.

In a large skillet heat the oil over moderately high heat until it is hot but not smoking and in it sauté half the tomatoes with half the garlic for 1 to 2 minutes on each side, or until they are browned lightly, transferring them as they are sautéed to a plate. Sauté the remaining tomatoes with the remaining garlic in the same manner.

Spread the custard evenly over the crust and arrange the tomatoes in rows on it. Bake the tart in the middle of a preheated 400° F. oven for 15 to 20 minutes, or until the custard is pale golden and set. Remove the tart carefully from the baking sheet with 2 spatulas and let it cool on a rack for 15 minutes. Garnish the tart with the basil sprigs and serve it at room temperature.

PHOTO ON PAGES 60 AND 61

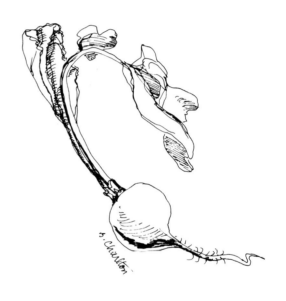

Turnip and Onion Gratin

½ pound turnips, peeled and grated

1 onion, chopped fine

2 teaspoons cornstarch

¼ cup plus 1 tablespoon freshly
   grated Parmesan

⅓ cup heavy cream

In a bowl toss the turnips and the onion with the cornstarch, ¼ cup of the Parmesan, and salt and pepper to taste and transfer the mixture to a buttered 9-inch-square baking dish, patting it down. Drizzle the cream evenly over the mixture, sprinkle the mixture with the remaining 1 tablespoon Parmesan, and bake the gratin in the middle of a preheated 375° F. oven for 25 to 30 minutes, or until the top is golden. Serves 2.

Turnip and Parsnip Purée

1½ pounds turnips, peeled and cut
    into ¾-inch pieces
1 pound parsnips, peeled and cut
    into ¾-inch pieces
3 tablespoons unsalted butter, cut into bits
freshly grated nutmeg to taste

In a large saucepan combine the turnips and the parsnips with salted water to cover, bring the water to a boil, and simmer the vegetables, covered, for 30 to 45 minutes, or until they are very tender. Drain the vegetables well, purée them in a food processor or force them through a food mill into a bowl, and stir in the butter, the nutmeg, and salt and pepper to taste. Makes about 4 cups, serving 6 to 8.

Glazed Turnips with Scallions and Parsley

1½ pounds turnips, peeled and cut into
    1-inch-thick wedges
1½ tablespoons unsalted butter
1¼ cups chicken broth
1 teaspoon sugar
1 scallion, minced
2 tablespoons minced fresh parsley leaves

In a saucepan cook the turnips in the butter over moderately low heat, stirring, until they are coated well with the butter and add the broth, the sugar, and salt to taste. Bring the mixture to a boil and simmer the turnips, covered, for 30 to 40 minutes, or until they are tender. Remove the lid and boil the turnips until almost all the liquid is evaporated and the turnips are glazed. Remove the pan from the heat, stir in the scallion and the parsley, and transfer the glazed turnips to a serving dish. Serves 6.

Grated Turnip Cakes with Ham

1 pound turnips, peeled
½ pound russet (baking) potatoes
⅓ cup all-purpose flour
2 large whole eggs, beaten lightly
1 large egg yolk
½ cup thinly sliced scallion
¼ pound coarsely ground cooked ham
about ⅓ to ½ cup vegetable oil for frying
    the cakes

Coarsely grate the turnips and the potatoes, peeled, and in a kitchen towel squeeze the grated vegetables to extract the excess liquid. In a bowl toss the grated vegetables with the flour, stir in the whole eggs, the egg yolk, the scallion, and the ham, and season the mixture with salt and pepper. In a large heavy skillet heat 2 tablespoons of the oil over moderate heat until it is hot but not smoking and in it fry rounded tablespoons of the turnip mixture in batches, flattening the cakes with a slotted spatula, for 1 to 2 minutes on each side, or until they are golden and tender, transferring the cakes as they are fried to a warm heatproof platter and adding more of the oil to the skillet as needed. If necessary, reheat the cakes on the platter in a preheated 300° F. oven for 5 to 10 minutes. Makes about 20 cakes, serving 6 to 8 as a side dish.

Sautéed Watercress

2 large garlic cloves, minced
3 tablespoons olive oil
6 bunches of watercress, coarse stems
    discarded and the watercress rinsed but not
    spun dry (about 16 cups)

In a large heavy skillet sauté the garlic in the oil over moderately high heat for 30 seconds, or until it is fragrant, add the watercress, and stir the mixture until it is combined well. Sauté the watercress, covered, for 2 to 3 minutes, or until it is just wilted, and season it with salt and pepper. Serves 8.

Marinated Vegetables

⅓ cup fresh lemon juice
½ cup olive oil
2 cups chicken broth
3 garlic cloves, crushed lightly with the
    flat side of a knife
a pinch of dried hot red pepper flakes,
    or to taste
¾ teaspoon salt, or to taste
2 teaspoons coriander seeds
2 fresh thyme sprigs or ¼ teaspoon dried
    thyme, crumbled
2 fresh orégano sprigs or ¼ teaspoon dried
    orégano, crumbled
1 teaspoon sugar

2 leeks (about ½ pound), trimmed, washed
    well, and cut crosswise into 1-inch pieces
1 yellow squash, trimmed, halved lengthwise,
    and cut crosswise into 1-inch pieces
4 ribs of celery, trimmed and cut into
    1-inch pieces
2 red bell peppers, cut into 1-inch pieces
¼ pound green beans, trimmed and cut into
    1-inch pieces
½ pound mushrooms, halved if large and the
    stems reserved for another use

In a kettle stir together the lemon juice, the oil, the broth, the garlic, the red pepper flakes, the salt, the coriander seeds, the thyme, orégano, the sugar, and pepper to taste, bring the mixture to a boil, and simmer it, stirring occasionally, for 5 minutes. Bring the mixture to a boil, add the leeks, and simmer them for 2 minutes. Add the squash and the celery and simmer the vegetables, stirring gently, for 2 minutes. Add the bell peppers and the green beans and simmer the vegetables, stirring gently, for 2 minutes. Add the mushrooms and simmer the vegetables, stirring gently, for 30 seconds.

Transfer the vegetables with a slotted spoon to a shallow baking dish or bowl, boil the cooking liquid for 2 minutes, or until it is reduced to ½ cup, and strain it through a fine sieve onto the vegetables. Let the vegetables marinate, covered and chilled, for at least 3 hours or overnight, season them with salt and pepper, and let them come to room temperature before serving. Serves 6 as a first course.

Vegetable Ribbons with Horseradish Lemon Butter

1 carrot, peeled
1 small zucchini, scrubbed
1 small yellow summer squash, washed well
1 tablespoon unsalted butter
½ teaspoon drained bottled horseradish
1 teaspoon fresh lemon juice

With a vegetable peeler cut the carrot, the zucchini, and the yellow squash lengthwise into "ribbons," reserving the center cores for another use. In a glass dish microwave the vegetables, covered, at high power (100%) for 2 minutes, or until they are crisp-tender. In a small glass dish or glass cup combine the butter, the horseradish, and the lemon juice and microwave the mixture at high power (100%) for 20 seconds, or until the butter is melted. Pour the horseradish butter over the vegetables, season the vegetables with salt and pepper, and toss them well. Serves 2.

Winter Vegetables with Horseradish Dill Butter

6 pounds small red potatoes, quartered and
    reserved in a bowl of cold water
3 pounds Brussels sprouts, trimmed
    and halved
1½ pounds parsnips, peeled and cut
    into 2-inch sticks
1½ pounds carrots, peeled and cut
    diagonally 1-inch-thick
1½ pounds small turnips, peeled and
    cut into sixths
3 sticks (1½ cups) unsalted butter
⅓ cup drained bottled horseradish
⅓ cup cider vinegar
⅓ cup minced fresh dill

In a large vegetable steamer set over boiling water steam separately the potatoes, the Brussels sprouts, the parsnips, the carrots, and the turnips for 8 to 12 minutes, or until they are just tender. In a saucepan melt the butter over moderate heat, stir in the horseradish, the vinegar, the dill, and salt and pepper to taste, and in a large baking pan toss the vegetables with the butter mixture. Keep the vegetables warm, covered, in a 200° F. oven. Serves 18.

PHOTO ON PAGE 14

SALADS AND SALAD DRESSINGS

ENTRÉE SALADS

Walnut Chicken Salad

For the dressing
2 tablespoons wine vinegar
2 shallots, minced
1 teaspoon Dijon-style mustard
⅓ cup walnut oil (available at specialty foods
    shops and some supermarkets)
3 tablespoons minced fresh parsley leaves
1 tablespoon minced fresh chervil leaves
    if desired

3 tablespoons unsalted butter
2 whole skinless boneless chicken breasts
    (about 1½ pounds total), halved and
    flattened slightly between sheets of
    plastic wrap
¼ cup chopped walnuts plus, if desired,
    walnut halves for garnish
2 tablespoons minced shallot, squeezed dry in
    a kitchen towel
1 red bell pepper, chopped fine
2 tablespoons drained bottled capers
1 small head of Boston lettuce, left whole,
    rinsed, and spun dry
½ bunch of watercress, coarse stems
    discarded and the watercress rinsed and
    spun dry
6 ounces mushrooms, sliced thin

Make the dressing: In a small bowl whisk together the
vinegar, the shallots, the mustard, and salt and pepper
to taste, add the oil in a slow stream, whisking, and
whisk the dressing until it is emulsified. Add the parsley
and the chervil and stir the dressing.

In a large heavy skillet melt the butter over moderately low heat, add the chicken, and turn it to coat it with
the butter. Season the chicken with salt and pepper and
cook it, covered with a buttered round of wax paper and
the lid, over low heat for 10 minutes, or until it is just
cooked through. Transfer the chicken with tongs to a
bowl and boil the liquid remaining in the skillet until it is
reduced to about 2 tablespoons. While the chicken is
still warm shred it into long strips and in a bowl combine
it with the reduced cooking liquid, the chopped walnuts, the shallot, the bell pepper, the capers, ¼ cup of
the dressing, and salt and pepper to taste.

Spread the head of lettuce open on a platter, remove
the heart, and shred it. In a small bowl toss the shredded
lettuce with 1 tablespoon of the remaining dressing,
mound the shreds in the center of the lettuce head, and
mound the chicken salad on it. In the small bowl toss the
watercress with the mushrooms, the walnut halves, and
the remaining dressing and arrange the mixture around
the chicken salad. Serves 4.

Warm Lentil Salad with Sausage

¾ cup lentils
4 cups water
1 bay leaf
1 onion, minced
1 carrot, grated coarse
1 rib of celery, chopped fine
2 garlic cloves, minced
¼ teaspoon dried thyme, crumbled
2 tablespoons olive oil
1½ tablespoons red-wine vinegar, or to taste
¼ cup minced fresh parsley leaves
¼ pound smoked *kielbasa* or other smoked
    sausage, cut crosswise into ¼-inch-thick
    slices

In a saucepan combine the lentils, the water, and the bay leaf, bring the water to a boil, and simmer the mixture, covered, for 15 minutes. Add salt to taste and simmer the mixture, covered, for 3 to 5 minutes, or until the lentils are just tender.

While the lentils are simmering, in a heavy skillet cook the onion, the carrot, the celery, the garlic, and the thyme with salt and pepper to taste in the oil over moderately low heat, stirring, until the vegetables are softened. Drain the lentils in a sieve, discarding the bay leaf. Add the lentils, the vinegar, and the parsley to the skillet, heat the mixture over low heat, stirring, until it is heated through, and keep the lentil mixture warm, covered. In another heavy skillet brown the *kielbasa* over moderate heat and transfer it to paper towels to drain. Divide the lentil mixture between 2 plates, mounding it, and top it with the *kielbasa*. Serves 2.

Middle-Eastern Pita Salad

½ cucumber, peeled and cut into ¼-inch dice
1½ large (7-inch) *pita* loaves (preferably
    Mediterranean-style pocketless), cut into
    ¾-inch pieces
¼ cup olive oil
1 tablespoon fresh lemon juice, or to taste
1 garlic clove, minced
½ red bell pepper, cut into ¼-inch dice
1 tomato, chopped fine
¼ cup thinly sliced scallion
2 tablespoons finely chopped fresh
    parsley leaves
3 tablespoons finely chopped fresh mint
    leaves or 2 teaspoons dried, crumbled, plus
    fresh mint sprigs for garnish
inner leaves of romaine, rinsed and spun dry,
    for garnish

In a sieve sprinkle the cucumber with a pinch of salt, let it drain for 20 minutes, and pat it dry. While the cucumber is draining, in a baking pan bake the *pita* pieces in the middle of a preheated 325° F. oven, shaking the pan occasionally, for 18 to 20 minutes, or until they are golden brown and crisp, and let them cool slightly.

In a large bowl whisk together the oil, the lemon juice, the garlic, and salt and pepper to taste, whisking until the dressing is emulsified, stir in the bell pepper, the tomato, the scallion, the parsley, the chopped mint, the *pita* pieces, the cucumber, and more salt and pepper to taste, and toss the salad to combine it well. Transfer the salad to a platter and garnish it with the romaine and the mint sprigs. Serves 2.

Macaroni and Salmon Salad

1 cup elbow macaroni
¾ cup thawed frozen peas
¼ cup mayonnaise
3 tablespoons minced fresh dill
3 tablespoons finely chopped scallion
1 tablespoon fresh lemon juice
a 7½-ounce can salmon, drained and flaked
    into large pieces
½ cup finely chopped celery

In a kettle of boiling salted water cook the macaroni until it is *al dente*, add the peas, and cook the mixture until the macaroni is just tender. Drain the mixture in a colander, rinse it under cold water until it is cold, and drain it well. In a bowl whisk together the mayonnaise, the dill, the scallion, the lemon juice, and salt and pepper to taste, add the macaroni mixture, the salmon, and the celery, and stir the salad until it is combined well. Serves 2.

*Smoked Salmon, Watercress, and Daikon Salad
with Ginger Vinaigrette*

a 1- to 2-inch length of fresh gingerroot
1½ tablespoons rice vinegar (available at
    Asian markets and some supermarkets)
¼ cup vegetable oil
a pinch of sugar
3 cups loosely packed watercress sprigs,
    rinsed and spun dry
¼ pound (about a 4-inch length) *daikon*
    (Oriental white radish, available at
    specialty produce markets and some
    supermarkets), peeled and sliced into
    paper-thin rounds
¼ pound smoked salmon, sliced thin

Grate the gingerroot into a fine sieve set over a bowl, press on the pulp to extract 2 teaspoons of the juice, and discard the pulp. To the bowl add the vinegar, the oil, the sugar, and salt and pepper to taste and whisk the dressing until it is emulsified. Divide the watercress among 4 salad plates and arrange some of the *daikon* rounds down the center of each plate. Roll the salmon into 8 rosettes, arrange 2 rosettes on each plate, and drizzle the dressing over the salads. Serves 4.

PHOTO ON PAGE 51

Shrimp, Feta, and Tomato Salad

6 tablespoons olive oil
1½ pounds small shrimp (about 68), shelled
    and, if desired, deveined
2 tablespoons fresh lemon juice
1 teaspoon white-wine vinegar
¼ teaspoon freshly grated lemon zest
1 tablespoon fresh orégano leaves,
    minced, or 1 teaspoon dried,
    crumbled
6 ounces Feta, crumbled coarse
3 tomatoes, seeded and chopped
1 cup thinly sliced celery
1 cup Kalamata or other brine-cured black
    olives, cut into slivers

In a large heavy skillet heat 2 tablespoons of the oil over moderately high heat until it just begins to smoke and in it sauté the shrimp, stirring, for 2 minutes, or until they are just firm. Transfer the shrimp to a large bowl and let them cool. In a small bowl whisk together the

lemon juice, the vinegar, the zest, the orégano, and salt and pepper to taste, whisk in the remaining 4 tablespoons oil, and whisk the dressing until it is emulsified. Toss the shrimp with the dressing, the Feta, the tomatoes, the celery, and the olives until the salad is combined well. *The salad may be made 1 day in advance and kept covered and chilled.* Serves 4.

PHOTO ON PAGE 57

*Grilled Tuna Salad with Sun-Dried
Tomato Dressing*

For the dressing
1 large garlic clove, minced and mashed to a
    paste with ½ teaspoon salt
2 tablespoons red-wine vinegar
1 tablespoon fresh lemon juice plus
    additional to taste
¼ cup finely chopped drained sun-dried
    tomatoes packed in oil
2 plum tomatoes, seeded and chopped
½ cup olive oil
2 tablespoons sour cream
½ cup packed fresh coriander

10 cups loosely packed *mesclun* (mixed baby
greens, available at specialty produce
markets)
1 cup cherry tomatoes, halved lengthwise
1 cup cooked fresh corn (cut from about
2 ears)
two 1-inch-thick tuna steaks (about
1½ pounds)
olive oil for brushing the tuna
nasturtium blossoms for garnish
if desired

Make the dressing: In a blender blend together the
garlic, the vinegar, 1 tablespoon of the lemon juice, the
sun-dried tomatoes, the plum tomatoes, and ¼ cup
water until the mixture is smooth and with the motor
running add the oil in a stream. Add the sour cream, the
coriander, the additional lemon juice, and salt and pepper to taste and blend the dressing until it is combined
well. *The dressing may be made 1 day in advance and
kept covered and chilled. Let the dressing return to
room temperature.*

In a large bowl toss the *mesclun* with the tomatoes
and the corn and divide the mixture among 4 plates.
Brush the tuna on both sides with the oil, season it with
salt and pepper, and grill it on an oiled rack set about
4 inches over glowing coals for 4 to 5 minutes on each
side for medium-rare, or until it is cooked to the desired
degree. Let the tuna stand for 3 minutes and cut it
against the grain into ¼-inch-thick slices. Divide the
tuna slices among the salads and pour about ¼ cup of the
dressing over each serving. Serve any remaining dressing separately and garnish the salads with the nasturtium blossoms. Serves 4.

PHOTO ON PAGE 48

SALADS WITH GREENS

*Avocado, Grapefruit, and Watercress Salad with
Roquefort and Paprika Dressing*

1½ grapefruits
1½ avocados (preferably California)
2 teaspoons red-wine vinegar
½ teaspoon Dijon-style mustard
½ teaspoon paprika
⅓ cup vegetable oil

3 cups packed watercress sprigs
⅓ cup crumbled Roquefort

With a serrated knife cut the zest and pith from the
grapefruits and working over a bowl cut the flesh into
sections, discarding the membranes and reserving
6 tablespoons of the juice. Peel and pit the avocados and
cut them into 12 wedges. In a bowl sprinkle the avocados with 3 tablespoons of the reserved grapefruit juice,
coating them thoroughly. In another bowl whisk together the remaining 3 tablespoons reserved grapefruit
juice, the vinegar, the mustard, the paprika, and salt and
pepper to taste, add the oil in a stream, whisking, and
whisk the dressing until it is emulsified. In a large bowl
toss the watercress with two thirds of the dressing and
divide it among 4 salad plates. Top the watercress decoratively with the avocado wedges, drained, and the
grapefruit sections, sprinkle the salads with the Roquefort, and drizzle them with the remaining dressing.
Serves 4.

PHOTO ON PAGE 39

*Escarole, Spinach, and Red Onion Salad with
Anchovy Garlic Dressing*

For the dressing
1 garlic clove, minced and mashed to a paste
with ¼ teaspoon salt
1 flat anchovy fillet, or to taste, chopped
2 teaspoons balsamic vinegar
1½ tablespoons fresh lemon juice
¾ teaspoon Dijon-style mustard
⅓ cup olive oil

8 cups packed escarole, rinsed, spun dry, and
torn into pieces
6 cups packed fresh spinach leaves, washed
well, spun dry, and torn into pieces
1 cup finely chopped red onion

Make the dressing: In a blender blend together the
garlic paste, the anchovy, the balsamic vinegar, the
lemon juice, the mustard, and salt and pepper to taste.
With the motor running add the oil in a stream and blend
the dressing well.

In a large bowl combine the escarole, the spinach, the
onion, and the dressing and toss the salad until it is combined well. Serves 6 to 8.

PHOTO ON PAGE 75

Fennel and Watercress Salad

1 teaspoon freshly grated orange zest
2 teaspoons fresh orange juice
2 tablespoons olive oil
½ fennel bulb, sliced thin lengthwise
2 cups watercress sprigs, the coarse stems
    discarded and the sprigs washed and
    spun dry

In a bowl whisk the zest and the orange juice with salt to taste, whisking until the salt is dissolved, add the oil in a stream, whisking, and whisk the dressing until it is emulsified. In another bowl toss the fennel with half the dressing until it is coated well. Add the watercress to the remaining dressing, toss it until it is just coated well, and divide it between 2 plates, mounding the fennel in the middle. Serves 2.

PHOTO ON PAGE 18

Frisée and Radicchio Salad with Bacon and Pine Nuts

a ¼-pound piece of slab bacon, cut crosswise
    into ⅓-inch-wide pieces
1½ tablespoons red-wine vinegar
⅓ cup olive oil
6 large *radicchio* leaves, rinsed, spun dry, and
    torn into pieces
6 cups torn *frisée* (French or Italian curly
    chicory, available at specialty produce
    markets), rinsed and spun dry
2 tablespoons pine nuts, toasted lightly

In a skillet cook the bacon over moderate heat, stirring, until it is crisp and transfer it with a slotted spoon to paper towels to drain. In a small bowl whisk together the vinegar and salt and pepper to taste, add the oil in a stream, whisking, and whisk the dressing until it is emulsified. In a salad bowl toss the *radicchio* and the *frisée* with the dressing and sprinkle the salad with the bacon and the pine nuts. Serves 6.

PHOTO ON PAGE 63

Salade Verte avec Croûtes de Roquefort
(Green Salad with Roquefort Toasts)

For the toasts
twelve ⅓-inch-thick diagonal slices of French
    or Italian bread

½ cup crumbled Roquefort (about 2 ounces),
    softened
2 tablespoons unsalted butter, softened
For the salad
1 tablespoon Sherry vinegar (available at
    specialty food shops and some
    supermarkets) or red-wine vinegar
1 teaspoon Dijon-style mustard
¼ cup extra-virgin olive oil
4 cups torn *frisée* (French or Italian curly
    chicory, available at specialty produce
    markets), rinsed and spun dry
4 cups torn *arugula*, rinsed well and spun dry

Make the toasts: Bake the bread slices on a baking sheet in one layer in the middle of a preheated 350° F. oven for 10 to 15 minutes, or until they are golden. *The toasts may be baked 1 day in advance and kept in an airtight container.* In a bowl cream the Roquefort with the butter and spread the mixture on the toasts.

Make the salad: In a large bowl whisk the vinegar with the mustard and salt and pepper to taste, add the oil in a stream, whisking, and whisk the dressing until it is emulsified. Add the *frisée* and the *arugula* and toss the mixture well to coat the greens with the dressing. Season the salad with pepper, divide it among 6 salad plates, and arrange 2 toasts on each plate. Serves 6.

Herbed Salad with Goat Cheese Toasts and Shallot Vinaigrette

two ½-inch-thick slices of round country-style
    bread, halved
3 tablespoons olive oil
2 ounces mild goat cheese, such as
    Montrachet
2 cups shredded chicory (curly endive)
2 cups shredded Boston lettuce
1 tablespoon white-wine vinegar
1 tablespoon finely chopped shallot
1 tablespoon minced fresh parsley leaves
a pinch of dried thyme, crumbled
a pinch of dried basil, crumbled

Toast the bread on a rack under a preheated broiler about 4 inches from the heat, turning it once, until it is lightly golden and brush the toasts with 2½ teaspoons of the oil. In a small bowl mash together the goat cheese and ½ teaspoon of the remaining oil and spread the toasts evenly with the mixture. Broil the toasts on the rack under the preheated broiler about 4 inches from the heat for 1 minute, or until the cheese is browned lightly, and keep them warm. In a large bowl toss together the chicory and the Boston lettuce. In another bowl whisk together the remaining 2 tablespoons oil, the vinegar, the shallot, the parsley, the thyme, the basil, and salt and pepper to taste and toss the salad greens well with the dressing. Divide the salad between 2 plates and arrange 2 goat cheese toasts on each serving. Serves 2.

Mâche Salad with Chiffonade of Beet and Radish

5 tablespoons white-wine vinegar
6 tablespoons olive oil
1 pound beets, cooked, chilled, peeled,
    and grated coarse
2 cups coarsely grated icicle or *daikon* radish
    (available seasonally at specialty produce
    markets and some supermarkets)
8 cups *mâche*, rinsed well and spun dry

In a small bowl whisk together the vinegar and salt and pepper to taste, add the oil in a stream, whisking, and whisk the dressing until it is emulsified. In a bowl toss the beets with one third of the dressing, in another bowl toss the radish with half the remaining dressing, and in a large bowl toss the *mâche* with the remaining dressing. Arrange the *mâche*, the beets, and the radish decoratively on 6 salad plates. Serves 6.

Radicchio, Fennel, and Arugula Salad with Roquefort and Walnuts

For the dressing
1 tablespoon fresh lemon juice
1 tablespoon white-wine vinegar
1 teaspoon Dijon-style mustard
⅓ cup olive oil

6 cups shredded *radicchio* (about ¾ pound)
2 cups thinly sliced fennel bulb
½ cup walnuts, toasted, cooled, and chopped
⅔ cup crumbled Roquefort (about 3 ounces)
6 cups *arugula*, coarse stems discarded and
    the leaves washed well and spun dry

Make the dressing: In a small bowl whisk together the lemon juice, the vinegar, the mustard, and salt and pep-

per to taste, add the oil in a stream, whisking, and whisk the dressing until it is emulsified.

In a bowl toss together the *radicchio*, the fennel, the walnuts, the Roquefort, and the dressing. On each of 8 plates arrange some of the *arugula* and divide the *radicchio* mixture among the plates. Serves 8.

Red-Leaf and Bibb Lettuce Salad with Scallion

1 head of red-leaf lettuce, rinsed, spun dry,
    and torn into small pieces
1 head of Bibb lettuce, rinsed, spun dry, and
    torn into small pieces
½ cup thinly sliced scallion
2 tablespoons white-wine vinegar
⅓ cup olive oil

In a large bowl toss together the lettuces and the scallion. In a small bowl whisk together the vinegar and salt and pepper to taste, add the oil in a slow stream, whisking, and whisk the dressing until it is emulsified. Toss the salad with the dressing. Serves 6.

PHOTO ON PAGE 33

Spinach Salad with Blue Cheese and Bacon

1 tablespoon fresh lemon juice
¾ teaspoon Dijon-style mustard
3 tablespoons olive oil
½ pound fresh spinach (about 6 cups packed
    leaves), coarse stems discarded and the
    leaves washed well and spun dry
1 cup thinly sliced mushrooms
3 slices of lean bacon, cooked and crumbled
½ cup thinly sliced red onion
½ cup crumbled blue cheese

In a small bowl whisk together the lemon juice, the mustard, and salt and pepper to taste, add the oil in a stream, whisking, and whisk the dressing until it is emulsified. In a bowl combine the spinach, the mushrooms, the bacon, the onion, the blue cheese, and the dressing and toss the salad until it is combined well. Serves 2.

Spinach Salad with Fried Blue Cheese

1 small garlic clove, halved
⅛ teaspoon salt
1 tablespoon red-wine vinegar
½ teaspoon Worcestershire sauce
3 tablespoons olive oil
½ pound fresh spinach, coarse stems
    discarded and the leaves washed well and
    spun dry (about 6 cups packed leaves)
2 tablespoons all-purpose flour
1 large egg
¼ cup plain bread crumbs
¼ pound chilled blue cheese (preferably
    Roquefort), cut into ¾-inch cubes
vegetable oil for frying the cheese cubes

In a large bowl with a fork mash the garlic to a paste with the salt, add the vinegar, the Worcestershire sauce, and the olive oil, and combine the dressing well. Add the spinach to the dressing and toss the salad well.

Have ready in separate bowls the flour, the egg, beaten lightly, and the bread crumbs. Dredge the cheese cubes in the flour, shaking off the excess, coat them thoroughly with the egg, and dredge them in the bread crumbs, patting the crumbs on to help them adhere. In a saucepan heat 2 inches of the vegetable oil to 350° F. on a deep-fat thermometer and in it fry the cheese cubes in batches for 45 seconds, or until they are golden, trans-

ferring them as they are fried with a slotted spoon to paper towels to drain. Divide the spinach salad between 2 bowls and top it with the fried cheese. Serves 2.

Spinach, Fennel, and Pink Grapefruit Salad

⅓ cup red-wine vinegar
⅔ cup fresh pink grapefruit juice
2½ teaspoons Dijon-style mustard
1¼ cups olive oil
18 cups small spinach leaves (from about
    4 pounds untrimmed spinach), washed well
    and spun dry
9 pink grapefruits, the zest and pith cut away
    with a serrated knife and the grapefruit cut
    into segments
4 small fennel bulbs, sliced thin crosswise and
    reserved in a bowl of cold water

In a blender blend together the vinegar, the grapefruit juice, the mustard, and salt and pepper to taste, add the oil, and blend the dressing until it is emulsified. On each of 18 salad plates arrange some of the spinach, arrange some of the grapefruit on it, and top the salad with some of the fennel, drained. Drizzle the dressing over the salads. Serves 18.

Wilted Spinach Salad with Warm Apple Cider and Bacon Dressing

5 slices of lean bacon, chopped fine
2 tablespoons minced shallot
½ cup finely chopped apple
2 tablespoons cider vinegar
1½ cups unpasteurized apple cider
1 teaspoon Dijon-style mustard
1 tablespoon olive oil
1 pound fresh spinach, coarse stems
    discarded and the leaves washed well
    and spun dry

In a large skillet cook the bacon over moderate heat, turning it, until it is crisp, transfer it to paper towels to drain, and discard all but 2 tablespoons of the fat. In the fat remaining in the skillet cook the shallot and the apple over moderate heat, stirring, for 1 minute, add the vinegar, the cider, and salt and pepper to taste, and boil the mixture, stirring occasionally, for 8 to 10 minutes, or until it is reduced to about ½ cup. Whisk in the mustard, the oil, and salt and pepper to taste. In a large bowl toss the spinach with the warm dressing until it is just wilted and sprinkle the salad with the bacon. Serves 4.

Watercress, Endive, and Goat Cheese Salad

enough Italian bread cut into ½-inch cubes to
  measure 1 cup
¼ cup olive oil
1½ tablespoons fresh lemon juice, or to taste
½ teaspoon Dijon-style mustard
1 teaspoon minced fresh thyme leaves or
  ¼ teaspoon dried thyme, crumbled
3 cups loosely packed watercress, the coarse
  stems discarded and the sprigs rinsed and
  spun dry
1 small Belgian endive, trimmed and sliced
  thin crosswise
2 ounces mild goat cheese such as
  Montrachet, crumbled (about ½ cup)

In a small bowl toss the bread cubes with 1 tablespoon of the oil and salt to taste and on a baking sheet toast them in the middle of a preheated 350° F. oven for 10 minutes, or until they are golden. Transfer the croutons to a salad bowl and let them cool. In another small bowl whisk together the lemon juice, the mustard, the thyme, and salt and pepper to taste, add the remaining oil in a stream, whisking, and whisk the dressing until it is emulsified. To the croutons add the watercress, the endive, the goat cheese, and the dressing and toss the salad well. Serves 2.

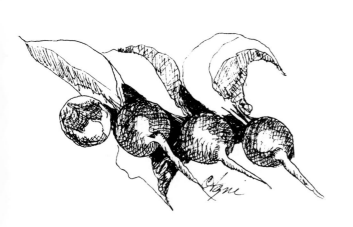

VEGETABLE SALADS

Beet Orange Salad

8 pounds beets, trimmed, leaving 3 inches of
  the stems intact and reserving the leaves for
  another use
1 teaspoon freshly grated orange zest
⅓ cup fresh orange juice
¼ cup sugar
½ cup distilled vinegar
1 small bay leaf
½ cup vegetable oil
1 onion, chopped fine

In a kettle combine the beets with enough cold water to cover them by 2 inches, bring the water to a boil, and simmer the beets, removing the small ones as they are done, for 40 to 50 minutes, or until they are tender. Drain the beets and let them cool. *The beets may be cooked 1 day in advance and kept covered and chilled.* Peel the beets and cut them into 1-inch wedges.

In a small saucepan combine the zest, the orange juice, the sugar, the vinegar, and the bay leaf and boil the mixture until it is reduced to about ¼ cup. Discard the bay leaf and let the mixture cool. In a large bowl whisk together the orange mixture, the oil, and salt and pepper to taste until the dressing is emulsified, add the beets and the onion, and combine the salad well. Serves 12.

PHOTO ON PAGES 42 AND 43

*Chopped Salad of Cucumber, Red Onion,
Lemon and Parsley*

½ seedless cucumber, cut into ⅓-inch dice
1 small red onion, cut into ⅓-inch dice
five ¼-inch-thick slices of lemon, the zest and
  pith discarded and the fruit cut into ¼-inch
  dice, plus whole slices for garnish
1 tablespoon minced fresh flat-leafed parsley leaves
2 tablespoons olive oil

In a bowl combine the cucumber, the onion, the lemon, and the parsley and season the mixture with salt and pepper. Drizzle the salad with the oil, toss it gently to coat it well, and serve it garnished with the lemon slices. Serves 2.

PHOTO ON PAGE 17

Mushroom, Currant, and Scallion Salad with Coriander and Mint Vinaigrette

½ pound mushrooms, the stems discarded and
   the caps chopped fine
1 teaspoon fresh lemon juice
1 scallion, sliced thin
2 tablespoons dried currants
1 tablespoon finely chopped fresh mint leaves
   or ½ teaspoon dried, crumbled, or to taste
1 tablespoon finely chopped fresh coriander
2 tablespoons olive oil
1 tablespoon white-wine vinegar
½ teaspoon sugar
soft-leafed lettuce for lining the plates

In a bowl toss the mushrooms with the lemon juice
and the scallion. In another bowl whisk together the currants, the mint, the coriander, the oil, the vinegar, the
sugar, and salt and pepper to taste. Toss the mushroom
mixture well with the vinaigrette and divide the salad
between 2 plates lined with the lettuce. Serves 2.

Potato Salad with Asian-Style Chili Dressing

2 pounds boiling potatoes (preferably yellow-
   fleshed), quartered lengthwise and cut
   crosswise into ¾-inch pieces
1 fresh *jalapeño* pepper, minced with some of
   the seeds (wear rubber gloves)
2 small garlic cloves, minced
1 tablespoon sugar
1 tablespoon white-wine vinegar
1½ tablespoons fresh lime juice
1 tablespoon anchovy paste
1½ teaspoons vegetable oil
¼ cup packed fresh coriander, chopped fine
¼ cup packed fresh mint leaves, chopped fine
2 ribs of celery, sliced thin crosswise

In a steamer set over boiling water steam the potatoes, covered, for 10 to 12 minutes, or until they are just
tender, transfer them to a bowl, and let them cool to
room temperature. In a small bowl whisk together the
jalapeño, the garlic, the sugar, the vinegar, the lime
juice, the anchovy paste, the oil, and salt to taste and let
the dressing stand at room temperature for 30 minutes.
Add the dressing to the potatoes with the coriander,
the mint, and the celery and combine the salad well.
Serves 6.

Arugula Pesto Potato Salad

2 pounds boiling potatoes (preferably yellow-
   fleshed), quartered lengthwise and cut
   crosswise into ¾-inch pieces
1 cup packed, washed, and spun dry
   arugula leaves
2 tablespoons pine nuts
3 tablespoons olive oil
¼ cup freshly grated Parmesan
1 tablespoon unsalted butter, cut into bits
   and softened
1 garlic clove, crushed

In a steamer set over boiling water steam the potatoes, covered, for 10 to 12 minutes, or until they are just
tender, transfer them to a bowl, and let them cool to
room temperature. In a blender purée the *arugula* with
the pine nuts, the oil, the Parmesan, the butter, the garlic, and salt and pepper to taste, add the *pesto* to the potatoes, and combine the salad well. Serves 6.

German-Style Hot Potato Salad

2 pounds boiling potatoes (preferably yellow-
fleshed), quartered lengthwise and cut
crosswise into ¾-inch pieces
½ pound *kielbasa* (Polish sausage), cut into
¼-inch-thick rounds
1 onion, chopped fine
½ cup distilled white vinegar
½ cup beef broth
⅓ cup minced fresh parsley leaves

In a steamer set over boiling water steam the potatoes, covered, for 10 to 12 minutes, or until they are just
tender, and transfer them to a bowl. While the potatoes
are steaming, in a heavy skillet cook the *kielbasa* over
moderate heat, stirring occasionally, until it is golden,
add the onion, and cook the mixture, stirring occasionally, until the onion is golden. Remove the skillet from
the heat and add the vinegar and the broth carefully.
Bring the mixture to a boil, scraping up the brown bits,
and boil it until the liquid is reduced to about ⅔ cup. Add
the *kielbasa* mixture to the potatoes with the parsley and
combine the salad well. Serves 4 to 6.

Fried Okra and Potato Salad

2 pounds boiling potatoes (preferably yellow-
fleshed), quartered lengthwise and cut
crosswise into ¾-inch pieces
½ pound okra (available seasonally at
specialty produce markets and many
supermarkets), trimmed and cut crosswise
into ¼-inch-thick rounds
½ cup cornmeal
vegetable oil for deep-frying
1½ tablespoons cider vinegar
1½ teaspoons honey
¾ cup mayonnaise
1 tomato, seeded and chopped coarse

In a steamer set over boiling water steam the potatoes, covered, for 10 to 12 minutes, or until they are just
tender, transfer them to a bowl, and let them cool to
room temperature. In another bowl toss the okra with
the cornmeal and salt and pepper to taste, transfer the
mixture to a sieve, and shake off the excess cornmeal. In
a deep skillet heat 1 inch of the oil to 375° F., in it fry the
okra, stirring, for 2 minutes, or until it is golden, and
transfer it to paper towels to drain. In a small bowl

whisk together the vinegar, the honey, the mayonnaise,
1 tablespoon water, and salt and pepper to taste. Add the
dressing to the potatoes with the okra and the tomato and
combine the salad well. Serves 6.

Parsleyed Yellow-Potato Salad

5 pounds yellow-fleshed potatoes
⅓ cup white-wine vinegar
½ cup vegetable oil
2 cups minced fresh parsley leaves

In a kettle combine the potatoes with enough salted
cold water to cover them by 2 inches, bring the water to
a boil, and simmer the potatoes, removing the small
ones as they are done, for 30 to 40 minutes, or until they
are tender. Drain the potatoes and let them cool until
they can be handled. Peel the potatoes and cut them into
bite-size pieces.

In a large bowl whisk together the vinegar and salt
and pepper to taste, add the oil in a stream, whisking,
and whisk the dressing until it is emulsified. Add the potatoes and the parsley and combine the salad well.
Serves 12.

PHOTO ON PAGE 43

Two-Potato Salad with Mustard Dressing

1 pound boiling potatoes (preferably yellow-
fleshed), quartered lengthwise and cut
crosswise into ¾-inch pieces
1 pound sweet potatoes, quartered lengthwise
and cut crosswise into ¾-inch pieces
1 tablespoon white-wine vinegar
2 tablespoons Dijon-style mustard
¼ cup olive oil
¼ cup finely chopped onion
¼ cup finely chopped red bell pepper
2 tablespoons finely chopped sweet gherkin

In a steamer set over boiling water arrange the boiling
potatoes, top them with the sweet potatoes, and steam
the potatoes, covered, for 10 to 12 minutes, or until they
are just tender. Transfer the potatoes to a bowl and let
them cool. In another bowl whisk together the vinegar,
the mustard, and salt and pepper to taste, add the oil in a
stream, whisking, and whisk the dressing until it is
emulsified. Add the dressing to the potatoes with the
onion, the bell pepper, and the gherkin and combine the
salad well. Serves 6.

Sweet Potato and Celery Salad

¾ pound sweet potato, peeled and cut into
    ½-inch dice
1 tablespoon white-wine vinegar
1½ tablespoons Dijon-style mustard
¼ cup vegetable oil
1 cup thinly sliced celery
¼ cup thinly sliced red bell pepper
¼ cup thinly sliced scallion
lettuce leaves for lining the plates

On a steamer rack set over boiling water steam the sweet potato, covered, for 6 to 8 minutes, or until it is tender, transfer it to a bowl, and let it cool. In a bowl whisk together the vinegar and the mustard, add the oil in a stream, whisking, and whisk the dressing until it is emulsified. To the sweet potato add the dressing, the celery, the bell pepper, the scallion, and salt and black pepper to taste and combine the salad well. Divide the salad between 2 plates lined with the lettuce. Serves 2.

Radish and Cucumber Salad with Yogurt Dressing

1 cup plain yogurt
1 cup finely diced radishes
1 cup finely diced cucumber
1 small garlic clove, minced and mashed to a
    paste with ½ teaspoon salt
2 tablespoons minced fresh mint or
    parsley leaves
soft-leafed lettuce or *pita* bread for serving

In a cheesecloth-lined sieve set over a bowl let the yogurt drain for 2 hours. In a bowl stir together the drained yogurt, the radishes, the cucumber, the garlic paste, the mint or parsley, and salt and pepper to taste. Divide the salad among individual salad plates lined with the lettuce or serve it as a sandwich filling for the *pita* bread. Serves 4.

Tomato Salad with Hard-Boiled Eggs

2 slices of day-old homemade-style white
    bread, crusts removed and the bread cut
    into ½-inch cubes
½ tablespoon unsalted butter, melted
1 tablespoon red-wine vinegar
¼ cup extra-virgin olive oil
2 tomatoes, seeded and chopped

¼ cup finely chopped scallion green
3 Kalamata or other brine-cured olives, cut
    into slivers
2 hard-boiled large eggs, sliced thin
    lengthwise

In a bowl toss the bread cubes with the butter and salt to taste, spread them in a jelly-roll pan, and bake them in a preheated 375° F. oven for 4 to 6 minutes, or until they are golden. In a bowl whisk together the vinegar, the oil, and salt and pepper to taste until the dressing is emulsified, add the tomatoes, the scallion green, the olives, and the croutons, and toss the salad until it is combined well. Divide the salad between 2 plates and top it with the egg slices. Serves 2.

SLAWS

Old-Fashioned Coleslaw

¼ cup mayonnaise
2 tablespoons sour cream
1½ teaspoons red-wine vinegar
1 teaspoon Dijon-style mustard
1 teaspoon grated onion
½ teaspoon sugar
2½ cups finely shredded cabbage
1 carrot, grated coarse

In a bowl whisk together the mayonnaise, the sour cream, the vinegar, the mustard, the onion, the sugar, and salt and pepper to taste. Add the cabbage and the carrot to the dressing and toss the coleslaw until it is combined well. Serves 2.

Corned Beef Coleslaw with Rye Croutons

¾ cup mayonnaise
¼ cup bottled chili sauce
1 teaspoon drained bottled horseradish
2 tablespoons minced onion
1 tablespoon minced bottled pimiento
¼ cup minced green bell pepper
10 cups finely shredded green cabbage
½ pound trimmed sliced cooked corned beef,
    cut into julienne strips
4 slices of rye bread, crusts discarded, the
    bread cut into ½-inch cubes and toasted

In a large bowl whisk together the mayonnaise, the chili sauce, the horseradish, the onion, the pimiento, the bell pepper, and salt and black pepper to taste, add the cabbage and the corned beef, and toss the mixture until it is combined well. Top the coleslaw with the rye croutons. Serves 4 to 6.

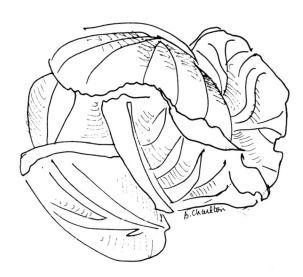

b. Charlton

Oriental-Style Coleslaw with Chicken

2 tablespoons soy sauce
1 tablespoon Oriental sesame oil
1 teaspoon white-wine vinegar
3 tablespoons peanut oil
2 teaspoons finely grated peeled fresh
    gingerroot
1 red bell pepper, cut into julienne strips
1 whole skinless boneless chicken breast
    (about ¾ pound), halved and cut crosswise
    into thin strips
12 cups finely shredded Napa cabbage
    (about 2½ pounds)
½ cup julienne strips of canned
    bamboo shoots
¼ pound snow peas, cut into julienne strips
    and blanched in boiling water for
    10 seconds
3 scallions, sliced thin
finely chopped salted roasted peanuts for
    sprinkling the coleslaw

In a bowl stir together the soy sauce, the sesame oil, the vinegar, and salt and black pepper to taste. Heat a large wok or large skillet over high heat until it is hot and add the peanut oil. When the oil is hot but not smoking add the gingerroot, the bell pepper, and the chicken and stir-fry the mixture over moderately high heat for 2 minutes. Add the cabbage, the bamboo shoots, the snow peas, and the scallions and stir-fry the mixture for 3 minutes. Make a well in the center of the mixture, pour in the soy sauce mixture, and reduce the heat to low. Simmer the mixture, stirring, for 3 minutes, or until the vegetables are crisp-tender. Transfer the coleslaw to a serving bowl with a slotted spoon and sprinkle it with the peanuts. Serves 4 to 6.

Warm Coleslaw with Kielbasa and Bacon

6 slices of lean bacon, cut crosswise into
    thin strips
1 small red onion,
    minced
1 garlic clove,
    minced
⅔ cup apple cider vinegar
⅔ cup white wine
a pinch of ground cloves
¼ teaspoon caraway seeds
1 unpeeled large Granny Smith apple
10 cups finely shredded red cabbage
    (about 2¼ pounds)
½ pound *kielbasa* or other
    ready-to-eat smoked sausage,
    halved lengthwise and
    sliced thin crosswise

In a large kettle cook the bacon, stirring, over moderate heat until it is crisp, transfer it with a slotted spoon to paper towels to drain, and pour off all but ¼ cup of the fat. To the fat in the kettle add the onion and the garlic and cook them over moderately low heat, stirring, until they are softened. Stir in the vinegar, the wine, the cloves, the caraway seeds, and the apple, cored and chopped fine, and simmer the mixture, stirring occasionally, for 3 minutes, or until the apple is softened. Stir in the cabbage, the *kielbasa*, and salt and pepper to taste and cook the mixture, stirring, for 3 minutes, or until the cabbage is wilted slightly. Transfer the coleslaw to a serving bowl and top it with the bacon. Serves 6 to 8.

Radish Slaw

½ pound radishes, trimmed and grated coarse
   (about 2 cups)
3 cups finely shredded cabbage
1 cup coarsely grated carrots
½ cup thinly sliced red onion
2 tablespoons fresh lemon juice
½ teaspoon sugar
2 tablespoons olive oil
2 tablespoons finely chopped fresh coriander,
   mint, or parsley leaves

In a bowl toss together the radishes, the cabbage, the carrots, the onion, the lemon juice, the sugar, the oil, the coriander, and salt and pepper to taste. Serves 4.

GRAIN SALADS

Two-Bean and Barley Salad with Pine Nuts

1 pound dried black beans, soaked in enough
   cold water to cover them by 2 inches
   overnight or quick-soaked (procedure on
   page 143) and drained
1 cup barley (not quick-cooking)
6 tablespoons fresh lemon juice
1 tablespoon Dijon-style mustard
¾ cup olive oil
1½ cups finely chopped red onion
1 pound green beans, trimmed
½ cup pine nuts, toasted lightly

In a kettle combine the black beans with enough cold water to cover them by 2 inches, simmer them, covered, for 1 hour, or until they are tender, and drain them well. While the beans are cooking, in a large saucepan combine the barley with 4 cups boiling salted water and simmer it, covered, for 45 minutes, or until it is cooked but still *al dente*. Drain the barley in a colander, rinse it, and drain it well. In a small bowl whisk together the lemon juice, the mustard, and salt and pepper to taste, add the oil in a stream, whisking, and whisk the dressing until it is emulsified. In a large bowl combine the black beans, the barley, and the onion, add the dressing, and toss the salad until it is combined well. *The salad may be prepared up to this point 1 day in advance and kept covered and chilled.* In a saucepan of boiling salted water cook the green beans for 4 to 5 minutes, or until they are just

tender, refresh them under cold water, and drain them well. Cut the beans crosswise into ¼-inch pieces, add them to the salad with the pine nuts and salt and pepper to taste, and toss the salad until it is combined well. Serve the salad chilled or at room temperature. Serves 6 to 8.

Bulgur Salad with Cucumber and Tomato

½ cup *bulgur*
½ teaspoon salt
1½ tablespoons fresh lemon juice, or to taste
2 tablespoons olive oil
¾ cup minced fresh parsley leaves
½ cup chopped seeded cucumber
½ cup quartered cherry tomatoes
1 scallion, sliced thin

In a small saucepan combine the *bulgur,* the salt, and ¾ cup water and simmer the mixture, covered, for 12 to 15 minutes, or until the water is absorbed. Transfer the *bulgur* to a bowl, let it cool for 10 minutes, and stir in the lemon juice, the oil, the parsley, the cucumber, the tomatoes, the scallion, and salt and pepper to taste. Serves 2.

Rice and Black Bean Salad

½ teaspoon salt
2 tablespoons plus 1 teaspoon olive oil
⅓ cup long-grain rice
1 cup chopped tomato
½ cup finely chopped green bell pepper
¼ cup finely chopped onion
1 tablespoon white-wine vinegar
1 tablespoon fresh lime juice
¼ cup finely chopped fresh coriander
a 15- to 16-ounce can black beans, rinsed well
   in a colander and drained well

In a small saucepan bring ⅔ cup water to a boil with the salt and 1 teaspoon of the oil, add the rice, and cook it, covered, over low heat for 20 minutes, or until the water is absorbed. Rinse the rice in a sieve under cold water and drain it well. In a bowl stir together the tomato, the bell pepper, the onion, the vinegar, the lime juice, the remaining 2 tablespoons oil, and the coriander, add the beans, the rice, and salt and pepper to taste, and stir the salad until it is combined well. Serves 2.

SALAD DRESSINGS

Blue Cheese Salad Dressing

1 large garlic clove, minced and mashed to a
   paste with ¼ teaspoon salt
1 tablespoon Dijon-style mustard
2 tablespoons fresh lemon juice
2 tablespoons white-wine vinegar
⅓ cup olive oil
⅓ cup sour cream
¾ cup crumbled blue cheese (about 3 ounces)
   plus additional to taste if desired

In a blender or small food processor blend together the garlic paste, the mustard, the lemon juice, the vinegar, and salt and pepper to taste. With the motor running add the oil and blend the mixture until it is combined well. Add the sour cream, ¾ cup of the cheese, and 2 tablespoons water, or enough to obtain the desired consistency, blend the dressing until it is combined well, and transfer it to a bowl. Stir in the additional cheese. The dressing keeps, covered and chilled, for about 1 week. Makes about 1⅓ cups.

Cranberry Vinaigrette

1 tablespoon maple syrup
½ teaspoon English-style dry mustard
1 tablespoon cider vinegar
2 tablespoons cranberry juice
½ cup vegetable oil

In a bowl whisk together the syrup, the mustard, the vinegar, the cranberry juice, and salt to taste, add the oil in a stream, whisking, and whisk the vinaigrette until it is emulsified. Makes about ⅔ cup.

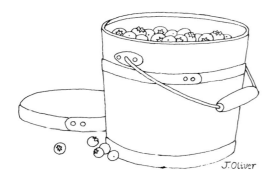

J. Oliver

Hard-Boiled Egg Dressing with Tarragon and Cornichons

1 hard-boiled whole large egg,
   mashed well
1 hard-boiled large egg yolk, mashed well
1 tablespoon Dijon-style mustard
2 tablespoons tarragon vinegar
½ cup olive oil
2 tablespoons chopped drained *cornichons*
   (French sour gherkins, available at
   specialty foods shops and some
   supermarkets)
2 tablespoons minced fresh tarragon

In a bowl whisk together the mashed whole egg and yolk, the mustard, and the vinegar and add the oil in a stream, whisking until the dressing is emulsified. Stir in the *cornichons*, the tarragon, and salt and pepper to taste. *The dressing keeps, covered and chilled, for several days.* Serve the dressing with cold meat, poultry, or vegetables. Makes about ¾ cup.

Basic French Vinaigrette

2 tablespoons white-wine vinegar or fresh
   lemon juice
½ teaspoon Dijon-style mustard
⅓ cup olive oil

In a bowl whisk together the vinegar, the mustard, and salt and pepper to taste, add the oil in a stream, whisking, and whisk the vinaigrette until it is emulsified. Makes about ½ cup.

French Vinaigrette with Hard-Boiled Egg

½ teaspoon Dijon-style mustard
3 tablespoons white-wine vinegar
⅓ cup olive oil
2 tablespoons minced fresh parsley leaves
1 hard-boiled large egg

In a bowl whisk together the mustard, the vinegar, and salt to taste, add the oil in a stream, whisking, and whisk the vinaigrette until it is emulsified. Stir in the parsley. Halve the egg lengthwise, reserving one half for another use, force the remaining half through a coarse sieve into the bowl, and stir the vinaigrette until it is combined well. Makes about ⅔ cup.

Garlic French Vinaigrette

2 garlic cloves
5 tablespoons heavy cream
½ teaspoon Dijon-style mustard
2 tablespoons fresh lemon juice
1 tablespoon olive oil

In a small saucepan boil the garlic in 2 inches water for 15 minutes, or until it is tender, and drain it. In a bowl mash the garlic to a paste and whisk in the cream, the mustard, the lemon juice, and salt and pepper to taste, whisking until the mixture is thickened slightly. Add the oil, drop by drop, whisking, and whisk the vinaigrette until it is emulsified. Makes about ½ cup.

Lime and Cumin Vinaigrette

2 tablespoons fresh lime juice
1 tablespoon fresh lemon juice
½ teaspoon cumin
½ teaspoon chili powder
½ teaspoon salt
⅓ cup vegetable oil

In a bowl whisk together the lime juice, the lemon juice, the cumin, the chili powder, and the salt, add the oil in a stream, whisking, and whisk the vinaigrette until it is emulsified. Makes about ½ cup.

Mustard and Dill Vinaigrette

1 teaspoon firmly packed brown sugar
1 teaspoon Dijon-style mustard
2 tablespoons white-wine vinegar
⅓ cup vegetable oil
1 tablespoon minced fresh dill

In a bowl whisk together the brown sugar, the mustard, the vinegar, and salt to taste, add the oil in a stream, whisking, and whisk the vinaigrette until it is emulsified. Stir in the dill. Makes about ½ cup.

JEANNE

Raspberry and Walnut Vinaigrette

½ teaspoon honey mustard*
2 tablespoons raspberry vinegar*
3 tablespoons walnut oil*
3 tablespoons olive oil
1 tablespoon minced fresh tarragon

In a bowl whisk together the mustard, the vinegar, and salt to taste, add the oils in a stream, whisking, and whisk the vinaigrette until it is emulsified. Stir in the tarragon. Makes about ½ cup.

*available at specialty food shops and
  some supermarkets

Sesame Soy Vinaigrette

½ teaspoon sugar
2 teaspoons soy sauce
2 tablespoons rice vinegar
2 tablespoons Oriental sesame oil
¼ cup vegetable oil
2 teaspoons sesame seeds,
  toasted lightly
  and cooled

In a bowl whisk together the sugar, the soy sauce, the vinegar, and salt to taste, add the oils in a stream, whisking, and whisk the vinaigrette until it is emulsified. Stir in the sesame seeds. Makes about ½ cup.

Sun-Dried Tomato Vinaigrette

2 sun-dried tomato halves
1½ tablespoons balsamic vinegar
1½ tablespoons red-wine vinegar
½ garlic clove, minced and
  mashed to a paste
  with ½ teaspoon salt
⅓ cup olive oil
1 tablespoon minced fresh basil leaves

In a saucepan simmer the sun-dried tomatoes in 2 inches water for 3 minutes, or until they are tender, drain them, and mince them. In a bowl whisk together the tomatoes, the vinegars, and the garlic paste, add the oil in a stream, whisking, and whisk the vinaigrette until it is emulsified. Stir in the basil. Makes about ⅔ cup.

SAUCES

SAVORY SAUCES

Spiced Cranberry Sauce

a 12-ounce bag of cranberries, picked over
½ cup honey
2 to 3 tablespoons firmly packed brown sugar,
    or to taste
two 3-inch cinnamon sticks
6 whole cloves
¼ teaspoon freshly grated nutmeg, or to taste
¾ cup water

In a saucepan combine the cranberries, the honey, the brown sugar, the cinnamon sticks, the cloves, the nutmeg, and the water and simmer the mixture, covered, stirring occasionally, for 5 to 10 minutes, or until the cranberries have burst and the mixture is thickened. Transfer the sauce to a bowl and let it cool. *The sauce may be made 2 days in advance and kept covered and chilled.* Serve the sauce at room temperature. Makes about 2¼ cups.

PHOTO ON PAGE 72

Jellied Cranberry and Port Sauce

a 12-ounce bag of cranberries, picked over
1½ cups sugar, or to taste
1 cup Tawny Port
1 teaspoon freshly grated lemon zest
2 tablespoons fresh lemon juice, or to taste

In a large saucepan combine the cranberries, the sugar, the Port, the zest, and the lemon juice, simmer the mixture, stirring occasionally, for 15 to 20 minutes, or until the berries have burst and the mixture has thickened, and let it cool. Spoon the mixture into a lightly oiled 1-quart decorative mold and chill it, covered, for at least 3 hours or overnight. Run a thin knife around the edge of the mold, dip the mold into warm water for 10 seconds, and invert it onto a serving plate. Serves 8.

Roquefort Sauce

¼ cup minced shallot
2 tablespoons unsalted butter
1 cup dry white wine
2 tablespoons all-purpose flour
¾ cup milk
1 cup crumbled Roquefort (about ¼ pound)
2 tablespoons minced fresh parsley leaves

In a small heavy saucepan cook the shallot in the butter over moderately low heat, stirring, until it is softened, add the wine, and boil the mixture until the liquid is reduced to about 1 tablespoon. Whisk in the flour and cook the mixture, whisking, for 3 minutes. Add the milk in a stream, whisking, and boil the mixture, whisking, for 2 minutes. Reduce the heat to low, whisk in the Roquefort, a little at a time, whisking until it is melted and being careful not to let the mixture boil, and strain the sauce through a fine sieve into a bowl. Stir in the parsley, season the sauce with salt and pepper, and serve it with roasted or grilled beef, veal, or pork. Makes about 1 cup.

CONDIMENTS

Apple Cider, Onion, and Raisin Chutney

6 cups apple cider
½ cup cider vinegar
two 10-ounce cartons of fresh pearl onions,
    blanched in boiling water for 3 minutes,
    drained, and peeled
¾ cup raisins
¼ cup firmly packed light brown sugar
a pinch of ground cloves

In a large saucepan combine the cider, the vinegar, the onions, the raisins, the brown sugar, the cloves, and salt and pepper to taste and boil the mixture, stirring occasionally, for 30 to 35 minutes, or until the liquid is reduced to a syrupy consistency. The chutney keeps, covered and chilled, for 1 week. Serve the chutney with roasted meats or poultry. Makes about 2 cups.

Cranberry and Pear Chutney

a 12-ounce bag of cranberries, picked over
½ cup firmly packed dark brown sugar
½ cup raisins
2 pears, peeled and chopped
2 teaspoons freshly grated lemon zest
¼ cup minced peeled fresh gingerroot
½ teaspoon dried hot red pepper flakes
1 cup chopped onion
¼ cup cider vinegar
1 teaspoon mustard seeds
⅛ teaspoon salt

In a heavy saucepan combine the cranberries, the brown sugar, the raisins, the pears, the zest, the gingerroot, the red pepper flakes, the onion, the vinegar, the mustard seeds, and the salt and simmer the mixture, stirring occasionally, for 20 to 25 minutes, or until the berries have burst. The chutney keeps, covered and chilled, for 2 weeks. Serve the chutney at room temperature. Makes about 4 cups.

Rhubarb, Onion, and Raisin Chutney

1½ pounds onions, halved lengthwise and cut
    crosswise into ¼-inch slices
3 tablespoons vegetable oil

1 cup golden raisins
3 tablespoons red-wine vinegar
⅛ teaspoon ground cloves
¼ cup sugar
1 pound rhubarb, trimmed and cut into
    ½-inch pieces (about 3 cups)

In a large saucepan cook the onions in the oil over moderately low heat, stirring occasionally, until they are softened. While the onions are cooking, in a bowl combine the raisins, ½ cup hot water, the vinegar, the cloves, and the sugar, let the mixture stand for 15 minutes, and stir it into the onions. Bring the mixture to a boil, stirring, top it with the rhubarb (do not stir in the rhubarb), and cook the mixture, covered, at a slow boil for 5 minutes. Stir the mixture, cook it, uncovered, for 3 to 5 minutes more, or until the rhubarb is just tender, and season the chutney with salt and pepper. *The chutney may be made 1 week in advance and kept in an airtight container and chilled.* Serve the chutney warm or at room temperature. Makes about 3½ cups.

PHOTO ON PAGE 24

Indonesian-Style Sambal
(Pineapple and Cucumber Condiment)

1 cup ¼-inch-thick chunks of fresh pineapple
1 cup ¼-inch-thick chunks of seedless cucumber
2 teaspoons sugar
1 large shallot, chopped fine
1 tablespoon soy sauce
1 tablespoon fresh lime juice

In a bowl combine well the pineapple, the cucumber, the sugar, the shallot, the soy sauce, the lime juice, and salt to taste and let the *sambal* stand, covered and chilled, for 1 hour to let the flavors develop. The *sambal* keeps, covered and chilled, for 2 days. Serve the *sambal* as an accompaniment to curries and grilled meats. Makes about 2 cups.

Cranberry, Onion, and Apricot Confit

2 pounds onions, sliced thin
⅓ cup sugar
½ stick (¼ cup) unsalted butter
2 teaspoons minced garlic
½ cup red-wine vinegar
¼ cup water

2 cups cranberries, picked over
⅛ teaspoon salt
½ cup chopped dried apricots

In a skillet cook the onions and the sugar in the butter over moderate heat, stirring, until the onions are pale golden, add the garlic, and cook the mixture, stirring, for 1 minute. Stir in the vinegar, the water, the cranberries, and the salt and cook the mixture, stirring, for 10 to 15 minutes, or until the berries have burst and are softened. Stir in the apricots and cook the *confit* for 1 minute. The *confit* keeps, covered and chilled, for 2 weeks. Serve the *confit* warm or at room temperature. Makes about 3½ cups.

Uncooked Cranberry, Orange, and Ginger Relish

2 teaspoons chopped peeled fresh
    gingerroot
1 large navel orange, including the rind,
    chopped
a 12-ounce bag of cranberries,
    picked over
¾ cup sugar, or to taste

In a food processor chop fine the gingerroot and the orange, add the cranberries, and pulse the motor until the berries are chopped fine. Transfer the mixture to a bowl and stir in the sugar. Chill the relish, covered, for at least 30 minutes. The relish keeps, covered and chilled, for 2 weeks. Makes about 3 cups.

DESSERT SAUCES

Butterscotch Cranberry Sauce

1 cup firmly packed light brown sugar
2 tablespoons light corn syrup
2 tablespoons unsalted butter
½ cup heavy cream
¼ teaspoon salt
1 cup cranberries,
    picked over

In a heavy saucepan combine the brown sugar, the corn syrup, the butter, the cream, and the salt, bring the liquid to a boil, stirring, and simmer the mixture for 5 minutes. Add the cranberries and simmer the mixture,

stirring occasionally, for 5 minutes, or until the berries have burst and the liquid is reduced to about 1½ cups. Serve the sauce warm over ice cream. Makes about 1½ cups.

Cranberry Apricot Pear Sauce

¾ cup cranberries, picked over
⅓ cup (about 2 ounces) chopped dried apricots
2 pears (about 1 pound), not peeled or cored,
    cut into 1-inch pieces
3 tablespoons sugar,
    or to taste
¼ teaspoon cinnamon
⅓ cup water
sour cream or plain yogurt as an
    accompaniment if desired

In a microwave-safe bowl combine the cranberries, the apricots, the pears, the sugar, the cinnamon, and the water, cover the bowl with microwave-safe plastic wrap, and microwave the mixture at high power (100%) for 5 minutes, or until the fruits are very tender. Remove the plastic carefully and force the mixture through the medium disk of a food mill into a bowl. Stir the purée, let it stand for 10 minutes (the purée will thicken as it stands), and serve the sauce warm or at room temperature with the sour cream or yogurt as a breakfast dish or dessert. Serves 2.

Cranberry Cassis Chocolate Sauce

¾ cup heavy cream
¼ cup sugar
1 cup cranberries, picked over
⅓ cup cassis
4½ ounces semisweet chocolate,
    chopped
1 ounce unsweetened chocolate,
    chopped

In a saucepan combine the cream, the sugar, the cranberries, and the cassis and simmer the mixture, stirring occasionally, for 10 to 15 minutes, or until the berries have burst. Remove the pan from the heat, stir in the chocolates, stirring until the mixture is smooth, and strain the mixture through a sieve into a bowl. The sauce keeps, covered and chilled, for 2 weeks. Serve the sauce warm over ice cream. Makes about 3 cups.

DESSERTS

CAKES

Chinese Almond Cakes

2½ cups all-purpose flour
¾ teaspoon double-acting baking powder
½ cup lard
½ cup vegetable shortening
1½ cups sugar
¼ teaspoon almond extract
2 tablespoons beaten egg
30 blanched whole almonds for garnish

Into a bowl sift together the flour and the baking powder and blend in the lard, the vegetable shortening, and the sugar until the mixture resembles coarse meal. Stir in the almond extract, the egg, and 1 tablespoon water, or enough to form the mixture into a soft dough, knead the dough several times, and let it stand in a cool place for 5 minutes. Form the dough into 1½-inch balls and press them down with the palm of the hand to form cakes about ½ inch thick. Press an almond into the center of each cake and bake the cakes in batches on floured baking sheets in the middle of a preheated 375° F. oven for 5 minutes. Reduce the temperature to 300° F. and bake the cakes for 8 to 10 minutes more, or until they are light golden brown. Makes 30 cakes.

Apple Cider Cupcakes with
Cider Cream Cheese Icing
For the cupcakes
3 cups unpasteurized apple cider

¾ cup vegetable shortening
1¾ cups sugar
2 large eggs
2 cups all-purpose flour, sifted
⅛ teaspoon ground cloves
1 teaspoon cinnamon
1 teaspoon baking soda
For the icing
2 cups apple cider
6 ounces cream cheese, cut into bits
    and softened
½ cup sifted confectioners' sugar

Make the cupcakes: In a large saucepan boil the cider until it is reduced to about 1½ cups and let it cool. In a large bowl with an electric mixer beat together the shortening and the sugar until the mixture is fluffy and beat in the eggs, 1 at a time. Into the bowl sift together the flour, the cloves, the cinnamon, the baking soda, and a pinch of salt, stir in the reduced cider, and combine the mixture well. Divide the batter among 18 paper-lined ½-cup muffin tins and bake the cupcakes in the middle of a preheated 375° F. oven for 25 minutes, or until a tester comes out clean. Transfer the cupcakes to a rack and let them cool in the tins. Remove the cupcakes from the tins.

Make the icing: In a saucepan boil the cider until it is reduced to about ¼ cup and let it cool. In a bowl with an electric mixer beat together the cream cheese, the confectioners' sugar, the reduced cider, and a pinch of salt until the icing is smooth.

Spread each cupcake with some of the icing. Makes 18 cupcakes.

Blackberry Jam Cake with Caramel Icing

For the cake

2 sticks (1 cup) unsalted butter
2 cups sugar
5 large eggs, beaten
3 cups plus 1 tablespoon sifted all-purpose flour
1½ teaspoons allspice
1½ teaspoons ground cloves
½ teaspoon cinnamon
¼ teaspoon salt
1 cup buttermilk
1 teaspoon baking soda
1 cup chopped raisins or dates
1 cup chopped pecans
1 cup seedless blackberry jam

For the icing

3 cups light brown sugar
1 cup evaporated milk
1 stick (½ cup) unsalted butter

Make the cake: In a large bowl with an electric mixer cream together the butter and the sugar until the mixture is light and fluffy. Add the eggs and combine the mixture well. Into a bowl sift together 3 cups of the flour, the allspice, the cloves, the cinnamon, and the salt. In another bowl combine the buttermilk and the baking soda. Add the flour mixture to the butter mixture in batches alternately with the buttermilk mixture, beating well after each addition. In a bowl toss together the raisins, the pecans, and the remaining 1 tablespoon flour and stir the mixture into the batter with the jam, stirring until the mixture is combined well. Line the bottoms of 2 buttered 9-inch cake pans with wax paper and butter the paper. Pour the batter into the pans and bake the layers in the middle of a preheated 325° F. oven for 40 minutes, or until a tester comes out clean. Let the layers cool in the pans on a rack for 15 minutes, invert them onto the rack, and let the layers cool completely.

Make the icing: In a saucepan combine the brown sugar, the evaporated milk, and the butter, cook the mixture over moderately low heat, stirring, until the sugar is dissolved, and cook it, undisturbed, washing down any sugar crystals clinging to the side of the pan with a brush dipped in cold water, until it registers 238° F. on a candy thermometer. Transfer the mixture to a bowl and beat it until it is of spreading consistency. If the icing gets too hard to spread, dip the icing spatula in hot water.

Transfer one of the layers, bottom up, to a cake plate, frost the top of the layer with the icing, and top it with the remaining layer, bottom down. Frost the top and side of this layer with the icing.

Chocolate Mousse and Raspberry Cream Dacquoise

For the meringues

1 cup hazelnuts, toasted and skinned
    (procedure follows) and cooled

2 cups sugar

½ teaspoon salt

1 cup egg whites (about 8 large egg whites)

3 ounces fine-quality bittersweet chocolate,
    melted

For the mousse

7 ounces fine-quality bittersweet chocolate,
    chopped

2 ounces unsweetened chocolate, chopped

3 tablespoons framboise

⅓ cup strong brewed coffee

1¼ cups sugar

4 large egg whites

¼ teaspoon cream of tartar

For the whipped cream

1 envelope (1 tablespoon) plus 2 teaspoons of
    unflavored gelatin

¼ cup framboise

4 cups well-chilled heavy cream

¼ cup sugar

1½ teaspoons vanilla

2½ cups picked-over raspberries

For garnish

3 ounces fine-quality bittersweet chocolate,
    melted

about 1 cup raspberries

Line 3 buttered baking sheets with parchment paper and trace an 11-inch circle on each sheet of parchment. (Alternatively, foil may be used.)

Make the meringues: In a food processor grind fine the hazelnuts with ½ cup of the sugar, transfer the mixture to a bowl, and stir in ½ cup of the remaining sugar and the salt, stirring and fluffing the mixture until it is combined well. In a large bowl with an electric mixer beat the egg whites with a pinch of salt until they hold soft peaks, add the remaining 1 cup sugar gradually, beating, and beat the egg whites until they hold stiff glossy peaks. Fold in the hazelnut mixture gently but thoroughly and transfer the meringue to a pastry bag fitted with a ½-inch plain tip. Starting in the middle of each parchment circle pipe the mixture in a tight spiral to fill in the circles and bake the meringues on 3 evenly spaced racks or in batches in a preheated 250° F. oven,

switching the meringues from 1 rack to another every 20 minutes, for 1 hour, or until they are firm when touched. Remove the parchment from the baking sheets, let the meringues cool on it, and peel off the parchment carefully. *The meringues may be made 1 day in advance and kept wrapped well in plastic wrap at room temperature.*

Trim the meringues to a uniform size if necessary with a serrated knife and reserve the best-looking meringue for the top layer. Spread the underside of 1 of the remaining meringues with the melted chocolate (this will be the middle layer), reserve it, chocolate side up, and put the remaining meringue (this will be the bottom layer) on a large flat cake platter.

Make the mousse: In a bowl set over barely simmering water melt the chocolates with the framboise and the coffee, whisking until the mixture is smooth, and let the mixture cool. In a small heavy saucepan combine the sugar with ½ cup water and bring the mixture to a boil, stirring until the sugar is dissolved. Boil the syrup, undisturbed, until it registers 248° F. on a candy thermometer and remove the pan from the heat. While the syrup is boiling, in the large bowl of an electric mixer beat the egg whites with a pinch of salt until they are foamy, and the cream of tartar, and beat the egg whites until they hold soft peaks. With the mixer running add the hot syrup in a stream and beat the mixture on medium speed for 20 minutes, or until it is cool. Whisk about 1 cup of the egg white mixture into the chocolate mixture to lighten it and fold the chocolate mixture into the remaining egg white mixture gently but thoroughly.

Mound the mousse in the middle of the bottom meringue layer, top it with the chocolate-covered meringue layer, chocolate side up, and press the layer down gently until the mousse almost reaches the edge. Chill the cake for 1 hour, or until the mousse is set.

Make the whipped cream: In a very small saucepan sprinkle the gelatin over the framboise and 2 tablespoons water, let it soften for 5 minutes, and heat the mixture over low heat, stirring, until the gelatin is dissolved. Let the gelatin cool as much as possible while still remaining liquid. In a chilled large bowl beat the cream with the sugar and the vanilla until it is thick and the beaters just begin to leave a mark. Add the gelatin mixture in a stream, beating, and beat the mixture until it just holds stiff peaks. (Be careful not to over beat.)

Reserve one fourth of the whipped cream and spread half the remaining whipped cream on top of the chocolate-covered meringue layer. Arrange the raspberries on top and spread the remaining half of the whipped cream on top. Put the reserved meringue on the whipped cream, pressing it down gently, and spread some of the reserved whipped cream on the side of the cake. Put the remaining reserved whipped cream in a pastry bag fitted with a star tip and pipe it decoratively on the top and bottom edges of the cake.

Garnish the cake: Put the melted chocolate in a small pastry bag fitted with a plain writing tip and pipe it in a spoke pattern on the top of the cake. Arrange the raspberries around the edge of the cake and in the center.

Chill the cake for at least 4 hours and up to 8 hours. Serves 18.

PHOTO ON PAGE 15

To Toast and Skin Hazelnuts

Toast the hazelnuts in one layer in a baking pan in a preheated 350° F. oven for 10 to 15 minutes, or until they are colored lightly and the skins blister. Wrap the nuts in a kitchen towel and let them steam for 1 minute. Rub the nuts in the towel to remove the skins and let them cool.

Chocolate Raspberry Shortcakes

For the shortcakes
2 tablespoons unsweetened cocoa powder
½ cup all-purpose flour
2 tablespoons granulated sugar
¾ teaspoon double-acting baking powder
¼ teaspoon baking soda
⅛ teaspoon salt
2 tablespoons cold unsalted butter, cut
    into bits
4 tablespoons heavy cream

1½ cups raspberries
2 tablespoons granulated sugar, or to taste
1 tablespoon framboise, or to taste, if desired
⅓ cup well-chilled heavy cream
confectioners' sugar for sprinkling the
    shortcakes
mint sprigs for garnish if desired

Make the shortcakes: Into a bowl sift together the cocoa powder, the flour, the sugar, the baking powder, the baking soda, and the salt, add the butter, and blend the mixture until it resembles coarse meal. Add the cream and stir the mixture with a fork until it forms a

dough. Divide the dough in half, arrange each half in a mound on a lightly greased baking sheet, and bake the shortcakes in the middle of a preheated 425° F. oven for 12 minutes, or until a tester inserted in the centers comes out with crumbs clinging to it. Transfer the shortcakes to a rack and let them cool.

In a bowl mash ¾ cup of the raspberries with a fork, stir in 1 tablespoon of the granulated sugar and the framboise, stirring until the sugar is dissolved, and stir in the remaining ¾ cup raspberries. In a small bowl with an electric mixer beat the cream until it holds soft peaks, add the remaining 1 tablespoon granulated sugar, and beat the cream until it holds stiff peaks. Carefully cut the shortcakes in half horizontally with a serrated knife and with a metal spatula transfer the bottom half of each to an individual plate. (The shortcakes are delicate and crumble easily.) Top each bottom half with half the raspberry mixture, divide the whipped cream between the 2 shortcakes, and with the spatula carefully top each serving with the top half of a shortcake. Sprinkle the shortcakes with the confectioners' sugar and garnish the plates with the mint sprigs. Serves 2.

Toasted-Coconut Streusel Coffeecake

For the streusel
¾ cup firmly packed light brown sugar
¾ cup all-purpose flour
1 tablespoon cinnamon
¾ stick (6 tablespoons) unsalted butter, cut
    into bits and softened
1 cup sweetened flaked coconut, toasted
    lightly and cooled

For the cake batter
2 sticks (1 cup) unsalted butter,
    softened
1 cup firmly packed light brown sugar
3 large eggs
1 tablespoon vanilla
3 cups all-purpose flour
2½ teaspoons double-acting baking powder
1 teaspoon baking soda
1 teaspoon salt
1¼ cups sour cream
2 cups sweetened flaked coconut, toasted
    lightly and cooled

Make the streusel: In a bowl stir together the brown sugar, the flour, and the cinnamon, add the butter, and blend the mixture until it resembles coarse meal. Stir in the coconut and reserve the streusel.

Make the cake batter: In a bowl with an electric mixer cream the butter, add the brown sugar, and beat the mixture until it is light and fluffy. Add the eggs, 1 at a time, beating well after each addition, and the vanilla and beat the mixture until it is combined well. In another bowl whisk together the flour, the baking powder, the baking soda, and the salt, add the flour mixture to the butter mixture alternately with the sour cream, beginning and ending with the flour mixture and beating the batter after each addition until it is just combined, and stir in the coconut.

Spoon half the batter into a buttered and floured tube pan, measuring 10 inches across the top and about 4 inches deep, with a removable bottom, spreading it evenly. Sprinkle half the reserved streusel over the batter and spoon the remaining batter into the pan, spreading it carefully over the streusel. Sprinkle the remaining streusel over the top and bake the cake in the middle of a preheated 350° F. oven for 1 to 1¼ hours, or until a tester comes out clean. Let the cake cool in the pan on a rack for 10 minutes, remove the tube section from the pan, and run a thin knife under the cake to release the bottom. Lift the cake off the tube section of the pan with 2 long spatulas, let it cool completely on the rack, and transfer it to a serving plate.

PHOTO ON PAGE 20

Gingersnap Mincemeat Torte

½ cup gingersnap crumbs
¾ teaspoon double-acting baking powder
2 large eggs, separated
⅓ cup sugar
¼ cup bottled mincemeat
coffee or vanilla ice cream as an
    accompaniment

Line a buttered 8-inch round cake pan with a round of wax paper, butter the paper, and dust the pan with flour, knocking out the excess. In a small bowl stir together the gingersnap crumbs and the baking powder. In a bowl with an electric mixer beat the egg yolks and the sugar until the mixture is thick and pale and beat in the mincemeat and the crumb mixture. In another bowl with cleaned beaters beat the whites with a pinch of salt until they just hold stiff peaks, stir one third of them into the batter to lighten the batter, and fold in the remaining whites gently but thoroughly. Turn the batter into the prepared pan, bake the torte in the middle of a preheated 350° F. oven for 20 minutes, or until it begins to shrink from the side of the pan, and transfer it to a rack. Let the torte cool for 15 minutes and invert it onto the rack. Discard the wax paper and invert the torte onto a plate. Serve the torte, cut into wedges, with the ice cream. Serves 2.

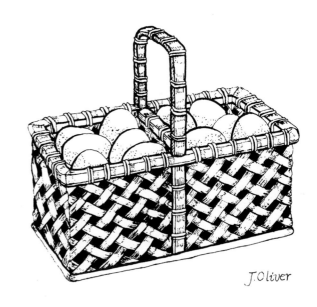

J. Oliver

Lady Baltimore Cake

For the cake layers

2 sticks (1 cup) unsalted butter, softened
2 cups sugar
1 teaspoon vanilla
½ teaspoon almond extract
3 cups all-purpose flour
1 tablespoon double-acting baking powder
½ teaspoon salt
1 cup milk
7 large egg whites
¼ teaspoon cream of tartar

2 cups sugar
¾ cup water
6 large egg whites
2 teaspoons vanilla
½ cup finely chopped dried figs plus sliced
    dried figs for garnish
1 cup pecans, toasted lightly and chopped
    fine, plus pecan halves for garnish
½ cup raisins, chopped

Make the cake layers: Line 3 buttered 9-inch round cake pans with rounds of wax paper, butter the paper, and dust the pans with flour, knocking out the excess. In a large bowl with an electric mixer cream the butter with the sugar until the mixture is light and fluffy and beat in the vanilla and the almond extract. In a bowl stir together the flour, the baking powder, and the salt, add the flour mixture to the butter mixture in batches alternately with the milk, and stir the batter until it is just combined. In another large bowl beat the egg whites with the cream of tartar and a pinch of salt until they just hold stiff peaks, stir one third of them into the batter, and fold in the remaining whites gently but thoroughly. Divide the batter among the prepared pans, smoothing the tops, and bake the cake layers, in batches if necessary, in the middle of a preheated 325° F. oven for 25 to 35 minutes, or until a tester comes out clean. Let the cake layers cool in the pans on racks for 5 minutes, turn them out onto the racks, and let them cool completely.

In a small saucepan combine the sugar and the water, bring the mixture to a boil, stirring until the sugar is dissolved, and boil the syrup until it registers 248° F. on a candy thermometer. While the syrup is boiling, in a large bowl with an electric mixer beat the egg whites with a pinch of salt until they hold soft peaks and with the mixer running add the hot syrup in a stream. Beat in

the vanilla and beat the icing until it is cool. Transfer 2 cups of the icing to a bowl, reserving the remaining icing, and fold in the chopped figs, the chopped pecans, and the raisins.

Arrange 1 of the cake layers, flat side up, on a serving plate, spread it with half the dried-fruit icing, and top the filling with another cake layer, flat side down. Spread the top layer with the remaining dried-fruit icing and top the filling with the remaining cake layer. Spread the top and side of the cake with the reserved plain icing and garnish the cake with the sliced figs and the pecan halves.

Maple Pecan Cheesecake

For the crust

2 cups finely ground gingersnaps
¾ stick (6 tablespoons) unsalted butter, melted

For the filling

2 pounds cream cheese, softened
1 cup firmly packed dark brown sugar
½ cup maple syrup
3 large eggs, separated
½ cup sour cream
½ teaspoon salt
1 teaspoon vanilla
¾ teaspoon maple extract
1 cup pecans, toasted lightly and chopped fine

Make the crust: In a bowl stir together the gingersnap crumbs and the butter until the mixture is combined well and press the mixture onto the bottom and halfway up the side of a 9-inch springform pan.

Make the filling: In a large bowl with an electric mixer cream together the cream cheese and the brown sugar until the mixture is light and fluffy and beat in the maple syrup. Add the egg yolks, 1 at a time, beating well after each addition, and beat in the sour cream, the salt, the vanilla, the maple extract, and the pecans. In a bowl with the electric mixer, beaters cleaned, beat the egg whites with a pinch of salt until they just hold stiff peaks, whisk about one fourth of them into the cream cheese mixture, and fold in the remaining whites gently but thoroughly.

Pour the filling into the prepared crust and bake the cheesecake in the middle of a preheated 350° F. oven for 1 hour. Turn off the oven, let the cheesecake cool completely in the oven with the door ajar, and chill it, covered, overnight.

Pineapple Apricot Upside-Down Cake

3 tablespoons unsalted butter, melted
½ cup firmly packed brown sugar
four ¼-inch-thick fresh pineapple rings plus
    2 tablespoons finely chopped fresh
    pineapple
6 dried whole apricots plus 2 tablespoons
    finely chopped
1 cup all-purpose flour
1¼ teaspoons double-acting baking powder
¼ teaspoon salt
⅓ cup vegetable shortening
½ cup granulated sugar
1 large egg
1 teaspoon vanilla
whipped cream as an accompaniment

In a buttered 9- by 1½-inch round cake pan combine well the butter and the brown sugar and press the mixture evenly onto the bottom of the pan. Cut the pineapple rings in half and arrange them, patted with paper towels, and the whole apricots, smooth sides down, decoratively on the sugar mixture.

Into a small bowl sift together the flour, the baking powder, and the salt. In a bowl with an electric mixer beat the shortening and the granulated sugar until the mixture is light and fluffy and beat in the egg and the vanilla. Add the flour mixture alternately with ⅓ cup water, beating after each addition, and stir in the chopped pineapple, patted dry, and the chopped apricots. Turn the batter into the pan, spreading it evenly, and bake the cake in the middle of a preheated 350° F. oven for 40 to 45 minutes, or until a tester comes out clean. Let the cake cool in the pan for 5 minutes, invert it onto a serving plate, and serve it warm or at room temperature with the whipped cream.

Pistachio Cake with Orange Syrup

For the syrup
½ cup sugar
two ¼-inch-thick orange slices
2 tablespoons dark rum
For the cake
1½ cups shelled unsalted pistachio nuts,
    ground fine in a blender
4 slices of zwieback, ground fine (about ⅓ cup)
3 large eggs, separated
⅓ cup sugar

½ teaspoon vanilla
1½ teaspoons finely grated orange zest
a pinch of cream of tartar

Make the syrup: In a saucepan combine 1 cup water, the sugar, and the orange slices, bring the water to a boil over moderate heat, stirring until the sugar is dissolved, and simmer the mixture for 1 minute. Add the rum, simmer the syrup for 1 minute, and let it cool completely.

Make the cake: In a small bowl stir together the pistachios and the zwieback. In a bowl with an electric mixer beat together the egg yolks, the sugar, and the vanilla until the mixture is thick and pale and beat in the zest. In another bowl with clean beaters beat the egg whites with the cream of tartar and a pinch of salt until they just hold stiff peaks. Stir one fourth of the whites into the yolk mixture and fold in the remaining whites alternately with the pistachio mixture gently but thoroughly. Turn the batter into a buttered 9-inch square baking pan, smoothing it, and bake the cake in the middle of a preheated 350° F. oven for 20 to 25 minutes, or until a tester comes out clean.

Transfer the cake in the pan to a rack and strain the syrup over it. Let it cool and cut into 1-inch diamonds.

PHOTO ON PAGE 56

Strawberry Lemon Bavarian Cake

For the shortbread
1 stick (½ cup) unsalted butter, softened
¼ cup sugar
½ teaspoon vanilla
1 cup all-purpose flour
½ teaspoon double-acting baking powder
¼ teaspoon salt
For the Bavarian
¾ cup strained fresh lemon juice
1 cup sugar
2 tablespoons orange-flavored liqueur
2 envelopes unflavored gelatin
2 cups well-chilled heavy cream
1½ pints strawberries, diced (about 3 cups)

about 24 strawberries, halved, for garnish

Make the shortbread: In a bowl cream together the butter, the sugar, and the vanilla, add the flour, the baking powder, and the salt, and stir the mixture until it forms a dough. Spread the dough evenly in the bottom of a 10-inch springform pan and bake it in the middle of a preheated 350° F. oven for 20 to 25 minutes, or until it is golden. Let the shortbread cool and chill it in the pan for 15 minutes.

Make the Bavarian: In a small saucepan stir together the lemon juice, the sugar, the liqueur, and 2 tablespoons water, sprinkle the gelatin over the mixture, and let it soften for 1 minute. Heat the mixture over moderately low heat, stirring, until the sugar and the gelatin are dissolved, set the pan in a bowl of cold water (do not add ice), and stir the mixture until it is just cool but still liquid. In a chilled large bowl with an electric mixer beat the cream until it holds soft peaks, with the motor running add the lemon mixture, beating until the mixture is just combined, and fold in the diced strawberries gently but thoroughly.

Pour the Bavarian into the springform pan and chill it, covered, for 4 hours, or until it is set. *The cake may be made 1 day in advance and kept covered and chilled.* Remove the side of the pan, transfer the cake to a plate, and garnish the top and side with the strawberries.

PHOTO ON PAGE 25

Swedish Meringue Cake with Strawberries and Orange Filling

1½ cups cake flour (not self-rising)
1½ teaspoons double-acting baking powder
¼ teaspoon salt
1½ sticks (¾ cup) unsalted butter, softened
1¾ cups sugar
6 large eggs, separated
1 teaspoon vanilla
½ cup milk
½ cup sliced blanched almonds, ground fine
  in an electric coffee or spice grinder
For the orange filling
½ cup sugar
3 tablespoons cornstarch
1 teaspoon freshly grated orange zest
½ teaspoon freshly grated lemon zest
¾ cup fresh orange juice
2 tablespoons fresh lemon juice
2 large egg yolks

1½ pints strawberries, reserve 11 whole for
  garnish, the remaining ones chopped fine
1 cup well-chilled heavy cream
2 tablespoons confectioners' sugar

Line the bottoms of 3 buttered 9- by 2-inch cake pans with rounds of wax paper, butter the paper, and dust the pans with flour, knocking out the excess. Into a bowl sift together the flour, the baking powder, and the salt. In the bowl of an electric mixer cream together the butter and ¾ cup of the sugar until the mixture is light and fluffy, add the egg yolks, 1 at a time, beating well after each addition, and beat in the vanilla. Add the flour mixture and the milk in batches, beginning and ending with the flour mixture and beating well after each addition, and divide the batter among the prepared pans, spreading and smoothing it.

In the cleaned bowl with cleaned beaters beat the egg whites with a pinch of salt until they hold soft peaks, add the remaining 1 cup sugar, a little at a time, and beat the meringue until it just holds stiff peaks. Fold in the almonds gently but thoroughly. (Do not beat in the almonds.) Spread the meringue over the batter, smoothing it, and bake the layers in the middle of a preheated 350° F. oven for 30 to 35 minutes, or until a tester comes out clean. Let the layers cool in the pans on a rack. Run a knife around the edges, invert the layers onto the rack, and discard the wax paper. *The cake layers may be made 1 day in advance and kept wrapped in plastic wrap.*

Make the orange filling: In a heavy saucepan whisk together the sugar, the cornstarch, and a pinch of salt. In a bowl whisk together the zests, the juices, and the yolks and whisk the yolk mixture into the sugar mixture until the mixture is combined well. Bring the mixture to a boil, whisking, boil it gently, whisking, for 2 minutes, and let it cool, whisking occasionally.

Arrange one of the layers, meringue side up, on a plate, spread half the orange filling on it, and spread half the chopped strawberries on the filling. Arrange another layer, meringue side up, on the strawberries, spread the remaining filling on it, and spread the remaining chopped strawberries on the filling. Arrange the remaining layer, meringue side up, on the strawberries.

In a bowl with an electric mixer beat the cream until it holds soft peaks, beat in the confectioners' sugar, and beat the cream until it holds stiff peaks. Transfer the cream to a pastry bag fitted with a star tip and pipe a circle of it decoratively around the top edge of the cake. Pipe another circle of cream 1 inch inside the first circle, pipe a rosette in the center, and pipe another circle of cream around the base of the cake. Quarter lengthwise 10 of the reserved strawberries, arrange them decoratively inside the concentric circles, and arrange the remaining strawberry on the rosette.

COOKIES

Cappuccino Brownies

For the brownie layer

8 ounces fine-quality bittersweet chocolate,
    chopped
1½ sticks (¾ cup) unsalted butter,
    cut into pieces
2 tablespoons instant espresso powder
    dissolved in 1 tablespoon boiling water
1½ cups sugar
2 teaspoons vanilla
4 large eggs
1 cup all-purpose flour
½ teaspoon salt
1 cup walnuts, chopped

For the cream cheese frosting

8 ounces cream cheese, softened
¾ stick (6 tablespoons) unsalted butter, softened
1½ cups confectioners' sugar
1 teaspoon vanilla
1 teaspoon cinnamon

For the glaze

6 ounces fine-quality bittersweet chocolate
2 tablespoons unsalted butter
½ cup heavy cream
1½ tablespoons instant espresso powder
    dissolved in 1 tablespoon boiling water

Make the brownie layer: In a metal bowl set over a pan of barely simmering water melt the chocolate with the butter and the espresso mixture, stirring until the mixture is smooth. Remove the bowl from the heat, let the mixture cool to lukewarm, and stir in the sugar and the vanilla. Stir in the eggs, 1 at a time, stirring well after each addition, stir in the flour and the salt, stirring until the mixture is just combined, and stir in the walnuts. Pour the mixture into a buttered and floured 13- by 9-inch baking pan, smooth the top, and bake the brownie layer in the middle of a preheated 350° F. oven for 22 to 25 minutes, or until a tester comes out with crumbs adhering to it. Let the brownie layer cool completely in the pan on a rack.

Make the cream cheese frosting: In a bowl with an electric mixer cream together the cream cheese and the butter until the mixture is light and fluffy, add the confectioners' sugar, sifted, the vanilla, and the cinnamon, and beat the frosting until it is combined well.

Spread the frosting evenly over the brownie layer and chill the brownies for 1 hour, or until the frosting is firm.

Make the glaze: In a metal bowl set over a pan of barely simmering water melt the chocolate with the butter, the cream, and the espresso mixture, stirring until the glaze is smooth, remove the bowl from the heat, and let the glaze cool to room temperature.

Spread the glaze over the frosting layer and chill the brownies, covered, for at least 3 hours or overnight.

Cut the brownies while they are cold with a sharp knife and serve them cold or at room temperature. The brownies keep, covered and chilled, for 3 days. Makes about 24 brownies.

Irish Lace Cookies

1 stick (½ cup) unsalted butter,
    softened
¾ cup firmly packed light brown sugar
2 tablespoons all-purpose flour
2 tablespoons milk
1 teaspoon vanilla
1¼ cups old-fashioned rolled oats

In a bowl cream the butter with the brown sugar until the mixture is light and fluffy and beat in the flour, the milk, and the vanilla. Stir in the oats, drop rounded teaspoons of the dough about 3 inches apart onto ungreased baking sheets, and bake the cookies in batches in the middle of a preheated 350° F. oven for 10 to 12 minutes, or until they are golden. Let the cookies stand on the sheets for 1 minute, or until they are just firm enough to be moved with a metal spatula. (If desired, turn the cookies upside down on the sheets and, working quickly, roll them into cylinders on the sheets. If the cookies become too hard to roll, return them to the oven for a few seconds and let them soften.) Transfer the cookies to a rack and let them cool completely. Makes about 40 cookies.

Lemon Almond Madeleines

4 large eggs
⅔ cup granulated sugar
½ teaspoon almond extract
1½ teaspoons freshly grated lemon zest
1 cup all-purpose flour
½ cup almonds with the skins, toasted lightly,
    cooled, and ground coarse

1 stick (½ cup) unsalted butter, melted and
  cooled slightly
confectioners' sugar for dusting the *madeleines*

In a bowl with an electric mixer beat the eggs with the granulated sugar until the mixture is thick and pale and forms a ribbon when the beaters are lifted and beat in the almond extract and the zest. Sift the flour in 4 batches over the mixture, folding it in gently after each addition, add the almonds and the butter, and fold them in gently but thoroughly. Spoon the batter into twenty-four 3- by 2-inch buttered *madeleine* molds and bake the *madeleines* in the lower third of a preheated 375° F. oven for 10 minutes, or until the edges are golden. Turn the *madeleines* out onto racks, let them cool, and sift the confectioners' sugar over them. Makes 24 *madeleines*.

Lemon Thins

1 stick (½ cup) unsalted butter, softened
⅔ cup firmly packed light brown sugar
1½ tablespoons freshly grated lemon zest
1 large egg yolk
¼ cup fresh lemon juice
¼ teaspoon vanilla
¼ teaspoon salt
¾ cup all-purpose flour

In a bowl with an electric mixer cream the butter with the brown sugar and the zest until the mixture is light and fluffy and beat in the yolk, the lemon juice, the vanilla, and the salt. Add the flour, sifted, and beat the mixture until it is just combined well. Drop teaspoons of the batter 2 inches apart onto well-buttered baking sheets and bake the cookies in batches in the middle of a preheated 350° F. oven for 8 to 10 minutes, or until they are golden around the edges. Let the cookies cool on the sheet for 1 minute, or until they are just firm enough to be removed, and transfer them to racks to cool. Makes about 50 cookies.

PHOTO ON PAGE 49

Oatmeal Trail Mix Cookies

½ stick (¼ cup) unsalted butter, softened
¼ cup vegetable shortening
½ cup firmly packed light brown sugar
¼ cup granulated sugar
1 large egg
½ teaspoon baking soda dissolved in
  1 tablespoon warm water
½ cup plus 2 tablespoons all-purpose flour
½ teaspoon salt
½ teaspoon vanilla
1½ cups old-fashioned rolled oats
½ cup sweetened flaked coconut
a 6-ounce package semisweet chocolate chips
⅓ cup roasted peanuts
½ cup raisins

In a bowl cream the butter and the shortening with the sugars and beat in the egg, the baking soda mixture, the flour, the salt, and the vanilla. Stir in the oats, the coconut, the chocolate chips, the peanuts, and the raisins. Drop rounded tablespoons of the dough about 4 inches apart onto greased baking sheets and with a fork flatten and spread each mound into a round, about 3 inches in diameter. Bake the cookies in batches in the middle of a preheated 375° F. oven for 8 to 10 minutes, or until they are golden, transfer them with a metal spatula to racks, and let them cool. Makes about 30 cookies.

Peanut Butter Cookies

½ cup vegetable shortening
1 cup chunky peanut butter
1 cup firmly packed light brown sugar
1 large egg
1½ cups all-purpose flour
½ teaspoon baking soda
½ teaspoon salt

In a bowl cream together the shortening, the peanut butter, and the brown sugar, beating until the mixture is light and fluffy, beat in the egg, and stir in the flour, the baking soda, and the salt. Form tablespoonfuls of the dough into balls, transfer the balls as they are formed to baking sheets, and with the tines of a fork flatten them, making a crosshatch pattern. Bake the cookies in batches in the middle of a preheated 400° F. oven for 8 to 10 minutes, or until they are golden, transfer them to racks, and let them cool completely. Makes about 36 cookies.

Peanut Butter Swirl Brownies

2½ sticks (1¼ cups) unsalted butter, softened
1 cup chunky peanut butter
½ cup firmly packed light brown sugar
3 large eggs
8 ounces cream cheese, softened
4 ounces unsweetened chocolate, chopped
2 cups granulated sugar
1 teaspoon vanilla
⅞ cup all-purpose flour

In a bowl cream together ½ stick of the butter, the peanut butter, and the brown sugar and beat in 1 of the eggs and the cream cheese, a little at a time, beating until the mixture is smooth. In a small saucepan melt 1 stick of the remaining butter with the chocolate over low heat, stirring until the mixture is smooth, and let the chocolate mixture cool. In another bowl cream together the remaining 1 stick butter and the granulated sugar, beating until the mixture is light and fluffy, and beat in the remaining 2 eggs, 1 at a time, beating well after each addition. Stir in the chocolate mixture, the vanilla, and the flour, sifted, and pour the batter into a buttered 13- by 9-inch baking pan. Drop dollops of the peanut butter mixture into the batter, swirling the peanut butter mixture to marble the batter, bake the brownies in the middle of a preheated 350° F. oven for 45 to 50 minutes, or until they pull away slightly from the sides of the pan and a tester comes out with crumbs adhering to it, and let them cool before cutting them into squares.

Spice Sugar Cookies

¾ cup vegetable shortening
   at room temperature
1 cup firmly packed light brown sugar
1 large egg, beaten lightly
¼ cup unsulfured molasses
2 cups all-purpose flour
2 teaspoons baking soda
1 teaspoon cinnamon
1 teaspoon ground ginger
½ teaspoon ground cloves
¼ teaspoon salt
granulated sugar for dipping the
   balls of dough

In a bowl cream the shortening with the brown sugar until the mixture is light and fluffy and stir in the egg and the molasses. Into another bowl sift together the flour, the baking soda, the cinnamon, the ginger, the cloves, and the salt, add the flour mixture in batches to the shortening mixture, and blend the dough well. Chill the dough, covered, for 1 hour.

Roll level tablespoons of the dough into balls, dip one side of each ball into the granulated sugar, and arrange the balls, sugared sides up, about 3 inches apart on greased baking sheets. Bake the cookies in batches in the middle of a preheated 375° F. oven for 10 to 12 minutes, or until they are puffed and cracked on top. Transfer the cookies with a metal spatula to racks and let them cool. Makes about 40 cookies.

JEANNE

PIES AND TARTS

Jumbleberry Pie
(Summer Berry Pie)

2 recipes *pâte brisée*
  (recipe follows)
3 cups blackberries, picked over
  and rinsed
3 cups blueberries, picked over
  and rinsed
2½ cups raspberries or other
  summer berries such as red currants or
  boysenberries, picked over
  and rinsed
⅓ cup cornstarch
1½ cups sugar plus additional for sprinkling
  the pie
¼ cup fresh lemon juice
⅛ teaspoon freshly grated nutmeg
⅛ teaspoon cinnamon
1 tablespoon unsalted butter,
  cut into bits
¼ cup half-and-half
peach and brown sugar ice cream
  (recipe follows) as an accompaniment
  if desired

Roll out half the dough ⅛ inch thick on a lightly floured surface, fit it into a 9-inch deep-dish (1-quart) pie plate, and trim the edge, leaving a ½-inch overhang. Chill the shell while making the filling. In a large bowl toss together the berries, the cornstarch, 1½ cups of the sugar, the lemon juice, the nutmeg, and the cinnamon until the mixture is combined well, mound the filling in the shell, and dot it with the butter bits.

Roll out the remaining dough into a 13- to 14-inch round on a lightly floured surface, drape it over the filling, and trim it, leaving a 1-inch overhang. Fold the overhang under the bottom crust, pressing the edge to seal it, and crimp the edge decoratively. Brush the crust with the half-and-half, make slits in the top crust, forming steam vents, and sprinkle the pie lightly with the additional sugar. Bake the pie on a large baking sheet in the middle of a preheated 425° F. oven for 20 minutes, reduce the heat to 375° F., and bake the pie for 35 to 40 minutes more, or until the crust is golden and the filling is bubbling. Serve the pie with the ice cream.

Pâte Brisée

1¼ cups all-purpose flour
¾ stick (6 tablespoons) cold unsalted butter,
  cut into bits
2 tablespoons cold vegetable shortening
¼ teaspoon salt

In a large bowl blend the flour, the butter, the vegetable shortening, and the salt until the mixture resembles meal. Add 2 tablespoons ice water, toss the mixture until the water is incorporated, adding more ice water if necessary to form a dough, and form the dough into a ball. Dust the dough with flour and chill it, wrapped in wax paper, for 1 hour.

Peach and Brown Sugar Ice Cream

2 pounds very ripe peaches (about 4), pitted
  and chopped
2 tablespoons granulated sugar
¾ cup firmly packed light brown sugar
3 large egg yolks
1 large whole egg
1½ cups half-and-half
¼ teaspoon cinnamon
¼ teaspoon freshly grated nutmeg
2 tablespoons peach schnapps or
  other peach-flavored liqueur

In a saucepan combine the peaches, the granulated sugar, and ¼ cup water and simmer the mixture, stirring occasionally, for 15 to 20 minutes, or until the peaches are soft. Purée the mixture in a food processor or blender, force the purée through a fine sieve into a bowl, and let it cool. In the pan, cleaned, cook the brown sugar with ¼ cup water over moderately low heat, stirring, until it is dissolved. In a large bowl with an electric mixer beat the yolks and the whole egg until they are frothy, beat in the brown sugar syrup, and beat the mixture until it is thick and pale. Stir in the half-and-half, scalded, pour the mixture into the pan, and cook it over moderately low heat, stirring with a wooden spoon, to 175° F. on a candy thermometer. Strain the custard through the fine sieve into another large bowl, let it cool, and stir in the peach purée, the cinnamon, the nutmeg, and the peach schnapps. Freeze the mixture in an ice-cream freezer according to the manufacturer's instructions. Makes about 1 quart.

Burnt-Sugar Pecan Pumpkin Pie

1 recipe *pâte brisée* (page 229)
⅓ cup sugar
1 cup light corn syrup
2 tablespoons dark rum
2 tablespoons unsalted butter, cut into bits
3 large eggs
1 teaspoon vanilla
⅔ cup fresh pumpkin purée (recipe follows)
   or canned pumpkin purée
1 teaspoon ground ginger
1 cup pecan halves
sweetened whipped cream as an
   accompaniment

Roll out the dough ⅛ inch thick on a lightly floured surface and fit it into a 9-inch (1-quart) pie tin. Crimp the edge of the dough decoratively and chill the shell for 30 minutes.

In a heavy saucepan cook the sugar over low heat, undisturbed, until it is melted, cook it over moderately low heat, swirling the pan occasionally, until it is a deep caramel color, and stir in the corn syrup, stirring the mixture until it is combined well. Add the rum and the butter and cook the mixture for 1 minute. Remove the pan from the heat and let the mixture cool until it stops bubbling.

In a bowl whisk together the eggs, the vanilla, and a pinch of salt and add the syrup mixture in a stream, whisking. In another bowl whisk together the pumpkin purée and the ginger and whisk in 1¼ cups of the egg mixture. Pour the pumpkin mixture into the prepared shell, arrange the pecan halves decoratively on the mixture, and spoon the remaining egg mixture over the pecans. (The pecans will float to the top.) Bake the pie in the middle of a preheated 350° F. oven for 45 to 50 minutes, or until the filling is set and the crust is pale golden, let it cool, and serve it warm or at room temperature with the whipped cream.

Fresh Pumpkin Purée

an 8-pound pumpkin (preferably a sugar pumpkin)
1½ tablespoons unsalted butter, melted

Slice off the stem end of the pumpkin 2½ inches from the top, reserving it, scrape out the seeds and the membranes, reserving the seeds for toasting (procedure on page 117) if desired, and brush the inside of the pumpkin with the butter. Top the pumpkin with the reserved stem end, bake it in a shallow baking pan in the middle of a preheated 375° F. oven for 1½ hours, or until the pulp is tender, and let it cool in the pan until it can be handled. Discard any liquid that may have accumulated in the pumpkin, scoop out the pulp, and in a blender purée it in batches, transferring it as it is puréed to a large sieve or colander lined with overlapping large coffee filters and set over a large bowl. Cover the surface of the purée with plastic wrap and let the purée drain, chilled, overnight. Makes about 4 cups.

Rhubarb Streusel Pie

1 recipe *pâte brisée* (page 229)
raw rice for weighting the shell
For the filling
1 cup sugar
3 tablespoons quick-cooking tapioca
½ teaspoon vanilla
5 cups ½-inch chunks trimmed fresh rhubarb
   (about 2 pounds) or thawed frozen rhubarb
2 tablespoons unsalted butter, cut into bits
For the streusel topping
¼ cup firmly packed light brown sugar
½ cup all-purpose flour
2 tablespoons unsalted butter, cut into bits
¼ teaspoon cinnamon
¼ cup finely chopped walnuts

an egg wash made by beating 1 large egg with
   1 tablespoon water
about ¼ cup red currant jelly, melted

Roll out the dough ⅛ inch thick on a lightly floured surface, fit it into a 9-inch (1-quart) pie plate, and crimp the edge decoratively. Line the shell with foil, fill the foil with the rice, and bake the shell in the middle of a preheated 425° F. oven for 10 minutes. Remove the rice and foil carefully and bake the shell for 3 to 5 minutes more, or until it is pale golden.

Make the filling: In a large bowl stir together the sugar, the tapioca, a pinch of salt, the vanilla, the rhubarb, and the butter until the mixture is combined well and let the filling stand, stirring occasionally, for 15 minutes.

Make the streusel topping: In a large bowl stir together the brown sugar, the flour, the butter, the cinnamon, the walnuts, and a pinch of salt and blend the mixture until it resembles coarse meal.

Spoon the filling into the shell, sprinkle the streusel topping around the outer 2 inches of the filling, leaving the center exposed, and brush the edge of the shell with some of the egg wash. Bake the pie on a baking sheet in the lower third of a preheated 450° F. oven for 15 minutes, reduce the heat to 350° F., and bake the pie for 50 minutes to 1 hour more, or until the filling is bubbling and the rhubarb is tender. Brush the exposed (center) portion of the filling with the jelly and let the pie cool on a rack for 2 hours.

PHOTO ON PAGE 32

Rum Cream Pie

1 recipe *pâte brisée* (page 229)
raw rice for weighting the shell
6 large egg yolks
1 cup sugar
2 cups well-chilled heavy cream
½ cup dark rum
1½ tablespoons unflavored gelatin
bittersweet chocolate shavings and curls
    for garnish

Roll out the dough ⅛ inch thick on a lightly floured surface and fit it into a 9-inch pie plate. Crimp the edge decoratively and prick the bottom with a fork. Line the shell with foil, fill the foil with the rice, and bake the shell in the lower third of a preheated 400° F. oven for 15 minutes. Remove the rice and foil carefully, reduce the oven temperature to 375° F., and bake the shell for 10 minutes more, or until it is pale golden.

In a bowl with an electric mixer beat the egg yolks, add the sugar gradually, beating, and beat the mixture until it is thick and pale. Beat in 1 cup of the cream, the rum, and ¼ cup water, transfer the mixture to the top of a double boiler or to a bowl set in a saucepan of gently simmering water, and cook the mixture, stirring constantly, until it registers 140° F. on a candy thermometer. Cook the mixture at 140° F., stirring constantly, for 3 minutes.

In a small saucepan sprinkle the gelatin over ¼ cup cold water, let it soften for 5 minutes, and heat the mixture over low heat, stirring, until the gelatin is dissolved. Whisk the mixture into the custard, set the bowl in a larger bowl of ice and cold water, and let the mixture cool, stirring it occasionally, until it is the consistency of raw egg white. *Do not let the mixture set.* In a bowl beat the remaining 1 cup cream until it just holds

stiff peaks, fold the whipped cream into the custard mixture gently but thoroughly, and pour the filling into the shell. Chill the pie for 3 hours, or until it is set, and garnish it with the chocolate.

J. Oliver

Apple Tarts

1 sheet (½ pound) frozen puff pastry, thawed
1 Granny Smith apple
2 tablespoons sugar
¼ teaspoon cinnamon
1 tablespoon cold unsalted butter, cut into bits
2 tablespoons apricot jam, heated and strained
vanilla ice cream or whipped cream as an
    accompaniment

Roll out the pastry ⅛ inch thick on a lightly floured surface, cut out two 7-inch rounds, and transfer them to a baking sheet. Peel, halve lengthwise, and core the apple, slice it thin crosswise, and arrange the slices, overlapping them slightly, on the pastry rounds. In a small bowl stir together the sugar and the cinnamon, sprinkle the mixture evenly over the apples, and dot the tarts with the butter. Bake the tarts in the middle of a preheated 400° F. oven for 25 minutes, or until the pastry is golden. Transfer the tarts to a rack, brush them with the jam, and serve them warm with the ice cream. Serves 2.

Cranberry Pear Tart with Gingerbread Crust

For the pear mixture

4 cups cranberry juice cocktail

½ cup sugar

a 4-inch cinnamon stick

2 tablespoons fresh lemon juice

4 large firm-ripe pears, halved lengthwise,
   peeled, cored, and reserved in a bowl
   of cold water acidulated with the juice
   of ½ lemon

⅓ cup dried cranberries*

For the crust

1½ cups all-purpose flour

3 tablespoons firmly packed brown sugar

2 teaspoons ground ginger

2½ teaspoons ground cinnamon

¾ teaspoon ground allspice

½ teaspoon salt

1 stick (½ cup) cold unsalted butter,
   cut into bits

1 large egg yolk

2 tablespoons dark molasses

raw rice for weighting the crust

3 large eggs

⅓ cup sugar

½ cup sour cream

¼ cup milk

¼ teaspoon vanilla

1 teaspoon freshly grated orange zest

*Dried cranberries are available at some
   specialty foods shops. They can be ordered
   directly from American Spoon Foods by
   calling (800) 222-5886.

Make the pear mixture: In a kettle combine the cranberry juice, the sugar, the cinnamon stick, and the lemon juice, bring the mixture to a boil, and add the pears. Heat the mixture until it just comes to a simmer and simmer the pears gently for 10 to 15 minutes, or until they are just tender. Remove the kettle from the heat, stir in the cranberries, and let the mixture cool. Chill the mixture, covered, for at least 8 hours. *The pear mixture may be made 2 days in advance and kept covered and chilled.*

Make the crust: In a food processor blend together well the flour, the brown sugar, the ginger, the cinnamon, the allspice, and the salt, add the butter, and blend the mixture until it resembles coarse meal. In a small bowl stir together the egg yolk and the molasses, add the mixture to the flour mixture, and pulse the motor, blending the mixture until it is combined well but still crumbly. Turn the mixture out into a 10-inch tart pan with a fluted removable rim and press it onto the bottom and up the side of the pan. Chill the crust for 30 minutes. Prick the crust with a fork, line it with foil, and fill the foil with the rice. Bake the crust in the lower third of a preheated 375° F. oven for 15 minutes, carefully remove the foil and the rice, and bake the crust for 10 minutes more. Let the crust cool in the pan on a rack.

Transfer the poached pears and half the cranberries with a slotted spoon to paper towels to drain, discard the cinnamon stick, and reserve the cranberry syrup with the remaining cranberries. In a small bowl whisk together the eggs, the sugar, the sour cream, the milk, the vanilla, the zest, and a pinch of salt, stir in the drained cranberries, and spoon half of the custard into the crust. Slice 4 of the pear halves crosswise on the diagonal, arrange them decoratively on the custard with the unsliced pear halves, and spoon the remaining custard around the pears. Bake the tart in the middle of a preheated 325° F. oven for 50 to 55 minutes, or until the custard is just set. Remove the rim of the tart pan and let the tart cool on a rack. *The tart may be prepared up to this point 8 hours in advance, cooled completely, and chilled.*

In a saucepan boil the reserved cranberry syrup and cranberries over moderately high heat until the syrup is reduced to about 1 cup and is jellylike in consistency and transfer the cranberries with a slotted spoon to a plate to cool. Brush the pears with some of the cranberry glaze and arrange the cranberries around the edge of the tart. Serve the tart warm or chilled.

Frangipane Tart with Strawberries and Raspberries

1 recipe *pâte brisée* (page 229)
¾ stick (6 tablespoons) unsalted butter,
    softened
½ cup sugar
1 large egg
¾ cup blanched almonds,
    ground fine
1 teaspoon almond extract
1 tablespoon Amaretto,
    or to taste
1 tablespoon all-purpose flour
2 cups strawberries,
    hulled
2 cups raspberries, picked over
    and rinsed
¼ cup strawberry or raspberry jam, melted
    and strained

Roll out the dough ⅛ inch thick on a lightly floured surface, fit it into an 11- by 8-inch rectangular or 10- or 11-inch round tart pan with a removable fluted rim, and chill the shell while making the frangipane. In a small bowl cream together the butter and the sugar and beat in the egg, the almonds, the almond extract, the Amaretto, and the flour. Spread the frangipane evenly on the bottom of the shell and bake the tart in the middle of a preheated 375° F. oven for 20 to 25 minutes, or until the shell is pale golden. (If the frangipane begins to turn too brown, cover the tart loosely with a piece of foil.) Let the tart cool. Cut the strawberries lengthwise into ⅛-inch-thick slices, arrange the slices, overlapping, decoratively with the raspberries in rows on the frangipane, and brush them gently with the jam.

Ginger Butterscotch Pear Tart

For the shell
¾ cup walnuts
2 tablespoons sugar
1¼ cups all-purpose flour
½ teaspoon salt
¾ stick (6 tablespoons) cold unsalted butter,
    cut into bits
raw rice for weighting the shell
For the poached pears
3 firm-ripe pears
2 cups dry red wine
1 cinnamon stick

1 cup sugar
For the ginger butterscotch pastry cream
3 large egg yolks
½ cup light brown sugar
3 tablespoons all-purpose flour
¼ cup milk
1 tablespoon unsalted butter
¼ teaspoon salt
2 teaspoons grated peeled fresh gingerroot

Make the shell: In a food processor grind coarse the walnuts with the sugar, add the flour, the salt, and the butter, and blend the mixture until it resembles coarse meal. Transfer the mixture to a bowl, add 3 tablespoons ice water, and toss the mixture until the water is incorporated. Press the dough into the bottom and up the side of a 7½-inch tart pan with a removable fluted rim, crimping the edge decoratively, and prick the bottom with a fork. Chill the shell for 30 minutes, line it with foil, and fill the foil with the rice. Bake the shell in the middle of a preheated 425° F. oven for 7 minutes, remove the rice and foil carefully, and bake the shell for 5 minutes more, or until it is golden. Let the shell cool in the pan on a rack.

Poach the pears: In a saucepan just large enough to hold the pears in one layer combine the wine, the cinnamon stick, and the sugar and bring the liquid to a boil over moderately high heat, stirring until the sugar is dissolved. Add the pears, peeled, and poach them, turning them occasionally, for 15 minutes, or until they are just tender. Let the pears cool in the syrup.

Make the ginger butterscotch pastry cream: In a bowl with an electric mixer beat lightly the egg yolks. Add the brown sugar, a little at a time, beating, beat the mixture until it ribbons when the beaters are lifted, and beat in the flour. Add the milk, scalded, in a stream, whisking, transfer the mixture to a heavy saucepan, and bring it to a boil over moderately low heat, stirring constantly. Boil the mixture, stirring constantly, for 2 minutes. Strain the pastry cream through a fine sieve into a bowl and stir in the butter, the salt, and the gingerroot. Let the pastry cream cool, its surface covered with a buttered round of wax paper, for 1 hour.

Remove the rim of the tart pan, set the shell on a platter, removing the bottom of the pan, and spread the pastry cream in the shell. Arrange the pears, drained, cut lengthwise into sixths, and cored, in a spoke pattern on top of the pastry cream.

PHOTO ON PAGE 19

Lemon Buttermilk Chess Tartlets

1 recipe *pâte brisée* (page 229)
½ stick (¼ cup) unsalted butter,
    softened
1 cup granulated sugar
3 large eggs
¼ cup buttermilk
2 tablespoons cornmeal
1 teaspoon freshly grated lemon zest plus
    thin strips of lemon zest tied into knots
    for garnish
3 tablespoons fresh lemon juice
¼ teaspoon salt
confectioners' sugar for dusting
    the tartlets

Roll out the dough ⅛ inch thick on a floured surface, fit it into 8 tartlet tins, each 3¾ inches across the top and ¾ inch deep, and roll a rolling pin over the edges of the tins to trim the excess dough. Chill the shells for 30 minutes.

In a bowl with an electric mixer cream the butter with the sugar until the mixture is light and fluffy, beat in the eggs, 1 at a time, beating well after each addition, and beat in the buttermilk, the cornmeal, the grated zest, the lemon juice, and the salt. Divide the mixture among the tartlet shells and bake the tartlets on a baking sheet in the lower third of a preheated 425° F. oven for 15 minutes. Reduce the oven temperature to 350° F. and bake the tartlets for 10 to 15 minutes more, or until they are golden and set. Let the tartlets cool in the tins on racks until they can be handled, remove them from the tins, and let them cool completely on the racks. *The tartlets may be made 1 day in advance and kept covered loosely in a cool place.* Dust the tartlets lightly with the confectioners' sugar and garnish them with the lemon zest knots. Makes 8 tartlets.

Pecan Chocolate Tart

1 recipe *pâte brisée* (page 229)
3½ ounces bittersweet chocolate,
    chopped
¾ cup firmly packed brown sugar
¾ cup light corn syrup
2 tablespoons unsalted butter,
    cut into bits
4 large eggs
1 teaspoon vanilla

1⅔ cups pecan halves
banana rum ice cream (recipe follows)

Roll out the dough ⅛ inch thick on a lightly floured surface, fit it into a 10-inch tart pan with a removable fluted rim, and trim the edge, leaving a ½-inch overhang. Fold the overhang inward onto the side of the shell, pressing it firmly, and chill the shell for 30 minutes. Spread the chocolate, melted, on the bottom of the shell and chill the shell for 15 minutes.

In a heavy saucepan combine the brown sugar and the syrup, bring the mixture to a boil, stirring, and simmer it for 5 minutes. Let the mixture cool until it is no longer bubbling, add the butter, and stir the mixture until the butter is melted. In a bowl whisk together the eggs, the vanilla, and a pinch of salt and add the syrup mixture in a slow stream, whisking. Add the pecans to the shell, pour in the egg mixture, and if necessary tap down the pecans to coat them with the egg mixture. Bake the tart in the middle of a preheated 350° F. oven for 40 to 45 minutes, or until the crust is pale golden, let it cool, and serve it warm with the banana rum ice cream.

Banana Rum Ice Cream

¾ cup sugar
1 tablespoon cornstarch
2 large egg yolks
1 large whole egg
2 cups milk
3 tablespoons dark rum
1 teaspoon vanilla
1 cup well-chilled heavy cream
5 bananas (about 1½ pounds)

In a bowl whisk together the sugar, the cornstarch, the yolks, and the whole egg and add the milk, scalded, in a stream, whisking. In a heavy saucepan bring the mixture to a boil over moderate heat, whisking, and boil it, whisking, for 1 minute. Add the rum, boil the custard for 1 minute more, and strain it through a fine sieve into a metal bowl set in a larger bowl of ice and cold water. Chill the custard until it is cold and stir in the vanilla and the cream. In a food processor purée the bananas, stir the purée into the custard, and chill the mixture until it is cold. Freeze the mixture in an ice-cream freezer according to the manufacturer's instructions. Makes about 1½ quarts.

FRONTISPIECE

234

DESSERT CRÊPES

Mint Chocolate Soufflé Crêpes

For the filling
⅓ cup cocoa powder
⅓ cup plus 2 tablespoons sugar
¼ cup cornstarch
1 cup milk
3 large egg whites
½ teaspoon mint extract

chocolate crêpe batter (recipe follows)
chocolate sauce (page 236)

Make the filling: In a saucepan stir together the cocoa powder, ⅓ cup of the sugar, the cornstarch, and a pinch of salt, add the milk in a stream, whisking, and bring the mixture to a boil, whisking until it is thick and smooth. Remove the pan from the heat and let the mixture cool. In a bowl beat the egg whites until they hold soft peaks, add the mint extract, and beat in the remaining 2 tablespoons sugar, a little at a time, beating until the whites hold stiff peaks. Stir one third of the whites into the cocoa mixture and fold in the remaining whites gently but thoroughly.

Make 8 crêpes (procedure follows) with the chocolate crêpe batter. Spread ⅓ cup of the filling onto half of each crêpe and fold the crêpes gently over the filling. Bake the crêpes on a baking sheet in a preheated 350° F. oven for 10 minutes, transfer them to plates, and serve them with the sauce, heated. Makes 8 filled crêpes, serving 8.

Chocolate Crêpe Batter

1 cup all-purpose flour
3 tablespoons unsweetened cocoa powder
3 tablespoons sugar
½ teaspoon salt
½ cup milk
3 large eggs
2 tablespoons unsalted butter,
   melted and cooled

In a blender or food processor blend the flour, the cocoa, the sugar, the salt, ½ cup plus 2 tablespoons water, the milk, the eggs, and the butter for 5 seconds. Turn off the motor, with a rubber spatula scrape down the sides of the container, and blend the batter for 20 seconds more. Transfer the batter to a bowl and let it stand, covered, for 1 hour. *The batter may be made 1 day in advance and kept covered and chilled.* Makes enough batter for about 18 crêpes.

To Make Crêpes

melted unsalted butter for brushing the pan
crêpe batter

Heat a crêpe pan or non-stick skillet measuring 6 or 7 inches across the bottom over moderate heat until it is hot. Brush the pan lightly with the butter, heat it until it is hot but not smoking, and remove it from the heat. Stir the batter, half fill a ¼-cup measure with it, and pour the batter into the pan. Tilt and rotate the pan quickly to cover the bottom with a thin layer of batter and return any excess batter to the bowl. Return the pan to the heat, loosen the edge of the crêpe with a spatula, and cook the crêpe for 1 minute, or until the top appears almost dry. Turn the crêpe, cook the other side lightly, and transfer the crêpe to a plate. Make crêpes with the remaining batter in the same manner, brushing the pan lightly with butter as necessary. *The crêpes may be made 3 days in advance, kept stacked, wrapped in plastic wrap, and chilled.*

daisy

Chocolate Sauce

2 ounces semisweet chocolate,
  chopped
⅔ cup heavy cream
½ cup unsweetened cocoa powder
⅓ cup firmly packed dark brown sugar
⅛ teaspoon salt
1 teaspoon vanilla

In a heavy saucepan heat the chocolate and the cream over moderately low heat, stirring, until the chocolate is melted, but do not let the mixture boil. In a small bowl combine the cocoa powder with the brown sugar. In a small heavy saucepan bring ¼ cup water to a simmer, add the cocoa powder mixture, a little at a time, stirring, and cook the mixture over moderately low heat, stirring, until the sugar is dissolved and the mixture is smooth. Add the chocolate cream mixture and the salt and cook the mixture, stirring, until it is smooth, but do not let it boil. Remove the pan from the heat, stir in the vanilla, and transfer the sauce to a bowl. *The sauce may be made 2 weeks in advance if cooled for at least 2 hours and then kept covered and chilled.* Serve the sauce warm. Makes about 1½ cups.

*Toasted Coconut Crêpe Cups with
Pineapple à la Mode*

toasted coconut crêpe batter (recipe follows)
1½ cups chopped drained canned pineapple
2 tablespoons unsalted butter
2 tablespoons dark rum
vanilla ice cream
¼ cup sweetened flaked coconut, toasted
  lightly

Make 6 crêpes (procedure on page 235) with the toasted coconut crêpe batter. Fit the crêpes into ½-cup muffin tins and put a ball of foil in the center of each cup to keep the crêpes open. Bake the cups in a preheated 400° F. oven for 4 minutes, remove the foil, and bake the cups for 6 to 8 minutes more, or until they are crisp.

In a skillet sauté the pineapple in the butter over moderately high heat, stirring, for 3 minutes, add the rum carefully, and boil the mixture for 3 minutes. Put a scoop of vanilla ice cream in each crêpe cup, spoon some of the pineapple sauce over it, and sprinkle the tops with the toasted coconut. Makes 6 crêpe cups, serving 6.

Toasted Coconut Crêpe Batter

⅓ cup all-purpose flour
1 tablespoon sugar
3 tablespoons milk
1 large egg
1 tablespoon unsalted butter, melted and
  cooled
¼ teaspoon salt
¼ teaspoon almond extract
¼ cup lightly toasted sweetened flaked
  coconut, chopped fine

In a blender or food processor blend the flour, the sugar, ½ cup water, the milk, the egg, the butter, the salt, and the almond extract for 5 seconds. Turn off the motor, with a rubber spatula scrape down the sides of the container, and blend the batter for 20 seconds more. Transfer the batter to a bowl, stir in the coconut, and let the batter stand, covered, for 1 hour. *The batter may be made 1 day in advance and kept covered and chilled.* Makes enough batter for about 6 crêpes.

Poppy-Seed Cheese Crêpes with Apricot Sauce
For the filling
two 1-pound containers of plain yogurt
¼ cup confectioners' sugar

½ teaspoon vanilla
For the sauce
6 ounces (about 1 cup) dried apricots
¼ cup firmly packed light brown sugar

poppy-seed crêpe batter
  (recipe follows)
melted butter for brushing the crêpes

Make the filling: In a large cheesecloth-lined sieve set over a bowl let the yogurt drain, covered and chilled, for 8 hours. Transfer the yogurt to a bowl, add the confectioners' sugar and the vanilla, and whisk the mixture until it is smooth.

Make the sauce: In a small heavy saucepan combine the apricots, the brown sugar, and 2½ cups water, bring the liquid to a boil, and simmer the mixture, covered, for 20 minutes. In a food processor or blender purée the mixture and force it through a sieve into a bowl. *The sauce may be made 3 days in advance and kept covered and chilled.* Serve the sauce either warm or at room temperature.

Make 12 crêpes (procedure on page 235) with the poppy-seed crêpe batter. Mound 2 tablespoons of the filling in the center of each crêpe and fold the bottom third of the crêpe up over the filling. Fold in 1 inch of each side and fold down the top third of the crêpe to enclose the filling completely, forming a rectangle. Arrange the crêpes in one layer in a shallow baking dish, brush them with the butter, and bake them in the middle of a preheated 450° F. oven for 10 minutes. Serve the crêpes with the apricot sauce. Makes 12 filled crêpes, serving 4 to 6.

Poppy-Seed Crêpe Batter

1 cup all-purpose flour
2 tablespoons sugar
½ cup milk
3 large eggs
2 tablespoons unsalted butter,
  melted and cooled
1 tablespoon poppy seeds
2 teaspoons freshly grated lemon zest
¼ teaspoon salt

In a blender or food processor blend the flour, the sugar, ½ cup plus 2 tablespoons water, the milk, the eggs, the butter, the poppy seeds, the zest, and the salt

for 5 seconds. Turn off the motor, with a rubber spatula scrape down the sides of the container, and blend the batter for 20 seconds more. Transfer the batter to a bowl and let it stand, covered, for 1 hour. *The batter may be made 1 day in advance and kept covered and chilled.* Makes enough batter for about 16 crêpes.

CUSTARDS, MOUSSES, AND PUDDINGS

Pots de Crème Javanaise
(*Coffee Custards*)

½ cup sugar
½ ounce semisweet chocolate, chopped fine
5 large egg yolks
1 large whole egg
2 cups milk
2 tablespoons instant espresso powder
1 teaspoon vanilla
whipped cream and 6 chocolate coffee beans
  for garnish if desired

In a small skillet cook ¼ cup of the sugar over moderate heat, stirring with a fork, until it is melted and a golden caramel, add carefully ¼ cup water (pour it into the side of the skillet), and simmer the mixture, stirring, until the caramel is dissolved. Remove the skillet from the heat and stir in the chocolate, stirring until it is melted. In a bowl whisk the yolks and the whole egg with the remaining ¼ cup sugar and add the chocolate mixture, whisking. Whisk in the milk, scalded, in a stream, the espresso powder, the vanilla, and a pinch of salt. Strain the custard through a fine sieve into another bowl, skim the froth, and divide the custard among six ⅔-cup *pots de crème* pots or ramekins.

Put the pots in a baking pan, add enough hot water to the pan to reach one third up the sides of the pots, and cover the pots with their lids or cover the pan tightly with foil. Bake the custards in the middle of a preheated 300° F. oven for 30 to 35 minutes, or until they are just set, let them cool completely, uncovered, and chill them, covered, for 3 hours, or until they are cold. *The custards may be made 1 day in advance and kept covered and chilled.* Garnish each custard with a rosette of whipped cream and a chocolate coffee bean. Serves 6.

PHOTO ON PAGE 37

Lemon Caramel Custard

1½ cups sugar
a pinch of cream of tartar
3½ cups milk
1 cup heavy cream
5 large whole eggs
5 large egg yolks
2 tablespoons fresh lemon juice
1 tablespoon freshly grated lemon zest
1 teaspoon vanilla

In a small heavy saucepan combine ¾ cup of the sugar, the cream of tartar, and ¼ cup water, bring the mixture to a boil, stirring until the sugar is dissolved, and boil the syrup, covered, for 1 minute. Remove the lid and boil the syrup, undisturbed, until it begins to turn golden. Continue to boil the syrup, swirling it and tilting the pan occasionally, until it is a deep golden caramel. Pour the caramel into a loaf pan, 9¼ by 5¼ by 3 inches, tilt the pan to coat the bottom and sides with the caramel, and let the caramel cool.

In a large saucepan scald the milk with the cream over moderate heat. In a large heatproof bowl whisk together the whole eggs, the egg yolks, and the remaining ¾ cup sugar until the mixture is light and frothy. Add the scalded milk mixture in a slow stream, stirring constantly, and stir in the lemon juice, the zest, and the vanilla. Set the loaf pan in a larger and deeper baking pan and strain the custard mixture into the loaf pan. Cover the loaf pan with heavy-duty foil and add enough hot water to the larger pan to come two thirds of the way up the sides of the loaf pan.

Bake the custard in the middle of a preheated 325° F. oven for 1 hour and 20 minutes, remove the loaf pan from the baking pan carefully, and remove the foil. (The custard will not appear set in the middle but it will continue to cook as it cools.) Let the custard cool and chill it, covered, overnight. Run a thin knife around the edge of the custard, invert a serving platter over the custard, and invert the custard onto it.

Tiramisù Parfaits

2 large egg whites
a pinch of cream of tartar
⅔ cup sugar
½ pound *mascarpone* (Italian-style cream
    cheese, available at specialty foods shops
    and some supermarkets)

2 tablespoons dark rum
2 ounces fine-quality bittersweet chocolate,
    chopped fine
1 cup coarsely crumbled butter cookies or
    pound cake
1 cup lukewarm brewed coffee
For garnish
2 ounces fine-quality bittersweet chocolate,
    chopped

Put the egg whites in the bowl of an electric mixer, put the bowl in a bowl of hot water, and let the whites stand, stirring occasionally, for 15 minutes. Add the cream of tartar and a pinch of salt and beat the whites until they just hold stiff peaks. While the whites are being beaten, in a small saucepan combine the sugar and ¼ cup water, bring the mixture to a boil, stirring to dissolve the sugar, and boil the syrup until it registers 240° F. on a candy thermometer. Add the sugar syrup to the whites in a stream, beating, and beat the mixture until it is cool. Add the *mascarpone*, the rum, and the chocolate and beat the mixture until it is combined well.

Divide half the cookie crumbs among 4 stemmed glasses, drizzle each portion with 2 tablespoons of the coffee, and top the soaked crumbs with half the *mascarpone* mixture. Layer the remaining cookie crumbs, coffee, and *mascarpone* mixture in the same manner. Chill the parfaits, covered, for at least 2 hours or overnight.

Make the garnish: In a metal bowl set over a pan of barely simmering water melt the chocolate. Line a baking sheet with foil and spread the chocolate about ⅛-inch thick on the foil. Chill the chocolate until it is just set but not hard and with a pastry wheel cut it into triangles. Chill the chocolate triangles on the baking sheet until they have hardened and peel the foil carefully from them. Garnish each parfait with a chocolate triangle. Serves 4.

PHOTO ON PAGE 55

Honeydew and Cantaloupe Mousse

For the honeydew mousse
1½ envelopes (about 1½ tablespoons)
    unflavored gelatin
¼ cup Midori (melon-flavored liqueur)
the flesh of half a 6- to 7-pound honeydew melon
¼ cup sugar
2 tablespoons fresh lemon juice
⅓ cup plain yogurt

For the cantaloupe mousse
1½ envelopes (about 1½ tablespoons)
    unflavored gelatin
3 tablespoons Port
the flesh of a 3-pound cantaloupe
3 tablespoons sugar
2 tablespoons fresh lemon juice
⅓ cup plain yogurt

small wedges of honeydew melon and
    cantaloupe for garnish

Make the honeydew mousse: In a small saucepan sprinkle the gelatin over the Midori and let it soften for 1 minute. Heat the mixture over low heat, stirring, until the gelatin is dissolved completely and let it cool. In a blender purée the honeydew with the sugar and the lemon juice and with the motor running add the Midori mixture in a stream. Transfer the mixture to a metal bowl set in a larger bowl of ice and cold water and stir it until it is the consistency of raw egg white. Remove the metal bowl from the ice, stir in the yogurt, and let the honeydew mousse stand while making the cantaloupe mousse.

Make the cantaloupe mousse: In a small saucepan sprinkle the gelatin over the Port and let it soften for 1 minute. Heat the mixture over low heat, stirring, until the gelatin is dissolved completely and let it cool. In a blender purée the cantaloupe with the sugar and the lemon juice and with the motor running add the Port mixture in a stream. Transfer the mixture to a metal bowl set in a larger bowl of ice and cold water and stir it until it is the consistency of raw egg white. Remove the metal bowl from the ice and stir in the yogurt.

In a 2-quart glass bowl or 8 dessert glasses layer the mousses, chilling them for 5 minutes between each layer, chill the mousse for at least 2 hours or overnight, and garnish it with the melon wedges. Serves 8.

Mango Yogurt Mousses

1 envelope (1 tablespoon) unflavored gelatin
2 cups fresh mango purée (about 2 peeled
    and pitted mangoes) plus mango slices
    for garnish
⅓ cup sugar
½ teaspoon vanilla
1 cup plain yogurt
1 cup well-chilled heavy cream

In a small saucepan sprinkle the gelatin over ¼ cup cold water, let it soften for 1 minute, and heat the mixture over low heat, stirring, until the gelatin is dissolved. In a blender blend together the mango purée, the sugar, and the vanilla, add the gelatin mixture, and blend the mixture well. Transfer the mixture to a bowl and stir in the yogurt. In a chilled bowl beat the cream until it holds stiff peaks, fold it into the mango mixture gently but thoroughly, and divide the mousse among 4 dessert glasses. Chill the mousses for at least 4 hours or overnight. Garnish the mousses with the mango slices. Serves 4.

PHOTO ON PAGE 38

Apple Cider Indian Pudding

1 cup milk
⅔ cup yellow cornmeal
3 cups unpasteurized apple cider
1 large egg, beaten lightly
½ cup firmly packed light brown sugar
1 teaspoon cinnamon
1 teaspoon salt
½ stick (¼ cup) unsalted butter, cut into bits
½ cup raisins
vanilla ice cream as an accompaniment

In the top of a double boiler set over simmering water scald ½ cup of the milk. In a bowl whisk together the cornmeal and the cider, stir the mixture into the scalded milk, and cook the mixture, stirring occasionally, for 20 to 25 minutes, or until it is thickened. (The mixture may appear slightly curdled.) Remove the pan from the heat, whisk in the egg, the brown sugar, the cinnamon, the salt, the butter, and the raisins, and pour the mixture into a buttered 13- by 9-inch baking pan. Whisk in the remaining ½ cup milk and bake the pudding in the middle of a preheated 325° F. oven for 1 hour. Serve the pudding warm with the ice cream. Serves 6 to 8.

Bread and Butter Pudding

1½ cups milk
½ vanilla bean, split lengthwise
twelve ½-inch-thick slices of French or
    Italian bread
2½ tablespoons unsalted butter, softened
2 large whole eggs
6 large egg yolks
½ cup plus 1 tablespoon sugar
1 cup heavy cream
¼ cup apricot jam

In a saucepan scald the milk with the vanilla bean and let the mixture stand for 15 minutes. Scrape the seeds from the pod into the milk and discard the pod. Spread one side of each bread slice with the butter and arrange the slices, buttered sides up, overlapping them, in a 1½-quart gratin dish or shallow flameproof baking dish. In a bowl whisk together the whole eggs, the egg yolks, and ½ cup of the sugar and whisk in the milk and the cream. Pour the custard over the bread and sprinkle the mixture with the remaining 1 tablespoon sugar. Put the gratin dish in a baking pan, add enough hot water to the pan to reach halfway up the side of the gratin dish, and bake the pudding in the middle of a preheated 350° F. oven for 30 minutes, or until the custard is set. Broil the pudding under a preheated broiler about 4 inches from the heat for 1 minute, or until the bread is golden.

In a small saucepan bring the jam to a simmer with 1 teaspoon water, force it through a fine sieve into a small bowl, and with a pastry brush brush it over the pudding. Serve the pudding warm or at room temperature. Serves 6.

PHOTO ON PAGE 62

Microwave Chocolate Puddings
with Rum-Soaked Golden Raisins

2 tablespoons golden raisins
3 tablespoons light rum,
    or to taste
3 tablespoons firmly packed light brown sugar
2 tablespoons cornstarch
1 large egg yolk, beaten lightly
1¼ cups milk
3 ounces semisweet chocolate,
    chopped fine
1 tablespoon unsalted butter, cut into bits
¼ teaspoon vanilla

In a 1-quart glass measure combine the raisins and the rum, microwave the mixture at high power (100%) for 30 seconds, and let it stand, covered. In a large bowl whisk together the brown sugar, the cornstarch, a pinch of salt, and the egg yolk, whisk in the milk slowly, and whisk the mixture until it is combined well. Transfer the mixture to another 1-quart glass measure or a large microwave-safe bowl. Microwave the mixture at high power (100%) for 2 minutes, whisking it well after each minute. Microwave the mixture for 2 minutes more and whisk in the chocolate, the butter, and the vanilla, whisking until the mixture is smooth. Whisk in the raisin mixture and divide the pudding between two 1-cup bowls. Serves 2.

Raspberry Summer Pudding

14 slices of very thin homemade-type white
    bread, crusts removed and 8 of the slices
    halved crosswise
4 cups raspberries plus additional for garnish
⅓ cup sugar, or to taste
¼ cup framboise or raspberry-flavored liqueur
whipped cream for garnish

Line a 1-quart charlotte mold with plastic wrap and trim 1 whole bread slice to fit the bottom of it. Arrange the halved slices, overlapping them slightly, around the sides of the mold and press the bread round into the bottom.

In a saucepan combine 4 cups of the raspberries, the sugar, and the framboise, bring the mixture to a simmer over moderate heat, stirring, and simmer it, stirring, for 3 minutes, or until the raspberries are crushed and the sugar is dissolved. Remove the pan from the heat and let the raspberry mixture cool.

Spoon one third of the raspberry mixture into the mold and top it with 1 slice of the remaining bread, trimming the bread if necessary. Spoon half the remaining raspberry mixture into the mold and top it with 1 slice of the remaining bread, trimming the bread if necessary. Spoon the remaining raspberry mixture into the mold and top it with enough of the remaining 3 slices of bread, cut into pieces, to cover the top completely. Cover the mold with a round of wax paper cut to fit the inside of the mold, top the wax paper with 1 round of stiff cardboard cut to fit the inside of the mold, and weight the pudding evenly with a 2-pound weight. Chill the pudding overnight.

Just before serving remove the weight, the cardboard, and the wax paper, run a thin knife around the edge of the mold to loosen the pudding, and invert a large round serving plate over the mold. Invert the raspberry pudding onto the plate, remove the plastic wrap, and garnish the pudding with the whipped cream and the additional raspberries.

PHOTO ON PAGE 44

FROZEN DESSERTS

Honeydew and Sake Granita

½ cup sugar
the flesh of a 3-pound honeydew melon
    plus, if desired, 8 thin round slices
    of honeydew melon
    for garnish
¼ cup *sake*
2 teaspoons fresh lime juice
pickled ginger and plum-wine granita
    (recipe follows)

In a small saucepan combine the sugar and 1¼ cups water and bring the mixture to a boil, stirring. In a blender purée the honeydew flesh with the syrup, the *sake*, and the lime juice. Transfer the mixture to 2 metal ice-cube trays without the dividers or to a shallow metal pan and freeze it, stirring and crushing the lumps with a fork every 30 minutes, for 2 to 3 hours, or until it is firm but not frozen solid. *The granita may be made 2 days in advance and kept covered and frozen.* Scrape the granita with a fork to lighten the texture. On each of 4 plates arrange 2 of the honeydew slices and top 1 of the slices on each plate with a scoop of the honeydew and *sake* granita. Top the other slices with a scoop of the pickled ginger and plum-wine granita. Serves 4.

PHOTO ON PAGE 50

Pickled Ginger and Plum-Wine Granita

⅔ cup sugar
2 tablespoons pickled ginger slices (available
    at Asian markets and some supermarkets),
    rinsed
¼ cup plum wine
2 drops of red food coloring if desired

In a small saucepan combine the sugar and 3½ cups water and bring the mixture to a boil, stirring. In a blender purée the ginger with the syrup, the wine, and the food coloring, chill the mixture until it is cold, and stir it. Transfer the mixture to 2 metal ice-cube trays without the dividers or to a shallow metal pan and freeze it, stirring and crushing the lumps with a fork every 30 minutes, for 2 to 3 hours, or until it is firm but not frozen solid. *The granita may be made 2 days in advance and kept covered and frozen.* Scrape the granita with a fork to lighten the texture. Serves 4.

PHOTO ON PAGE 50

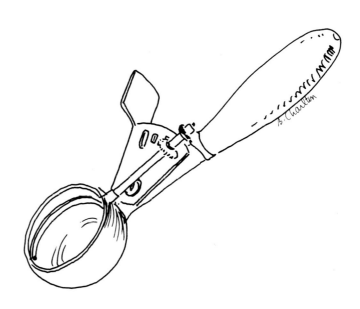

Strawberry Italian Ice

1 pint fresh strawberries, trimmed
¼ cup sugar
2 teaspoons fresh lemon juice
2 cups ice cubes (about 11)

Put a 9- or 10-inch metal cake pan in the freezer. In a blender blend the strawberries, the sugar, and the lemon juice until the mixture is smooth and the sugar is dissolved. Add the ice cubes, blend the mixture until it is smooth, and pour it into the cold pan. Freeze the mixture for 30 to 40 minutes, or until it is frozen around the edge but still soft in the center, stir the strawberry ice, mashing the frozen parts with a fork, and spoon it into 2 bowls. Serves 2.

Cinnamon Cocoa Meringues with Vanilla Ice Cream and Cinnamon Chocolate Sauce

2 large egg whites
a pinch of cream of tartar
½ cup sugar
2 teaspoons unsweetened cocoa powder
½ teaspoon cinnamon
vanilla ice cream
cinnamon chocolate sauce (recipe follows)

In a bowl with an electric mixer beat the egg whites until they are foamy, add the cream of tartar, and beat the whites until they hold soft peaks. Add the sugar, 1 tablespoon at a time, beating, and beat the meringue until it holds stiff peaks. Sift the cocoa powder and the cinnamon over the meringue and fold them in gently but throughly. Transfer the mixture to a pastry bag fitted with a ½-inch star tip and pipe it into 5-inch rounds on baking sheets lined with parchment paper. Bake the meringues in the middle of a preheated 250° F. oven for 1½ hours and let them cool on the sheets. *The meringues may be made 10 days in advance and kept, separated with sheets of wax paper, in an airtight container.* Arrange 1 meringue on each of 2 plates and top each meringue with a scoop of the ice cream and some of the cinnamon chocolate sauce. Serves 2.

Cinnamon Chocolate Sauce

¾ cup heavy cream
⅓ cup firmly packed light brown sugar
3 ounces bittersweet chocolate, chopped
3 ounces unsweetened chocolate, chopped
½ stick (¼ cup) unsalted butter, softened
½ teaspoon cinnamon

In a small heavy saucepan combine the cream and the brown sugar, bring the mixture to a boil over moderately high heat, whisking occasionally, and boil it, whisking, until the brown sugar is dissolved. Remove the pan from the heat, add the chocolates, and whisk the mixture until they are melted. Whisk in the butter and the cinnamon, whisking until the sauce is smooth, and let the sauce cool slightly. *The sauce may be made 1 week in advance and kept covered and chilled. Reheat the sauce over very low heat, stirring occasionally, until it is warm.* Makes about 1½ cups.

Raspberry Swirl Parfaits

two 10-ounce packages frozen raspberries in light syrup, thawed
3 large eggs
2½ tablespoons sugar
2½ tablespoons honey
¾ cup well-chilled heavy cream
½ cup walnuts, toasted lightly, cooled, and chopped
6 chocolate curls for garnish if desired
fresh raspberries if available for garnish

In a food processor purée the thawed raspberries with the syrup, force the mixture through a fine sieve into a heavy saucepan, pressing hard on the solids, and boil the raspberry purée, stirring occasionally, until it is reduced to about 1 cup. Let the raspberry purée cool and chill it.

In a metal bowl beat together the eggs, the sugar, and the honey, set the bowl over a saucepan of simmering water, and beat the mixture until it is pale, thickened, and registers 160° F. on a candy thermometer. Beat the mixture set over a larger bowl of ice and cold water until it is cold, in another bowl beat the cream until it just holds stiff peaks, and fold the cream and the walnuts into the egg mixture gently but thoroughly. Spoon the raspberry purée and the egg mixture decoratively into 6-ounce glasses, make swirls with a wooden skewer, and freeze the parfaits, covered, overnight. *The parfaits may be made 2 days in advance and kept covered and frozen.* Let the parfaits stand for 15 minutes before serving. Arrange the chocolate curls and the fresh raspberries decoratively on the parfaits. Serves 6.

Buttermilk Sherbet

4 cups buttermilk
1½ cups light corn syrup
½ cup fresh lemon juice
½ cup sugar
the freshly grated zest of 4 lemons plus, if desired, strips of zest, removed with a vegetable peeler and sliced thin, for garnish
a few drops of green food coloring if desired

In a bowl combine well the buttermilk, the corn syrup, the lemon juice, the sugar, the zest, and the food coloring and freeze the mixture in an ice-cream freezer according to the manufacturer's instructions. Pack the sherbet into an airtight container and freeze it until it is firm. Serve scoops of the sherbet garnished with the strips of zest. Makes about 1½ quarts.

Fresh Pineapple Sherbet

½ cup sugar
1 pineapple, cored, trimmed, reserving
   6 large wedges for garnish, puréed in a
   blender, and forced through a fine sieve
   (3 cups strained purée)
1½ cups well-chilled milk
2 tablespoons fresh lemon juice
fresh mint sprigs for garnish if desired

In a small saucepan combine the sugar and ½ cup water, bring the mixture to a boil, and simmer it for 5 minutes, or until it is reduced to ½ cup. Let the sugar syrup cool completely. In a bowl whisk together the pineapple purée, the sugar syrup, the milk, the lemon juice, and a pinch of salt. Chill the mixture until it is cold and freeze it in an ice-cream freezer according to the manufacturer's instructions. Serve the sherbet in scoops on dessert plates garnished with the reserved pineapple wedges and the mint. Makes 1 quart.

Mulled Apple Cider Sorbet

6 cups unpasteurized apple cider
a 3-inch cinnamon stick
½ cup sugar
2 teaspoons strained fresh lemon juice

In a large saucepan combine the cider, the cinnamon stick, the sugar, and a pinch of salt and boil the mixture for 5 to 10 minutes, or until the liquid is reduced to about 4 cups. Stir in the lemon juice, strain the mixture through a fine sieve into a bowl, and chill it, covered, until it is cold. Freeze the mixture in an ice-cream freezer according to the manufacturer's instructions. Makes about 1¼ quarts.

Coconut Mint Sorbet

¾ cup sugar
2 bags of peppermint herbal tea
1 large coconut without any cracks and
   containing liquid
2 or 3 drops of green food coloring if desired

In a saucepan bring 2 cups water to a boil with the sugar, stirring until the sugar is dissolved, add the tea bags, and let the tea steep, covered, for 15 minutes. Discard the tea bags.

With an ice pick test the 3 eyes of the coconut to find the weakest one and pierce it to make a hole. Drain the liquid and reserve it. Bake the coconut in a preheated 400° F. oven for 15 minutes, break it with a hammer, and remove the flesh from the shell, levering it out carefully with the point of a strong knife. Cut the coconut meat into small pieces, transferring it as it is ground to a bowl. Return the ground coconut to the blender.

Strain the reserved coconut liquid through a fine sieve into a large measure and add enough water to measure a total of 2 cups liquid. In a saucepan bring the liquid to a boil, add it to the ground coconut, and blend the mixture for 1 minute. Let the coconut mixture cool, strain it through a large sieve lined with a double thickness of cheesecloth into a bowl, pressing hard on the solids, and squeeze the coconut in the cheesecloth to extract as much of the milk as possible.

Stir the tea into the coconut milk with the food coloring, if using, and chill the mixture, covered until it is cold. Freeze the mixture in an ice-cream freezer according to the manufacturer's instructions and store the *sorbet* in freezer containers. *The sorbet may be made 5 days in advance and kept frozen, covered. Let the sorbet stand in the refrigerator for 30 minutes or microwave it at 30% power for 1 minute to soften lightly before serving.* Makes about 1 quart.

Black Plum Sorbet

1½ pounds black plums, pitted and chopped
3 tablespoons fresh lemon juice, or to taste
½ cup sugar
2 tablespoons kirsch

In a saucepan combine the plums, the lemon juice, and ¼ cup water and cook the mixture over moderate heat, stirring occasionally, for 10 to 15 minutes, or until the plums are soft. While the plums are cooking, in a small saucepan combine the sugar and ¾ cup water, cook the mixture over moderate heat, stirring, until the sugar is dissolved, and stir in the kirsch. In a blender or food processor purée the plums with the kirsch syrup. Strain the purée through a fine sieve into a bowl, let it cool, and freeze it in an ice-cream freezer according to the manufacturer's instructions. Makes about 1 quart.

FRUIT FINALES

Cinnamon Baked Apples with Yogurt Cheese

2 cups plain yogurt
6 apples, such as Empire, Red Delicious,
    Granny Smith, or Golden Delicious
the juice of ½ lemon
¾ cup firmly packed light brown sugar
¾ cup water
½ teaspoon cinnamon
⅛ teaspoon black pepper
1 tablespoon unsalted butter, cut into 6 pieces
¼ cup chopped almonds

In a sieve, lined with a rinsed and squeezed paper towel or cheesecloth and set over a bowl, let the yogurt drain, covered and chilled, overnight.

Core the apples, peel the top third of each apple decoratively, and drop the apples into a large bowl of cold water acidulated with the lemon juice. In a saucepan combine the brown sugar, the water, the cinnamon, and the pepper, bring the mixture to a boil, stirring, and boil the syrup for 6 minutes. Arrange the apples, patted dry, in a baking dish just large enough to hold them, top them with the butter pieces, and pour the syrup over them. Bake the apples in the middle of a preheated 375° F. oven, basting them with the syrup once or twice, for 40 minutes, or until they are just tender. Baste the apples with the syrup, transfer them with a slotted spoon to a platter, reserving the syrup in a small bowl, covered, and let the apples and the syrup cool. *The baked apples may be made 1 day in advance and kept covered and chilled. Let them stand at room temperature for 1 hour before serving.*

Top each apple with some of the yogurt cheese. Whisk the syrup to combine it, drizzle it over the apples, and sprinkle the almonds on top. Serves 6.

PHOTO ON PAGE 68

Sour Cherry Cobbler

4 cups sour cherries, picked over, rinsed, and
    drained well
2 tablespoons cornstarch
⅔ cup plus 2 tablespoons sugar
2 tablespoons fresh lemon juice
¼ teaspoon almond extract
1 cup all-purpose flour

1 teaspoon double-acting baking powder
½ teaspoon salt
¾ stick (6 tablespoons) cold unsalted butter,
    cut into bits
peach and brown sugar ice cream (page 229)
    or vanilla ice cream as an accompaniment
    if desired

Working over a bowl pit the cherries, discarding the pits and reserving the cherries and any juices in the bowl, and into the cherries stir the cornstarch, ⅔ cup of the sugar, the lemon juice, and the almond extract. In a small bowl stir together the flour, the baking powder, the salt, the remaining 2 tablespoons sugar, and the butter, blend the mixture until it resembles coarse meal, and stir in ¼ cup boiling water, stirring until the batter is just combined. In an 8-inch cast-iron skillet or flameproof baking dish bring the cherry mixture to a boil, drop the batter by heaping tablespoons onto it, and bake the cobbler in the middle of a preheated 350° F. oven for 45 to 50 minutes, or until the top is golden. Serve the cobbler with the ice cream.

Lime Soufflés

5 tablespoons sugar plus additional for dusting
    the ramekins
2 large eggs, separated
2 teaspoons freshly grated lime zest
2 tablespoons fresh lime juice

Cut two 1½- by 12-inch foil strips, butter them, and wrap the strips, buttered sides in, around two ⅔-cup buttered ramekins to form ½-inch collars, tying the collars with kitchen string. Dust the ramekins with the additional sugar, shaking out the excess. In a small bowl whisk the egg yolks with 3 tablespoons of the sugar until the mixture ribbons when the whisk is lifted and whisk in the zest and the lime juice. Transfer the mixture to a small heavy saucepan and cook it over moderately low heat, stirring constantly with a wooden spoon, until it thickens and coats the back of the spoon. *Do not let the mixture boil.* Remove the pan from the heat and transfer the mixture to a bowl.

In a bowl beat the egg whites with a pinch of salt until they hold soft peaks, add the remaining 2 tablespoons sugar gradually, and beat the meringue until it just holds stiff peaks. Stir one fourth of the meringue into the lime mixture and fold in the remaining meringue gently but thoroughly. Divide the mixture between the ramekins. Bake the soufflés in the middle of a preheated 400° F. oven for 8 to 10 minutes, or until they are puffed and the tops are golden. Serves 2.

B. Charlton

Peach and Blackberry Crisp

1½ pounds peaches (about 3), pitted and cut
    into ½-inch-thick wedges
2 cups blackberries, picked over and rinsed
1 tablespoon cornstarch
2 tablespoons fresh lemon juice
⅓ cup granulated sugar
⅔ cup all-purpose flour
¾ cup firmly packed light brown sugar
½ cup old-fashioned rolled oats
½ teaspoon salt
1 teaspoon cinnamon
½ teaspoon freshly grated nutmeg
¾ stick (6 tablespoons) cold unsalted butter,
    cut into bits
¾ cup coarsely chopped lightly toasted pecans
peach and brown sugar ice cream (page 229)
    or vanilla ice cream as an accompaniment

In a large bowl toss the peaches and the blackberries gently with the cornstarch, the lemon juice, and the granulated sugar until the mixture is combined well. In a small bowl stir together the flour, the brown sugar, the oats, the salt, the cinnamon, and the nutmeg, add the butter, blending the mixture until it resembles coarse meal, and stir in the pecans. Spread the peach mixture in a 13- by 9-inch (3-quart) baking dish, sprinkle the pecan mixture evenly over it, and bake the crisp in the middle of a preheated 375° oven for 45 to 50 minutes, or until the top is golden. Serve the crisp with the ice cream.

Broiled Peaches with Cookie-Crumb Topping

2 ripe peaches (about 1 pound),
    peeled, pitted, and cut
    into ¼-inch-thick slices
2 teaspoons fresh lemon juice
4 teaspoons firmly packed light brown sugar
1 tablespoon unsalted butter,
    cut into bits
2 shortbread or butter cookies, crumbled
    (about ¼ cup crumbs)
heavy cream as an accompaniment

In a bowl toss together the peaches, the lemon juice, and 1 tablespoon of the brown sugar and in a buttered flameproof baking pan large enough to hold the peaches in one layer broil the mixture about 6 inches from a preheated broiler for 5 to 7 minutes, or until the peaches are tender. In a small bowl combine the remaining 1 teaspoon brown sugar, the butter, and the cookie crumbs and sprinkle the topping over the peaches. Broil the mixture for 1 to 2 minutes, or until the topping is pale golden. Divide the mixture between 2 dishes and serve it with the cream. Serves 2.

Poached Pear and Dried Apricots
with Chocolate Sauce

¼ cup sugar
1 tablespoon dark rum
1 large pear
6 whole dried apricots,
    chopped
½ ounce fine-quality bittersweet chocolate,
    chopped
¼ teaspoon vanilla

In a heavy saucepan combine the sugar, the rum, and ½ cup water and simmer the mixture for 2 minutes. Add the pear, peeled, halved, and cored, and the apricots and poach the fruit, covered, spooning the syrup over the pear occasionally, for 8 to 10 minutes, or until the pear is tender. In a small heavy saucepan combine the chocolate, 2 tablespoons water, and the vanilla and heat the mixture over low heat, stirring constantly, until it is smooth. Transfer the pear halves to a work surface. Cut the pears diagonally into ¼-inch-thick slices, and fan them onto 2 plates. Sprinkle the apricots over the pear slices and spoon the chocolate sauce around the fruit. Serves 2.

Pineapple Banana Fritters

1⅓ cups all-purpose flour
1½ teaspoons double-acting baking powder
3 tablespoons granulated sugar
1 teaspoon ground ginger
¾ cup chopped fresh pineapple, drained
¾ cup chopped banana
½ cup milk
1 large egg, beaten lightly
vegetable oil for deep-frying
confectioners' sugar for dusting the fritters

Into a bowl sift together the flour, the baking powder, the granulated sugar, the ginger, and a pinch of salt. In a bowl combine well the pineapple, the banana, the milk, and the egg, add the flour mixture, and stir the batter until it is combined. In a kettle heat 1½ inches of the oil until it registers 375° F. on a deep-fat thermometer, drop the batter by tablespoonfuls into the oil in batches, and fry the fritters, turning them, for 1 to 1½ minutes, or until they are golden. Transfer the fritters with a slotted spoon to paper towels to drain and sift the confectioners' sugar over them. Makes 22 fritters.

Pineapple Ginger Preserves

3½ cups sugar
two 4-pound pineapples, peeled, cut into
    ¼-inch-thick rings, cored, and chopped coarse
¼ cup finely chopped peeled fresh gingerroot

In a heavy kettle combine the sugar and 2 cups water, bring the mixture to a boil, stirring until the sugar is dissolved, and boil the syrup until it registers 220° F. on a candy thermometer. Stir in the pineapple and the gingerroot and simmer the mixture, uncovered, stirring to prevent scorching, for 1 hour, or until the mixture registers 220° F. on a candy thermometer. Remove the kettle from the heat and ladle the preserves into 5 sterilized ½-pint Mason-type jars (sterilizing procedure on page 157), filling the jars to within ¼ inch of the tops. Wipe the rims with a dampened towel and seal the jars with the lids. Put the jars in a water bath canner or on a rack set in a deep kettle, add enough hot water to the canner or kettle to cover the jars by 2 inches, and bring the water to a boil. Process the jars, covered, for 10 minutes, transfer them with tongs to a rack, and let them cool completely. Store the jars in a cool dark place. Makes five ½-pint jars.

Chocolate and Prune Marquise with Armagnac Crème Anglaise

½ pound pitted prunes, chopped fine
½ cup Armagnac
1 pound bittersweet chocolate, chopped
1 stick (½ cup) unsalted butter, cut into pieces
1½ teaspoons freshly grated orange zest
1 cup well-chilled heavy cream
2 cups Armagnac *crème anglaise* (recipe follows)
candied orange zest (page 247) for garnish

In a small bowl let the prunes macerate in the Armagnac for at least 2 hours, or until they have absorbed most of the liquid. In a metal bowl set over a pan of barely simmering water combine the chocolate and the butter and heat the mixture, stirring occasionally, until the chocolate is melted and the mixture is smooth. Remove the bowl from the heat, stir in the prune mixture and the grated zest, and let the mixture cool completely. In a bowl with an electric mixer beat the heavy cream until it just holds stiff peaks, whisk about one fourth of it into the chocolate mixture, and fold in the remaining cream gently but thoroughly.

Line an oiled 5- to 6-cup terrine or loaf pan with plastic wrap and pour the chocolate mixture into it, smoothing the top. Cover the terrine with plastic wrap and chill it overnight. Remove the plastic wrap from the top of the terrine, invert the terrine onto a plate, and peel off the remaining plastic wrap. Pour ¼ cup of the Armagnac *crème anglaise* onto each of 8 dessert plates, cut the marquise into ¾-inch-thick slices with a sharp knife, and arrange a slice on each plate. Garnish the desserts with the candied orange zest. Serves 8.

Armagnac Crème Anglaise

2 cups half-and-half
1 vanilla bean, split lengthwise
2 large eggs
½ cup sugar
2 tablespoons Armagnac, or to taste

In a small heavy saucepan combine the half-and-half and the vanilla bean, bring the half-and-half just to a boil, and remove the pan from the heat. In a bowl whisk together the eggs and the sugar until the mixture is combined well and add the scalded half-and-half mixture in a slow stream, whisking. Transfer the mixture to a heavy saucepan and cook it over moderately low heat, stirring constantly with a wooden spoon, until it thickens (175° F. on a candy thermometer), but do not let it boil. Strain the *crème anglaise* through a fine sieve into a metal bowl set in a larger bowl of ice and cold water, let it cool, stirring, and stir in the Armagnac. Chill the sauce, covered, until it is very cold. Makes 2 cups.

Candied Orange Zest

⅔ cup julienne strips of fresh orange zest
⅔ cup Cointreau or other clear orange liqueur

In a heavy saucepan combine the zest and the liqueur, simmer the mixture until the liquid is just evaporated, and spread the zest on a sheet of wax paper, separating the pieces with a fork. Let it cool. Makes ½ cup.

Strawberries and Cantaloupe with Yogurt and Honey-Almond Brittle

1 cup plain yogurt
3 tablespoons sliced almonds
3 tablespoons honey
1 teaspoon unsalted butter
¼ teaspoon vanilla
8 strawberries, quartered
1 cantaloupe, halved and seeded

In a sieve lined with rinsed and squeezed cheesecloth or a paper towel and set over a bowl let the yogurt drain, chilled, for 30 minutes. While the yogurt is draining, in a skillet combine the almonds, 1 tablespoon of the honey, the butter, and a pinch of salt, cook the mixture over moderately high heat, stirring, for 3 minutes, or until it is golden, and transfer it to a piece of foil. Let the brittle cool and break it into small pieces. In a small bowl stir together the drained yogurt, the remaining 2 tablespoons honey, and the vanilla. Divide the strawberries between the cantaloupe halves, top them with the yogurt mixture, and sprinkle the brittle on top. Serves 2.

Summer Fruit Terrine

1 cup dry white wine
½ cup sugar
3 tablespoons fresh lemon juice
4 large peaches (about 2 pounds)
2 envelopes unflavored gelatin
16 strawberries, hulled and halved lengthwise
½ cup raspberries
½ cup blueberries
½ cup seedless green grapes, halved lengthwise
2¼ cups raspberry peach sauce (page 248)
mint sprigs for garnish if desired

In a saucepan combine the wine, the sugar, the lemon juice, and ½ cup water, bring the mixture to a boil, stirring until the sugar is dissolved, and add 2 of the peaches, peeled, halved, and pitted, cut sides down. Simmer the peaches for 10 to 15 minutes, or until they are very tender, and transfer them with a slotted spoon to a blender. Add 1 cup of the cooking liquid and blend the mixture until it is smooth. In a small saucepan sprinkle the gelatin over ⅓ cup cold water, let it soften for 5 minutes, and heat the mixture over low heat, stirring, until the gelatin is dissolved. With the motor running add the gelatin mixture in a stream to the peach mixture and blend the mixture until it is combined well.

Line a 5- to 6-cup terrine or loaf pan with plastic wrap and pour into it about ¼ cup of the peach purée, or enough to just cover the bottom. Arrange half the strawberries, cut sides down, in one layer on the peach purée and pour enough of the peach purée over the strawberry layer to just cover it. Peel, halve, and pit the remaining 2 peaches, slice them thin, and in a bowl toss them with ¼ cup of the peach purée. Arrange half the peach slices, overlapping them slightly, over the strawberry layer and pour enough of the remaining peach purée over the peach layer to just cover it.

In a small bowl toss the raspberries and the blueberries with ¼ cup of the peach purée and arrange the berries in one layer over the peaches. Pour enough of the remaining peach purée into the terrine to just cover the berries, in the bowl toss the grapes with about 2 tablespoons of the remaining purée, and arrange them in one layer over the berries. Pour enough of the remaining purée into the terrine to just cover the grape layer, arrange the remaining peaches in one layer, overlapping them slightly, over the grapes, and pour enough of the remaining purée over the peaches to just cover them. Arrange the remaining strawberries, cut sides up, in one layer over the peaches and cover them with the remaining purée. Chill the terrine for 1 hour, or until it is just set, cover it with plastic wrap, and chill it overnight.

Remove the wrap from the top of the terrine, invert the terrine onto a plate, and serve it with the sauce and the mint sprigs. Serves 4.

PHOTO ON PAGE 49

Raspberry Peach Sauce

¼ cup sugar
3 tablespoons fresh lemon juice
2 large peaches
    (about 1 pound)
1½ cups raspberries

In a saucepan combine the sugar, the lemon juice, and ¼ cup water and bring the mixture to a boil, stirring until the sugar is dissolved. In a blender purée the peaches, peeled, pitted, and chopped, and the raspberries with the sugar syrup until the mixture is smooth and force the mixture through a fine sieve set over a bowl, discarding the solids. Chill the sauce, covered, for at least 1 hour or overnight. Makes 2¼ cups.

PHOTO ON PAGE 49

CONFECTIONS

Chocolate Almond Truffle Squares

16 ounces fine-quality bittersweet chocolate
½ cup heavy cream
3 tablespoons Amaretto,
    or to taste
⅓ cup coarsely chopped almonds

Chop fine 12 ounces of the chocolate. In a small saucepan bring the cream just to a boil, remove the pan from the heat, and whisk in the chopped chocolate, whisking until the chocolate is melted completely. Whisk in the Amaretto, whisking until the mixture is smooth, and let the truffle mixture cool slightly.

In a small heatproof bowl set over a saucepan of barely simmering water melt the remaining 4 ounces chocolate. Line the bottom of an 8-inch-square baking pan with wax paper and spread half of the melted chocolate in a thin layer on the paper. Freeze the chocolate layer for 5 minutes and top it with the truffle mixture, smoothing the surface. Drizzle the truffle mixture with the remaining melted chocolate, spreading it lightly, and sprinkle the melted chocolate with the almonds, pressing them lightly. Chill the mixture for 3 hours, or until it is firm. Turn the mixture out onto a cutting board, peel off the wax paper, and with a long sharp knife cut the mixture into ¾-inch squares. The truffle squares keep, chilled in an airtight container, for 2 weeks. Makes about 100 truffle squares.

Chocolate Peanut Butter Balls

¾ cup firmly packed light brown sugar
½ stick (¼ cup) unsalted butter, melted and
    cooled, plus ¾ stick (6 tablespoons)
¾ cup graham cracker crumbs
1 cup creamy peanut butter
a 12-ounce bag semisweet chocolate chips

In a bowl stir together the brown sugar, ½ stick of the butter, the graham cracker crumbs, and the peanut butter until the mixture is smooth and chill the mixture, covered, for 1 hour, or until it is firm enough to form into balls. Form teaspoonfuls of the mixture into balls and transfer the balls as they are formed to a baking sheet lined with wax paper. In a metal bowl set over a pan of barely simmering water melt the chocolate chips with the remaining ¾ stick butter, stirring until the mixture is smooth, and let the chocolate mixture cool. Dip the balls into the chocolate mixture with a fork, coating them well and letting the excess drip off, transfer them as they are coated to the baking sheet, and chill them, covered loosely, for at least 1 hour or overnight. (The balls may be double-dipped if desired.) Makes about 40 chocolate peanut butter balls.

Pumpkin Walnut Fudge

4 cups sugar
1 cup milk
3 tablespoons light corn syrup
1 cup fresh pumpkin purée (page 230) or
    canned pumpkin purée
3 tablespoons unsalted butter, cut into bits
1 teaspoon vanilla
2 cups chopped walnuts

In a 4-quart heavy saucepan combine the sugar, the milk, the corn syrup, the pumpkin purée, and a pinch of salt, cook the mixture over moderate heat, stirring, until the sugar is dissolved, and cook it, undisturbed, until a candy thermometer registers 238° F. Remove the pan from the heat, add the butter (do not stir it into the mixture), and let the mixture cool until it is 140° F. Stir in the vanilla and the walnuts, beat the mixture with a wooden spoon for 30 seconds to 1 minute, or until it begins to lose its gloss, and pour it immediately into a buttered 9-inch-square pan. Let the fudge cool until it begins to harden, cut it into squares, and let it cool completely. Makes about 2 pounds.

BEVERAGES

ALCOHOLIC

Lemon Margaritas
⅓ cup fresh lemon juice
1 cup white Tequila
⅓ cup triple sec
coarse salt for coating the rims
   of the glasses

Dip the rims of 4 long-stemmed glasses in the lemon juice and put the glasses in the freezer. In a sealable bottle or pitcher combine the Tequila, the triple sec, the remaining lemon juice, and about 2 cups crushed ice, seal the bottle, and shake the Margarita vigorously until it is very cold and the ice is almost melted. Remove the glasses from the freezer, dip the rims in the salt, shaking off the excess, and fill the glasses with ice cubes. Divide the Margaritas among the glasses. Makes 4 drinks.

Pineapple Grapefruit Punch
two 4-pound pineapples, peeled and cut
   into pieces
2½ cups fresh pink grapefruit juice
2 tablespoons sugar
3 cups chilled seltzer or
   club soda
1 cup rum

In a food processor purée the pineapple in batches and strain the purée through a fine sieve into a bowl, pressing hard on the solids. Stir in the grapefruit juice and the sugar and stir the mixture until the sugar is dissolved. Chill the mixture, covered, until it is cold and stir in the seltzer and the rum. Makes about 10 cups.

Minted White Sangría
1 cup packed fresh mint leaves plus mint
   sprigs for garnish
¼ cup sugar
a chilled 750-ml. bottle dry white wine
¼ cup brandy

In a pitcher combine the mint, the sugar, and 3 tablespoons hot water and with a wooden spoon combine the mixture well, bruising the mint. Stir in the wine and the brandy and chill the sangría, covered, for 1 hour. Strain the sangría into tall glasses filled with ice cubes and garnish each drink with a mint sprig. Makes 6 drinks.

To Freeze a Bottle of Aquavit
a 750-ml. bottle of aquavit, such as
   O.P. Anderson, Linie, or Aalborg
flowers such as roses or tulips if desired
distilled water or springwater

Open fully the top of a cleaned half-gallon milk carton to extend the length of the carton, wrap the outside and bottom of the carton with foil, and put the aquavit in the carton close to one side, leaving as much space as possible for the flowers. Cut the flower stems to various lengths to fit the space, fill the carton with the distilled water to within ½ inch of the top, and arrange the flowers carefully in the water, using the bottle to wedge them if they begin to float. Transfer the carton to the freezer, spoon in enough of the water to reach the top of the carton, and freeze the aquavit overnight. *The aquavit may be frozen 1 week in advance.*

Remove the foil and let the aquavit stand at room temperature for 15 minutes. Peel the carton and put the aquavit on a napkin-covered surface.

PHOTO ON PAGE 42

NONALCOHOLIC

Cranberry, Pear, and Grapefruit Juice

2 cups cranberry juice
2 cups pear nectar
1 cup grapefruit juice

In a pitcher stir together the juices and chill the mixture until it is cold. Serves 6.

Mocha Hot Chocolate

1 cup unsweetened cocoa powder
1 cup sugar
¼ cup instant espresso powder
1 tablespoon vanilla
6 cups milk, scalded
2 cups half-and-half, scalded

In a large heavy saucepan combine the cocoa powder, the sugar, the espresso powder, the vanilla, a pinch of salt, and 1 cup cold water and heat the mixture over low heat, whisking, until the cocoa powder is dissolved and the mixture is a smooth paste. Gradually add the milk and the half-and-half, and heat the mixture over moderately low heat, whisking, until it is hot, but do not let it boil. (For frothy hot chocolate, in a blender blend the mixture in batches until it is frothy.) Serves 8.

PHOTO ON PAGE 20

Mulled Apple Cider with Orange and Ginger

8 cups unpasteurized apple cider
a 3-inch cinnamon stick
10 whole cloves
1 navel orange, peeled and
   sliced crosswise
a 2-inch piece of peeled fresh gingerroot, cut
   into 6 slices

In a large saucepan combine the cider, the cinnamon stick, the cloves, the orange, and the gingerroot and simmer the mixture for 20 minutes. Strain the mixture through a fine sieve into a heatproof pitcher and serve the mulled cider warm. Makes about 8 cups.

Pineapple Citrus Juice

2½ cups fresh pink grapefruit juice
2½ cups fresh orange juice
1 pineapple, peeled, cored, and chopped
   (about 4 cups)

In a blender blend half the grapefruit juice, half the orange juice, and half the pineapple, until the mixture is smooth and transfer the mixture to a large pitcher. Blend the remaining juices and pineapple in the same manner, transfer the mixture to the pitcher, and chill it, covered, overnight. Stir the juice before serving. Serves 8.

PHOTO ON PAGE 21

PART THREE

CUISINES OF THE WORLD

THE FLAVORS OF
France

Few would deny that France is one of the most beautiful countries of the world, and fewer still would dismiss the suggestion that the finest cuisine can be found there. Her bordering seas offer not only breathtaking coastlines, but an abundance of fresh seafood; her picturesque, rolling vineyards provide outstanding wines; and her lush, green farmlands produce an array of the freshest vegetables, the healthiest livestock, and, consequently, the finest dairy products. But this is not enough to secure France's place at the pinnacle of the culinary world. Such international renown comes from the country's everlasting love affair with food.

French cuisine can be as simple or as fancy as the cook desires, but quality is never compromised. Unlike Americans who cultivate bland corn on the cob and tasteless strawberries in the off-season for year-round availability, the discerning French happily let nature take its course, and enjoy its bounty only at the point of perfection. A vigilant eye is kept on crops to determine peak harvest times. For the thin French bean this means an early harvest, when it is most tender. Also, to ensure freshness the shipment of all food cargo is given top priority, for chefs as well as everyday cooks demand the freshest ingredients.

On the following pages we present French cuisine as it is enjoyed in France today. We begin with recipes and tips for basic stocks and pastry doughs (with shortcuts for both), and a discussion on cheese and its ever-important role in French cuisine. Three diverse menus that introduce a variety of French cooking techniques follow and put all of these essentials to use. We include all of your favorites, as well as classic dishes with an updated twist. *Nouvelle cuisine* of the 1970s, while now passé, gave chefs the freedom to experiment with exotic foods from around the globe. Once started, the quest for new flavors never ended. Mangos, papayas, ginger, and star anise are jut a few of the surprises that have recently surfaced in the restaurants of Paris, and here you will find these and other foreign accents.

Let our Summer Dinner *à la Campagne* take you to southern France, where fresh herbs, juicy tomatoes, firm eggplant, and baby greens combine to produce the aromas and flavors of the region. From the flaky Provençale tart, to the sautéed herb-coated chicken with *shiitake* mushroom and wine sauce, to the frozen orange mango soufflé, this innovative meal truly captures the freshness of summer.

Our next menu honors the French custom of Sunday Lunch *en Famille*, a time set aside for families to gather and enjoy hours of good food and conversation. A seafood soup delicately flavored with fennel, orange peel, and saffron is followed by succulent braised pork and cabbage with a savory lentil vinaigrette side dish. We then present a "salade courante" of three garden herbs—light, simple, and punctuated with fresh goat cheese! And for dessert, our very pretty apple tart is sure to please every member of your family.

Finally, we offer an inspired *Buffet de Fête* for a very special occasion. Our artichoke and cheese won ton starters add a touch of Eastern flair and can be either passed as an hors d'oeuvre or added to the buffet table. The feast continues with a fanciful tricolor fish terrine, a hearty beef bourguignon, and a robust cheese tray. (See our discussion on French cheeses, page 260, for selection ideas.) Our colorful tropical fruit mosaic and miniature éclairs with *ganache* lightly satisfy the sweet tooth as we bring our gathering to a close.

Perhaps these pages will unlock a few mysteries of French cooking and allow you to enjoy it all the more. As our photographs of the land and its cuisine indicate, a bit of France could enrich all our lives. We invite you to experience the sights, flavors, and aromas of this exceptional country.

Essentials of French Cooking

BASIC STOCKS

Classic French chefs refer to their basic stock preparations as *fonds de cuisine* (foundations of cooking) because they simply could not cook without them. For that matter, even the most unassuming French cooks consider homemade stocks the basis of many of their dishes.

While everyone knows that these basic stocks are instrumental in producing delicious soups, they go far beyond this service. For example, a stock becomes an essence, or a glaze, when it is boiled down. When a *roux* or other binding substance is added to a basic stock, a fundamental sauce is created, and a host of different sauces are derived from these stocks. Our menus use the stock recipes below in a variety of ways: to make a marvelous soup (Seafood Soup with Pistou, page 274); to flavor a delightful mushroom and wine sauce (Sautéed Chicken Breasts with Shiitake Mushrooms and Herbes de Provence, page 266); to braise a tender entrée (Braised Pork and Savoy Cabbage, page 275); and to prepare a hearty, well-seasoned stew—the French *ragôut* (Beef Bourguignon with Star Anise and Ginger, page 284).

Below are three of the most essential stocks—chicken, beef, and fish—the only ones you will need to prepare our three menus. They are easily made from fowl, meat, or fish bones, with vegetables, herbs, and water, and they simmer on your stove-top with minimal supervision.

Homemade stocks keep in the refrigerator for days (see recipes for procedure) or freeze for several weeks. To freeze, cool the stock, skim off the fat, and divide the chilled stock among small containers so it can be thawed quickly. You may even want to make frozen stock cubes in ice trays to have smaller amounts of stock readily available for handy use in sauces and soups. Remove the frozen cubes from the trays and store them in sealed plastic bags for easy access.

Taking the time to prepare these essential stocks "from scratch" will make a remarkable difference in the finished dish. If, however, you simply do not have the time to attend to a simmering pot for hours, we offer quick alternatives that take a fraction of the cooking time. While not quite as "full-bodied" as the classic stocks, these short-cuts provide a homemade taste that is fresher, lighter, and often less salty than the canned variety.

CHICKEN STOCK

It is perfectly acceptable to collect and freeze chicken parts and bones on an "as you go" basis until you have enough of them to make a stock. If you don't have a supply in your freezer, however, packaged chicken necks and backs have meaty bones that make a good stock.

Chicken Stock

4 pounds meaty chicken bones, and chicken backs, wings, necks, or a combination, chopped into 2-inch pieces
2 cups (about 1 large) white and pale green part of leek, well washed and chopped
1 whole onion, peeled and stuck with 3 cloves
2 carrots, peeled and quartered
2 celery ribs, including the leaves, cut into 1-inch pieces
8 parsley stems
½ teaspoon dried thyme, crumbled
½ teaspoon peppercorns
2 bay leaves

In a kettle combine all of the ingredients with 3 quarts cold water and simmer the mixture, partially covered, skimming the froth, for 3 hours. Add boiling water if necessary to keep the ingredients barely covered. Strain the stock through a fine sieve into a bowl, pressing hard on the solids, and let it cool. Chill the chicken stock and remove the fat. The stock keeps, covered and chilled, for 1 week if it is brought to a boil every 2 days and then allowed to cool to warm, uncovered, before being chilled again. The stock keeps, frozen, for 3 months. Makes about 8 cups.

Quick Chicken Stock

1 cup finely chopped onion or the white part of leek
⅓ cup finely chopped celery
2 tablespoons finely chopped carrot
⅓ cup dry white wine
3 cups canned low-sodium chicken broth
8 parsley stems
¼ teaspoon dried thyme, crumbled
6 peppercorns
2 cloves
1 bay leaf

In a saucepan combine all of the ingredients and simmer the mixture, partially covered, for 20 minutes. Strain the stock through a fine sieve into a bowl, pressing hard on the solids. Makes about 3 cups.

BEEF STOCK

When choosing meaty beef bones for your stock, the tougher, less expensive cuts of meat should be used. Remember to ask your butcher to saw the beef bones into 2-inch pieces for maximum flavor. As our recipe indicates, the bones are baked in a hot oven until they turn a deep brown to ensure a nicely browned stock.

Beef Stock

4 pounds meaty beef bones (cut from the shank, neck leg, or knuckle), sawed into 2-inch pieces
1 pound unpeeled onions (about 2 large), quartered
2 unpeeled carrots, quartered
1 unpeeled garlic bulb, halved crosswise
2 ribs of celery, cut into 1-inch slices
1½ cups chopped tomatoes or a 28-ounce can tomatoes, drained and chopped
12 parsley stems
2 teaspoons dried thyme, crumbled
1 teaspoon peppercorns
6 cloves
3 bay leaves

Spread the beef bones, the onions, the carrots, and the garlic in a flameproof baking pan, brown them well in a preheated 450° F. oven, for 25 to 30 minutes, and transfer them to a kettle. Add 2 cups water to the pan, deglaze the pan over high heat, scraping up the brown bits, and add the liquid to the kettle with 14 cups cold water and the remaining ingredients. Bring the liquid to a boil and skim the froth. Simmer the mixture, partially covered, adding boiling water to keep the ingredients barely covered, for 4 to 5 hours, or until the stock is reduced to about 8 cups. Strain the stock through a fine sieve into a bowl, pressing hard on the solids, and let it cool. Chill the beef stock and remove the fat. The stock keeps, covered and chilled, for 1 week if it is brought to a boil every 2 days and then allowed to cool to warm, uncovered, before being chilled again. The stock keeps, frozen, for 3 months. Makes about 8 cups.

Quick Beef Stock

1 cup finely chopped onion
½ cup finely chopped celery
¼ cup finely chopped carrot
1 to 2 garlic cloves, chopped
1 tablespoon unsalted butter
½ cup dry white wine
3 cups canned low-sodium beef broth
2 teaspoons tomato paste
8 parsley stems
½ teaspoon dried thyme, crumbled
12 peppercorns
2 cloves
1 bay leaf

In a saucepan cook the onion, the celery, the carrot, and the garlic in the butter over moderate heat, stirring often, until the vegetables are golden brown. Add the remaining ingredients and simmer the mixture, partially covered, for 20 minutes. Strain the stock through a fine sieve into a bowl, pressing hard on the solids, and skim the surface to remove the fat. Makes about 3 cups.

FISH STOCK

If possible, choose a variety of fish bones, heads, and trimmings to make your stock. Just remember to avoid fatty fish (mackerel, shad, herring, and bluefish) which will create an oily stock. Remove any traces of the liver and cut out and remove the gills. And, finally, be careful not to overcook the fish stock; it can turn bitter if cooked for more than the 20 minutes we prescribe.

2 cups (about 1 large) white and pale green
    part of leek, well washed and chopped
1 medium onion, sliced
¼ pound mushrooms, sliced
1 tablespoon unsalted butter

2 pounds bones and trimmings of any white
    fish such as sole, flounder, or whiting,
    chopped into 2-inch pieces
1 cup dry white wine
12 parsley stems
½ teaspoon dried thyme, crumbled
½ teaspoon peppercorns
2 bay leaves

In a large saucepan cook the leek, the onion, and the mushrooms in the butter over moderate heat, stirring occasionally, until the onion is softened. Add the remaining ingredients and 9 cups cold water, bring the liquid to a boil, skimming the froth, and cook the stock over moderate heat for 20 minutes. Strain the stock through a fine sieve into a bowl, pressing hard on the solids, let it cool to warm, and chill it, covered. The stock keeps, covered and chilled, for 1 week if it is brought to a boil every 2 days and then allowed to cool to warm, uncovered, before being chilled again. The stock keeps, frozen, for 3 months. Makes about 8 cups.

Quick Fish Stock

1 cup bottled clam juice
½ cup dry white wine
1 small onion or the white part of 1 leek, sliced
8 parsley stems
¼ teaspoon dried thyme, crumbled
6 peppercorns
1 bay leaf

In a saucepan combine all of the ingredients and 2 cups cold water, bring the liquid to a boil, and simmer the stock for 20 minutes. Strain the stock through a fine sieve into a bowl and let it cool. Makes about 2½ cups.

If time is very short, simply combine the clam juice, the white wine, and 2 cups water and use it in place of the fish stock. It will not be as flavorful as the above recipe, but in a pinch it will work.

BASIC PASTRY DOUGHS

B. Charlton

*T*here are three types of pastry doughs that appear again and again in French cooking—plain, puff, and *choux*. You may already be familiar with *pâte brisée* (page 229), the plain dough used throughout our recipe collection. Now we would like to introduce you to the sweet version of this tender dough, *pâte sucrée*, which is widely used in France for tart-making. Perhaps the ease of our warm Apple Tart recipe (page 276) will entice you to make this sweet dough. When it comes to puff pastry, the busy cook may want to leave the classic recipe to a pastry chef. Instead we would like to share a "quick" puff pastry recipe that is more accessible than its classic counterpart. You will need this flaky pastry to make our Pissaladière (page 266), a fabulous fresh herb, tomato, and roasted garlic tart from Provence. Fi-

nally, we provide a simple recipe for *pâte à chou*, a dough that makes those famous cream puffs, as well as our Miniature Éclairs with Ganache (page 286). But this is just the beginning! *Choux* pastry can be piped into many different shapes and filled with various heavenly creams; it also appears in *quenelles* (fish dumplings), classic fish mousses, and *pommes dauphine* as a binding agent.

How often have you seen a perfectly decorated and glazed French tart, or a spectacular pyramid of *profiteroles*, or glorious *bouchées* (puff pastry shells) filled with everything from seafood to fresh fruit, and dismissed making them yourself because it all looked much too difficult? The insights and recipes that follow will give you confidence, and prove that these dishes are, indeed, very doable.

PÂTE SUCRÉE

Pâte sucrée is a sweet, rich, firm dough used in classic tart recipes. Unlike its unsweetened cousin, *pâte brisée*, an egg is added for richness and color, and it is combined with sugar for a cookie-like texture. We encourage you to blend the pastry dough with your hands, especially if you have never done so before. Just remember to use well-chilled butter and to work quickly using only your fingers (warm palms will soften the dough and make it sticky).

After the dough is combined and formed into a ball, you will knead it briefly. The correct method is called *fraisage*: simply smear about ¼ cup of the dough away from you with the heel of your hand to blend the dough ingredients thoroughly. This process should be continued until the whole ball of dough is completely blended in this manner.

Pâte Sucrée

1½ cups all-purpose flour
¼ cup sugar
¼ teaspoon salt
1 stick (½ cup) cold unsalted butter,
    cut into bits
1 large egg, beaten lightly
¼ teaspoon vanilla
1 to 2 tablespoons ice water

In a large bowl with your fingertips or with 2 knives blend the flour, the sugar, the salt, and the butter until the mixture resembles coarse meal. Add the egg, the vanilla, and 1 tablespoon of the water, toss the mixture until the liquid is incorporated, adding 1 more tablespoon of water if the mixture is dry, and form the dough into a ball. Knead the dough lightly with the heel of your hand against a smooth surface for a few seconds to distribute the fat evenly and re-form it into a ball. Chill the dough, wrapped in wax paper or plastic wrap, for 1 hour.

To Roll Out Plain Dough
(Pâte Brisée and Pâte Sucrée)

Place the dough on a lightly floured, smooth surface, (marble is ideal as it keeps the dough cool). If the butter in the dough is too hard, beat the dough with the rolling pin to soften it slightly. Knead the dough quickly into a flat circle. Roll out the dough, always rolling from center to edge, and flour the round. (Place the pin just below the center of the dough and apply gentle pressure. With a firm stroke, and rolling away from you, roll the dough to within 1 inch of the far edge. Lift and turn the dough one-quarter turn and continue the process, lightly flouring the surface when necessary, until the circle is ⅛-inch thick and 2 inches larger than your baking pan.) Brush off excess flour from the top of the dough, loosely roll the dough up on a rolling pin, and transfer it to your pan. Unroll the dough and brush off the excess flour.

PÂTE À CHOU

Pâte à chou is a simple dough made in minutes on the stove-top. This paste is typically used to make cream puff cases, but it can also be piped into different shapes to make everything from tiny appetizers, to chocolate éclairs, to a giant pastry ring. The only tricky part of making *choux* pastry is gauging the amount of egg to be added to the cooked ball of dough. The number of eggs needed will vary depending upon the size of the eggs, the type of flour, and the amount of water that evaporates as the dough forms in the saucepan. Just enough egg must be added to the batter to form a paste that stands in soft peaks and falls easily from the spoon. As the dough is heated in the oven, the eggs cause the dough to puff into a case that is crusty on the outside, and soft and doughy on the inside.

Pâte à Chou

1 stick (½ cup) unsalted butter, cut into pieces
¼ teaspoon salt
1 cup all-purpose flour
4 to 5 large eggs

In a heavy saucepan bring 1 cup of water to a boil with the butter and the salt over high heat. Reduce the heat to moderate, add the flour all at once, and beat the mixture with a wooden spoon until it leaves the sides of the pan and forms a ball. Transfer the mixture to a bowl and beat in 4 eggs, one at a time, beating well after each addition (the batter should be stiff enough to just hold soft peaks). If the batter is too stiff, break the remaining egg into a small bowl, beat lightly, and add just enough of it to the batter to thin it to the proper consistency. Makes about 2½ cups dough.

QUICK PUFF PASTE

Puff pastry dough bakes into crisp, light, flaky perfection many times its original thickness. Making classic puff paste can be a trying ordeal that requires a marathon of rolling, folding, and waiting before the buttery dough is distributed into hundreds of individual layers. Even the French rely on professional pastry chefs to make their beloved pastries, so we feel justified in offering a shortcut to this delicate pastry dough.

Our quick puff paste recipe saves half the preparation time of the classic dough by blending the butter into the flour in coarse meal-sized pieces. The result is less rolling and folding, and therefore less resting time (required to ease the elasticity built up in the dough between "turns," see recipe below).

Remember to form the dough with well-chilled butter and ice water. This will ensure a cold dough that is easy to handle. Also, try to handle the dough as little as possible to prevent overworking, and to use as little flour as possible when rolling out the dough for a more tender pastry. If the dough becomes too difficult to handle, chill it for about 20 minutes before proceeding.

A cold surface is vital when making a dough that contains so much butter. A piece of marble is ideal; it should be large enough to roll out the 12- by 6-inch rectangles of dough, but small enough to chill in the refrigerator before and while the dough chills and rests.

Quick Puff Paste

2 cups all-purpose flour sifted with
  ½ teaspoon salt
2 sticks (1 cup) cold unsalted butter,
  cut into bits
½ cup ice water

In a large bowl with your fingertips or with 2 knives blend the flour mixture and the butter until the mixture resembles very coarse meal. Add the ice water and form the dough into a ball. Dust the dough with flour and chill it, wrapped in wax paper, for 1 hour.

On a floured surface roll the dough into a 12- by 6-inch rectangle, dusting it with flour if it sticks to the rolling pin. Fold the top third of the rectangle over the center and the bottom third over the top, forming a 6- by 4-inch rectangle. Press down the top edge of the rectangle with the rolling pin so it adheres, turn the dough seam side down, and brush any excess flour from the dough. With an open side facing you roll the dough out again into a 12- by 6-inch rectangle and fold it into thirds as before. This completes 2 "turns." Make 2 more turns, chilling the dough until it is firm but not hard (about 20 to 30 minutes between turns) and always starting with the seam side down and an open end facing you. Chill the dough, wrapped in wax paper, for at least 30 minutes or up to 3 days. The dough may be frozen.

THE CHEESE COURSE

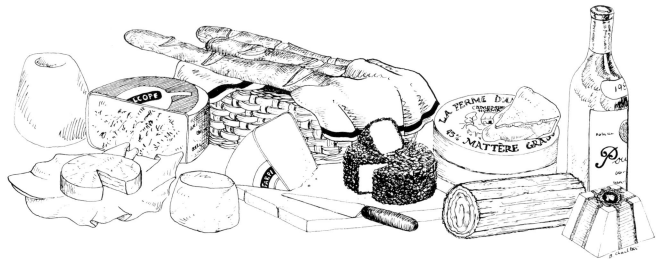

General Charles de Gaulle once quipped: "No one can simply bring together a country that has 265 kinds of cheese," and indeed the bounty of French cheeses seems to be ever growing. With now over 370 varieties, the French take a special pride in this happy abundance, and as with their vineyards, they consider cheese a gift from nature. In the United States we often think of cheese as a pleasant offering at a buffet table or a convenient snack at a cocktail party, but to the average Frenchman, who consumes 40 pounds of cheese each year, it is a way of life and worthy of its own honored place as a separate course in any complete menu.

Usually served after the salad and before dessert, the cheese course is a natural reflection of the typical French meal containing several small-portioned courses of various flavors. Plain, crusty French bread is always offered to ensure that the flavor of the cheese is highlighted, while fruit is served separately or with dessert, leaving the palate free to savor the nuances of different varieties.

Depending upon the size of the gathering, a varying number of different types of cheeses must be carefully chosen. Deciding which cheeses to serve with the meal can be an elaborate process, but there are a few guidelines that should be followed with any menu. The French emphasize the importance of the cheese course as a part of a whole menu, where the flavors must complement, not overwhelm, other parts of the meal. Therefore, it is important to serve milder cheeses such as creamy Vacherin Mont d'Or after a light veal or chicken entrée, while you may include a stronger

cheese, such as spicy Dauphin, after a heavier beef entrée or a highly seasoned meal. (Also, the wine that is served with your cheese should not be lighter than the wine served with the entrée, but it can be bolder if the cheese, such as Roquefort, requires it.)

When choosing cheeses for your tray, a mixed assortment should be selected to provide for the varying tastes of your guests, and an effort should also be made to combine different types, textures, and shapes. Your cheese tray should include an interesting mixture, such as a soft cheese, a *double-* or *triple-crème*, a hard cheese, and a blue; or a cow's milk, a goat's milk, and a sheep's milk cheese.

The incredible array of French cheeses can be overwhelming, but you can purchase an intelligent variety without being a cheese expert. If possible, try to establish a relationship with your local cheese shop owner, who will allow you to taste the cheese before you buy it. Also be aware that the flavor of a particular type of cheese may change depending on the time of year it is made. For example, "the French Cheddar," Cantal, is fruitier in the summer than in the fall. The character and flavor of any cheese depends on individual cheese-making methods within a particular geographical area. Vegetation, climate, rainfall, subsoil, breed of cow, goat, or sheep, and length of aging all contribute to the flavor of the final product. Although it is not generally known, cheeses are just as seasonal as produce, and French chefs meticulously choose cheeses that are at their peak at any given time of year. Brie, for example, is best from December through March. This does not mean that the cheese is not available at other times of the year, but if it is not at its prime, why settle for less than the best?

Also, especially when purchasing soft cheeses, try to buy only as much as you will need for a day or two, and keep them wrapped at room temperature. Once a soft cheese is refrigerated it loses its moisture and will never regain its proper consistency. If you must store cheeses, they should be tightly wrapped in plastic, chilled, and rewrapped in fresh plastic after every use to lock in moisture.

Attaining the fullest flavor of cheese may begin with your purchase at the cheese shop, but serving your cheese properly is just as important. Cheese is always best when served at room temperature. Soft cheeses, such as Camembert, warm up in a third of the time as hard cheeses. So, if you have refrigerated your cheeses, be aware that you may have to allow different amounts of time for them to reach room temperature.

When arranging your tray, avoid mixing flavors by placing the mild cheeses well apart from the stronger varieties, and provide a separate serving knife for each cheese as well. Since the proper moisture of cheese is so important to its flavor, do not cut the cheese into pieces ahead of time. If you have a whole wheel and feel that your guests will be reluctant to make the first cut, do so yourself to start them off.

For our *Buffet de Fête* for twelve, we have selected the six cheeses below for a total of about three pounds. This will give your guests a pleasant variety, and yet not spoil the dessert that will follow. The flavorful artichoke and cheese won ton starters and hearty beef bourguignon entrée call for a full array of cheeses that allows us to combine the mild Explorateur *triple-crème* with the full-flavored Livarot. The cheeses should be tasted in ascending order to fully appreciate the subtleties of each.

• *Explorateur* (*triple-crème*): Made in the Ile-de-France, this creamy cow's milk cheese has a slightly tart aftertaste. It has a supple, edible rind and the interior is a pale yellow color. When ripe, it should be rich and buttery, but not oozing. If Explorateur is unavailable, the more widely available St. André is a good substitute.

• *Crottin de Chavignol* (goat's milk): From Chavignol in the province of Berry, this nugget-sized cheese is widely available fresh or aged. Younger crottins may be creamy enough to spread, but as they age they become firm to hard in texture and sharper in taste.

Shaped like a small flattened ball, it has a pale tan rind with white patches and a strong smell. Any *chèvre frais* (fresh goat's cheese) that is available would also be a good choice.

• *Mimolette Français* (cow's milk): The clean, nutty flavor of this cow's milk cheese from Normandy is a pleasant accompaniment to any tangy cheese. It is a mild cheese with a deep orange color and a firm, slightly oily texture. Avoid cracks in the rind, holes in the cheese, and a rancid or sharp flavor.

• *Pyrénées Bredis* (sheep's milk): This firm and oily *bredis* (sheep's milk) cheese from the Pyrénées region in the south of France should be requested by brand name, such as "Prince de Claverolle" or "Etorki," to avoid confusion with the cow's milk cheese from the same area. This mild-flavored cheese has a thin, inedible, pale tan rind and a yellow interior.

• *Livarot* (washed): This hearty, spreadably soft Normandy cheese comes in rust-colored rounds that are typically covered with five blades of grass. It is often called "Le Colonel" because the grass matches the stripes on a colonel's cuff. This cheese has a pronounced, pungent flavor and a strong smell. Avoid a dry or sticky rind, holes, runniness, or a putrid odor. If unavailable, Pont l'Eveque and Chaumes are both good substitutes.

• *Fourme d'Ambert* (blue): This creamy cow's milk cheese from the Auvergne region has a pronounced savoriness. Less crumbly and sharper than Roquefort, this blue cheese may be slightly bitter. Watch out for a cracked or sticky rind, a grainy texture, and excessive bitterness. If Fourme d'Ambert is unavailable, the less sharp Bleu d'Auvergne from the same region is a good substitute.

Of course you may choose other cheeses of similar flavor that will also complement our *Buffet de Fête*. If you do not have a cheese shop nearby, do not be disheartened—cheese is available through mail order. From the mild Camembert of Normandy to the spicy Castillon of the Pyrénées, the French are blessed with cheeses for every taste, whim, or fancy, and no menu that truly celebrates the flavors of France should be without them.

A SUMMER DINNER
À LA CAMPAGNE

Pissaladière

Rosé de Bandol   *Suprêmes de Poulet Sautés aux Shiitakes et aux Herbes de Provence*
Domaine Tempier '90

Gratin d'Aubergines, Courgettes, et Tomates

Purée de Pommes de Terre au Fenouil

Salade Mesclun

Muscat de   *Soufflé Glacé de Mangues et Sauce au Gingembre*
Beaumes-de-Venise

Gordes in the Lubéron

Suprêmes de Poulet Sautés
aux Shiitakes et aux
Herbes de Provence; Gratin
d'Aubergines, Courgettes, et
Tomates; Purée de Pommes
de Terre au Fenouil

Pissaladière

Soufflé Glacé de Mangues et Sauce au Gingembre

Pissaladière
(Provençale Onion, Tomato, and Anchovy Tart)

quick puff paste (page 259)
1 pound onions (about 3 medium), sliced thin
mixed herbs, 1½ teaspoons each minced fresh
    basil, thyme, and rosemary, or ½ teaspoon
    of each dried, crumbled
4 tablespoons olive oil
a 14½-ounce can tomatoes, drained and
    chopped
1 head roasted garlic (procedure follows),
    halved crosswise and flesh pressed out
2 tablespoons minced fresh basil leaves or
    parsley
⅓ cup freshly grated Parmesan
½ pound firm ripe tomatoes (about 2 medium),
    seeded and cut into ⅛-inch-thick slices
a 2-ounce can flat anchovies, drained and
    halved lengthwise
20 pitted black Niçoise or Kalamata olives
mixed minced fresh basil, thyme, or rosemary
    to taste for garnish

On a lightly floured surface roll the chilled quick puff paste into a rectangle about 12 by 16 inches and ⅛-inch thick. Gently roll the pastry onto the rolling pin, unroll it onto a dampened baking sheet, and chill the dough for 30 minutes.

In a skillet cook the onion with the mixed herbs and salt and pepper to taste in 2 tablespoons of the olive oil over moderate heat, stirring occasionally, until it is golden. Add the tomatoes and cook the mixture, over moderate heat, stirring until the liquid is evaporated. Stir in the garlic and the fresh basil. *The onion mixture may be prepared 1 day ahead, covered, and chilled.*

Brush the edges of the pastry with water and fold them over to form a border about 1-inch wide. With the tines of a fork score the border and prick the center of the tart at ¼-inch intervals.

Sprinkle the inside of the tart with 2 tablespoons of the cheese and distribute the onion mixture over it. Sprinkle the onions with 2 more tablespoons of the cheese, top with the sliced tomatoes, and brush the tomatoes with the remaining oil. Decorate the top of the tart with the anchovies and the olives. Bake the tart in a preheated 450° F. oven for 30 to 35 minutes, or until the pastry is golden and crisp. Sprinkle the warm tart with the remaining Parmesan and fresh herbs. Serve the tart warm or at room temperature. Serves 6.

Roasted Garlic

1 medium head of garlic
1 tablespoon olive oil

Remove the papery outer skin of the garlic without separating the cloves, put it on a piece of aluminum foil, and spoon the oil over it. Wrap the garlic in the foil and bake it in a preheated 350° F. oven for 1 hour.

Suprêmes de Poulet Sautés aux Shiitakes et aux Herbes de Provence
(Sautéed Chicken Breasts with Shiitake Mushrooms and Herbes de Provence)

3 whole chicken breasts (about 3¾ pounds),
    halved, boned, but not skinned
2 tablespoons olive oil
2 tablespoons unsalted butter
1 tablespoon herbes de Provence or
    1 teaspoon each dried thyme, marjoram,
    and rosemary, crumbled
¼ teaspoon fennel seed, crushed
⅓ cup minced shallot
½ pound *shiitake* mushrooms, sliced
2 large garlic cloves, minced
½ cup dry white wine
1½ cups chicken stock (page 255) combined
    with 2 teaspoons arrowroot
2 tablespoons finely chopped fresh chives

Pat the chicken dry and season it with salt and pepper. In a large skillet heat the olive oil and 1 tablespoon of the butter over moderately high heat until it is hot. Add the chicken, skin side down, and sauté it for 3 minutes, or until the skin is golden. Turn the chicken, sprinkle it with the herbes de Provence and the fennel seed, and cook it, covered, over moderate heat for 6 to 8 minutes more, or until it is springy to the touch. Transfer the chicken to a platter and keep it warm, covered loosely.

Add the shallot to the skillet and cook it, stirring, over moderate heat for 1 minute. Add the mushrooms and the garlic and cook the mixture, stirring occasionally, for 2 minutes. Add the wine and boil it until it is reduced to 2 tablespoons. Stir the stock mixture, add it to the skillet, and boil it until it is reduced by half. Swirl in the remaining butter and the chives. Drain the chicken juices from the platter into the skillet, stir the sauce, and spoon it over the chicken. Serves 6.

Gratin d'Aubergines, Courgettes, et Tomates
(Eggplant, Zucchini, and Tomato Gratin)

2 medium onions, chopped
4 tablespoons olive oil
1 green or red bell pepper (about ½ pound),
    cut into 1-inch pieces
1 eggplant (about 1 pound), trimmed and
    cut into 1-inch pieces
mixed fresh herbs, 1½ teaspoons each,
    minced savory, basil, and rosemary, or
    ½ teaspoon of each dried, crumbled
a 14½-ounce can tomatoes, drained and
    chopped
3 garlic cloves, minced
2 tablespoons minced fresh basil
1 tablespoon drained capers
1 tablespoon tomato paste
1 pound firm ripe tomatoes, seeded and cut
    into ⅛-inch-thick slices
1 zucchini (about ½ pound), trimmed and cut
    diagonally into ⅛-inch-thick slices
2 tablespoons freshly grated Parmesan

In a saucepan cook the onion with salt and pepper in 2 tablespoons of the oil over moderate heat, stirring occasionally, until it is golden. Add the bell pepper, the eggplant, and half the mixed herbs to the saucepan and cook the mixture, stirring occasionally until the bell pepper is softened. Add the canned tomatoes and the garlic and simmer the mixture, covered, stirring occasionally, for 5 minutes. Increase the heat to medium high and cook the mixture, stirring, until the liquid is evaporated. Stir in the fresh basil, the capers, and the tomato paste. *The vegetable mixture may be prepared up to this point 1 day in advance, covered, and chilled.*

Spoon the vegetable mixture into a 13- by 9- by 2-inch gratin dish and arrange the tomato slices and zucchini slices in alternate rows over the vegetables. Brush the tomatoes and the zucchini with the remaining oil and sprinkle them with the remaining mixed herbs and the Parmesan. Bring the gratin to a simmer over moderate heat and bake it in a preheated 400° F. oven for 30 minutes, or until the zucchini is tender. Broil the gratin under a preheated broiler about 4 inches from the heat for 1 minute or until golden. Serves 6.

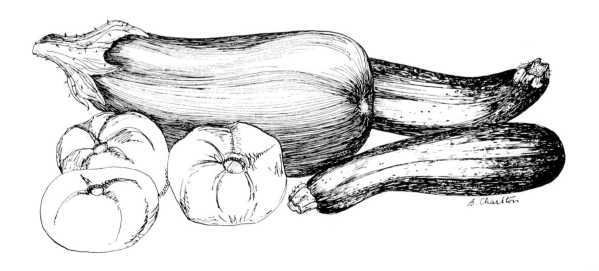

Purée de Pommes de Terre au Fenouil
(Potato Purée with Fennel)

2½ pound russet (baking) potatoes
a ¾ pound fennel bulb, trimmed, cored, and
    chopped, reserving 4 tablespoons minced
    feathery fennel tops
1 teaspoon crushed fennel seed, or to taste
1 tablespoon unsalted butter
3 to 4 tablespoons heavy cream or half-and-half

In a saucepan combine the potatoes, peeled and cut into 1-inch pieces, the fennel, and the fennel seed with salted water to cover, and simmer the mixture, covered, for 20 to 25 minutes, or until very tender. Drain the potato mixture and force it through the medium disk of a food mill into the saucepan. Stir the purée over moderately low heat until it is thick and completely dry and beat in the butter, the heavy cream, the reserved fennel tops, and salt and pepper to taste. Serves 6.

Salade Mesclun
(Salad of Mixed Baby Greens)

1 tablespoon tarragon or white wine vinegar
1 teaspoon Dijon-style mustard
¼ cup extra-virgin olive oil
½ pound mixed baby greens, such as lambs lettuce,
    bibb, red oak, dandelion, nasturtium, and arugula
2 tablespoons mixed minced fresh herbs, such
    as tarragon, chervil, basil, or chives

In a large bowl whisk the vinegar with the mustard and salt and pepper to taste, add the oil in a stream, whisking, and whisk the dressing until it is emulsified. Add the greens and the herbs and toss them well to coat them with the dressing. Serves 6.

Soufflé Glacé de Mangues et
Sauce au Gingembre
(Iced Orange Mango Soufflé with
Gingered Mango Sauce)

flavorless vegetable oil for oiling the collar
2 firm ripe mangoes (about 1½ pounds)
3 tablespoons orange juice
1 teaspoon freshly grated orange zest, or to taste
½ cup sugar
3 large egg whites
1 cup heavy cream
½ cup chopped macadamia nuts, lightly toasted, or
    chopped blanched almonds, lightly toasted

For the sauce
¼ cup coarsely grated fresh gingerroot
¼ cup sugar
2 firm ripe mangoes (about 1½ pounds)
4 tablespoons orange juice
1 teaspoon freshly grated orange zest
whipped cream, fresh mint leaves, chopped
    macadamia nuts, or candied orange peel for
    garnish, if desired

Fit a 1-quart soufflé dish with a 6-inch-wide band of wax paper, doubled and brushed with the oil to form a collar extending 3 inches above the rim.

Peel the mangoes and cut the flesh from the pits. In a food processor combine the mango with the orange juice and the orange zest and purée the mixture until it is smooth. Transfer the purée to a bowl.

In a small heavy saucepan combine the sugar with ¼ cup water, bring the water to a boil over moderate heat, stirring until the sugar is dissolved. Boil the syrup until it registers 240° F. on a candy thermometer (the soft ball stage) and remove the pan from the heat.

While the syrup is boiling, in a bowl with an electric mixer beat the egg whites until they hold soft peaks. With the motor running add the hot syrup in a stream, beating, and beat the whites until cool. In a chilled bowl beat the heavy cream with the electric mixer until it holds soft peaks. Stir the nuts into the mango purée and gently but thoroughly fold the purée mixture into the egg whites, one-third at a time. Fold in the whipped cream. Spoon the mixture into the soufflé dish, swirl the top of the soufflé with the back of a spoon, and freeze it, loosely covered, for 3 hours or until it is frozen. *The soufflé may be made 1 day in advance and kept loosely covered and frozen.*

Make the sauce: In a saucepan combine the gingerroot with the sugar and ½ cup water. Simmer the mixture for 10 minutes and strain the syrup into a bowl. Let the syrup cool.

Peel the mangoes and cut the flesh from the pits. In a food processor combine the mango with the orange juice and purée the mixture until it is smooth. Strain the purée through a medium sieve into a bowl and stir in 3 to 4 tablespoons of the syrup and the orange zest. Chill the sauce, covered, until ready to serve the soufflé. *The sauce may be made 1 day in advance.*

Remove the collar from the soufflé dish and refrigerate the soufflé for 20 minutes before serving. Garnish the soufflé as desired and serve it with the sauce.

SUNDAY LUNCH EN FAMILLE

Riesling d'Alsace '90   *Soupe de Poissons au Pistou et Croûtons à la Parmesane*

Côte de Brouilly
  Domaine du Pavillon   *Porc Braisé au Chou Vert*
    de Chavannes '90

Lentilles Vinaigrette

Salade aux Trois Herbes

Vouvray Moelleux '83   *Tarte aux Pommes*

Tarte aux Pommes, Crème Chantilly

*Soupe de Poissons au Pistou et
Croûtons à la Parmesane
(Seafood Soup with Pistou and
Parmesan Croûtes)*

1½ cups white part of chopped leek
1 cup chopped onion
½ cup minced fennel bulb
4 to 6 large garlic cloves, chopped
¼ cup olive oil
½ cup dry white wine
8 cups white fish stock (page 256) or quick
  white fish stock (page 256)
3 cups peeled, seeded, and chopped fresh
  tomatoes or 3 cups drained and chopped
  canned tomatoes
2 tablespoons tomato paste
2 teaspoons dried basil, crumbled
1 teaspoon dried thyme, crumbled
½ teaspoon fennel seed, crushed
1 bay leaf
a 3-inch strip of orange peel
⅛ teaspoon crumbled saffron threads
6 hard-shelled clams, scrubbed well
6 mussels, scrubbed well and beards removed
2 pounds skinned firm-fleshed white fish
  steaks or fillets, such as monkfish, halibut,
  red snapper, or cod, cut into 2-inch pieces
pistou (recipe follows)
Parmesan croûtes (recipe follows) as an
  accompaniment, if desired

In a large kettle cook the leek, the onion, the fennel, and the garlic in the olive oil over moderate heat, stirring occasionally, for 5 minutes. Add the wine, the fish stock, the tomatoes, the tomato paste, the herbs, the orange peel, the saffron, and salt and pepper to taste, bring the liquid to a boil, and simmer the mixture, stirring and skimming occasionally, for 45 minutes. Force the soup through the medium disk of a food mill into a bowl, or purée it in batches, in a food processor.

Return the soup to the kettle and bring it to a simmer. Add the clams and the mussels, cover, and cook over moderately high heat for 5 to 6 minutes, or until the clams and mussels have opened. Discard any clams or mussels that have not opened. With a slotted spoon transfer the shellfish to a bowl and keep it warm, covered loosely. Add the white fish to the kettle and simmer the mixture, stirring occasionally, for 5 to 7 minutes, or until the white fish is just firm to the touch.

Divide the shellfish among six bowls and ladle the white fish and soup into the bowls. Drizzle the pistou over each bowl or serve it separately. Serve the soup with Parmesan croûtes, if desired. Serves 6.

Pistou

3 garlic cloves
¼ teaspoon salt
1 cup packed fresh basil leaves,
  minced
¼ cup freshly grated Parmesan
⅓ cup olive oil

In a mortar with pestle purée the garlic with the salt, mashing it to a fine paste. Add the basil and the Parmesan and continue to mash the mixture until it is blended well. Transfer the mixture to a small bowl and whisk in the oil, a little at a time. Continue to whisk the mixture until it is a thick paste.

Alternatively, in a blender or food processor purée the garlic, the salt, the basil, and the Parmesan together, scraping down the sides of the bowl, until the mixture is blended well. With the motor running, add the oil in a stream until the mixture is a thick paste. Makes about ½ cup.

*Croûtons à la Parmesane
(Parmesan Croûtes)*

3 tablespoons unsalted butter
3 tablespoons olive oil
1 loaf of French or Italian bread, cut
  diagonally into ½-inch-thick slices
⅔ cup freshly grated Parmesan

In a small saucepan add the butter and the oil and cook the mixture over moderate heat, stirring, until the butter is melted. Brush the butter mixture on one side of the bread slices, arrange the slices on a baking sheet, and bake them in a preheated 375° F. oven for 10 minutes. Remove the baking sheet from the oven, sprinkle the toasts with the Parmesan, and broil them under a preheated broiler about 6 inches from the heat for 30 seconds to 1 minute, or until the outer edges are golden and the Parmesan begins to melt. Makes about 16 toasts.

Porc Braisé au Chou Vert
(Braised Pork and Savoy Cabbage)

To prepare the pork

1½ teaspoons each minced fresh thyme,
    rosemary, and sage leaves, or ½ teaspoon
    each dried, crumbled
1 garlic clove, minced
a 3-pound rib-end boneless pork loin, rolled
    and tied

2 tablespoons vegetable oil
1 large onion, sliced
1 garlic clove, chopped
3 tablespoons all-purpose flour
½ cup dry white wine
4 cups beef stock (page 255), quick beef stock
    (page 256), or beef broth
1½ teaspoons each minced fresh thyme,
    rosemary, and sage leaves, or ½ teaspoon
    each dried, crumbled
1 bay leaf
4 cloves

For the cabbage

1 large onion, sliced
1 tablespoon vegctable oil
a 2½-pound Savoy cabbage, cored and
    shredded
1½ teaspoons caraway seed
½ cup dry white wine
2 tablespoons white wine vinegar

2 to 3 teaspoons Dijon-style mustard

Prepare the pork: In a bowl combine the thyme, the rosemary, the sage, the garlic, and salt and pepper to taste. Rub the mixture into the pork and chill it, covered with plastic wrap, for several hours or overnight.

In a heavy kettle heat the oil over moderately high heat until it is hot. Season the pork with salt and pepper, and brown it on all sides. Transfer the pork to a platter. Add the onion to the pan and cook it, stirring occasionally, until it is golden. Add the garlic and cook the mixture, stirring, for 1 minute more. Add the flour and cook the mixture, stirring, over moderately low heat for 2 minutes. Add the remaining ingredients and salt and pepper to taste, return the pork to the pan, and bring the liquid to a simmer on top of the stove. Braise the pork, covered, in a preheated 325° F. oven for 1½ hours.

Meanwhile prepare the cabbage: In a large saucepan cook the onion in the oil over moderate heat, stirring, for 5 minutes. Add the cabbage, the caraway seed, and salt and pepper to taste and cook the mixture, stirring, for 3 minutes. Add the white wine and simmer the cabbage, covered, stirring occasionally, for 20 minutes. Add water if the mixture becomes too dry. Add the vinegar to the cabbage and toss to combine. Set aside.

Transfer the braised pork to a platter, strain the stock into a bowl, and skim the surface of fat. Return the stock to the pan, add the cabbage and the pork, and bring the liquid to a simmer on top of the stove. Continue to braise the pork in the oven for 30 minutes more, or until a meat thermometer registers 170° F.

Transfer the pork to a platter, discard the strings, and with a slotted spoon arrange the cabbage around the pork. Boil the stock until it is lightly thickened and whisk in the mustard. Spoon some of the sauce over the pork. Serve the remaining sauce separately. Serves 6.

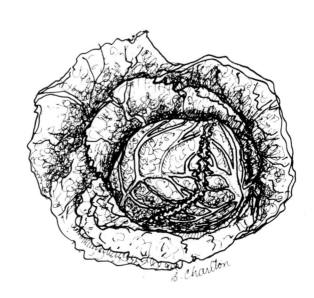

B. Charlton

Lentilles Vinaigrette
(Savory Lentils with Onions, Carrots, Celery, and Chives)

1 cup minced onion
½ cup diced carrot
½ cup diced celery
4 tablespoons olive oil
¾ pound green lentils (about 2 cups), rinsed
　　and picked over
3 cups chicken stock (page 255), quick
　　chicken stock (255), or chicken broth
1½ teaspoons minced fresh thyme, or
　　½ teaspoon dried, crumbled
2 to 3 teaspoons fresh lemon juice
2 to 3 teaspoons Dijon-style mustard
3 tablespoons minced fresh chives, or fresh
　　basil, or fresh parsley leaves

In a large saucepan cook the onion, the carrot, the celery, and salt and pepper to taste in 2 tablespoons of the oil over moderate heat, stirring, until the onion is softened. Add the lentils, the chicken stock, the thyme, and salt and pepper to taste and simmer the mixture, covered, stirring occasionally, for 20 to 25 minutes, or until the lentils are just tender.

In a bowl whisk together the lemon juice and the mustard. Add the remaining oil in a stream, whisking, and whisk until combined. Gently fold the dressing and the chives into the lentil mixture and season it with salt and pepper to taste. Serves 6.

Salade aux Trois Herbes
(Salad of Three Garden Herbs)

6 to 8 tablespoons extra virgin
　　olive oil
lemon juice to taste
1 head soft leaf lettuce, such as Boston, red
　　leaf, or green leaf, separated into leaves,
　　rinsed and patted dry
3 ounces of any three mixed young fresh
　　herbs such as parsley, chervil, tarragon,
　　dill, or fennel, rinsed and patted dry
French cheese, such as goat cheese, Brie, or
　　Camembert

In a large bowl combine 3 tablespoons of the oil, or to taste, with a sprinkling of the lemon juice and salt and pepper to taste. Add the lettuce leaves and gently toss

them to lightly coat them with the dressing. Arrange the leaves on six salad plates.

In a bowl toss the herbs with just enough of the remaining oil to lightly coat them, sprinkle them with lemon juice and salt and pepper to taste, and mound them on the lettuce leaves. Arrange 1 or 2 slices of cheese on each plate. Serves 6.

Tarte aux Pommes
(Apple Tart)

pâte sucrée (page 258)
6 McIntosh apples (about 2 pounds)
2 tablespoons unsalted butter
½ cup sugar
½ teaspoon freshly grated lemon zest
½ teaspoon cinnamon
½ teaspoon freshly grated nutmeg

For the glaze
½ cup apricot preserves, sieved
1 tablespoon Cognac, Calvados, or rum

Crème Chantilly (recipe follows) as an
　　accompaniment, if desired

Roll out the pastry on a lightly floured surface into a round ⅛-inch thick and fit it into a 10-inch tart pan, fluting the edge. Prick the bottom of the shell and chill it for 30 minutes. Reserve any pastry scraps for decorative cutouts, if desired.

Peel, core, and slice three of the apples. In a skillet combine the apples, 1 tablespoon of the butter, ¼ cup of the sugar, the lemon zest, and ¼ teaspoon each of the cinnamon and the nutmeg over moderately low heat, stirring occasionally for 7 to 10 minutes, or until the apples are soft. Gently mash the apples with the back of a spatula or spoon and stir the mixture until most of the liquid is evaporated. Let cool.

Spoon the apple mixture into the tart shell smoothing it into an even layer. Peel, core, and thinly slice the remaining 3 apples and in a bowl toss the slices with the remaining ¼ teaspoon each cinnamon and nutmeg. Arrange the apple slices in concentric circles over the cooked apples, sprinkle the top with 3 tablespoons of the remaining sugar, and dot with the remaining 1 tablespoon butter. Bake the tart on a baking sheet in the lower third of a preheated 400° F. oven for 30 minutes. Transfer the tart to the middle of the oven and continue to bake it for 10 minutes more, or until it is golden and bubbling. Sprinkle the tart with the remaining 1 tablespoon of sugar, cover the edges with foil, and broil it under a preheated broiler about 4 inches from the heat until it is golden.

Make the glaze: In a small saucepan combine the apricot preserves with the Cognac, bring the mixture to a boil over moderate heat, stirring, and simmer the glaze until it is thick. Spoon the glaze over the tart and garnish it with pastry cutouts if desired.

To make the pastry cutouts: Gather the pastry scraps into a ball and roll out the dough on a lightly floured surface into a round ⅛-inch-thick. Stamp out the pastry with a decorative cutter, and place the pastry on a baking sheet. Bake the cutouts in a preheated 400° F. oven for 5 to 7 minutes or until they are golden. Serve the tart warm or at room temperature with Crème Chantilly, if desired.

Crème Chantilly

1 cup chilled heavy cream
2 tablespoons confectioner's sugar
½ to 1 teaspoon vanilla extract

In a chilled bowl whip together the cream, the sugar, and the vanilla to taste with an electric mixer until it holds soft peaks. Serve the cream with the tart. Makes about 2 cups.

BUFFET DE FÊTE

Màcon Lugny '90

Beignets d'Artichauts au Fromage
Sauce aux Poivrons Rouges Grillés

Terrine Tricolore de Poisson
Sauce Concombre aux Herbes

Savigny-les-Beune '87

Boeuf Bourguignon à la Badiane et au Gingembre

Riz au Saffran

Asperges, Tomates, et Poireaux
à l'Huile d'Olive au Basilic

Gevrey-Chambertin '85

Fromages

Mosaïque de Fruits Exotiques avec Sauce Melba

Vin Crèmant de Bourgogne

Éclairs à la Crème Ganache

Talloires on Lake Annecy

From Left to Right: Terrine Tricolore de Poisson; Sauce Concombre aux Herbes;
Beignets d'Artichauts au Fromage; Sauce aux Poivrons Rouges Grillés;
Riz au Saffran; Asperges, Tomates, et Poireaux à l'Huile d'Olive au Basilic;
Boeuf Bourguignon à la Badiane et au Gingembre

Beignets d'Artichauts au Fromage
(Artichoke and Cheese Won Tons)

½ cup finely minced scallion
3 tablespoons unsalted butter
2 tablespoons all-purpose flour
1 cup milk
a 9-ounce package frozen artichoke hearts,
    cooked according to package directions,
    drained well, patted dry, and chopped
⅓ cup freshly grated Gruyère
⅓ cup freshly grated Parmesan
2 teaspoons Dijon-style mustard
48 won ton wrappers (available at Oriental
    markets and many supermarkets), thawed
    if frozen, covered with a dampened
    kitchen towel
vegetable oil for deep-frying
roasted red pepper dip as a accompaniment
    (recipe follows)

In a saucepan cook the scallion in the butter over moderate heat, stirring, until it is softened. Stir in the flour and cook the *roux* over low heat, stirring, for 3 minutes. Add the milk in a stream, whisking vigorously until the mixture is thick and smooth, simmer the sauce for 10 minutes, and transfer it to a bowl. Add the artichoke hearts, the cheeses, the mustard, and salt and pepper to taste to the bowl and stir the mixture until it is combined well. *The filling may be prepared 1 day in advance, covered, and chilled.*

Put 1 won ton wrapper on a work surface with a corner pointing toward you. Put 1 slightly rounded teaspoon of the filling in the center of the wrapper, brush the two adjacent sides lightly with water, and fold the opposite corner over the filling to form a triangle, pressing out the air. Press the edges together firmly, sealing them well. Pick up the pasta, bring together the points at the ends of the long side, and press them together firmly, moistening them if necessary. Make won tons in the same manner with the remaining wrappers and filling, and place them as they are formed in one layer on a floured dish towel. *The won tons may be prepared up to 3 hours in advance, covered with a dampened kitchen towel, and chilled.*

In a deep fryer or kettle fry the won tons in batches in 2 inches of 360° F. vegetable oil, turning them, for 3 to 4 minutes, or until they are golden, and transfer them to paper towels to drain. Serve the won tons with the roasted red pepper dip. Makes about 48 won tons.

Sauce aux Poivrons Rouges Grillés
(Roasted Red Pepper Dip)

1½ pounds red bell peppers (about 3 large),
    roasted (procedure on page 126)
2 tablespoons extra virgin olive oil
1 tablespoon fresh lime juice or lemon juice
cayenne to taste

In a food processor or blender blend the peppers until they are smooth. With the motor running, add the olive oil, the lime juice, the cayenne, and salt to taste. Transfer the dip to a bowl and chill it, covered, for 2 hours or overnight. Serve the dip at room temperature. Makes about 1½ cups.

Terrine Tricolore de Poisson
(Tricolor Fish Terrine)

For the sole and scallop mousseline
¾ pound sole fillet, cut into 1-inch pieces
¾ pound sea scallops
1 teaspoon salt
¼ teaspoon freshly grated nutmeg
¼ teaspoon freshly grated white pepper
1 egg white
1½ cups well-chilled heavy cream

For the salmon mousseline
¾ pound salmon fillet, cut into 1-inch pieces
½ teaspoon salt
⅛ teaspoon freshly grated nutmeg
⅛ teaspoon freshly grated white pepper
1 egg white
½ cup well-chilled heavy cream
¼ pound smoked salmon, diced fine

For the herb mousseline
2 cups loosely packed trimmed spinach
    leaves, rinsed well and drained
¼ cup minced shallot
1 tablespoon unsalted butter
¼ cup minced mixed fresh herbs, such as
    basil, chives, tarragon, chervil, or dill, or a
    combination

fresh herbs such as basil sprigs and chervil
    leaves for the garnish if desired
herbed cucumber sauce (recipe follows) as an
    accompaniment

Make the sole and scallop *mousseline*: In a food processor purée the sole, the scallops, the salt, the nutmeg, and the white pepper until the mixture is smooth. With the motor running add the egg white and purée the mixture until it is combined well. With the motor running add the cream in a stream, and blend the mixture until it is just combined. Transfer the *mousseline* to a bowl and chill it, covered.

Make the salmon *mousseline*: In a food processor purée the salmon, the salt, the nutmeg and the white pepper until the mixture is smooth. With the motor running add the egg white and purée the mixture until it is combined well. With the motor running add the cream in a stream, and blend the mixture until it is just combined. Transfer the *mousseline* to a bowl, fold in the smoked salmon, and chill it, covered.

Make the herb *mousseline*: In a skillet steam the spinach in the water clinging to its leaves, covered, stirring occasionally, over moderately high heat for 30 to 60 seconds until the leaves have wilted. Drain the spinach, refresh it under cold running water, and gently squeeze it dry between paper towels. In the skillet cook the shallot in the butter over moderate heat, stirring occasionally, until it is softened. Add the spinach and cook the mixture, stirring, until it is dry. In a food processor purée the spinach mixture, transfer it to a bowl, and mix it with half of the sole and scallop *mousseline*, the fresh herbs, and salt and white pepper to taste. Chill the herb *mousseline*, covered.

Assemble the terrine: Butter a 2-quart terrine or loaf pan, line the bottom with wax paper, and butter the paper. Spoon the remaining sole and scallop *mousseline* into the terrine and smooth it with a rubber spatula onto the sides and bottom of the pan creating a layer about 1-inch-thick. Add the salmon *mousseline* to the terrine, spreading it into an even layer, and rap the terrine on a hard surface several times to expel any air bubbles. Finally, add the herb *mousseline*, spread it into an even layer and rap the terrine on a hard surface. Cover the terrine with buttered wax paper and seal it tightly with foil.

Put the terrine in a baking pan, add enough water to the pan to come halfway up the sides of the terrine, and bake the terrine in the middle of a preheated 275° F. oven for 1½ hours, or until it is firm to the touch and has shrunk slightly from the sides of the pan. Let the terrine cool to room temperature and chill it overnight. Discard the foil and paper, and pour off the excess liquid. Invert a platter over the terrine and invert the terrine onto it. Blot up the excess liquid with paper towels and let the terrine come to room temperature.

Garnish the terrine with the fresh herbs, if desired. Serve the terrine with the herbed cucumber sauce. Serves 12.

Sauce Concombre aux Herbes
(Herbed Cucumber Sauce)

1 cup plain yogurt
1 cup sour cream
½ pound cucumber (about 1 medium), peeled, seeded, grated, and squeezed dry
⅓ cup finely minced scallion
1 to 2 tablespoons tarragon-flavored vinegar or white wine vinegar
1 to 2 teaspoons Dijon-style mustard
¼ cup minced fresh herbs such as dill, basil, or tarragon
1 to 2 garlic cloves, minced fine
sliced cucumbers and dill sprigs for garnish

In a sieve lined with a double thickness of rinsed and squeezed-dry cheesecloth set over a bowl, let the yogurt drain for 20 minutes.

Meanwhile, in a bowl combine the remaining ingredients and salt and pepper to taste. Stir in the drained yogurt, transfer the sauce to a serving dish, and garnish the top with sliced cucumber and dill sprigs. Cover and chill the sauce until ready to serve. *The sauce may be prepared 4 to 6 hours in advance, covered and chilled.* Makes about 2½ cups.

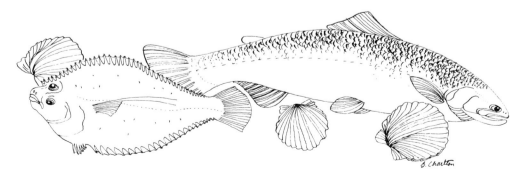

Boeuf Bourguignon à la Badiane et au Gingembre
(Beef Bourguignon with Star Anise and Ginger)

5 pounds lean beef chuck, cut into 2-inch
    pieces

For the marinade
3 cups dry red wine
4 cups beef stock (page 255), quick beef stock
    (page 256), or beef broth
1 large onion, chopped coarse
1 carrot, sliced
6 garlic cloves, sliced
1 teaspoon dried thyme, crumbled
6 whole cloves
1 star anise, or to taste (available at
    Oriental markets and some specialty
    foods shops)
12 parsley stems
¼ teaspoon black peppercorns
2 bay leaves
a 1½-inch piece of fresh gingerroot, peeled
    and cut into slices

4 slices thick-sliced bacon (about 6 ounces),
    chopped
1 tablespoon tomato paste
1¼ pounds pearl onions, peeled
1 tablespoon unsalted butter
1 tablespoon vegetable oil
1¼ pounds mushrooms,
    quartered
3 tablespoons arrowroot

To marinate the beef: In a large bowl combine the beef, the wine, enough of the beef stock to cover the beef, and the remaining marinade ingredients. Chill the mixture, covered, for 4 hours or overnight. Drain the beef, reserving the marinade and vegetables separately, pat the beef dry, and season it with salt and pepper.

In a kettle cook the bacon over moderate heat until it is crisp. Remove the bacon from the kettle, reserving the cooking fat, and set it aside. Heat the bacon fat in the kettle over moderately high heat until it is hot, but not smoking, and cook the beef in it, in batches, over moderately high heat, until it is browned. Transfer the beef as it is browned to a plate. Pour off all but 1 tablespoon of the fat from the kettle. Add the reserved vegetable mixture to the kettle and cook the mixture, stirring, for 3 minutes. Add the reserved marinade liquid, the

remaining beef stock, and the tomato paste, bring the liquid to a boil, and braise the meat, covered, in a preheated 325° F. oven for 2 hours.

Skim the fat from the stew and drain the meat and vegetables, reserving the braising liquid. Return the braising liquid and the meat to the kettle, discarding the vegetables. Add the onions to the kettle, bring the liquid to a boil, and braise the mixture, covered, in the oven for 20 minutes, or until the meat and onions are tender.

Meanwhile, heat the butter and the oil in a large skillet until it is hot, add the mushrooms, and salt and pepper to taste, and cook the mushrooms over moderately high heat, stirring occasionally, for 7 minutes, or until they are firm and have given off their liquid. Add the mushrooms and the reserved bacon to the kettle. *The stew may be prepared up to this point 2 days in advance, covered and chilled. To reheat, simmer the mixture, covered, until it is heated through.*

With a slotted spoon transfer the meat and vegetables to a serving dish, cover it loosely, and keep it warm in a slow oven. Bring the braising liquid in the kettle to a boil and boil it until it is reduced to 3 cups. In a small bowl combine the arrowroot with ¼ cup water and stir it into the simmering liquid. Simmer the sauce, stirring, until it is lightly thickened. Before serving spoon the sauce over the meat and vegetables. Serves 10 to 12.

Riz au Saffran
(Saffron Rice Pilaf)

¼ teaspoon crumbled saffron threads
4½ cups chicken stock (page 255) or quick
    chicken stock (page 255), heated
1½ cups minced onion
3 tablespoons unsalted butter
2½ cups long-grain rice
1 bay leaf
parsley sprigs for garnish if desired

Soak the saffron in the chicken stock for 5 minutes. In a flameproof baking dish cook the onion in the butter over moderate heat, stirring occasionally, until it is softened. Add the rice and cook the mixture, stirring, for 1 minute. Add the chicken stock mixture, the bay leaf, and salt to taste. Bring the liquid to a simmer and bake the rice, covered with a buttered round of wax paper and the lid, in a preheated 350° F. oven, for 20 minutes, or until it is tender. Garnish with parsley sprigs if desired. Serves 10 to 12.

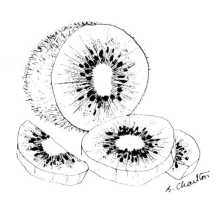

Arrange the asparagus, the tomato slices, and the leeks on a platter, strain the basil oil over the vegetables, and season them with salt and pepper. *The vegetables may be prepared 4 to 6 hours in advance, covered and chilled. Bring them to room temperature before serving.* Sprinkle the vegetables with the lemon juice and minced fresh basil. Serves 10 to 12.

Mosaïque de Fruits Exotiques avec Sauce Melba
(Tropical Fruit Mosaic with Melba Sauce)

1 small pineapple, peeled, cored,
    and sliced
1 papaya, peeled, seeds removed, and sliced
1 mango, peeled and sliced
2 blood oranges or navel oranges, peeled
    and sliced
2 kiwis, peeled and sliced
1 pint strawberries, hulled and halved or
    quartered if large
1 pint raspberries
1 star fruit, sliced
2 tablespoons fresh lemon juice
Melba sauce (recipe follows) as an
    accompaniment

On one large platter or two small platters arrange the fruit decoratively, sprinkle it with the lemon juice, and chill it, covered with plastic, until ready to serve. *The fruit may be assembled 3 to 4 hours in advance.* Serve the fruit with the Melba sauce. Serves 10 to 12.

Sauce Melba
(Raspberry Sauce)

four 10-ounce packages frozen raspberries,
    thawed and drained
1 to 2 tablespoons fresh lemon juice
2 tablespoons superfine granulated sugar,
    or to taste

In a food processor or in a blender purée the raspberries with the lemon juice and strain the sauce through a fine sieve into a bowl, pressing hard on the solids. Stir in the sugar to taste. Cover with plastic wrap and chill until ready to serve. Makes about 2 cups.

Asperges, Tomates, et Poireaux à l'Huile d'Olive au Basilic
(Poached Asparagus with Tomatoes and Leek in Basil Oil)

For the basil oil
2 cups basil leaves, washed and drained
¾ cup extra virgin olive oil

2 pounds asparagus, peeled if large, and
    trimmed
the white and pale green part of 3 leeks, cut
    into ¼-inch-thick diagonal slices, washed
    well and drained (about 2 cups)
6 firm ripe tomatoes (about 1½ pounds) cored
    and cut into ¼-inch slices
fresh lemon juice to taste
1 to 2 tablespoons minced fresh basil

Make the basil oil: In a saucepan of boiling water, blanch the basil leaves for 20 seconds, drain them, and refresh them under cold running water. Gently squeeze dry the basil leaves and transfer them to a blender. With the motor running add the olive oil in a stream and blend the mixture until it is combined well. Transfer the mixture to a bowl. *The basil oil may be prepared up to 1 day ahead, covered and stored in a cool place.*

Tie the asparagus into bundles of about eight spears. In a large saucepan of simmering salted water add the asparagus and simmer them for 6 to 8 minutes, or until they are just tender. With tongs transfer the asparagus to a bowl of ice water and let them cool. Drain them and pat them dry.

Bring the water in the saucepan to a boil, add the leeks, and blanch them for 30 seconds. Drain the leeks, refresh them under cold water, and pat them dry.

Éclairs à la Crème Ganache
(Miniature Éclairs with Ganache)

For the ganache

8 ounces bittersweet chocolate

1 cup heavy cream

1 tablespoon orange-flavored liqueur or
   Cognac, if desired

½ recipe *pâte à chou* (page 258)

egg wash made by beating 1 egg with
   1 teaspoon water

½ cup sliced blanched almonds, chopped
   coarse

confectioners' sugar for garnish

Make the *ganache*: Chop the chocolate into pieces and transfer it to a small bowl. In a saucepan bring the cream to a simmer, add it to the chocolate in a stream, stirring, and stir the mixture until it is smooth. Stir in the liqueur and chill the *ganache*, covered, until it is firm enough to hold shape when piped, about 1½ to 2 hours.

Make the *pâte à chou* and transfer it to a pastry bag fitted with a ½-inch plain tip. Pipe out small éclairs about 2 inches long and 2 inches apart on buttered and floured baking sheets. Brush the tops of the éclairs with the egg wash and sprinkle them with the almonds. Bake the éclairs in a preheated 425° F. oven for 10 minutes. Reduce the heat to 375° F. and bake them for 10 minutes more. Pierce the end of each éclair with the tip of a sharp knife and let the éclairs stand in the turned-off oven for 10 minutes. Transfer them to a rack and let them cool completely. *The éclairs may be made 1 day in advance and kept in an airtight container.*

Assemble the éclairs: With the end of a chopstick or similar instrument make a hole in the end of each éclair. Transfer the *ganache* to a pastry bag fitted with a small plain tip and pipe it into the éclairs through the hole. Chill the éclairs, uncovered, until ready to serve. Before serving, sift the confectioners' sugar over the éclairs. Serves 12.

PART FOUR

A GOURMET ADDENDUM

COOKING WITH SPICES

ature has given us many wonderful gifts, but perhaps one of the most delightful is her treasure trove of spices. Throughout the ages, man has been enchanted by their ethereal qualities. Even the smallest measure of these gems, with their intriguing aromas and lively flavors, adds ''spice'' to our lives.

Every nation of the world has gathered spices native to its land and put them to various uses—in dyes, perfumes, medicines, and eventually in the cuisine. Since ancient times, Europeans traded goods for spices from the Arabian peninsula and East Africa to supplement their limited spice supply. In the Middle Ages ''exotic'' spices of the Far East were brought home by the Crusaders, and an active spice trade that would last for centuries began. Cinnamon, pepper, ginger, turmeric, cardamom, cloves, nutmeg, and mace were brought thousands of miles by camel caravan from their source in the Asian tropics to India, then to Arabia and Egypt, to reach the West.

Europeans were eager to find their own sea route to the East, and many exploratory voyages ensued. One such expedition led by Christopher Columbus resulted in the discovery of the New World instead! There he found allspice and chilies and brought them back to Europe. In 1498, Portuguese explorer Vasco da Gama discovered a sea route to the Spice Islands, making Eastern spices more accessible to the West.

The discovery of different cuisines, and therefore ''new'' spices, is ongoing. During World War II, American soldiers fell in love with the foods of the Mediterranean and the Orient and brought back home a demand for the spices in these cuisines. Shortly thereafter, as international travel became more affordable, Americans travelled abroad in greater numbers. They, too, returned home with a craving for foreign spices, and today the United States is the world's largest spice importer.

In the 1991 edition of *The Best of Gourmet*, our Addendum featured garden herbs and their ability to naturally enhance foods. This year we turn to spices, also natural food awakeners, to reveal their culinary potential. We have selected a variety of spices to please all palates—from sweet cinnamon to hot chilies. You will find those spices that you have known for years, as well as those that you may have never tried.

Spices and herbs are not easily differentiated. *The Oxford English Dictionary* describes a spice as a "strongly flavored or aromatic substance of vegetable origin, obtained from tropical plants, commonly used as condiments . . . aromatic dried roots, bark, buds, seeds, berries, and other fruits." This is not inclusive of all spices, nor is it exclusive of all herbs. Our collection of spices may include a plant or two that you consider an herb, and countless books have been written that will both agree and disagree with you.

As with our discussion of herbs, we have organized spices by botanical family name. Sometimes spice family members have similar physical characteristics, but more often these plants are distant cousins and do not resemble one another. Also, within a family, one plant might be used for its berries, while another is used for its roots or leaves. Usually, however, a spice family shares a similar degree of pungency, and our discussion begins with the milder, aromatic families and progresses to those with more stimulating, sharper flavors. The recipes are an eclectic mix of beverages, hors d'oeuvres, starters, entrées, side dishes, and desserts.

Unfortunately, most spices come from tropical plants that can only grow in torrid climates, but they are readily available at specialty food shops and most supermarkets. Spices should be kept in airtight containers in a cool, dark, dry place. Since they are often displayed on well-lit store shelves, it is best to buy spices where there is a heavy turnover so they can be properly stored as soon as possible. Rarer spices, if found in supermar-

kets, may have lingered on shelves for some time; it is best to purchase them in busy specialty foods shops where they will be readily available and fresh.

If possible, buy spices in whole form to assure that they have not been tampered with—often powdered spices contain inferior ground plants. Also, once a spice is ground, it begins to lose its flavor and aroma, so whenever possible, grind the spice yourself immediately before use. A spice grinder or a mortar and pestle are ideal, as is a coffee grinder, if it is kept for this use only. Whole spices, if properly kept, will stay fresh for a long time. Before purchasing them, however, it is best to make sure that they have not lost their original form and that they do not have a musty smell. Certain spices, such as turmeric and paprika, are not available in whole form and must be bought as a powder. When buying these and other ground spices, make sure that they have not faded in color. Whole or ground, spices should be bought often and in small amounts. Finding a spice market that allows you to buy tiny packets is most desirable.

Spices are generally very potent flavorings, and you will only need a small amount for each recipe. Once you try a spice, you may wish to increase or decrease the quantity for your personal taste. Several of our recipes contain blends of various spices, a practice followed in many different cultures for optimum flavor. Spice blends are used in curries, chili sauces, chutneys, and various condiments.

More and more Americans are experimenting with new spices, and a trip to your local market will show that the variety of available spices is ever-growing. As your own culinary prowess grows, we hope that the following pages will make you take a second look at the spices you know—and entice you to test the unknown. So explore with confidence and let spices bring your cooking to life!

THE MYRTLE FAMILY

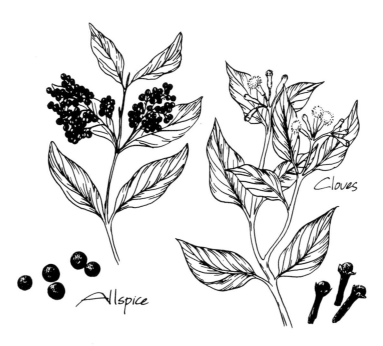

Allspice and cloves, two members of the Myrtle Family, have made their way from native island homes to become popular spices in Western cuisine. Known for their enticing aromas, these tropical flavorings from opposite ends of the globe are used in both sweet and savory dishes.

One of the few native spices of the western hemisphere, allspice was discovered in the Caribbean Islands by Columbus, and carried back to Europe. The spice became particularly popular in England and Scandinavia (where it appears in virtually every dish of a Swedish smorgasbord). Although its name implies that it is made up of more than one spice, allspice is simply the dried berry of the evergreen allspice tree. The berry itself is the "all-spice," containing the flavors of cloves, cinnamon, and nutmeg. Today, Jamaica and Mexico produce most of the world's supply.

The versatility of allspice is seen in traditional British favorites, such as pork and game pies and Christmas puddings. It is also a delightful beverage enhancer. We add allspice to an already flavorful cinnamon and clove brew in our Spiced Tea and Apple Refresher. This naturally sweetened iced tea drink (without sugar) is full of spicy apple flavor—a delicious thirst-quencher on a warm summer's day.

From the Spice Islands in Indonesia, cloves are the nail-shaped unopened flower buds of the evergreen clove tree. These buds are picked as they turn from pale green to pink, and then dried to a deep brown. They were used as a perfume, in medicines, and as a culinary spice by the Chinese in the 3rd century BC. In the Middle Ages, Europeans also used cloves as an antiseptic, and in pomanders as an air-freshener.

Although sweet-smelling, cloves are quite pungent so they should be used sparingly for culinary purposes. Studding a glazed ham with cloves is one of the spice's most popular uses, and our Red Currant and Mustard Glazed Ham with Cloves combines the spice with the sweetness of jam and the sharpness of mustard for an impressive entrée. And, for a bite of sweetness perfumed with the taste of cloves, you must try our Clove-Studded Snowball Cookies (just remember to remove the clove before eating).

Spiced Tea and Apple Refresher

1 cinnamon stick, cracked
2 teaspoons allspice berries
2 teaspoons grated dried orange peel,
    or 1 tablespoon freshly grated orange zest
4 whole cloves
3 teaspoons Darjeeling tea leaves
3 cups apple juice or cider
lemon slices and sprigs of mint for garnish

In a saucepan combine 5 cups of water with the cinnamon, the allspice, the orange peel, and the cloves, bring the liquid to a boil, and simmer the mixture for 10 minutes. Add the tea, cover the pan, and let the tea steep for at least 5 minutes, or until it is cool. Strain the tea into a pitcher and stir in the apple juice. Chill the tea, covered, until ready to serve. Serve the tea over ice cubes and garnish with a slice of lemon and a sprig of mint. Makes 8 cups.

Red Currant and Mustard Glazed Ham with Cloves

a 6½-pound (butt end) ham
40 to 45 whole cloves
½ cup Dijon-style mustard
½ cup red currant jelly
2 tablespoons cider vinegar

With a sharp knife score the ham in a criss-cross pattern and stud it at 1-inch intervals with the cloves. Wrap the ham in foil and bake it in a baking pan in the middle of a preheated 325° F. oven for 1½ hours.

Meanwhile, in a saucepan whisk together the mustard, the red currant jelly, and the vinegar and simmer the glaze mixture, stirring, until it is smooth.

Remove the ham from the oven and increase the oven temperature to 425° F. Unwrap the ham, set it on a rack in the baking pan, and brush it with the glaze. Bake the ham in the oven, basting it frequently with the glaze, for 30 minutes, or until it is deeply browned and crisp. Serves 10 to 12.

Clove-Studded Snowball Cookies

2 sticks (1 cup) unsalted butter, softened
½ cup confectioners' sugar, plus additional
    for sprinkling the cookies
1 egg yolk
1 tablespoon milk
2 teaspoons vanilla
2¼ cups sifted all-purpose flour
30 whole cloves

In a bowl with an electric mixer cream the butter until it is light in color. Add the sugar, a little at a time, and beat the mixture until it is fluffy. In a small bowl whisk together the egg yolk, the milk, and the vanilla. Add the egg yolk mixture to the butter mixture and continue to beat the dough until it is combined. Add the flour, a little at a time, and beat the mixture until it is smooth. Chill the dough, wrapped in plastic, for 1 hour, or until it is firm.

Form the dough into ½-inch balls, arrange the balls about 1 inch apart on baking sheets, and stick a clove in the top of each cookie. Bake the cookies in the middle of a preheated 350° F. oven for 17 to 20 minutes, or until they are firm and very lightly golden. Let the cookies cool on the baking sheets for 5 minutes and transfer them to racks to cool completely. Dust the cookies liberally with the confectioners' sugar and store them in an airtight container. Remove the cloves before eating. Makes about 30 cookies.

THE NUTMEG FAMILY

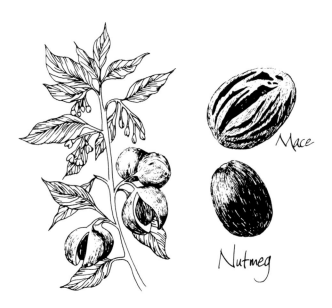

Mace

Nutmeg

utmeg and mace are two distinct spices that come from the fruit of an evergreen tree native to New Guinea and the Spice Islands of Indonesia. Nutmeg is the 1½-inch oval gray-brown kernel found enclosed in a dark brown shell, while mace is the outer crimson-colored lacy growth, or "aril," that surrounds the shell. The aril is dried to a rusty brown and broken into pieces, or "blades."

   Both spices were part of the caravan trade to Alexandria in the 6th century and were probably first brought to Europe by the Crusaders. In the 17th and 18th centuries, Europeans carried silver graters with them to add the freshly grated, sweet-flavored nutmeg to their food, mulled wine, and possets (curdled milk drinks). But this was not all that gave nutmeg its allure. The spice was also consumed in large quantities to create feelings of euphoria as well as hallucinations.

   Mace has a similar taste that combines the flavors of cinnamon and nutmeg. The spice is more powerful in strength than nutmeg, however, and should be used in small amounts. Mace, not gratable at home, is usually sold in ground form; nutmeg, easily gratable, should always be bought in whole kernel form for the fullest flavor.

   Throughout India and Southeast Asia nutmeg is used to flavor meats, while Westerners utilize it in both sweet and savory dishes. The spice adds a warm, sweet taste to our Holiday Eggnog with Nutmeg, as well as to our Rice Pudding with Dried Fruits and Nutmeg, a delicious, creamy dessert. Mace is ideal for adding a touch of smoky flavor to savory dishes such as our Fresh and Smoked Potted Salmon, and to prove the spice's versatility, our colorful Spiced Pumpkin Muffins blend it with ginger and cinnamon for a sweet bread of Eastern flavors.

Rice Pudding with Dried Fruits and Nutmeg

⅔ cup long grain rice
⅛ teaspoon salt
3 large eggs
2 cups milk
½ cup sugar
2 teaspoons vanilla
½ teaspoon freshly grated nutmeg, plus
    additional for garnish
1 package unflavored gelatin (about
    1 tablespoon)
1 cup raisins, chopped dried apricots, dried
    peaches, or other dried fruit, or a
    combination
1 cup heavy cream

In a large heavy saucepan combine the rice and the salt with 4 cups water, bring the mixture to a boil, and boil it, stirring occasionally, until almost all the liquid has evaporated. In a bowl whisk together the eggs, the milk, the sugar, the vanilla, and the nutmeg. Stir the egg mixture into the rice mixture and cook it over moderately low heat, stirring, until it is slightly thickened and reaches 140° F. on a candy thermometer. Do not let the mixture boil. In a small bowl sprinkle the gelatin over ¼ cup cold water and let it soften for 10 minutes. Add the gelatin mixture to the rice mixture and stir until it is combined well.

Transfer the rice mixture to a large bowl and stir in the dried fruit. Chill the mixture, covered with plastic wrap, stirring it occasionally for about 20 minutes, or until it is cool. In a small bowl with an electric mixer whip the heavy cream until it holds soft peaks and fold it into the rice mixture. Chill the pudding for 2 to 3 hours, or until it is cold. The pudding keeps for 3 to 4 days, covered and chilled. Garnish each serving with freshly grated nutmeg. Makes 8 cups.

Holiday Eggnog with Nutmeg

8 large egg yolks
⅔ cup sugar
4 cups milk, scalded
1 teaspoon freshly grated nutmeg, plus
    additional for garnish
1 cup bourbon, whiskey, or brandy, or to taste
2 cups heavy cream

In a bowl with an electric mixer beat the egg yolks until they are thick. Add the sugar, a little at a time, and beat the mixture until it is light and fluffy. Add the scalded milk in a stream, whisking until the mixture is combined, and transfer the mixture to a saucepan. Whisk in the nutmeg and cook the mixture over moderately low heat, whisking, until it is slightly thickened and it reaches 140° F. on a candy thermometer. Do not let the mixture come to a boil. Transfer the mixture to a large bowl and stir in the bourbon to taste. Chill the mixture, covered with plastic wrap, for at least 3 hours or overnight.

Just before serving, in a bowl with an electric mixer whip the heavy cream until it holds soft peaks and fold it into the eggnog. Garnish each serving with freshly grated nutmeg. Makes about 10 cups, serving 16.

Fresh and Smoked Potted Salmon

two 8-ounce salmon steaks, each 1 inch thick
¼ cup dry white wine
3 tablespoons minced shallot
¼ teaspoon ground mace, plus a pinch for
    final seasoning
1 bay leaf
1 stick (½ cup) unsalted butter
¼ pound smoked salmon, chopped
fresh lemon juice to taste
3 tablespoons clarified butter (procedure
    follows) for covering the potted salmon
crackers, melba thins, or toasted croûtes as an
    accompaniment

Arrange the salmon steaks in a buttered flame-proof gratin dish just large enough to hold them in one layer, sprinkle them with the wine, the shallot, the mace, and salt to taste, and top them with the bay leaf and 4 tablespoons of the butter cut into pieces. Bring the wine mixture to a simmer and bake the salmon steaks, covered with foil, in a preheated 350° F. oven for 20 to 25 minutes, turning them once, or until they just flake. With a slotted spoon transfer the salmon steaks to a plate, discard the bay leaf, and remove the skin and bones. Strain the cooking liquid into a bowl and reserve it.

In a food processor combine the salmon steaks and the cooking liquid and process the mixture until it is combined. Add the smoked salmon and process the mixture until it is smooth. With the motor running add the remaining 4 tablespoons butter, 1 tablespoon at a time, and process the mixture until it is combined well. Season the mixture with a pinch of mace, the lemon juice, and salt and white pepper to taste.

Transfer the mixture to a crock, smooth the top, and spoon the clarified butter over it. Chill the potted salmon, covered with plastic wrap, overnight. Serve the potted salmon with crackers, melba thins, or toasted croûtes. *The potted salmon may be prepared 5 days in advance, covered with plastic wrap, and chilled.* Makes about 3 cups.

To Clarify Butter

½ stick (¼ cup) unsalted butter, cut into
    1-inch pieces

In a heavy saucepan melt the butter over low heat. Remove the pan from the heat, let the butter stand for 3 minutes, and skim the froth. Strain the butter through a sieve lined with a double thickness of rinsed and squeezed cheesecloth into a bowl, leaving the milky solids in the bottom of the pan. Pour the clarified butter into a jar or crock and store it, covered, in the refrigerator. The butter keeps, covered and chilled, indefinitely. Makes about 3 tablespoons.

Spiced Pumpkin Muffins

2 cups all-purpose flour
2 teaspoons double-acting baking powder
½ teaspoon baking soda
½ teaspoon salt
¼ teaspoon ground mace
¼ teaspoon ground ginger
¼ teaspoon ground cinnamon
⅔ cup firmly packed dark brown sugar
1 cup unsweetened pumpkin purée
⅔ cup sour cream
1 large egg
6 tablespoons unsalted butter,
    melted
2 teaspoons freshly grated orange zest
½ cup chopped pecans
½ cup chopped pitted dates

For the topping
¼ cup sugar
¼ cup ground pecans
⅛ teaspoon ground mace
⅛ teaspoon ground cinnamon
⅛ teaspoon ground ginger

Into a large bowl sift together the flour, the baking powder, the baking soda, the salt, the mace, the ginger, the cinnamon, and the brown sugar. In another bowl whisk together the pumpkin purée, the sour cream, the egg, the butter, and the orange zest. Add the pumpkin mixture to the flour mixture and stir the mixture until it is just combined. Add the pecans and the dates and stir them in until they are combined.

In a small bowl combine the topping ingredients and stir the mixture until it is combined well. Divide the batter among 12 buttered ½-cup muffin tins, filling them ⅔ full, and sprinkle the muffins with the topping. Bake the muffins in the upper third of a preheated 400° F. oven for 18 to 25 minutes, or until a tester inserted in the center comes out clean. Makes 12 muffins.

THE LAUREL FAMILY

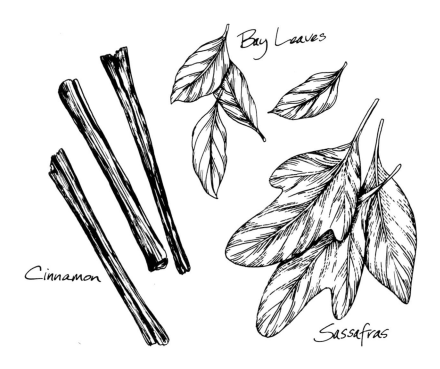

erhaps the most diverse group of spices we have assembled belong to the Laurel Family—bay leaf, cinnamon, and sassafras come from different parts of the world and have varying culinary roles.

The bay tree, native to the Mediterranean area, was so loved by the Greeks and Romans, they used its leaves to crown emperors and honored countrymen. Sometimes referred to as an herb, the bay leaf has been featured for centuries in the cuisines that surround the Mediterranean basin. Also known as Sweet Bay or Bay Laurel, bay leaf must not be confused with common laurel, which is poisonous. Fresh bay leaf has a slightly bitter, resinous, and pungent flavor that is modified when it is dried. Bay leaves are sold both fresh and dried, whole and ground, but avoid buying the ground variety, as its flavor fades more quickly. Our Cauliflower and Mushroom à la Grecque is suffused with the taste of the fresh leaves.

A native to Sri Lanka and Southeast Asia, cinnamon possesses a sweetness and warmth that have made it one of the most sought-after spices of the world. Paper-thin bark slices from young shoots of the tropical evergreen cinnamon tree are rolled by hand into sticks or "quills" of cinnamon. The quills are then dried until dark tan colored, smooth, thin, and brittle. Our Cinnamon-Flavored Couscous Salad with Sautéed Vegetables and Chick-Peas demonstrates the aromatic union of cumin and cinnamon in a savory dish from the East.

And, from our corner of the world, we introduce sassafras. Native to the eastern United States, it is one of the few existing North American spices, a relative newcomer to the spice world. The aromatic leaves of the sassafras tree are dried and powdered to form *filé* powder, a spice that is often used in lively Creole dishes from America's deep South. *Filé* powder, however, has a mild flavor; it is primarily used as a thickener that is stirred into a dish just before serving. (Be sure to avoid boiling the mixture once *filé* powder is added—doing so will ruin the texture of a dish.) Our Shrimp Gumbo combines garlic, onion, cayenne, bay leaf, and *filé* powder to create a feast for the senses.

Cauliflower and Mushrooms à la Grecque

½ cup olive oil
10 ounces pearl onions, peeled
½ pound mushrooms, quartered
1 small head of cauliflower, separated
    into flowerets (about 5 cups)
a 14½- to 16-ounce can tomatoes, puréed with
    the liquid
⅔ cup chicken broth
½ cup dry white wine
⅓ cup fresh lemon juice
a cheesecloth bag containing 3 bay leaves,
    2 tablespoons coriander seeds,
    1 tablespoon peppercorns, 2 teaspoons
    dried thyme, crumbled
minced fresh parsley leaves for garnish,
    if desired

In a large deep skillet or sauté pan heat the olive oil over moderate heat until it is hot but not smoking and in it cook the onions, stirring, until they are golden brown. Add the mushrooms and cook the mixture, stirring, for 3 minutes more. Add the cauliflower, the tomatoes, the broth, the wine, the lemon juice, the cheesecloth bag, and salt to taste, bring the liquid to a boil, and boil the mixture, shaking the pan occasionally, for 15 to 20 minutes, or until the liquid is slightly thickened and the vegetables are tender. Transfer the mixture to a bowl and let it cool. *The vegetable mixture may be prepared up to this point 1 day in advance, covered and chilled.* Squeeze the cheesecloth bag over the vegetables, discard the bag, and sprinkle the vegetables with the parsley. Serve the dish at room temperature. Serves 4.

Cinnamon-Flavored Couscous Salad with Sautéed Vegetables and Chick-Peas

1¾ cups chicken broth
2 tablespoons unsalted butter
½ teaspoon salt
1 cinnamon stick (about 4 inches), cracked
1 cup couscous
5 tablespoons olive oil
a ¾ pound eggplant, trimmed and cut
    into 1-inch pieces
1 red bell pepper, cut into 1-inch pieces
2 zucchini (about ¾ pound), trimmed, halved
    lengthwise, and cut into ½-inch-thick slices
3 garlic cloves, minced

½ teaspoon ground cinnamon
½ teaspoon ground cumin
2 tablespoons white wine vinegar
a 15½-ounce can chick-peas, drained
2 tomatoes, seeded and cut into cubes
1 cup minced scallion
¼ cup minced fresh mint leaves
3 tablespoons fresh lemon juice

In a saucepan combine 1½ cups of the chicken broth, the butter, the salt, and the cinnamon stick and bring the mixture to a boil. Stir in the couscous and let the mixture stand, off the heat, covered, for 5 minutes. Transfer the couscous to a large bowl, discard the cinnamon stick, and fluff the mixture with a fork.

In a large non-stick skillet heat 2 tablespoons of the oil over moderately high heat until it is hot but not smoking. Add the eggplant and the bell pepper and cook the vegetables, stirring, for 2 minutes. Add the zucchini, the garlic, the cinnamon, the cumin, and salt and pepper to taste and cook the mixture, stirring, for 1 minute more. Add the remaining ¼ cup chicken broth and the vinegar and simmer the mixture, covered, for 2 minutes, or until the vegetables are just tender. Raise the heat to high and cook the mixture, stirring, until all the liquid is evaporated. Let the mixture cool and add it to the bowl of couscous.

Add the chick-peas, the tomatoes, the scallion, and the mint to the couscous and sprinkle the salad with the remaining 3 tablespoons oil, the lemon juice, and salt and pepper to taste. Toss the salad until it is combined well. *The salad may be made 6 hours in advance, covered and chilled.* Serve the salad at room temperature. Serves 6.

Shrimp Gumbo

4 tablespoons unsalted butter
¼ cup flour
2 cups chopped onion
1½ cups chopped green
   bell pepper
1 cup chopped celery
1 tablespoon minced garlic
6 cups fish stock
a 28-ounce can crushed tomatoes,
   puréed
1½ teaspoons minced fresh thyme leaves, or
   ½ teaspoon dried, crumbled
1½ teaspoons minced fresh orégano, or
   ½ teaspoon dried, crumbled
½ teaspoon cayenne
1 bay leaf
1½ pounds large shrimp, shelled
   and deveined

2 teaspoons gumbo *filé* powder (ground dried
   sassafras leaves, available at specialty food
   shops)
cooked rice as an accompaniment

In a large saucepan over moderately low heat melt the butter. Add the flour and cook the *roux*, whisking, until it is golden. Add the onion, the bell pepper, and the celery and cook the vegetables over moderate heat, stirring, until the onion is softened. Stir in the garlic and cook it, stirring, for 1 minute. Add the fish stock, the tomatoes, the thyme, the orégano, the cayenne, the bay leaf, and salt to taste and simmer the mixture, stirring occasionally, for 1 hour.

Bring the liquid to a boil, add the shrimp, and simmer the mixture, stirring, for 1 minute. Remove the pan from the heat, stir in the *filé* powder, and let the gumbo stand, covered, for 10 minutes. Serve the gumbo with the rice. Serves 6.

THE GINGER FAMILY

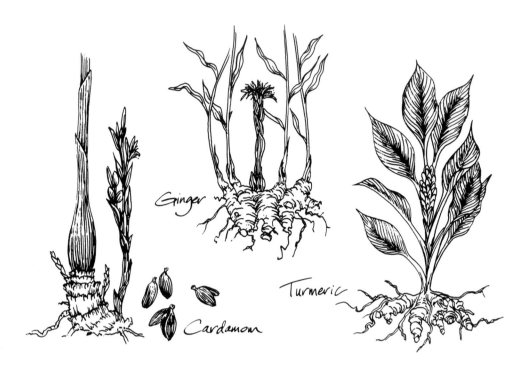

Ginger *Cardamom* *Turmeric*

inger, turmeric, and cardamom, members of the eclectic Ginger Family, are among the oldest and most prized spices of the world. Each plays an essential role in Eastern cuisine and they often are used together, as in Indian curry. Today, the West would also be at a loss without them.

The Ginger plant is indigenous to southeast Asia and India, and its knobbed root, both durable and transportable, proved to be a popular condiment in Europe— by the 9th century the spice was being used on the table as we use salt and pepper today. Gingerroot is commonly sold in two forms: fresh gingerroot, called "green ginger," with its brown or buff-colored covering and pale yellow flesh; and the bottled ground ginger, the beige-colored, grated, dried gingerroot. The flavor of green ginger is hot and spicy, but it adds a refreshing taste to many dishes; ground ginger has a diminished taste. Our recipes employ fresh gingerroot in savory dishes as is the custom in Eastern cuisines. It flavors an aromatic Oriental sauce in our Gingered Shrimp Salad with Baby Corn and Sugar Snap Peas, and it is combined with other Eastern spices in our chicken and rice recipes for the more piquant tastes of India.

Turmeric, like ginger, is native to tropical southeast Asia, and its roots have been used for centuries.

The turmeric root, however, is difficult to grind at home, so it is usually sold in ground form. This inexpensive, fine yellow powder carries a woody aroma and a distinctive, pungent taste. It is an excellent food colorant, as seen in our bright yellow Golden Indian Rice Pullao with Shiitake Mushrooms and Turmeric.

Cardamom, native to the tropical rain forests of India, was first used in Europe for its digestive properties, in perfumes, and as a breath freshener. Unlike its cousins, which are used for their roots, the cardamom plant has ground-crawling stalks that bear pods of precious aromatic seeds with a sweet flavor and a hint of eucalyptus. One of the most expensive spices of the world, cardamom is sold in pod form in three varieties: green, the most desirable; white, which are simply bleached green cardamoms; and brown, with seeds coarser in texture and flavor. Although the spice can be found in ground form, it is preferable to buy the pods and extract the seeds yourself to avoid the camphorous flavor of adulterated versions. Indian cuisine enjoys cardamom in a variety of ways and our recipes reflect a few of its Eastern ideas. Our Chicken Braised in Yogurt and Cardamom combines cardamom seeds, gingerroot, cloves, bay leaf, and coriander in a creamy yogurt sauce that is fragrant rather than hot; and in our Cardamom and Orange Baked Apples the spice provides a lemony flavor.

*Gingered Shrimp Salad with Baby Corn
and Sugar Snap Peas*

1½ pounds large shrimp, shelled and deveined
¼ pound sugar snap peas or snow peas,
    trimmed
a 15-ounce can baby corn, drained
1 tablespoon chopped, peeled, fresh
    gingerroot
1 large garlic clove, chopped
3 tablespoons fresh lemon juice
2 teaspoons Dijon-style mustard, or to taste
⅓ cup vegetable oil, or to taste
3 tablespoons sour cream or yogurt
¼ cup minced scallion
½ cup diced cucumber
2 tablespoons minced fresh coriander leaves,
    snipped chives, or dill, or a combination
green leaf lettuce leaves for garnish

In a large saucepan of boiling salted water cook the shrimp, stirring for 1 minute, or until they are opaque and firm but still springy to the touch. Drain the shrimp and let them cool. *The shrimp may be prepared up to 3 hours in advance and kept covered and chilled.*

In a saucepan of boiling salted water add the sugar snap peas and the baby corn and bring the liquid back to a boil over high heat, stirring. Drain the vegetables, refresh them under cold water and pat them dry. *The vegetables may be prepared up to 3 hours in advance and kept covered and chilled.*

In a food processor or blender combine the gingerroot, the garlic, the lemon juice, the mustard, and salt and pepper to taste. With the motor running add the oil in a stream and process the dressing until it is combined well. Transfer the dressing to a large bowl, add the shrimp, the sour cream, the scallion, the cucumber, and the fresh herbs, and gently stir until the shrimp is coated with the dressing.

Arrange the shrimp on a platter lined with the lettuce leaves and garnish it with the sugar snap peas and the baby corn. Serves 6.

*Golden Indian Rice Pullao with Shiitake Mushrooms
and Turmeric*

1 cup minced onion
3 tablespoons vegetable oil
1 tablespoon minced, peeled, fresh gingerroot
1 tablespoon minced garlic
1 teaspoon ground turmeric
1 teaspoon ground coriander
1 teaspoon cuminseed
½ pound *shiitake* mushrooms, stemmed and
    sliced
2 cups long-grain rice
3 cups chicken broth
1 small green chili, seeded and minced (wear
    rubber gloves)
1 bay leaf
2 tablespoons minced fresh coriander leaves
2 tablespoons sliced toasted almonds

In a saucepan cook the onion in the oil over moderate heat, stirring frequently, for 5 minutes, or until it is lightly golden. Add the gingerroot, the garlic, the turmeric, the ground coriander, and the cuminseed and cook the mixture, stirring, for 1 minute. Add the mushrooms and salt to taste and cook the mixture, stirring, for 3 minutes. Add the rice and stir until it is coated with the spices. Add the chicken broth, the green chili, and the bay leaf, bring the liquid to a boil, and simmer the rice, covered, for 20 minutes, or until it is tender. Remove the pan from the heat and let the rice stand for 5 minutes. Transfer the rice to a serving dish and sprinkle it with the coriander leaves and the almonds. Serves 6.

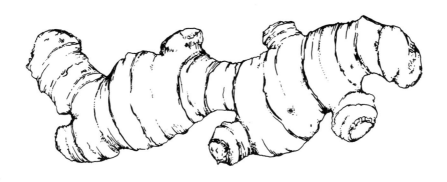

Chicken Braised in Yogurt and Cardamom

2 cups minced onion
4 tablespoons vegetable oil
1 tablespoon minced, peeled, fresh gingerroot
1 tablespoon minced garlic
seeds from 10 green cardamom pods (about
    ½ teaspoon) (available at specialty food
    shops and some supermarkets)
6 whole cloves
1 bay leaf
½ teaspoon ground coriander
4 skinless boneless chicken breast halves
    (about 1½ pounds)
½ cup chicken broth
½ cup plain yogurt
⅓ cup heavy cream
2 tablespoons minced fresh coriander leaves
    for garnish

In a large saucepan cook the onion in 3 tablespoons of the oil over moderate heat, stirring frequently, for 5 to 7 minutes, or until it is golden. Add the gingerroot, the garlic, the cardamom seeds, the cloves, the bay leaf, and the coriander and cook the mixture, stirring, for 2 minutes. Transfer the onion mixture to a bowl.

Add the remaining oil to the saucepan and cook the chicken, patted dry, with salt and pepper to taste over moderate heat for 1 to 2 minutes on each side, or until it is no longer pink. Return the onion mixture to the pan, add the chicken broth and the yogurt, and simmer the mixture, covered, for 10 to 12 minutes, or until the chicken is firm but still springy to the touch. Transfer the chicken with a slotted spoon to a platter.

Discard the bay leaf from the braising liquid and in a blender or food processor blend the mixture until it is smooth. Return the mixture to the saucepan, stir in the heavy cream, and bring the liquid to a simmer. Add the chicken and any juices that have accumulated on the platter to the saucepan and simmer the mixture until the chicken is heated through. Transfer the chicken to a platter, nap it with the sauce, and garnish it with the minced coriander leaves. Serves 4.

Cardamom and Orange Baked Apples

4 large apples, such as Rome Beauty,
    McIntosh, or Granny Smith, cored to
    within ½ inch of the bottom and the
    top half peeled
fresh lemon juice to taste
⅓ cup chopped pecans
⅓ cup firmly packed light brown sugar
⅓ cup raisins
2 tablespoons unsalted butter, softened
2 teaspoons freshly grated orange zest
½ teaspoon ground cardamom
½ cup orange juice
2 tablespoons honey
lightly whipped cream or vanilla ice cream
    as an accompaniment if desired

Sprinkle the inside and outside of the apples with the lemon juice to taste. In a bowl combine well the pecans, the brown sugar, the raisins, the butter, the orange zest, and the cardamon and mound the mixture into the cavities of the apples.

Arrange the apples in a 1-quart shallow flameproof baking dish and pour the orange juice and honey over them. Add ½ cup water to the baking dish and bring the liquid to a simmer over moderate heat. Bake the apples, basting them frequently, in a preheated 400° F. oven for 40 minutes, or until they are golden and tender.

Transfer the apples to a serving dish and bring the remaining pan juices to a boil over moderately high heat, stirring occasionally, until the liquid is syrupy. Pour the syrup over the apples and serve them with lightly whipped cream or vanilla ice cream if desired. Serves 4.

THE PEPPER FAMILY

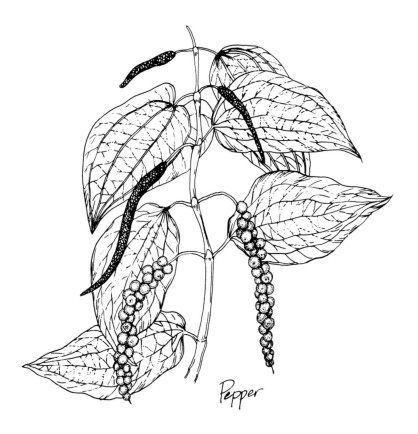

Pepper

epper is the most widely used spice in the world, and it is difficult to imagine cooking without it. At one time Europeans were so keen to have this tropical spice with its hot pungent flavor that they traded an ounce of gold for an ounce of pepper. In the 16th century pepper became readily available in Europe after a sea route was discovered to southwest India, pepper's native home. Pepper will only grow in tropical forests, and today it is cultivated in Brazil, the East and West Indies, Indonesia, and Malaysia.

The pepper plant, *piper nigrum*, is responsible for true pepper, although many other varieties of the plant exist. It is a woody-stemmed, climbing plant with trailing vines and white flowers that give way to globular berries. These berries become peppercorns that are commonly sold in three varieties: green, or unripe ber-

ries, which are freeze-dried (fresh green berries are also sold bottled in brine); black, the most popular form, which are the dried, semi-ripe red berry; and white, the ripe red berries which are immersed in water and husked before drying. Ground pepper quickly loses its aroma and flavor, so it is essential to buy whole berries and have a peppermill at the ready! Black peppercorns are stronger than white, and green peppercorns are the mildest of all.

Our Three-Pepper Goat Cheese displays the colorful trio of peppercorns for a full pepper taste that complements the strong flavor of Boucheron or any other goat cheese. For a robust entrée, our Grilled Peppered Sirloin with Green Peppercorn Sauce uses a liberal dose of whole and crushed black peppercorns to season the beef and the sauce, and green peppercorns for fresh pepper taste and color.

Three-Pepper Goat Cheese

2 teaspoons whole white peppercorns,
  ground coarse
2 teaspoons whole freeze-dried green
  peppercorns, ground coarse
2 teaspoons whole black peppercorns,
  ground coarse
a ½-pound piece of Boucheron, Montrachet,
  or any goat cheese

In a small bowl combine the white, green, and black peppercorns. Press the peppercorn mixture onto the cheese, coating it completely, and chill the cheese, wrapped in plastic, overnight. Serve the cheese with toasted croûtes or crackers.

Grilled Peppered Sirloin with Green Peppercorn Sauce

a 2½-pound boneless sirloin steak (about
  1½ inches thick)
4 teaspoons whole black peppercorns

For the sauce
½ cup dry white wine
½ cup minced shallot
1 teaspoon crushed black peppercorns
3 cups beef broth
½ cup heavy cream
4 teaspoons arrowroot
1 to 2 teaspoons Dijon-style mustard
1 to 2 tablespoons drained canned green
  peppercorns (available at specialty food
  shops and some supermarkets)

Pat dry the meat, season it with salt, and coat it evenly with the whole black peppercorns, pressing them onto both sides of the meat. *The meat may be prepared up to 6 hours in advance and kept covered and chilled.*

Make the sauce: In a saucepan combine the wine, the shallot, and the crushed black peppercorns, bring the mixture to a boil, and boil it until it is reduced to 3 tablespoons. Add the beef broth and simmer the mixture, stirring occasionally, for 30 minutes, or until the sauce is reduced to 2 cups. In a small bowl combine the heavy cream and the arrowroot until it is smooth and whisk the mixture into the simmering sauce until it is slightly thickened. Whisk in the mustard and salt to taste. Strain the sauce into another saucepan and add the green peppercorns. Keep the sauce warm over low heat, covered with a buttered round of wax paper. *The sauce may be prepared up to 4 hours in advance, covered with a round of wax paper and chilled. Bring the sauce to a simmer until heated through before serving.*

Grill the sirloin on a rack set about 4 to 5 inches over glowing coals for 8 to 10 minutes on each side for medium-rare meat. Let the steak stand for 5 minutes and cut it into thin slices. Serve the sauce with the steak. Serves 6.

THE MUSTARD FAMILY

Black Mustard

Horseradish

ustard and horseradish have been known to man for thousands of years as strong, pungent condiments and as healers. These two flavorful spices come from different parts of the world, but they are often used in similar ways.

In medieval times, mustard seed was used by commoners throughout Europe as an affordable spice to flavor foods and to concoct love potions. The Italians pursued its culinary virtues by mixing it with honey, nuts, vinegar, and spices to create exciting sauces, and the French and British mixed mustard seeds with unfermented grape juice to form "prepared mustard." Ground mustard was not developed until the 18th century in England.

Three varieties of mustard plants are named for the color seed they carry: black, originally from southern Europe and western Asia; brown, from India and China; and white (or yellow), which has long been naturalized in Europe and North America. All three plants have yellow flowers and long pods containing round, hard seeds. In our Grated Carrot Salad with Mustard Seeds

and Roasted Cashews, black mustard seeds are fried for a surprisingly sweet and nutty taste; Dijon mustard stars in our Sautéed Turkey Scallops with Tarragon Mustard Sauce, a classical French use of the world's most popular prepared mustard.

The horseradish plant's hot-tasting root is similarly used as a flavoring in sauces and as a condiment for red meat. Native to eastern Europe, horseradish is grown today in northern Europe, Great Britain, and the United States. The plant carries tiny, white, scented flowers and has a thick, buff-colored root that spreads laterally, taking over the whole garden if not contained. When it is scraped the root has a penetrating aroma; when grated, it has a distinct, sharp flavor and aroma that brings tears to the eyes. As with mustard seeds, however, horseradish looses much of its pungency when heated. The root can be found whole or grated, as well as in bottled sauces. Often, it is used to flavor vegetables, as in our recipe for Beet and Apple Salad with Horseradish Dressing. Here the varying tastes and textures of apple, celery, and beet are combined with a pleasantly pungent cream sauce for an exceptional dish.

Grated Carrot Salad with Mustard Seeds and Roasted Cashews

2 tablespoons vegetable oil
1 teaspoon black mustard seeds (available at specialty food shops and some supermarkets)
1 tablespoon minced, peeled fresh gingerroot
½ cup minced scallion
1 pound carrots, grated coarse
1 teaspoon freshly grated lemon zest
2 tablespoons fresh lemon juice
2 tablespoons minced fresh coriander
½ cup chopped roasted cashews

In a large skillet heat the oil over moderate heat until it is hot but not smoking. Add the mustard seeds and the gingerroot, cover the pan, and shake it over the stove for 30 seconds, or until the seeds have stopped popping. Add the scallion and cook the mixture, stirring, for 1 minute. Add the carrots, the lemon zest, and salt and pepper to taste and cook the carrots, stirring, for 3 to 4 minutes, or until they are just tender. Transfer the mixture to a bowl and let it cool to warm. Add the lemon juice and the coriander to the mixture and toss it to combine it well. Sprinkle the salad with the cashews. Serves 4.

Sautéed Turkey Scallops with Tarragon Mustard Sauce

four ½-inch-thick turkey cutlets (about 1¼ pounds)
1 cup fresh bread crumbs
½ cup freshly grated Parmesan
2 tablespoons minced fresh tarragon, or 2 teaspoons dried, crumbled
2 large eggs
1 tablespoon Dijon-style mustard
2 tablespoons olive oil
2 tablespoons unsalted butter

For the sauce
½ cup minced shallot
½ cup dry white wine
1 cup chicken broth
1 cup heavy cream
4 to 5 teaspoons Dijon-style mustard
2 tablespoons minced fresh tarragon, chives, or parsley leaves

Pat dry the turkey cutlets. In a shallow bowl combine the bread crumbs, the Parmesan, and the tarragon. In another shallow bowl beat together the eggs, the mustard, and 2 teaspoons of the oil. Dip the turkey cutlets in the egg mixture, letting the excess drip off, and coat them on each side with the bread crumb mixture. *The scallops may be prepared up to this point 3 hours in advance, covered with plastic wrap, and chilled.*

In a non-stick skillet heat the remaining 4 teaspoons oil and the butter over moderately high heat until it is hot but not smoking. Add the scallops without crowding them and cook them for 2 minutes on each side, or until they are golden and the juices run clear. Transfer the scallops to a platter and keep them warm, covered.

Make the sauce: In a small saucepan combine the shallot and the white wine and boil the mixture until it is reduced to 2 tablespoons. Add the chicken broth and boil the mixture until it is reduced by half. Add the heavy cream and boil the mixture until it is slightly thickened. Remove the pan from the heat and whisk in the mustard and the tarragon. *The sauce may be prepared 2 to 3 hours in advance, covered with a buttered round of wax paper and chilled. Warm the sauce before serving.* Serve the sauce with the scallops. Serves 4.

Beet and Apple Salad with Horseradish Dressing
For the salad
1⅔ cups diced, cooked, and peeled beets, or a 1-pound jar, drained
1 Granny Smith apple, peeled and diced (about 1⅓ cups)
⅔ cup diced celery (about 2 stalks)
½ cup minced onion

For the dressing
½ cup sour cream
¼ cup mayonnaise
2 tablespoons white wine vinegar
2 tablespoons peeled and grated fresh horseradish, or 2 to 4 tablespoons drained bottled horseradish
2 tablespoons snipped fresh dill

In a bowl combine all of the salad ingredients. In another bowl whisk together all of the dressing ingredients and salt and pepper to taste. Add the dressing to the salad and stir the mixture until it is combined well. Chill the salad, covered with plastic wrap, until ready to serve. *The salad may be made 1 day in advance, covered and chilled.* Serves 4.

THE NIGHTSHADE FAMILY

Paprika

Chili Pepper

aprika, chili peppers, cayenne, and chili powder come from a variety of capsicum plants that are indigenous to Central and South America and the West Indies. Today, capsicums are grown in tropical and sub-tropical regions throughout the world. The paprika plant looks very much like a bell pepper plant with its large green (unripe) and red (ripe) fruits hanging down. The mild red powder that we all recognize as paprika comes from the dried ripe fruits. Chili plants, however, usually have spear-shaped fruits that are ¼ to 12 inches long with various colored fruits: green when unripe, and red, orange, yellow, and purple when ripe. The pungency of these chilies ranges from relatively mild to ferociously hot—generally, the smaller, darker, and narrower the chili, the greater its heat. Unripe chilies are milder than ripe ones, and dried chilies are the most pungent of all. The tiny white seeds and flesh of

''Bird Chili'' fruits are dried and ground to produce powerfully hot cayenne pepper. Chili powders are made from unspecified dried and ground chilies and vary in pungency.

Our Paprika Cheese Straws, the perfect complement to a long, cool drink, combine a generous amount of Cheddar and Parmesan with cayenne for cheese flavor with a bit of mild piquancy, while the Hungarian paprika colors the puff pastry a rosy pink. This stronger flavored paprika appears again in our Veal Paprikash as a colorant and a spice. As the veal slowly braises, the paprika reddens the sauce and permeates the meat, adding moderate heat to the dish. For a spicier entrée, try our Shellfish in Piquant Red Pepper Sauce, where a generous amount of cayenne results in a lively seafood dish. *Jalapeño* chilies are featured in both our Jalapeño and Cheddar Cornbread and Chili Tortilla Soup recipes to demonstrate the stimulating flavors of Mexico.

Paprika Cheese Straws

quick puff paste (page 259), or a 1-pound
    package frozen puff paste
1 cup (¼ pound) grated sharp Cheddar
1 cup freshly grated Parmesan
3 tablespoons paprika, preferably Hungarian
⅛ teaspoon cayenne, or to taste
an egg wash, made by beating 1 egg with
    1 teaspoon water and ⅛ teaspoon salt

Halve the quick puff paste and reserve one half, wrapped in plastic wrap and chilled for later use. In a bowl stir together and combine well the Cheddar, the Parmesan, the paprika, and the cayenne. On a lightly floured surface roll out the dough into a 14- by 10-inch rectangle about ⅛-inch thick, brush it with some of the egg wash, and sprinkle it with about ½ cup of the cheese mixture. Gently press the cheese mixture into the pastry by rolling the rolling pin across the dough. Turn over the dough, brush it with some of the egg wash, and sprinkle it with another ½ cup of the cheese mixture, making sure the pastry is completely covered with cheese. Roll the cheese into the pastry in the same manner. With a pastry wheel or knife cut the dough crosswise into ½-inch-wide strips. Twist the strips and arrange them on baking sheets lined with parchment paper, pressing the ends of the strips down firmly onto the parchment. Bake the strips in the middle of a preheated 425° F. oven for 10 to 12 minutes, or until they are golden. Make more cheese straws in the same manner with the remaining dough, egg wash, and cheese. Trim the ends of the cheese straws and store the straws in an airtight container until ready to serve. The straws will keep for up to 3 days. Makes about 48 straws.

Veal Paprikash

2 pounds lean veal shoulder, cut into 1-inch
    pieces
2 tablespoons vegetable oil
1½ cups minced onion
1 green bell pepper, minced
2 garlic cloves, minced
2 tablespoons Hungarian paprika
⅓ cup dry white wine
⅓ cup beef broth
½ cup peeled, seeded, and chopped tomato
½ cup sour cream

nokedli (Hungarian-style *spätzle*, available at
    Hungarian food shops) or buttered egg
    noodles as an accompaniment

Pat the veal dry and season it with salt and pepper. In a large, heavy saucepan heat the oil over moderately high to high heat until it is hot but not smoking and brown the veal, in batches, transferring it to a platter as it is browned. Add the onion to the pan and cook it over moderate heat, stirring occasionally, until it is golden. Add the bell pepper, the garlic, and the paprika to the saucepan and cook the mixture, stirring, for 1 minute. Return the veal to the saucepan, add the wine, the beef broth, and the tomato and bring the mixture to a boil. Simmer the veal, covered, for 1½ hours, or until it is tender. Boil the juices in the saucepan until they are thickened, if necessary, and stir in the sour cream. Heat the mixture until it is heated through, but do not let it boil. Serve the veal with the *nokedli* or the egg noodles. Serves 4.

Shellfish in Piquant Red Pepper Sauce

1 cup minced onion
⅔ cup minced green bell pepper
½ cup minced celery
2 tablespoons unsalted butter
2 teaspoons minced garlic
1 tablespoon flour
¼ to ½ teaspoon cayenne
1 cup fish stock (page 256) or chicken broth
1 cup peeled, seeded, and chopped tomatoes
½ cup low-salt tomato sauce
½ teaspoon dried basil, crumbled
½ teaspoon dried thyme, crumbled
½ teaspoon freshly grated lemon zest
1 pound large shrimp, shelled and deveined,
    or sea scallops
rice or fettuccine as an accompaniment

In a large non-stick skillet cook the onion, the bell pepper, the celery, and salt and pepper to taste in the butter over moderate heat, stirring occasionally, until the onion is golden. Stir in the garlic, the flour, and the cayenne and cook the mixture, stirring, for 1 minute. Add the fish stock, the tomatoes, the tomato sauce, the basil, the thyme, and the lemon zest and simmer the sauce, stirring occasionally, for 20 minutes.

Add the shrimp or scallops and cook them for approximately 1 to 2 minutes, stirring, until they are opaque and firm but still springy to the touch. Serve the shellfish with rice or fettuccine. Serves 4.

Chili Tortilla Soup

1 cup minced onion
2 tablespoons vegetable oil
2 garlic cloves, minced
1½ teaspoons ground chili powder
1½ teaspoons ground cumin
5 cups chicken broth
a 14½- to 16-ounce can tomatoes, including
    the juice, puréed
1 tablespoon tomato paste
a 4-ounce can chopped mild green chilies,
    drained
1 tablespoon seeded and minced *jalapeño*
    chilies (about 2 chilies), or to taste
    (wear rubber gloves)
vegetable oil for frying the tortillas
4 corn tortillas, cut into ½-inch wide strips
2 tablespoons minced fresh cilantro
freshly grated Monterey Jack as an
    accompaniment

In a saucepan cook the onion in the oil over moderate heat, stirring, until it is softened. Add the garlic, the chili powder, and the cumin and cook the mixture, stirring, for 1 minute. Add the chicken broth, the tomatoes, the tomato paste, the green chilies, the *jalapeño* chilies, and salt to taste, bring the mixture to a boil, and simmer it, covered, for 20 minutes.

Meanwhile, in a large non-stick skillet heat ½ inch vegetable oil until it is hot. Add the tortilla strips in batches, and fry them, stirring, for about 1 minute or until they are crisp. Transfer the tortilla strips to a baking sheet lined with paper towels to drain.

Skim the surface of the soup and stir in the fresh cilantro. Divide the tortilla strips among four soup bowls and ladle the soup over the tortillas. Serve the soup with the Monterey Jack. Serves 4.

Jalapeño and Cheddar Cornbread

1 cup yellow cornmeal
1 cup all-purpose flour
2 teaspoons double-acting baking powder
½ teaspoon salt
1 cup milk
2 large eggs
5 tablespoons unsalted butter, melted and
    cooled
1 cup fresh corn, or frozen corn, thawed and
    drained
1¼ cups grated sharp Cheddar
2 to 3 *jalapeño* chilies, seeded and minced
    (wear rubber gloves)

Into a bowl sift the cornmeal, the flour, the baking powder, and the salt and set aside. In another bowl beat together the milk, the eggs, and 4 tablespoons of the butter. Stir the milk mixture into the flour mixture until it is just combined and fold in the corn, 1 cup of the Cheddar, and the *jalapeño* chilies. Pour the mixture into a buttered 8-inch square baking pan, sprinkle the top with the remaining Cheddar, and drizzle it with the remaining butter. Bake the cornbread in a preheated 425° F. oven for 25 to 30 minutes, or until it is golden and a tester inserted in the center comes out clean. Serves 6.

GUIDES TO THE TEXT

GENERAL INDEX

Page numbers in *italics* indicate color photographs
(M) indicates a microwave recipe

INDEX OF 45-MINUTE RECIPES

* Starred entries can be prepared in 45 minutes or less
but require additional unattended time

Page numbers in *italics* indicate color photographs

(M) indicates a microwave recipe

INDEX OF RECIPE TITLES

Page numbers in *italics* indicate color photographs

(M) indicates a microwave recipe

TABLE SETTING ACKNOWLEDGMENTS

To avoid duplication below of table setting information within the same menu, the editors have listed all such credits for silverware, plates, linen, and the like in its most complete form under "Table Setting."

Any items in the photographs not credited are privately owned.

All addresses are in New York City unless otherwise indicated.

Front Jacket

Cheese and Won Ton Ravioli Triangles with Tomato Sauce and Confetti Vegetables: "Tiger Raj" porcelain dinner plate by Lynn Chase—Geary's, 351 N. Beverly Drive, Los Angeles, California 90210.

Frontispiece

Banana Rum Ice Cream (page 2): Ridgeway ironstone dessert plates, circa 1840—Bardith Ltd., 901 Madison Avenue. American sterling serving spoon, Sheffield, circa 1875; English silver-plate basket, circa 1870—S. Wyler, Inc., 941 Lexington Avenue. See additional Table Setting credits for A New Orleans-Style Dinner below.

The Menu Collection

Table Setting (page 10): See Table Setting credits for A Masquerade Dinner below.

Our Anniversary Party

Table Setting (pages 12 and 13): "Vienne Gold" crystal wineglasses and Champagne flutes—Baccarat, Inc., 625 Madison Avenue. "Tabriz" porcelain dinner plates and salad plates—Christian Dior, Art de la Table, 41 Madison Avenue. "Malmaison" sil-

ver-plate flatware—Pavillon Christofle, 680 Madison Avenue. Crystal and continental silver open salts and continental silver pepper pots, circa 1900—S. Wyler & Son, 941 Lexington Avenue. Italian embroidered tablecloths with filet lace inserts, circa 1900; Spanish seventeenth-century silk velvet panel with embroidered appliqué border; Czechoslovakian damask napkins—Françoise Nunnallé Fine Arts, 105 West 55th Street. French mahogany console with white marble top, circa 1818—Yale R. Burge Antiques, 305 East 63rd Street. Nineteenth-century mirrored cachepot—James II Galleries, Ltd., 15 East 57th Street. Kashmiri handmade wool crewel-work rugs—Kamdin Designs, 791 Lexington Avenue. "Les Guirlandes" wallpaper (available through decorator)—Clarence House, 211 East 58th Street. Flowers and votive candles—Zezé, 398 East 52nd Street.

Chocolate Mousse and Raspberry Cream Dacquoise (page 15): English silver-plate salver, Sheffield, circa 1870—S. Wyler & Son, 941 Lexington Avenue. English silver-plate cake knife, circa 1870; Staffordshire porcelain plates, circa 1840 (from a dessert service of 5 serving pieces and 11 dessert plates)—James II Galleries, Ltd., 15 East 57th Street. French nineteenth-century ormolu and Baccarat crystal candelabra—Bardith Ltd., 31 East 72nd Street.

Opera Broadcast Luncheons

Poached Chicken with Vegetables, Coriander, and Saffron Couscous; Chopped Salad of Cucumber, Red Onion, Lemon, and Parsley (page 17): Ceramic dinner plates and salad plates—Conran's, 160 East 54th Street. German sterling flatware by H. Meyen & Co., circa 1925—F. Gorevic & Son, Inc., 635 Madison Avenue. "Aura" wineglasses—Cardel Ltd., 621 Madison Avenue. Linen napkins—Henri Bendel, Frank McIntosh Shop, 10 West 57th Street. Tulip wood and mahogany table, circa 1930; upholstered mohair club chairs, circa 1870—Howard Kaplan Antiques, 827 Broadway. Karabagh Caucasian rug, 1910—The Rug Warehouse Inc., 220 West 80th Street.

Risotto with Artichoke Hearts, Prosciutto, and Red Pepper; Fennel and Watercress Salad (page 18): Ceramic dinner plate by Jacques Molin—Henri Bendel, Frank McIntosh Shop, 10 West 57th Street. "Dashes" porcelain hors d'oeuvre plate by Robert Venturi for Swid Powell—Bloomingdale's, 1000 Third Avenue. Glass tumbler by Gilles Derain—Modern Age, 795 Broadway. Hand-painted linen napkins by Liz Wain—Geary's, 351 North Beverly Drive, Beverly Hills, California.

Ginger Butterscotch Pear Tart (page 19): Glass plate by Judy Smilow (from a set of 3 different plates)—MoMA Design Store, 44 West 53rd Street. Orange glass bowl by Baldwin & Guggisberg;

"Papilio" glass table; "Salon" leather chaise; "Harlequin" hand-tufted wool rug by Christine Van Der Hurd—Modern Age, 795 Broadway. Wool and polyester throw—Bloomingdale's, 1000 Third Avenue.

A Pre-Ski Breakfast

Toasted-Coconut Streusel Coffeecake, Mocha Hot Chocolate (page 20): "Claire" ceramic cake stand designed by Ralph Lauren—Polo/Ralph Lauren, 867 Madison Avenue.
Vegetable and Cheese Strata, Herbed Home-Fried Potatoes, Spicy Sausage Patties, Pineapple Citrus Juice (page 21): "Claire" ceramic platters; "Emma" glass tumblers; "Homestead" ceramic dinner plates and cups and saucers; cotton napkins; and chambray tablecloth, all designed by Ralph Lauren—Polo/Ralph Lauren, 867 Madison Avenue. Three-tiered yellow shelf; nineteenth-century painted tole box—Gail Lettick's Pantry & Hearth Antiques, 121 East 35th Street.

Easter Dinner

Table Setting (pages 22 and 23): "Nantucket Basket" bone-china soup and dinner plates by Wedgwood; "Normandie" crystal wineglasses by Baccarat—Bluck's, 4 Front Street, Hamilton, Bermuda. "Sea Shell" sterling flatware by Angela Cummings—Bergdorf Goodman, 754 Fifth Avenue. Cotton piqué and lace napkins—Henri Bendel, Frank McIntosh Shop, 10 West 57th Street. "Basket" ceramic votive candle holders; flower basket—Williams-Sonoma, 20 East 60th Street. "Crackle II" cotton chintz fabric (for tablecloth and cushions, available through decorator)—Woodson, 979 Third Avenue. Straw hat—Bloomingdale's, 1000 Third Avenue. Ribbon (on hat)—Hyman Hendler and Sons, 67 West 38th Street.
Ginger Rum–Glazed Ham; Rhubarb, Onion, and Raisin Chutney; Garlic Bread Puddings; Asparagus with Walnut-Chive Vinaigrette (page 24): "Nantucket Basket" bone-china serving dishes by Wedgwood—Bluck's, 4 Front Street, Hamilton, Bermuda.
Strawberry Lemon Bavarian Cake (page 25): Crystal cake stand—

Bluck's, 4 Front Street, Hamilton, Bermuda.

An East Indian Dinner

Red Lentil Soup with Spiced Oil; Pappadams (page 26): Stoneware bowl and dinner plate—Platypus, 126 Spring Street. Ceramic bowl by Christina Salusti—Zona, 97 Greene Street. "Arak" paisley cotton fabric (available through designer)—Brunschwig & Fils, 979 Third Avenue.
Braised Lamb with Spinach; Spiced Saffron Rice; Cauliflower with Ginger and Mustard Seeds (page 27): Bronze serving bowl and ceramic serving dishes—Zona, 97 Greene Street. Flower arrangement—Castle & Pierpont, 1441 York Avenue.

A New Orleans-Style Dinner

Table Setting (pages 28 and 29): Mason's ironstone dinner plates, circa 1810; English rummers, circa 1820; English engraved wineglasses, circa 1840; English cut-glass dessert wineglasses, circa 1840; Coalport porcelain jug, circa 1830—Bardith Ltd., 901 Madison Avenue. "Empire" sterling flatware by the Durgin Division of Gorham; sterling salts, Dublin, 1809; sterling salt spoons, Exeter, 1822—F. Gorevic & Son, Inc., 635 Madison Avenue. English engraved claret jug, circa 1865; eighteenth-century Bavarian mirrored sconces—James II Galleries, Ltd., 15 East 57th Street. French gilt bronze candlesticks, circa 1840; English decorative cushion (one of a pair); nineteenth-century William and Mary–style armchair (one of a pair); Queen Anne–style settee, circa 1920; pastel of a boy in a sailor suit, circa 1880—Yale R. Burge Antiques, Inc., 305 East 63rd Street. Nineteenth-century Romanian embroidery and lace tablecloth—Françoise Nunnalle, 105 West 55th Street. Flowers—Castle & Pierpont, 1441 York Avenue. English painted wood and metal birdcage, circa 1860; English mahogany stand, circa 1760; portrait of Ina Wiggan by Alfred Hartley, 1855-1933; English brass easel, circa 1870—Kentshire Galleries, 37 East 12th Street. "Etruscan Wall" handmade wallpaper; Lincrusta relief wall covering (available through decorator)—

Norton Blumenthal, Inc., 979 Third Avenue.
Crown Roast of Pork with Dirty Rice Stuffing and Creole Mustard Sauce; Sweet Potato Purée; Okra and Onion Pickle (pages 30 and 31): Sterling tray—F. Gorevic & Son, Inc., 635 Madison Avenue. Sterling tablespoon, London, 1839 (one of a pair)—S. Wyler, Inc., 941 Lexington Avenue. Caughley porcelain sauceboat, circa 1780; pair of Derby porcelain dishes, circa 1790; Newhall porcelain dish with pink and gilt border, circa 1800—Bardith Ltd., 901 Madison Avenue.

Pasta Dinners

Rhubarb Streusel Pie (page 32): Hand-painted raw-silk cloth—Bergdorf Goodman, 754 Fifth Avenue.
Pasta with Spring Vegetables and Prosciutto; Red-Leaf and Bibb Lettuce Salad with Scallion (page 33): Porcelain dinner plates by Les Georgique Cinq; acrylic flatware; Italian wineglasses; hand-painted linen napkins by A²—Barneys New York, Seventh Avenue at 17th Street. Pressed-glass salad plates (from a twenty-piece service for four); ceramic vase with metal handle and removable grid for flower arranging—D.F. Sanders & Co., 952 Madison Avenue. Flower arrangement—Castle & Pierpont, 1441 York Avenue. Reproduction "Serpent" glass-topped metal table—Yale R. Burge Antiques, Inc., 305 East 63rd Street. Eighteenth-century Italian painted hall bench (one of a pair)—Florian Papp, Inc., 962 Madison Avenue.

Dinner à la Française

Table Setting (pages 34 and 35): "Revolution" French hand-painted faience soup and dinner plates; French hand-blown wineglasses by Biot—Faïence, 104 Lewis Street, Greenwich, Connecticut. "Baguette" French silverplate flatware by Chambly—Wolfman • Gold & Good Company, 116 Greene Street. Cotton fabric for napkins—Pierre Deux, 870 Madison Avenue. Flower arrangements—Castle & Pierpont, 1441 York Avenue. "Four Seasons" French handmade terra-cotta wall plaques (from a set of four) by C. Robichon—Ségriès à Solanée, 866

Lexington Avenue. English nineteenth-century *faux* bamboo chairs with rush seats (from a set of six)—Stebbins & Company, 79 East Putnam Avenue, Greenwich, Connecticut. French marble-top serving table on polished iron base, circa 1840; French pine bistro table on iron and brass base, circa 1840—Howard Kaplan Antiques, 827 Broadway. "Luneville Niche" series wallpaper (available through decorator)—Brunschwig & Fils, 979 Third Avenue. *Poulet au Vinaigre à l'Estragon, Pommes Anna, Haricots Verts à la Vapeur* (page 36): "Revolution" hand-painted faience platter and vegetable dish—Faïence, 104 Lewis Street, Greenwich, Connecticut.

A Luncheon in Bermuda

Mango Yogurt Mousses (page 38): Glass compotes; "Peony" ceramic saucers (teacups not shown)—The Pottery Barn, 117 East 59th Street.
Onion Tart with Sherry Peppers Sauce; Tomato Basil Concassé; Avocado, Grapefruit, and Watercress Salad with Roquefort and Paprika Dressing (page 39): "Seashell" ceramic dinner plates (special order only); acrylic and stainless-steel flatware; linen napkins—Henri Bendel, Frank McIntosh Shop, 712 Fifth Avenue. "Lily" crystal salad plate by Hoya; "Prelude" crystal wineglasses by Orrefors—A.S. Cooper & Sons, Ltd., 59 Front Street, Hamilton, HM11 Bermuda.

A Swedish Midsummer Dinner

Table Setting (pages 40 and 41): Rörstrand "Ostindia" porcelain dinner plates; covered vegetable dishes; platter; jug—Robin Importers, 510 Madison Avenue. Gense "Triad" stainless-steel flatware—Scan-Agent, Inc., P.O. Box 220, Purchase, NY 10577. "Reijmyre" hand-engraved wineglasses and decanter; Swedish pewter candlesticks and plate (in cupboard); Swedish nineteenth-century wooden dough bowl; "Cavalier Check" cotton tablecloth; "Mansion Stripe" cotton seat cushions; "Gotland" birch chairs; Swedish wool apron (on flower table); Swedish eighteenth-century lap desk (in cupboard); Swedish "Mora" clock, circa 1850; Swedish nineteenth-century cor-

ner cupboard with new finish; "Stezenska" wallpaper—Country Swedish, 35 Post Road West, Westport, CT 06880. Swedish flower table, circa 1850—Evergreen Antiques, 120 Spring Street. Swedish cotton rag rugs, circa 1930—Evergreen Antiques, 1249 Third Avenue. Ivy plants and flowers—Castle & Pierpont, 1441 York Avenue.
Assorted Canapés, Aquavit (page 42): "Reijmyre" hand-engraved aquavit glasses—Country Swedish, 35 Post Road West, Westport, CT 06880. Kosta Boda crystal bowl—Royal Copenhagen Porcelain/Georg Jensen Silversmiths, 683 Madison Avenue.
Oven-Poached Salmon Steaks, Mustard Dill Sauce, Beet Orange Salad, Parsleyed Yellow-Potato Salad (pages 42 and 43): Stelton stainless-steel serving dish with wooden board; Orrefors "Linea" crystal bowl—Royal Copenhagen Porcelain/Georg Jensen Silversmiths, 683 Madison Avenue.

An Elegant Stove-Top Dinner

All items in the photographs are privately owned.

Dinner Alfresco

Table Setting (pages 46 and 47): Porcelain dinner plates by Laure Japy; linen napkins by Carol Becker for Cargo—Barneys New York, Seventh Avenue and 17th Street. Glass bowls—Annieglass Studio, (408) 426-5086. Lacquer chargers and lacquer and stainless-steel flatware by Nancy Calhoun; Italian crystal wineglasses by Mariposa; painted iron candlesticks by Faroy; wood napkin rings by L.A. Settings; Kenyan cotton tablecloth—The Dining Room Shop, 7645 Girard Avenue, La Jolla, California 92037.
Grilled-Tuna Salad with Sun-Dried Tomato Dressing; Bruschetta with Caponata (page 48): Glass plate by Annieglass Studio—Barneys New York, Seventh Avenue and 17th Street.

Luncheon in a Japanese Garden

Pickled Ginger and Plum-Wine Granita, Honeydew and Sake Granita (page 50): Lacquer plates—Katagiri, 226 East 59th Sreet. Stainless flatware designed by Ward Bennett for Sasaki—

Barneys New York, Seventh Avenue and 17th Street.
Smoked Salmon, Watercress, and Daikon Salad with Ginger Vinaigrette, Chilled Japanese Noodles with Grilled Chicken and Vegetables, Sake (page 51): "Yoshino I" and "Yoshino II" crystal salad plates by Hadfumi Ishihara; "Quintet" crystal bowls (2 from a set of 5); "Zenith" crystal glasses on acrylic bases—Hoya Gallery, 450 Park Avenue. Lacquer chopsticks—Katagiri, 226 East 59th Street. Linen napkins—Barneys New York, Seventh Avenue and 17th Street.

Dinner by the Pacific

Table Setting (pages 52 and 53): "Petro" handmade glass soup bowls by Annieglass—Annieglass Studio, Tel. (408) 426-5086. Hand-painted ceramic dinner and service plates by Antheor; hand-painted linen napkins by Liz Wain; handmade glass candelabrum by Glassworks of London—Barneys New York, Seventh Avenue and 17th Street. "Integrale" stainless-steel flatware—Pavillon Christofle, 680 Madison Avenue. "Trifid" hand-forged sterling seafood forks—James Robinson, 15 East 57th Street. "Column" handmade goblets by Melanie Guernsey—The Elements, 14 Liberty Way, Greenwich, Connecticut. Glasses (holding flowers); handmade stained and lacquered rattan chairs—The Pottery Barn, 117 East 59th Street. "Valencia" cotton fabric (tablecloth) and "Cordoba" cotton fabric (pillows), both available through decorator—Brunschwig & Fils, Inc., 979 Third Avenue.
Tiramisù Parfaits (page 55): Parfait glasses—The Pottery Barn, 117 East 59th Street.

Picnic in the Olive Grove

The Picnic (page 57): Pewterex plates—Portico, 379 West Broadway. Bronze bowls; cotton napkins—Zona, 97 Greene Street. Plastic wineglasses; acrylic container—Williams-Sonoma, 20 East 60th Street. Copper salt and pepper shakers—Bridge Kitchenware Corporation, 214 East 52nd Street. Italian paisley wool throw—Wolfman • Gold & Good Company, 116 Greene Street.

A Labor Day Cocktail Buffet

Table Setting (pages 58 and 59): "Evasion" faience platter and salad plates by Gien—Baccarat, Inc., 625 Madison Avenue. Baldelli ceramic platters (in plate stand)—Zona, 97 Greene Street. "Verlaine" French stainless-steel forks (in basket); "Shovel" wood and silver-plate salad servers; "Savannah" glass salad bowl; hand-painted glass bowl with pewter base (in plate stand); small glass bowl—Keesal & Mathews, 1244 Madison Avenue. Ribbed goblets; three-tiered hand-forged iron plate stand; painted copper wine cooler; cotton napkins—Wolfman • Gold & Good Company, 116 Greene Street. Wire basket by Dal Mondo—Ad Hoc Softwares, 410 West Broadway. Flowers—Zezé, 398 East 52nd Street.

Szechwan-Style Eggplant with Pita Wedges; Goat Cheese and Tomato Tart; Smoked Trout Canapés; Shredded Pork with Tomato Salsa on Tortilla Chips; Olive, Rosemary, and Onion Focaccia; Savory Mascarpone Cheesecake with Sun-Dried Tomato Pesto (pages 60 and 61): Wire cake stand by Dal Mondo—Ad Hoc Softwares, 410 West Broadway. Silver-plate pie server—Keesal & Mathews, 1244 Madison Avenue.

A Fishing Picnic in Scotland

Bread and Butter Pudding (page 62): Porcelain baking dish—Jenner's, Princes Street, Edinburgh, Scotland.
The Picnic (page 63): Fitted picnic basket; ceramic bowl (yellow) and ramekins; wool blanket—Jenner's, Princes Street, Edinburgh. Fishing gear—Kate Fleming, 26 Allan Street, Blairgowrie, Perthshire, Scotland.

A Masquerade Dinner

Table Setting (pages 64 and 65): Puiforcat "Galuchat" porcelain dinner plates—Puiforcat, 811 Madison Avenue. Laure Japy acrylic and stainless-steel flatware; cotton napkins—Barneys New York, Seventh Avenue and 17th Street. "Massena" crystal water goblets and wineglasses—Baccarat, Inc., 625 Madison Avenue. "Marcel" crystal and gilt vase and wineglasses by Borek Sipek—Driade, 212 East 57th Street. English bronze lustres, circa 1820—James II Galleries, Ltd., 15 East 57th Street. Handmade masks—Arnold S. Levine Theatrical Millinery, 250 West 54th Street. "Les Plumes Enchantes" silk fabric (on table) and "Epingle Poiret" cotton and polyester fabric (on cushion and pillows in window seat), both available through decorator—Clarence House, 211 East 58th Street.
Radicchio, Fennel, and Arugula Salad with Roquefort and Walnuts (page 66): "Harcourt" crystal plates—Baccarat, Inc., 625 Madison Avenue. French nineteenth-century beadwork tray—James II Galleries, Ltd., 15 East 57th Street.

Country Breakfast

Cinnamon Baked Apples with Yogurt Cheese (page 68): "Poynter" ironstone platter, teapot, sugar, and creamer by Recollections—The Victoria & Albert Museum Gift Shop, South Kensington, London SW7 2RL, England. Dedham pottery reproduction mugs—The Potting Shed, Box 1287, Concord, MA 01742. Twig tray—Gordon Foster, 1322 Third Avenue.
Cheddar French Toast with Dried Fruit in Syrup; Honey-Marinated Canadian Bacon (page 69): "Poynter" ironstone dinner plates—The Victoria & Albert Museum Gift Shop, South Kensington, London SW7 2RL, England. Handmade "Twig" flatware by Doug Benoit—The Whitney Museum's Store Next Door, 943 Madison Avenue. Cotton and crocheted lace napkins—Wolfman • Gold & Good Company, 116 Greene Street. Handwoven pumpkin-vine trays—William-Wayne & Co., 324 East 9th Street. Flowers—Zezé, 398 East 52nd Street. "Lafayette" chestnut-finish desk-table with gessoed cabriole legs—The Farmhouse Collection, Inc., (208) 788-3187. "Madeline" hand-carved and hand-painted buffet from The Farmhouse Collection (available through decorator)—Circa David Barrett, Ltd., 232 East 59th Street. "Log Cabin" wool challis quilt, circa 1880 (84 by 82 inches)—Thos. K. Woodard American Antiques & Quilts, 835 Madison Avenue.

A Maryland Thanksgiving

Table Setting (pages 70 and 71): Spode china dinner plates, circa 1820; English amethyst-glass wineglasses, circa 1865; Chamberlin-Worcester porcelain candlesticks, circa 1820; English nineteenth-century earthenware pitchers (on mantelpiece)—James II Galleries, Ltd., 15 East 57 Street. English silver-plate service plates; English sterling basket, London, 1912—S. Wyler, Inc., 941 Lexington Avenue. "Maryland Engraved" sterling flatware—Kirk Stieff, 800 Wyman Park Drive, Baltimore, MD 21211. Irish glass rummers, circa 1790; Wedgwood Jasperware hurricane lamps, circa 1820—Bardith, Ltd., 901 Madison Avenue. Linen and lace napkins; Italian *pointe de Venise* lace place mats, circa 1900—Françoise Nunnallé, 105 West 55th Street. English cranberry-glass salt and pepper cellars, circa 1870—Kentshire Galleries, 37 East 12th Street.
Roast Turkey with Country Ham Stuffing and Giblet Gravy; Spiced Cranberry Sauce; Candied Sweet Potatoes; Kale-Stuffed Onions; Potato Parsnip Purée; Sauerkraut with Apples and Caraway (pages 72 and 73): Gorham well-and-tree silver-plate platter; sterling gravy boat and tray; English silver-plate rectangular entrée dish (with cover), circa 1900; silver-plate carving knife and fork; English Sheffield coaster, circa 1815—F. Gorevic & Son, Inc., 635 Madison Avenue. English silver-plate oval entrée dish, circa 1880; German Art Deco porcelain and silver-plate tray, circa 1930; Coalport "Imari" footed porcelain dish, circa 1810—James II Galleries, Ltd., 15 East 57th Street. Spode china "shell" dish, circa 1820; Spode "Egg and Spinach" porcelain compote, circa 1810; English classical glass decanter, circa 1770—Bardith Ltd., 901 Madison Avenue. "Maryland Engraved" sterling serving spoons and ladle—Kirk Stieff, 800 Wyman Park Drive, Baltimore, MD 21211.

Dinner After the Game

Mixed Antipasto; Baked Pasta with Tomatoes, Shiitake Mushrooms, and Prosciutto; Escarole, Spinach, and Red Onion Salad with Anchovy Garlic Dressing (pages 74 and 75): Ceramic platter; Le Creuset 3½-quart enameled cast-iron casserole (lid not shown); glass salad bowl—Bloomingdale's, 1000 Third Avenue. French ceramic dinner plates by Molin—Jonal, 25 East 73rd Street. "Beechwood" wood-handled flatware; wineglasses; cotton napkins—Conran's Habitat, 160 East 54th Street. Nineteenth-century wood and brass candlesticks—Bob Pryor Antiques, 1023 Lexington Avenue. Fonthill "Kirby" cotton fabric from the Viceroy Plaid Collection (available through decorator)—Fonthill, 979 Third Avenue. Flower arrangement—Castle & Pierpont, 1441 York Avenue. Oil painting by W. J. Chapman, 1871 (one of a pair)—Karen Warshaw Ltd., 167 East 74th Street.

A Nantucket Christmas Dinner

Table Setting (pages 76 and 77): Davenport ironstone plates, circa 1850; ruby glass tumblers, circa 1880; acid-engraved wineglasses, circa 1875—James II Galleries, Ltd., 15 East 57th Street. Old Newbury Crafters "Moulton" hand-forged sterling flatware—Cardel, Ltd., 621 Madison Avenue. Linen damask napkins, circa 1840; Russian embroidered silk and linen runner, circa 1860—Françoise Nunnallé Fine Arts, (212) 246-4281. Handmade Nantucket skiff (on table) and sailing dory (on windowsill) by Mark Sutherland exclusively for Nantucket Looms; hand-loomed cotton and rayon stole; hand-painted wooden "bait" fish (on Christmas tree)—Nantucket Looms, 16 Main Street, Nantucket, MA, 02554. Birch bark votive candles, pine rope, and wreaths—Zezé, 398 East 52nd Street. New England birdcage Windsor chairs, circa 1820 (from a set of 6)—Wayne Pratt & Co., 28 Main Street, Nantucket, MA, 02554. Woodard Weave "Roxbury" flat-woven cotton carpet—Thos. K. Woodard

American Antiques and Quilts, 835 Madison Avenue.
Roast Beef with Glazed Onions and Worcestershire Gravy, Buttered Brussels Sprouts and Chestnuts, Mashed Celery Potatoes, Acorn Squash Purée, Cornmeal Rolls (pages 78 and 79): English pearlware platter, circa 1820—Bardith Ltd., 901 Madison Avenue. Wedgwood creamware sauce tureen, circa 1840 (cover not shown); silver-plate ladle, circa 1880—James II Galleries, Ltd., 15 East 57th Street. Old Newbury Crafters "Moulton" hand-forged sterling carving set and serving spoon—Cardel Ltd., 621 Madison Avenue.

An Elegant Little Christmas

Roasted Poussins with Fennel; Potato and Carrot Gratin Diamonds; Sage Cloverleaf Rolls (pages 80 and 81): "Ruby Ulander" bone china dinner plates by Wedgwood—Cardel Ltd., 621 Madison Avenue. "Empire" sterling flatware; sterling bread basket and open salt and pepper by Buccellati—Buccellati, Inc., 46 East 57th Street. "Montaigne Optic Gold" crystal water goblets and wineglasses—Baccarat, Inc., 625 Madison Avenue. "Harley Gold" cotton damask place mats by Brook Hill—Bergdorf Goodman, 754 Fifth Avenue. Flowers—Zezé, 398 East 52nd Street. Twig wreaths studded with leaves and dried fruit—Relic, 158 North LaBrea, Los Angeles, California 90036.

The Recipe Compendium

Roasted Chicken Legs with Plum Salsa and Mexican Chicken and Vegetable Casserole (page 82): Ceramic platter by Hartstone; ceramic bowls by Gilda Weinstein; gratin dish by Apilco; porcelain pitcher by Mottahedeh; and cotton dish towel, all from Dean and DeLuca, 560 Broadway.

A Summer Dinner à la Campagne

Suprêmes de Poulet Sautés aux Shiitakes et aux Herbes de Provence; Gratin d'Aubergines, Courgettes, et Tomates; Purée de Pommes de Terre au Fenouil (page 265): Hand-painted dinner plates and salad plates; water goblets and wine glasses; cotton fabric for tablecloth and curtains—Pierre Deux, 870 Madison Avenue. Cotton napkins—Williams-Sonoma, 20 E. 60th Street. Flower arrangement—Castle & Pierpont, 1441 York Avenue.

Sunday Lunch en Famille

Soupe de Poissons au Pistou et Croûtons à la Parmesane (page 272): Ceralene porcelaine plates and bowls; Baccarat crystal goblet and vase; Christofle "Perles" silverplate flatware—Baccarat, Inc., 625 Madison Avenue.
Tarte aux Pommes, Crème Chantilly (page 273): Ceralene porcelaine dessert plates; Christofle "Perles" silverplate spoon—Baccarat, Inc., 625 Madison Avenue. Glass bowl and plate—Williams-Sonoma, 20 E. 60th Street.

Buffet de Fête

Terrine Tricolore de Poisson; Sauce Concombre aux Herbes; Beignets d'Artichauts au Fromage; Sauce aux Poivrons Rouges Grillés; Riz au Saffran; Asperges, Tomates, et Poireaux à l'Huile d'Olive au Basilic; Boeuf Bourguignon à la Badiane et au Gingembre (pages 280 and 281): "Strasbourg Coq" faience dinner plates and serving pieces; hand-woven linen and rayon napkins; French cotton fabric by Les Olivades (on wall); cotton and linen throw (used as tablecloth)—Faïence, 104 Mason Street, Greenwich, Connecticut 06830.